Conserving and Valuing Ecosystem Services and Biodiversity

Conserving and Valuing Ecosystem Services and Biodiversity

Economic, Institutional and Social Challenges

Edited by K. N. Ninan

with foreword by Dr Achim Steiner
UN Under-Secretary General
and Executive Director
United Nations Environment Programme
Nairobi

publishing for a sustainable future

London • Washington, DC

First published in hardback by Earthscan in 2009
Published in paperback in 2011

Earthscan Ltd, Dunstan House, 14a St Cross Street, London EC1N 8XA, UK
Earthscan LLC, 1616 P Street, NW, Washington, DC 20036, USA
Earthscan publishes in association with the International Institute for Environment and Development

For more information on Earthscan publications, see www.earthscan.co.uk or write to earthinfo@earthscan.co.uk

ISBN: 978-1-84971-173-9

Typeset by Domex e-data Pvt Ltd
Cover design by Rob Watts

A catalogue record for this book is available from the British Library

Library of Congress Cataloging-in-Publication Data

Conserving and valuing ecosystem services and biodiversity : economic, institutional, and social challenges / [edited by] K. N. Ninan ; with foreword by Dr Achim Steiner.
    p. cm.
  ISBN 978-1-84407-651-2
  1. Biodiversity conservation–Economic aspects. 2. Biotic communities–Economic aspects. 3. Environmental degradation–Economic aspects. I. Ninan, K. N. (Karachepone Ninan), 1950–
  QH75.C6817 2008
  333.95'16–dc22

                          2008036285

At Earthscan we strive to minimize our environmental impacts and carbon footprint through reducing waste, recycling and offsetting our CO_2 emissions, including those created through publication of this book. For more details of our environmental policy, see www.earthscan.co.uk.

Printed and bound in the UK by CPI Antony Rowe.
The paper used is FSC certified.

Dedicated
to
the memory of
my parents

Behanan and Annamma Ninan

and

aunts

Mary Ponnamma George
Elisabeth Baby Mathews

Who sacrificed their todays
to secure our tomorrows,
Who have now blended with nature,
that nurtures and sustains our lives

Contents

PART 1 BIODIVERSITY, ECOSYSTEM SERVICES AND VALUATION

PART 5 CLIMATE CHANGE, BIODIVERSITY AND ECOSYSTEM SERVICES

List of Figures, Tables and Boxes

FIGURES

TABLES

Appendix Figures and Tables

Figures

Tables

Boxes

List of Contributors

I. J. Bateman is Professor of Environmental Economics, School of Environmental Sciences and Deputy Director of the Centre for Social and Economic Research on the Global Environment (CSERGE), University of East Anglia, Norwich, UK.

Regina Birner is Senior Research Fellow, International Food Policy Research Institute, Washington DC, USA.

Lucy Emerton is Chief Economist, Environment Management Group, Sri Lanka.

S. Georgiou is Associate Fellow, CSERGE, School of Environmental Sciences, University of East Anglia, Norwich UK.

Timothy C. Haas is Associate Professor in the Lubar School of Business Administration, University of Wisconsin at Milwaukee, USA.

A. Jones is Senior Lecturer, School of Environmental Sciences, University of East Anglia, Norwich, UK.

Jane Kabubo-Mariara is Associate Director and Senior Lecturer, School of Economics, University of Nairobi, Kenya.

Randall A. Kramer is Professor of Environmental Economics, Nicholas School of the Environment, Duke University, Durham, North Carolina, 27708, USA.

I. H. Langford (deceased) was formerly Senior Research Fellow, CSERGE, University of East Anglia, Norwich, UK.

John Loomis is Professor of Agricultural and Resource Economics, Colorado State University, Fort Collins, USA.

Marhawati Mappatoba is a faculty member in the Universitas Tadulako, Palu, Indonesia.

N. G. N. Matias is former Research Associate, School of Environmental Sciences, University of East Anglia, Norwich, UK.

Jeffrey A. McNeely is Chief Scientist, IUCN, Gland, Switzerland.

Ernest L. Molua is a Lecturer, Department of Economics and Management, University of Buea, Cameroon.

K. N. Ninan is Professor of Ecological Economics, Institute for Social and Economic Change, Bangalore, India and Visiting Professor, Donald Bren School of Environmental Science and Management, University of California, Santa Barbara, USA.

Unai Pascual is Environmental Economist in the Department of Land Economy, University of Cambridge, UK.

Subhrendu K. Pattanayak is Associate Professor, Sanford Institute of Public Policy and Nicholas School of the Environment, Duke University, Durham, North Carolina, 27708 USA.

Charles Perrings is Professor of Environmental Economics, ecoSERVICES Group, School of Life Sciences, Arizona State University, Tempe, USA.

Ray Purdy is Research Fellow, Centre for Law and Environment, University College, London, UK.

Leslie Richardson is Graduate Research Assistant, Department of Agricultural and Resource Economics, Colorado State University, Fort Collins, USA.

Erin O. Sills is Associate Professor and Director of International Programmes, Department of Forestry and Environmental Resources, North Carolina State University, Raleigh, North Carolina, USA.

L. Subramanian is former Research Associate, School of Environmental Sciences, University of East Anglia, Norwich, UK.

Timothy Swanson is Professor of Law and Economics, University College London, UK.

Krystyna Swiderska is Researcher in the International Institute for Environment and Development, London, UK.

Clem Tisdell is Professor Emeritus, School of Economics, The University of Queensland, Brisbane, Australia.

R. K. Turner is Professor of Environmental Economics and Management, School of Environmental Sciences and Director of CSERGE, University of East Anglia, Norwich, UK.

Ana Lea Uy is Corporate Secretary and Legal Counsel, Ana Lea Uy Law Office, Manila, Philippines.

Foreword

Biological diversity continues to decline at an alarming rate and by some estimates we are now in a sixth wave of extinctions. Over the past 20 or so years the world has rolled out the multilateral machinery in order to counter these declines. There are global and regional treaties covering trade in endangered species and migratory species up to biological diversity itself.

There are also many shining examples of intelligent management. For example:

- Paraguay, which until 2004 had one of the world's highest rates of deforestation, has reduced rates in its eastern region by 85 per cent.
- South East Asia has set aside close to 15 per cent of its land for protection, above the world average which in 2003 stood at 12 per cent.
- In Fiji, no take zones and better management of marine areas has increased species like mangrove lobsters by 250 per cent a year with increases of 120 per cent annually in nearby waters.
- A United Nations Environment Programme (UNEP) project, funded by the government of Japan, is assisting to restore the fabled Marshlands of Mesopotamia while providing environmentally sustainable drinking water and sewage systems for up to 100,000 people.

But the fact is that despite all these activities the rate of loss of biodiversity seems to be intensifying rather than receding, and the pace and magnitude of the international response is failing to keep up with the scale of the challenge. It is clear that one of the key shortcomings of humankind's existing relationship with its natural or nature-based assets is one of economics. There remains a gulf between the true value of biodiversity and the value perceived by politicians; business and perhaps even the public. There is an urgent need to shift into a higher gear in order to bridge this divide between perception and reality.

Some progress is being made towards a new compact with the world's nature-based resources in part as a result of the pressing need to combat climate change. Deforestation accounts for some 20 per cent of the greenhouse gas emissions and is also a major threat to biodiversity. Governments are now moving to include reduced emissions from degradation and deforestation (REDD) in a new climate deal either through a funding mechanism or via the carbon markets. This potentially represents a new multi-billion dollar avenue for funding, especially for tropical countries, for conservation and community livelihoods.

Another important development needs to be agreement on the outstanding issue of an international regime on Access and Benefit Sharing under the Convention on Biological Diversity (CBD). This remains the weak pillar of the convention and yet the greatest potential source of funding for conservation under the provisions of this treaty. It would allow researchers and companies access to the genetic treasure trove of the developing world in return for a share in the profits of the products and goods that emerge. But brokering the international regime has proved elusive: over the past five or so years there has been increasingly no access and no benefit sharing in the absence of an international deal. This spells a potentially huge economic, environmental and social loss to both the developed and developing world – losses in terms of breakthroughs in new pharmaceuticals, foods and biologically based materials and processes and biological pest controllers. There are losses also in terms of conservation. For an intelligently designed international access and benefit sharing (ABS) regime offers the chance for poorer countries, with the lion's share of the globe's remaining genetic resources to begin to be paid properly for maintaining and conserving them. At the CBD in 2008 in Bonn governments finally agreed to put aside vested interests and fractious debate by agreeing to a negotiating deadline of 2010 on the ABS question.

There are other promising developments which are opening the eyes of big business to the economic possibilities of biodiversity in ways that go beyond the traditional sectors of say forestry and timber and marine resources and fish products. One example of this comes under the umbrella of a new initiative called Nature's 100 Best – a partnership between an organization called Zero Emission Research and Initiatives (ZERI); the Biomimicry Guild; IUCN and the UNEP. The initiative is the brainchild of the Biomimicry Guild and the ZERI in partnership with UNEP and IUCN. It is aimed at showcasing how tomorrow's economy can be realized today by learning, copying and mimicking the way nature has already solved many of the technological and sustainability problems confronting humankind.

Let me give you a few examples.

Two million children die from vaccine-preventable diseases like measles, rubella and whooping cough each year. By some estimates, breakdowns in the refrigeration chain from laboratory to village means half of all vaccines never get to patients. Enter *Myrothamnus flabellifolia* – a plant found in central and southern Africa whose tissues can be dried to a crisp and then revived without damage, courtesy of a sugary substance produced in its cells during drought. And enter Bruce Roser, a biomedical researcher who, along with colleagues, recently founded Cambridge Biostability Ltd to develop fridge-free vaccines based on the plant's remarkable sugars called trehaloses. The product involves spraying a vaccine with the trehalose coating to form inert spheres or sugary beads that can be packaged in an injectable form and can sit in a doctor's bag for months or even years. The development, based on mimicking nature, could lead to savings of up to US$300 million a year in the developing world while cutting the need for kerosene and photovoltaic powered fridges. Other possibilities include new kinds of food preservation up to the storage of animal and human tissues that bypass storage in super cold liquid nitrogen.

A further case in point: the two main ways of reducing friction in mechanical and electrical devices are ball bearings and silicon carbide or ultra nanocrystalline diamond. One of the shortcomings of silicon carbide is that it is manufactured at temperatures of between 1600 and 2500 degrees Fahrenheit (°F) – in other words it is energy intensive involving the burning of fossil fuels. The synthetic diamond product can be made at lower temperatures and coated at temperatures of 400°F for a range of low friction applications. But it has drawbacks too. Enter the shiny Sandfish lizard that lives in the sands of north Africa and the Arabian Peninsula and enter a team from the Technical University of Berlin. Studies indicate that the lizard achieves its remarkable, friction-free life by making a skin of keratin stiffened by sugar molecules and sulphur. The lizard's skin also has nano-sized spikes. It means a grain of Sahara sand rides atop 20,000 of these spikes spreading the load and providing negligible levels of friction. Further tests indicate that the ridges on the lizard skin may also be negatively charged, effectively repelling the sand grains so they float over the surface rather like a hovercraft over water. The researchers have teamed up with colleagues at the Science University of Berlin and a consortium of three German companies to commercialize the lizard skin findings. The market is potentially huge, including in micro-electronic-mechanical systems where a biodegradable film made from the relatively cheap materials of kerotene and sugar and manufactured at room temperature offers an environmentally friendly 'unique selling proposition'.

And finally the issue of superbugs and bacterial resistance and a possible solution from an Australian Red Algae. Seventy per cent of all human infections are a result of biofilms. These are big congregations of bacteria that require 1000 times more antibiotic to kill them and are leading to an 'arms race' between the bugs and the pharmaceutical companies. It is also increasing antibiotic resistance and the rise of 'super bugs' like methicillin resistant Staphylococcus aureus that now kills more people than die of AIDS each year. Enter *Delisea pulchra*, a feathery red alga or seaweed found off the Australian coast and a team including researchers at the University of New South Wales. During a marine field trip, scientists noticed that the algae's surface was free from biofilms despite living in waters laden with bacteria. Tests pinpointed a compound – known as halogenated furanone – that blocks the way bacteria signal to each other in order to form dense biofilm groups. A company called Biosignal has been set up to develop the idea which promises a new way of controlling bacteria like golden staph, cholera and legionella without aggravating bacterial resistance. Products include contact lenses, catheters and pipes treated with algae-inspired furanones alongside mouthwashes and new therapies for vulnerable patients with diseases like cystic fibrosis and urinary tract infections. The work may also reduce pollution to the environment by reducing or ending the need for homeowners and companies to pour tons of caustic chemicals down pipes, ducts and tanks and onto kitchen surfaces to keep them bug-free.

The 20th century was an industrial century – the 21st will increasingly be a biological one but only if we can bring the wide variety of compelling economic arguments to the in-boxes of the world's political, civic and corporate leaders. The importance of the globe's nature-based assets go beyond dollars and cents: they are important culturally and spiritually for many people. But in a world where economics and trade dominate and define so many choices, it is crucial that we put the economic case clearly and convincingly if we are to make a difference.

This new publication, *Conserving and Valuing Ecosystem Services and Biodiversity: Economic, Institutional and Social Challenges* is therefore a welcome contribution to transforming the way we do business on this planet. I would like to congratulate the editor and contributors. It should be essential reading for all those who wish to realize truly sustainable development in this new millennium.

Achim Steiner
UN Under-Secretary General
and Executive Director
United Nations Environment Programme
Nairobi
12 July 2008

Preface

Conserving biodiversity and the ecosystem services that they provide is part of the larger objective of promoting human well-being and sustainable development. The Millennium Ecosystem Assessment (MEA) 2005 has brought about a fundamental change in the way that scientists perceive the role and value of biodiversity, and recognizes the dynamics and linkages between people, biodiversity and ecosystems. Human activities have direct and indirect impacts on biodiversity and ecosystems, which in turn affects the ecosystems services that they provide, and ultimately human well-being. The MEA and the World Summit on Sustainable Development held in Johannesburg in 2002, while endorsing the 2010 target of reducing biodiversity loss resolved by the Conference of the Parties to the Convention on Biological Diversity in 2002, also highlighted the essential role of biodiversity in meeting the millennium development goals, especially the target of halving the incidence of poverty and hunger by the year 2015. Ecosystem services directly support more than one billion people living in extreme poverty. However, the MEA review shows that the rates of biodiversity loss have remained steady, if not accelerated. About 60 per cent of the world's ecosystem services are degraded.

This book addresses the economic, institutional and social challenges confronting scientists and policy makers in conserving biodiversity and ecosystem services that are critical for sustaining human well-being and development. The contributors to the volume are leading experts in the world who have made significant contributions to biodiversity research and policy. The volume covers a wide range of themes and issues such as the economics and valuation of biodiversity and ecosystem services, social aspects of conservation, incentives and institutions including payments for ecosystem services, governance, intellectual property rights (IPRs) and protection of indigenous knowledge, climate change and biodiversity, etc. The book includes chapters with an international focus as well as case studies from North and South America, Europe, Africa, Asia and Australia covering ecosystems as diverse as tropical forests, wetlands, aquatic and marine ecosystems, dry ecosystems, etc. In addition, the book includes applications of environmental economics such as the contingent valuation method, benefit transfer, new institutional economics, game theory, etc. For convenience, the chapters are organized under the following broad themes: biodiversity, ecosystem services and valuation; incentives and institutions; governance; IPRs and protection of indigenous knowledge; and climate change, biodiversity and ecosystem services. However, some of the chapters address issues which overlap across these themes.

I had conceived of this book after the publication of my book *The Economics of Biodiversity Conservation: Valuation in Tropical Forest Ecosystems* by Earthscan in 2007. Unlike my earlier book which focused primarily on the economics of biodiversity conservation in the context of tropical forest ecosystems, I had visualized this volume to cover a broad canvas of issues, and also other ecosystems. I am glad that these efforts over the span of about one and a half years have borne fruit. I would like to thank all the eminent contributors to this volume for readily responding to my invitation to contribute a chapter despite their several commitments, for putting up with my frequent emails and reminders for sending their chapters, revising them in the light of reviewers' comments and responding to my several queries and giving clarifications. This book would not have been possible but for their unstinted support and cooperation.

Most of the chapters in this volume are products of on-going or completed larger research projects sponsored by several national and international agencies such as The World Bank, the International Food Policy Research Institute (IFPRI), the International Institute for Environment and Development (IIED), GTZ, IUCN and others. All these contributions have been reviewed by the projects as part of the review process of these institutions. Besides reviewing all the chapters myself, I also had the chapters reviewed by other experts. I would like to express my immense gratitude and appreciation to Professors Clem Tisdell (University of Queensland, Australia), John Loomis (Colorado State University, USA), Sebastian Hess (Institute of Environmental Studies, Amsterdam), Jane Kabubo-Mariara (University of Nairobi, Kenya), and B. P. Vani (ISEC, Bangalore) for their time and effort in reviewing these chapters and offering detailed comments to the authors.

I would like to thank the following organizations and publishers for very kindly giving me permission to publish the following: American Institute of Biological Sciences (Table 1.3 in the book), Elsevier Publishers for the article by Unai Pascual and Charles Perrings on 'Developing incentives and economic mechanisms for *in situ* biodiversity conservation in agricultural landscapes' (*Agriculture, Ecosystems and Environment*, vol 121, 2007, pp256–268), and Springer Publication (Berlin) for the article by Turner et al on 'An ecological economics approach to the management of a multi-purpose coastal wetland' (*Regional Environmental Change*, vol 4, 2004, pp86–99).

I would also like to thank Director Professor N. Jayaram, my colleagues and especially CEENR staff for the cooperation and support extended during the preparation of this book. My immense thanks to Ms. S. Padmavathy, our Centre Secretary, for her ungrudging assistance and support and for undertaking several drafts of the chapters of this book.

I would like to express my sincere gratitude to Dr Achim Steiner, UN Under-Secretary General, and Executive Director, United Nations Environment

Programme (UNEP), Nairobi, who despite his onerous responsibilities and several commitments has found time to write the foreword to this book. It is indeed an honour and a privilege to have his foreword.

My immense thanks also to Earthscan and the entire Earthscan team for their tireless efforts and care in bringing out this book. I have enjoyed working with the entire Earthscan team and deem it an honour to have another book from Earthscan.

K. N. Ninan
Bangalore
9 July 2008

List of Acronyms and Abbreviations

AAFC	Atlantic Africa Fisheries Conference
ABS	access and benefit sharing
ACC	auction contracts for conservation
ACF	Australian Conservation Foundation
ADB	Asian Development Bank
AOGCMs	atmosphere-ocean global circulation models
APFIC	Asia-Pacific Fisheries Commission
ARA	academic research agreement
ARTES	Africa rainfall and temperature evaluation system
ASALs	arid to semi-arid lands
ASEAN	Association of South East Asian Nations
BA	Broads Authority
BCH	bio-cultural heritage
BDI	beliefs, desires and intentions
BCOW	Behavioural Correlates of War
BIC	Bamusso–Isangele Creeks
BTNLL	Balai Taman Nasional Lore Lindu
CAP	Common Agricultural Policy
CBA	cost–benefit analysis
CBD	Convention on Biological Diversity
CCAMLR	Commission for the Conservation of Antarctic Marine Living Resources
CCC	Canadian Climate Center
CCSBT	Commission for the Conservation of Southern Bluefin Tuna
CCSR	Center for Climate System Research
CDF	cumulative distribution function
CDM	Clean Development Mechanism
CECAF	Fishery Committee for the Eastern Central Atlantic
CEEPA	Centre for Environmental Economics and Policy in Africa
CER	carbon emission reduction
CGCM	coupled general circulation model
CGIAR	Consultative Group on International Agricultural Research
CIP	International Potato Centre
CIPRA	Community Intellectual Property Rights Act
COREP	Regional Fisheries Committee for the Gulf of Guinea (not yet in force)

CPPS	South Pacific Permanent Commission
CRA	commercial research agreement
CSERGE	Centre for Social and Economic Research on the Global Environment
CSIRO	Commonwealth Scientific and Industrial Research Organisation model
CTMFM	Joint Technical Commission for the Argentina/Uruguay Maritime Front
CVM	contingent valuation method
CWP	Coordinating Working Party on Fishery Statistics
DCP	direct compensation payments
DOST	Department of Science and Technology
DPC	Douala–Pongo Creeks
DPSIR	driving forces–pressure–state–impact–response
EA	Environmental Agency
EBM	ecosystem-based management
ECHAM	European Centre Hamburg model
EDD	Empowered Deliberative Democracy
EEZ	exclusive economic zone
EFR	environmental fiscal reform
EMS	ecosystem management system
EPA	Environmental Protection Agency
ES	environmental service
ESV	ecosystem service value
FAO	Food and Agriculture Organisation
FAS	flood alleviation scheme
FDI	foreign direct investment
FFA	South Pacific Forum Fisheries Agency
FONAFIFO	National Fund for Forest Financing
FSC	Forest Stewardship Council
GATT	General Agreement on Tariffs and Trade
GDP	gross domestic product
GEF	Global Environment Facility
GFCM	General Fisheries Commission for the Mediterranean
GIS	geographical information systems
GNP	gross national product
GPS	global positioning system
GR	genetic resources
GRID	Global Resources Information Database
HADCM	Hadley Centre coupled model
IAC	Inter-Agency Committee
IACBGR	Inter Agency on Biological and Genetic Resources
IATTC	Inter-American Tropical Tuna Commission

IB	interactive bidding questions
IBSFC	International Baltic Sea Fishery Commission
ICCAT	International Commission for the Conservation of Atlantic Tuna
ICDP	integrated conservation and development project
ICEM	International Centre for Environmental Management
ICES	International Council for the Exploration of the Sea
ICRAF	World Agroforestry Centre
ID	influence diagram
IETA	International Emissions Trading Association
IFAD	International Fund for Agricultural Development
IFOAM	International Federation of Organic Agriculture Movements
IHRP	International Habitat Reserve Programme
IIED	International Institute for Environment and Development
IKEA	Swedish home products retail chain
IntIDS	interacting influence diagrams
IOTC	Indian Ocean Tuna Commission
IPCC	Intergovernmental Panel on Climate Change
IPHC	International Pacific Halibut Commission
IPO	Intellectual Property Office
IPR	intellectual property rights
IPRA	Indigenous Peoples Rights Act
ITQ	individual transferable quota
IUCN	International Union for the Conservation of Nature
IWC	International Whaling Commission
KKM	Kepasakapatan Konservasi Masyarakat
LME	large marine system
LPMS	least practical management strategy
LUCC	land use and land cover change
MAB	Man and the Biosphere Programme
MDG	Millennium Development Goal
MEA	Millennium Ecosystem Assessment
MPMS	most practical management strategy
NAFO	Northwest Atlantic Fisheries Organization
NAMMCO	North Atlantic Marine Mammal Commission
NASCO	North Atlantic Salmon Conservation Organization
NCGR	National Commission on Genetic Resources
NCIP	National Council for Indigenous Peoples
NEAFC	North-East Atlantic Fisheries Commission
NEPL	Nam Et-Phou Loei
NFF	National Farmers Federation (Australia)
NGO	non-governmental organization
NNP	Nagarhole National Park

NOAA	National Oceanic and Atmospheric Administration
NPAFC	North Pacific Anadromous Fish Commission
NPV	net present value
NRA	National Rivers Authority
NTFP	non timber forest product
OE	open-ended questions
OECD	Organisation for Economic Co-operation and Development
OLDEPESCA	Latin American Organization for the Development of Fisheries
OOHB	one and a half bound elicitation method
P(R)ES	payments/rewards for environmental services
PA	protected area
PAER	predicted actions error rate
PBR	plant breeders' rights
PCAARD	Philippine Council for Agriculture, Forestry and Natural Resources Research and Development
PCM	parallel climate model
PDF	probability density function
PDPF	Probability density probability function
PEFC	Programme for the Endorsement of Forest Certification Schemes
PIC	prior informed consent
PICES	North Pacific Marine Science Organization
PITAHC	Philippine Institute for Traditional and Alternative Health Care
PMF	probability mass function
PPP/PFI	public and private funding unitiative
P(R)ES	payments/rewards for environmental services
PSC	Pacific Salmon Commission
PVP	plant variety protection
PVPA	Plant Variety Protection Act
R&D	research and development
RECOFI	Regional Commission for Fisheries (not yet in force)
REDD	reduced emissions from degradation and deforestation
RFMO	Regional Fishery Management Organisation
RMSPE	root mean squared prediction error
RUPES	Rewarding Upland Poor for Environmental Services
SCBD	Secretariat of the Convention on Biological Diversity
SCM	subsidies and countervailing measures
SDE	stochastic differential equations
SEAFO	South East Atlantic Fishery Organization (not yet in force)
SEARICE	South East Asia Regional Initiatives for Community Development
SEDP	Socio-Economic Development Plan
SIOFA	South Indian Ocean Fisheries Agreement

SPC	Secretariat of the Pacific Community
SPS	sanitary and phytosanitary measures
SRCF	Sub-regional Commission on Fisheries
SRES	Special Report on Emissions Scenarios
STORMA	Stability of Rainforest Margins
SWIOFC	South West Indian Ocean Fishery Commission (not yet finalized)
TAMA	Traditional and Alternative Medicine Act
TBT	technical barriers to trade
TC	travel cost
TDR	transferable development right
TEV	total economic value
TK	traditional knowledge
TMC	Tiko–Mungo Creeks
TRIPs	trade related intellectual property rights
UNCBD	United Nations Convention on Biological Diversity
UNCLOS	UN Convention on the Law of the Seas
UNEP	United Nations Environment Programme
UNESCO	United Nations Educational, Scientific and Cultural Organization
UNFCCC	United Nations Framework Convention on Climate Change
UNPFII	United Nations Permanent Forum on Indigenous Issues
UPOV	International Convention for the Protection of New Varieties of Plants
USFWS	United States Fish and Wildlife Service
WCPFC	Western and Central Pacific Fisheries Commission (not yet in force)
WECAFC	Western Central Atlantic Fishery Commission
WIOTO	Western Indian Ocean Tuna Organization
WIPO	World Intellectual Property Organisation
WTA	willingness to accept
WTO	World Trade Organization
WTP	willingness to pay
WWF	Worldwide Fund for the Conservation of Nature
YEP	yellow-eyed penguin
YEPT	Yellow-eyed Penguin Trust
ZERI	Zero Emission Research and Initiatives
1DC	Single-bound dichotomous choice

1

Introduction

K. N. Ninan

Biodiversity, ecosystem services and human well-being

The Millennium Ecosystem Assessment (MEA) 2005 has brought about a fundamental change in the way that scientists perceive the role and value of biodiversity. While the arguments to support biodiversity conservation hitherto relied on its intrinsic, use and non-use values, the MEA broadened its scope by emphasizing the importance of biodiversity as a source of ecosystem services, and for human well-being. By identifying the role of biodiversity in the provision of services with demonstrable value to people, it has broadened the range of motivations for conservation, and has established an obligation to identify the consequences of change in biodiversity to the well-being of people (Kinzig et al, 2007). Justifying conservation no longer relies solely on the notion of biodiversity for biodiversity's sake, or the spiritual or ethical consideration of a right of species to exist independent of their use by people (sometimes referred to as 'intrinsic value'). While this remains an important motivation for conservation it significantly underestimates the value of biodiversity, and is one reason why it has been difficult to secure even the minimum level of protection needed to stem the accelerating wave of species extinctions (Kinzig et al, 2007). The MEA recognizes the dynamics and linkages between people, biodiversity and ecosystems. Human activities have direct and indirect impacts on biodiversity and ecosystems, which in turn affects the ecosystem services they provide, and ultimately impacts on human well-being. The MEA, however, also notes that many other factors, independent of changes in biodiversity and ecosystems, affect human conditions and that biodiversity and ecosystems are also influenced by many natural factors that are not associated with humans (MEA, 2005). While people and human well-being are the pivot around which the MEA revolves, it does acknowledge that biodiversity and ecosystems also have intrinsic value – value of something in and for itself, irrespective of its utility for someone else – and that people make decisions concerning ecosystems based on consideration of their own well-being and that of others as well as on intrinsic value (MEA, 2005).

The MEA identifies four types of ecosystem services that contribute to human well-being. These are: provisioning services such as food, water, timber and fibre; regulating services such as the regulation of climate, floods, disease, wastes and water quality; cultural services such as recreation, aesthetic enjoyment, and spiritual fulfilment; and supporting services such as soil formation, photosynthesis and nutrient cycling (MEA, 2005). Information on the main ecosystem types and services that they provide are furnished in Table 1.1. Human well-being as conceived by the MEA refers to not only material welfare and livelihoods but also security, resiliency, social relations, health, and freedom of choice and action. Biodiversity loss affects the critical ecosystem services that sustain human life and well-being. Besides human impacts, biodiversity loss also has non-human impacts, and inter-generational and intra-generational impacts (Ninan et al, 2007).

Figure 1.1 depicts the conceptual framework of the interactions that exist between biodiversity, ecosystem services, human well-being and drivers of change. Drivers are any natural or human induced factors that directly or indirectly cause a change in an ecosystem such as habitat change, climate change, invasive species, overexploitation and pollution. Indirect drivers are the real cause of ecosystem changes such as change in economic activity, demographic change, socio-political, cultural and religious factors, scientific and technological change, etc. (MEA, 2005). Changes in drivers that indirectly affect biodiversity, such as population, technology and lifestyle, can lead to changes in drivers directly affecting biodiversity such as fish catch, fertilizer use, etc. These lead to changes in biodiversity and ecosystem services, and ultimately human well-being. These interactions can take place at local, regional or global scales as well as across different timescales. For instance, international demand for timber may lead to a regional loss of forest cover, which increases flood magnitudes along a local stretch of water (MEA, 2005). Overharvesting of fish resources by the present generation will have an adverse impact on fish abundance and biodiversity, the spillover costs of which will be borne by future generations.

Conserving biodiversity and the ecosystem services that they provide is part of the larger objective of promoting human well-being and sustainable development. It also has implications for the poor and for poverty reduction. The poor depend on nature's bounties and services to sustain their livelihoods, and the degradation of these services threatens their livelihoods and survival. Ecosystem services directly support more than one billion people living in extreme poverty (World Bank, 2006, vide Turner et al, 2007). The degradation of biodiversity and ecosystems also imperils achieving the Millennium Development Goals (MDG) of reducing poverty, hunger, ill health and nutrition, by the year 2015. The World Summit on Sustainable Development held in Johannesburg in 2002, while endorsing the 2010 target of reducing biodiversity loss, also highlighted the essential role of biodiversity in meeting the millennium development goals, especially the target of halving the incidence of poverty and hunger by the year

Table 1.1 *Main ecosystem types and their services*

Ecosystem service	Ecosystem									
	Cultivated	Dryland	Forest	Urban	Inland water	Coastal	Marine	Polar	Mountain	Island
Freshwater	•		•		•	•		•	•	•
Food	•	•	•	•	•	•	•	•	•	
Timber, fuel and fibre	•	•	•			•	•			
Novel products	•	•	•	•		•	•	•	•	•
Biodiversity regulation	•	•	•	•	•	•	•	•	•	•
Nutrient cycling	•	•	•		•	•	•	•		•
Air quality and climate	•	•	•	•	•	•	•		•	
Human health		•	•	•	•	•	•			
Detoxification		•	•	•	•	•				
Natural hazard regulation			•		•	•			•	
Cultural and amenity	•			•	•	•	•	•	•	•

Source: Millennium Ecosystem Assessment, vide Pagiola et al, 2004.

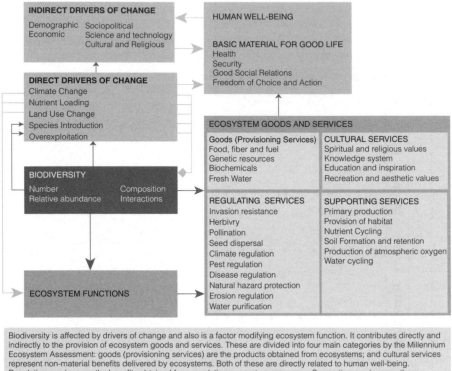

Biodiversity is affected by drivers of change and also is a factor modifying ecosystem function. It contributes directly and indirectly to the provision of ecosystem goods and services. These are divided into four main categories by the Millennium Ecosystem Assessment: goods (provisioning services) are the products obtained from ecosystems; and cultural services represent non-material benefits delivered by ecosystems. Both of these are directly related to human well-being. Regulating services are the benefits obtained from regulating ecosystem processes. Supporting services are those necessary for the production of all other ecosystem services.

Figure 1.1 Biodiversity, ecosystem functioning, ecosystem services and drivers of change

Source: Secretariat of the Convention on Biological Diversity, *Global Biodiversity Outlook 2*, Montreal, 2006.

2015 (Baillie et al, 2004). Although there could be trade-offs between achieving the 2015 target of the MDG, and the 2010 target of reducing the rate of biodiversity loss resolved by the Conference of the Parties to the Convention on Biological Diversity (CBD) in 2002, there are also potential synergies between achieving the internationally agreed goals of reducing biodiversity loss, and promoting environmental sustainability and development.

Since biodiversity and ecosystem services are public goods, the private incentive to exploit them beyond socially optimum levels is tremendous. Although the CBD, to which 188 countries are signatories, has set a target of achieving a significant reduction in the current rate of biodiversity loss by the year 2010, the MEA report paints a grim picture. Far from reducing, the MEA review shows that the rates of biodiversity loss have remained steady, if not accelerated. Approximately 35 per cent of mangroves, 30 per cent of coral reefs,

50 per cent of wetlands, 40 per cent of global forest cover (in the last 300 years) have either disappeared or degraded (MEA, 2005, vide EC, 2008). Approximately 60 per cent of the world's ecosystems services are degraded. Of 24 ecosystem services reviewed, the MEA observed that only four services, i.e. crop, livestock and aquaculture production, and carbon sequestration (that helps global climate regulation) have increased. Two other services, i.e. fisheries and freshwater, were found to be beyond sustainable levels; while all other remaining services were declining or degraded. To give a sense of the scale of environmental deterioration that has taken place, the MEA notes that more land has been converted to agriculture since 1945 than in the 18th and 19th centuries combined. The MEA notes that current extinction rates are up to 1000 times higher than the fossil record of less than one species per 1000 mammal species becoming extinct every millennium. The projected future extinction rate is more than ten times higher than the current rate. It is also reported that 12 per cent of bird species, 25 per cent of mammals and 32 per cent of amphibians are threatened with extinction over the next century (Baillie et al, 2004; MEA, 2005). Regional case studies show that freshwater fish species may be more threatened than marine species (Baillie et al, 2004). For example, 27 per cent of freshwater species in Eastern Africa were listed as threatened. About 42 per cent of turtles and tortoises are also listed as threatened. Of plants, only conifers and cycads have been completely assessed with 25 and 52 per cent respectively categorized as threatened. The Living Planet Index – a measure of the state of the world's biodiversity based on trends from 1970 to 2003 and covering 695 terrestrial species, 274 marine species and 344 freshwater species in the world – compiled by WWF (2006) notes an overall decline of 30 per cent in the index over the 33-year period under review, and similarly for terrestrial, marine and freshwater indices. The Ecological Footprint – a measure of humanity's demand on the Earth's biocapacity for meeting consumption needs and absorbing wastes – has exceeded the earth's biocapacity by 25 per cent as of 2003 (WWF, 2006). The IUCN Red List contains 784 documented extinctions and 60 extinctions of species in the wild since AD 1500 (Baillie et al, 2004). Over the past 20 years 27 documented extinctions or extinctions in the wild have occurred (Baillie et al, 2004). These numbers certainly underestimate the true number of extinctions in historic times as the majority of the species have not been described, most described species have not been comprehensively assessed, and proving that a species has gone extinct can take years to decades (Baillie et al, 2004). Moreover the IUCN Red List is based on an assessment of less than 3 per cent of the world's 1.9 million described species. What is more alarming to note is that while the vast majority of extinctions since AD 1500 have occurred on oceanic islands, continental extinctions are now as common as island extinctions. For instance, it is noted that 50 per cent of extinctions over the past 20 years have occurred on continents (Baillie et al, 2004). This is because most terrestrial species are continental. Habitat loss is the most pervasive threat, impacting on between

86–88 per cent of threatened birds, mammals and amphibians. These unprecedented rates at which species extinctions and environmental degradation are taking place threaten the very survival and well-being of human societies. Reversing these trends, therefore, pose a major challenge to scientists and governments.

Economic valuation of biodiversity and ecosystem services will help in assessing their benefits and contribution to the economy and human welfare. It will aid decision making by weighing the trade-offs between conservation and development, and ecosystem management options. Besides, it speaks in the economic language to which policy makers listen (O'Neill, 1997, vide Ninan et al, 2007). But, as stated earlier, biodiversity and ecosystem services have the characteristics of a public good and hence are treated as free or zero valued goods. However, merely because biodiversity and ecosystem services are not traded, or their values are not reflected in conventional markets does not imply that they have zero values. A few examples are worth citing to illustrate the economic or financial value of ecosystem services. For instance, New York city avoided spending US$6–8 billion on the construction of new water treatment plants by protecting the upstate Catskill watershed that traditionally accomplished these purification services but which had been degraded due to agricultural and sewage wastes, and instead spent US$1.5 billion on buying land around its reservoirs and instituting other protective measures, with the additional offshoot of enhancing recreation, wildlife habitats and other ecological benefits (Stapleton, 1997, vide www.earthtrends.wri.org). Similarly much of the Mississippi River Valley's natural flood protection services were destroyed when adjacent wetlands were drained and channels altered. As a result, the 1993 floods resulted in property damages estimated at US$12 billion, partly due to the inability of the valley to fulfil its natural flood protection services (www.esa.org). A study in the Hadejia-Jama'are flood plain region in northern Nigeria noted that the net benefit to the local people from the flood plains remaining in their current state in terms of agricultural, fishing, grazing, wild products benefits, etc., even without counting wildlife habitat benefits, was higher (US$167 per ha) than the benefits from a proposed irrigation project (US$29 per ha) that sought to divert water from the wetlands for irrigation (Barbier et al, 1993, vide www.earthtrends.wri.org). Eighty per cent of the world's population relies upon natural medicinal products. Of the top 150 prescription drugs used in the US, 118 originate from natural sources: of this 74 per cent are sourced from plants, 18 per cent from fungi, 5 per cent from bacteria and 3 per cent from snake species. To give another illustration, over 100,000 different species including bats, bees, flies, moths, beetles, birds and butterflies provide free pollination services. A third of human food comes from plants pollinated by wild pollinators. The value of pollination services from wild pollinators in the US alone is estimated at US$4–6 billion per year (www.esa.org). Several studies establish the economic values of biodiversity, habitats and ecosystem services to be high and significant (cf. Pearce and Moran, 1994;

Perrings, 2000; Ninan et al, 2007). For instance about 80–90 per cent of the total economic value (TEV) of tropical forests is attributable to indirect use values such as watershed protection, carbon sequestration and non-use values (Ninan et al, 2007). Economic valuation has enabled us to assess and value the non-market benefits of biodiversity and ecosystems. Natural scientists and others are, however, sceptical about the use of economic valuation, and according to them the intrinsic value of biodiversity and the inherent right of all species to exist regardless of their material value to humans is itself a justification for biodiversity conservation (IUCN, 1990 vide ODA, 1991; Gowdy, 1997, vide Ninan et al, 2007). Some cite the limitations of economic valuation and conventional cost–benefit analysis to justify biodiversity conservation (cf. Gowdy and McDaniel, 1995; Gowdy, 1997). According to them, owing to the complexities, uncertainty and irreversibilities characteristic of a public good such as biodiversity, the limitations of the market and substitutability between biodiversity and monetized goods, and conflicts between economic and biological systems, relying on the precautionary principle or safe minimum standard is the most prudent option to conserve biodiversity and ecosystem services. Establishing a proportion of forests as protected areas is an example of observing the safe minimum standard to conserve biodiversity. Those who justify economic valuation are not denying the importance of relying on the precautionary principle or safe minimum standard to conserve biodiversity. However, establishing and maintaining protected areas is not a costless activity and requires money and for bio-rich developing countries in particular this has to compete with alternate uses (Ninan et al, 2007). This is where economic valuation has a major role to play in conserving biodiversity and ecosystem services.

One of the first attempts to estimate the economic value of the world's ecosystem services was by Costanza et al (1997a). They estimated the current economic value of 17 ecosystem services for 16 biomes at US$16–54 trillion per year, with an average value of over US$33 trillion per year. Of this, soil formation alone accounted for over 51 per cent of this value (see Table 1.2). However, these estimates have attracted wide criticism. For instance, it was noted that the estimates based on willingness to pay (WTP) measures were almost twice the global gross national product (GNP) of US$18 trillion per year, and further that they have ignored the ecological feedbacks and non-linearities that are central to the processes that link all species to each other and to their respective habitats (Smith, 1997). Also, their estimates whereby WTP estimates were converted into per ha equivalents were questioned since it assumes that all hectares within ecosystems are perfect substitutes (Smith, 1997). However, the shortcomings of traditional GNP and willingness to pay measures are well known (Costanza et al, 1997b). David Pearce argues that from an economic perspective what is important is not the 'total value' but the 'marginal value', i.e. what is the value of a small or a discrete change in the provision of goods and services through, say, the loss or gain of a given increment or decrement in forest cover (SCBD, 2001, p9). In the context of securing both conservation of species and ecosystem services, a recent study (Turner et al, 2007) tried to examine the

Table 1.2 *Estimated value of the world's ecosystem services, 1997*

Ecosystem services	Estimated value (Trillion US$)
Soil formation	17.1
Recreation	3.0
Nutrient cycling	2.3
Water regulation and supply	2.3
Climate regulation (temperature and precipitation)	1.8
Habitat	1.4
Flood and storm protection	1.1
Food and raw materials	0.8
Genetic resources	0.8
Atmospheric gas balance	0.7
Pollination	0.4
All other services	1.6
Total value of ecosystem services	33.3

Source: Costanza et al, 1997a, vide www.earthtrends.wri.org.

concordance between these two conservation objectives, by analysing global (terrestrial) biodiversity conservation priority areas vis-à-vis ecosystem service values (ESV). They used a global ESV map (Sutton and Costanza, 2002, vide Turner et al, 2007) and published biodiversity conservation maps for this purpose. Their results indicate wide variations across priority areas (Table 1.3). The study observed concordance between high biodiversity priority areas with high ESV such as Congo, the Amazon, Central Chile, Western Ghats in India, parts of South East Asia, etc. (Turner et al, 2007). However, there were also areas with high biodiversity values and low ESV (such as South Africa's Succulent Karoo), high ESVs and low biodiversity values (e.g. temperate countries), low biodiversity value and ESV (e.g. desert and polar regions), all of which call for different conservation strategies. The study noted evergreen broadleaf forests to be the leading source of ESV in all biodiversity prioritization templates accounting for a mean of 59.5 per cent of ESV among the nine templates. Further, of 17 services, just four (nutrient cycling, waste treatment, food production and climate regulation) accounted for 54–66 per cent of the ESV of each template. Overall tropical forests offered the greatest opportunities for synergy where the overlap of the two conservation priorities is highest.

Areas which are rich in biodiversity and environmentally sensitive are also home to most of the world's poor and indigenous communities who depend on the forest and other ecosystems for their livelihoods. Unless the poor and indigenous communities have a stake in conservation or are provided with sustainable livelihood options, these adverse social impacts can affect the quality of success of conservation policies. Establishing an institutional environment and incentives conducive to conserving biodiversity and ecosystem management, and balancing developing goals with conservation, therefore, pose a major challenge to

Table 1.3 *Estimated ecosystem service value (ESV) within templates for global biodiversity conservation*

Global template	Area (million km²)	Mean ESV (US$ km² per year)	Total ESV (billion US$ per year)			Percentage above random[c]	Concordance index[d] (percentage)
			Observed	Random[a]	Maximum[b]		
High-biodiversity wilderness areas (Mittermeier et al, 2003)	11.5	200,720	2314	701	4708	230	40.3
Frontier forests (Bryant et al, 1997)	13.2	188,224	2487	803	5151	210	38.7
Most proactive	7.6	217,356	1659	464	3681	257	37.1
Global 200 ecoregions (Olson and Dinnerstein, 1998)	53.8	86,857	4671	3270	7466	43	33.4
Last of the wild (Sanderson et al, 2002)	35.0	98,356	3440	2127	6838	62	27.9
Megadiversity countries (Mittermeier et al, 1997)	49.8	77,457	3860	3031	7340	27	19.2
Endemic bird areas (Stattersfield et al, 1998)	13.8	88,710	1222	838	5301	46	8.6
Centres of plant diversity (WWF and IUCN 1994–1997)	12.2	83,779	1023	743	4888	38	6.8
Most reactive	12.1	76,057	917	734	4849	25	4.5
Biodiversity hotspots (Mittermeier et al, 2004)	23.0	69,071	1588	1398	6289	14	3.9
Random terrestrial km²	—	60,813	—	—	—	—	0.0
Crisis ecoregions (Hoekstra et al, 2005)	42.7	46,038	1967	2598	7112	−24	−14.0

Note: All monetary values are in 2005 US dollars

a. ESV in randomly selected 1km² cells, with the total area equivalent to that of each template.
b. Maximum ESV attainable for the total area equivalent to that of each template.
c. Significance of percentage deviation from random is evaluated with a randomization test ($N = 10,000$, $p\ 0.001$ in all cases).
d. Percentage of ESV represented beyond that expected at random, relative to the maximum attainable.
e. References in the table are cited in Turner et al, 2007.

Source: Will R. Turner et al (2007) 'Global conservation of biodiversity and ecosystem services', *Bioscience*, vol. 57, no. 10, November, pp. 868–873; Reproduced with permission. Copyright, American Institute of Biological Sciences.

governments, nations and societies. Apart from finding the right mix of incentives and institutions, the social costs of conservation also need to be accounted for. Other issues such as intellectual property rights cannot overlook the issue of the rights of indigenous communities and the protection of indigenous knowledge. The most important direct drivers of biodiversity loss and ecosystem services changes are habitat change, climate change, invasive alien species, overexploitation and pollution. Understanding the dynamics and linkages between the drivers behind loss of biodiversity and ecosystem services is another challenge that also needs to be addressed.

About this book

This book addresses the economic, institutional and social challenges confronting scientists and policy makers in conserving biodiversity and ecosystem services that are critical for sustaining human well-being and development. The contributors to the volume are leading experts in the world who have made significant contributions to biodiversity research and policy. It covers a wide range of themes and issues such as the economics and valuation of biodiversity and ecosystem services, the social aspects of conservation, incentives and institutions including payments for ecosystem services, governance, intellectual property rights (IPRs) and the protection of indigenous knowledge, climate change and biodiversity, etc. The volume includes chapters with an international focus (e.g. Chapters 2, 3, 4, 8, 9) as well as case studies from North and South America, Europe, Africa, Asia and Australia (e.g. Chapters 2, 3, 5, 6, 7, 9, 11–17) covering diverse ecosystems such as tropical forests, wetlands, aquatic and marine ecosystems, dry ecosystems, etc. In addition, the book includes applications of environmental economics such as the contingent valuation method, benefit transfer, and new institutional economics, game theory, etc. For convenience, the chapters are organized under the following broad themes: biodiversity, ecosystem services and valuation; incentives and institutions; governance; IPRs and protection of indigenous knowledge; and climate change, biodiversity and ecosystem services. However, some of the chapters address issues which overlap across these themes (e.g. Chapters 4, 7, 11).

Biodiversity, ecosystem services and valuation

The economics and valuation of biodiversity and ecosystem services, social aspects including biodiversity–poverty linkages, factors causing biodiversity loss and degradation of ecosystems are the main issues addressed in the chapters in this section. Economic valuation has emerged as a powerful tool to value the benefits of biodiversity and ecosystem services. The contingent valuation method (CVM) in particular has been widely used to value species, habitats and ecosystem services.

Richardson and Loomis (Chapter 2) summarize and review contingent valuation studies of the total economic value of endangered species worldwide. They compare US estimates with rest of the world estimates and developed versus developing countries for broad species groups, and individual species, and by type of CVM method used (i.e. open-ended versus dichotomous choice method, annual versus lump sum payment). Their review covers about 43 studies. They also try to identify 'standard practices' as well as assess whether there are consistent differences in how CVM is applied in developed versus developing countries. The average values per household for species are presented individually and by groups of similar species (e.g. marine mammals, birds, etc.). Comparisons are made between average values for similar species between developed and developing countries both in terms of absolute monetary values and as a percentage of income to control for differences in income. To make the estimates comparable, all WTP estimates were converted into constant (2006) US$. Their analysis reveals that US studies using lump sum payment elicit very high average WTP values as compared to the rest of the world estimates for marine mammals and birds. This is because the species surveyed in the US are charismatic mammals (e.g. monk seal, humpback whale, bald eagle) whereas the rest of the world studies are based on less charismatic species such as water vole, red squirrel, brown hare. However, the rest of the world studies that elicit WTP using an annual payment report higher values on average than US studies using the same annual payment horizon. Lower income respondents' WTP is more when the WTP elicits annual payment and less in the case of lump sum payment. They also compare the WTP estimates of individual species across selected countries to see how the WTP estimates fare for similar species, and their results are quite revealing. For instance, the value placed on wolves in Sweden is much higher than the value placed on wolves in the US. Similarly, the value placed on seals in Greece appeared to be higher than the value placed on seals in the US. The WTP values for similar species differ significantly depending on country where the study was conducted. Interestingly, respondents in developing countries are willing to pay more as a percentage of their income for nationally symbolic species, whereas in the US, it appears that only visitors and not necessarily households' WTP on average is more for nationally symbolic species. Most CVM studies reviewed used similar practices in conducting the CVM survey, WTP estimates on average seem to be higher when respondents are presented with a dichotomous choice format compared to an open-ended format. Their review, however, is not exhaustive, and especially so for developing countries where only three studies are reviewed. There are several CVM studies on African and Asian elephants, and some on Royal Bengal tigers in India (for a review see Ninan et al, 2007) which the review does not cover.

Unlike terrestrial ecosystems, aquatic and marine ecosystems have received relatively less attention. Tisdell (Chapter 3) traces the development of aquaculture and its impact on fish biodiversity. While genetic selection and the cultivation of organisms, particularly in agriculture, have helped to support a larger human population at a higher standard of living than otherwise, these developments have also led to a loss of biodiversity, particularly in the wild. The biodiversity of cultivated crops and domestic livestock has declined considerably in recent decades. The more recent development of aquaculture continues this development process. The aquaculture practices that are likely to lead to biodiversity loss are listed and their consequences specified. Trends in fish supplies from aquaculture are compared to supplies from the wild. These indicate an increasing replacement of supplies from the wild by aquaculture. For instance, since the late 1980s aquaculture has been the sole source of the increase in global supplies of fish, whereas production from wild catch has been virtually stagnant since that time. While in 1950 supplies of fish from aquaculture were negligible relative to wild catch, by 2004 they accounted for 60 per cent. China is the largest producer of aquaculture fish in the world. By 1983 China's production from aquaculture had overtaken its wild catch; by 2004 aquaculture fish supplies were two and a half times its wild catch. While domestic wild catch has been falling, China has increased its supplies from distant water fishing, apart from aquaculture. The role and environmental consequence of aquaculture, commercial and recreational fishing in accelerating biodiversity loss in wild fish stocks are discussed. While the development of aquaculture and of genetic selection has its economic advantages, considerable uncertainty exists about how much genetic alteration is desirable from an economic point of view. While development of aquaculture has started to reduce genetic diversity in wild fish stocks, the genetic diversity of farmed fish may also eventually decline as has happened to crop and livestock biodiversity.

Perrings (Chapter 4) discusses the problem of biodiversity conservation in the High Seas which have characteristics of open access resources. It starts from the premise that the aim of conservation is the sustainable use of marine resources, and that this implies maintenance of the resilience of large marine areas. While there are many threats to the resilience of marine ecosystems such as pollution, transmission of pests and pathogens in ballast water, bottom trawling, habitat disruption, climate change, etc., by far the most frequently cited stress in marine ecosystems is commercial overexploitation of fish and other marine animal resources. Lack of effective institutional and governance mechanisms are the underlying social causes of over exploitation. Perrings discusses the challenges and options for regulating access to large marine ecosystems so as to protect their resilience in order to maintain a desirable flow of ecosystem services over a range of conditions. Overfishing is associated with poorly regulated access, the net effect of which is a decline in yields of many of the world's major fisheries. Over the 54-year period 1950–2003, the rate of fisheries collapse in the 64 large marine areas which supply 83 per cent of global fish catches has accelerated; 29 per cent of fished species were in a state of collapse in 2003. Overfishing of deep-water species is a matter of particular concern. Demand for high-valued species in the export sector, such as southern blue finned tuna, have driven overexploitation of these species. Within coastal fisheries there has been a switch from large high-valued predator fish to smaller low-valued planktivorous fish, and from mature to immature fish. The level of fishing effort in oceanic species and deep-water species has increased relatively to that for other capture fisheries. The weaknesses of the UN Convention on the Law of the Seas (UNCLOS) multilateral agreement that enshrines open access as a fundamental right, the merits of regional seas programmes and their role in supporting conservation goals, property rights and governance issues in the context of large marine ecosystems is discussed.

Three case studies (Chapters 5, 6, 7) from Asia examine the biodiversity, poverty, livelihood linkages and local or indigenous communities' attitudes and support to conservation and establishment of protected areas. Emerton (Chapter 5) contends that economic and development concerns, and especially the targets towards global poverty reduction that are articulated in the MDGs, cannot in reality be separated from the need to conserve and sustainably use biodiversity – in relation to policy formulation, funding decisions and on-the-ground implementation. Failing to understand that biodiversity offers a basic tool for reducing poverty, and forms a key component of investments in development infrastructure, leads to the risk of incurring far-reaching economic and development costs – especially for the poorest and most vulnerable sectors of the world's population.

Emerton provides concrete examples of the linkages between biodiversity, poverty reduction and socio-economic development in Lao PDR. It articulates the economic contribution that biodiversity makes to local livelihoods and national development indicators, and in particular its value for the poorest and most vulnerable groups in the country. Biodiversity contributes directly or indirectly to three-quarters of per capita GDP in Lao PDR, over 90 per cent of employment, about 60 per cent of exports and foreign exchange earnings and nearly half of foreign direct investment (FDI) flows. Wild resources contribute 50–60 per cent of the livelihoods of the poorest households who face recurrent rice deficits, have little or no crop land and own few or no livestock. As poverty levels rise, forest products make a progressively greater economic contribution to livelihoods. The author also describes how, over the last decade, both domestic and overseas funding for biodiversity has declined dramatically in Lao PDR. At the same time, many of the policy instruments that are being used in the name of promoting development have acted to make conservation financially unprofitable and economically undesirable. The case of Lao PDR illustrates a situation, and highlights an apparent paradox, that is also found in many other parts of the world. If biodiversity has such a demonstrably high economic and livelihood value, especially for the poorest, then why is it persistently marginalized by the very economic policies and funding flows that are tied to strengthening livelihoods, reducing poverty and achieving sustainable socio-economic development? The chapter argues that a shift in the way in which development and conservation trade-offs are calculated is required – moving from approaches which fail to factor in ecosystem costs and benefits, to those which recognize and count natural ecosystems as a key component of development infrastructure.

A study of tribals in a protected area in India by Ninan (Chapter 6) analyses the economics of non timber forest products (NTFPs) and the economic values appropriated by them. Using primary data covering a cross section of tribals in the Nagarhole National Park (NNP), South India, the study notes that the economic values appropriated by the tribals are quite high. Even after including external costs (i.e. wildlife damages costs and defensive expenditures to protect against wildlife attacks) the net present value (NPV) of NTFP benefits derived by the tribal households was high and significant. Interestingly when the external costs borne by third parties (i.e. coffee growers) are taken into account, the net NTFP benefits turned negative. In other words, although from the NTFP extractors viewpoint NTFP extraction is a viable activity, from the society's viewpoint this is not so. The estimated net NTFP benefits from NNP after including the external costs borne by NTFP extractors was estimated at US$33.5–167.5 per ha per year using alternate assumptions regarding the park's area that is accessed by the tribals. The tribals have a positive attitude towards biodiversity conservation. Asked to justify and rank the reasons why biodiversity needs to be conserved, the tribals emphasized its livelihood and ecosystem functions. Using the contingent valuation method, the study notes that those with income from coffee estates and forest employment, and those residing in the core zone of the national park are less willing to accept compensation and relocate outside the national park. The study suggests improving the incentive structure in order to obtain the support and participation of tribals in biodiversity conservation strategies.

Integrated conservation and development projects (ICDP) have been promoted since the 1970s as an alternative to traditional park models with a view to linking conservation and development goals and also benefiting local communities. Over the past 25 years, considerable funds have been invested in ICDP projects associated with parks in developing countries. These projects count on local support, but the degree and distribution of such support is difficult to gauge. Kramer et al (Chapter 7) study two ICDP projects in Indonesia to gauge local support for the projects. Using the contingent valuation method, they found strong local support for the two projects. Household support for the projects varied with both socio-economic characteristics and use of park resources. Given the high cost of survey implementation, the authors also explored ways to predict support for park projects at other sites based on a survey at a single site. Their analysis reveals that the potential for such benefit transfer is limited by the difficulty of accounting for households who do not support the project.

Incentives and institutions

Establishing an institutional environment and incentives conducive to biodiversity conservation is a major challenge (Ninan et al, 2007). The recent past has witnessed several initiatives to popularize market-based and other incentives to secure biodiversity conservation.

The concept of payments for ecosystem services – an idea which has gained currency – implies that those who are providing the services deserve to be compensated when they manage ecosystems to deliver more services to others. It is being developed as an important means of providing a more diverse flow of benefits to people living in and around forests. McNeely (Chapter 8) provides an international perspective of some new approaches to building efficient markets for ecosystem services. Payment of conservation incentives can reward forest managers and farmers for being good stewards of the land and ensure that payments are made by those who are receiving benefits. Similarly those who degrade ecosystems and reduce the supply of ecosystem services should pay for the damages they cause based on the 'Polluter Pays Principle'. The Kyoto Protocol under the United Nations Framework Convention on Climate Change (UNFCCC) includes the Clean Development Mechanism, which provides for payments for certain forms of carbon sequestration. Other market-based approaches for paying for carbon sequestration services outside the Kyoto framework are being promoted in various parts of the world. Another common form of payment for ecosystem services is compensating upstream landowners for managing their land in ways that maintain downstream water quality. While biodiversity itself is difficult to value, it can be linked to other markets, such as certification in the case of sustainably produced forest products. McNeely discusses some of the markets for forest ecosystem services, identifies relevant sources of information, and highlights some of the initiatives linking such markets to poverty alleviation. Four categories of market and payment schemes are discussed in detail. These are (i) eco-labelling of forest/farm products; (ii) open trading under a regulatory cap or floor such as carbon trading or mitigation banking; (iii) user fees for environmental and cultural services such as hunting licenses or entry to protected areas; and (iv) public payment schemes to encourage forest owners to maintain or enhance ecosystem services such as 'conservation banking' and watershed protection. Making markets work for ecosystem services requires an appropriate policy framework, government support, operational institutional support, and innovation at scales from the site level to the national level.

Pascual and Perrings (Chapter 9) focus on agrobiodiversity and its effects on the multiple services that agriculture provides to society, especially those related to the provision of food and fibre production within agricultural landscapes. The interest is to shed light about the fundamental causes of agrobiodiversity loss by focusing upon the institutional or meso-economic environment that mediates farmers' decentralized decisions. Since the causes of farmers' decisions to 'disinvest' in agrobiodiversity as an asset lie in the incentives offered by current markets and other institutions, the solution lies in corrective institutional design. Changes in agrobiodiversity are the product of explicit or implicit decentralized farm-level decision whose effects include both farm and landscape level changes in a range of ecosystem services. The solution is to develop mechanisms that provide a different set of incentives. The institutional issues involved in establishing market-like mechanisms for agrobiodiversity conservation are discussed. Three steps are highlighted in such a process: demonstration (valuation), capture, and sharing of conservation benefits (mechanism design). This information is then used to examine the potential success of nascent market creation incentive mechanisms for biodiversity conservation, such as: (i) payments/rewards for environmental services; (ii) direct compensation payments; (iii) transferable development rights; and (iv) auctions for biodiversity conservation that can recreate decentralized markets to foster agrobiodiversity conservation and their implications for the conservation of agrobiodiversity. The potential gains to society from their use with regard to agrobiodiversity conservation are discussed and some illustrative examples involving their application in different parts of the world are also described.

Non-governmental conservation organizations are an important stakeholder in biodiversity conservation and their conservation behaviour and strategies will impact on the conservation of biodiversity and ecosystem services. Tisdell (Chapter 10) draws mostly on new institutional economics to consider the likely behaviours of conservation non-governmental organizations (NGOs) and their implications for biodiversity conservation. It considers: how institutional factors may result in the behaviour of conservation NGOs diverging from their objectives, including their support for biodiversity conservation; their role as political pressure groups trying to influence public policy by lobbying and by strategic dissemination of information; examines aspects of rent capture and conservation alliances; specifies social factors that may restrict the diversity of species supported by NGOs for conservation; bounded rationality in relation to the operation of conservation NGOs; and, using game theory, shows how competition between NGOs for funding can result in economic inefficiencies and narrow the diversity of species supported for conservation. For instance, conservation NGOs may favour the promotion of a narrow range of wildlife species, usually charismatic species, for conservation, since funds are easier to obtain than otherwise. Although the koala, a charismatic species, is not endangered, funding for its conservation is greater than for the critically endangered hairy-nosed wombat in Australia. Of course there may be some other rationale for this conservation behaviour. Given the large habitat requirements of flagship and umbrella species such as elephants and tigers, conserving them also benefits other species. The chapter also considers how the social role of conservation NGOs might be assessed and emphasizes a multidimensional approach to assess the role of such bodies in society.

Governance

Growing international attention to biodiversity in the 1990s has brought governance issues to the fore. The complexity of the governance issues involved in reconciling biodiversity conservation with competing interests makes it very difficult to manage protected areas and the resources they contain. The question of which institutional set up or management regime (or governance type) is most appropriate for protected areas cannot be easily resolved (Ninan, 1996; Ninan et al, 2007). While some argue that state or government managed protected areas are most suitable for biodiversity conservation and wildlife protection, others argue the case for community managed protected areas, especially in areas where indigenous or local communities depend heavily on these forests for their livelihoods; still others favour co-management where different stakeholders are represented, or privately managed wildlife reserves (as in Southern Africa).

Wetlands account for about 6 per cent of the global land area and are among the most threatened ecosystems. They provide various goods and services and generate substantial economic values. Turner et al (Chapter 11) analyse three interrelated management problems – eutrophication of multiple use shallow lakes, sea level rise and flood risk mitigation and tourism pressures – in the context of an internationally important wetland area, the Norfolk and Suffolk Broads in the UK. They present the results of valuation studies which seek to find out what individuals are willing to pay to prevent eutrophication of rivers and lakes through sewage treatment programmes, and elicit the views of recreational visitors to Broadlands to assess their WTP to preserve the existing Broads landscape, ecology and recreational possibilities, and these values are quite significant. The ecological-economic research findings presented should provide essential information to underpin the regulatory and management process in this internationally important conservation area. The authors state that the relevant authority needs to integrate the maintenance of public navigation rights, nature conservation and tourism promotion in a highly dynamic ecosystems setting. Because of the stakeholder conflicts, potential and actual, a more inclusive decision-making procedure is required, and is currently being implemented.

The decision to implement ecosystem protection options is ultimately a political one. Depending on the political mechanisms operating, a country may or may not heed the most reliable scientific analysis of an ecosystem's future health. A predictive understanding of the political processes that result in ecosystem management decisions can help guide the formulation of ecosystem management policy. To this end, Haas in Chapter 12 develops a stochastic, temporal model of how political processes influence and are influenced by ecosystem processes. This model is realized in a system of interacting influence diagrams that model the decision making of country presidents, environmental protection agencies and rural inhabitants. Decisions from these models affect the decisions of like models of groups in other countries, a model of a conservation-focused NGO and a model of the ecosystem enclosed by the interacting countries. As an example, a set of such models is constructed to represent cheetah management across Kenya, Tanzania and Uganda. These models are fitted to political decision and wildlife count data from these countries. The practical payoff of this fitted model is demonstrated by how it is used to find the most politically acceptable management strategy for conserving an at-risk ecosystem. Using the model, Haas shows how it can help in finding a practical management strategy for avoiding the extinction of cheetahs in East Africa.

The co-management of protected areas is widely considered to be a promising approach to overcome conflicts between different stakeholder and interest groups as well as an alternative to other management options. Community agreements are a major approach to the co-management of protected areas and natural resources. Negotiated agreements between local communities and state agencies concerning the management of natural resources have gained increasing importance in recent years. Birner and Mappatoba (Chapter 13) take the case of community agreements on conservation in Lore Lindu National Park, a world heritage site in Indonesia, rich in biodiversity and high endemism, as an example. The national park faces several threats such as conversion to agriculture, extraction of rattan, logging, hunting of protected and endemic animals, and collection of eggs of a protected bird. The authors analyse such agreements from two perspectives: (i) from the perspective of environmental economics, negotiated agreements are considered as a policy instrument that represents the bargaining solution proposed by Coase to solve externality problems; and (ii) from the perspective of policy analysis, the chapter analyses to what extent the agreements can be considered as an example of empowered deliberative democracy, a model suggested by Fung and Wright. The empirical analysis shows that the agreements differed considerably, depending on the value orientation and objectives of the NGOs promoting the agreements. Three NGOs were studied: an international NGO focusing on rural development, an international NGO specialized in nature conservation with a local sister organization focusing on community development, and a local NGO with a strong emphasis on advocacy for indigenous rights. Using a participatory approach, interviews with stakeholders, state agencies, NGOs and semi-structured interviews of random households in the selected villages, the analysis shows that both the Coase model and the deliberative democracy model offer useful insights into the logic behind the different agreements promoted by these organizations. The approaches to establish community agreements differed across the NGOs. While the advocacy NGO focused on indigenous people's rights, the rural development NGO viewed management of protected areas and natural resources as part of a broader community development programme that included, among other things, provision of physical infrastructure, whereas the conservation NGO focused on establishing co-management where all stakeholders had a say. The authors conclude that community agreements on conservation represent a promising approach to improve the management of protected areas, and especially for decentralized natural resource management even though the internal differentiation within the communities represents a challenge to this approach.

IPRs and protection of indigenous knowledge

The Convention on Biological Diversity, while recognizing the sovereign rights of nations over their biological resources, also called for equity in access and benefit sharing. Access and benefit sharing have, however, not made much headway due to problems and conflicts, especially in the areas of intellectual property rights and the protection of indigenous knowledge. There are conflicts between western and local legal systems regarding the use and management of genetic resources, and social and equity issues, especially the rights of indigenous communities and protection of their traditional knowledge.

The Philippines is home to a large indigenous population comprising almost 20 per cent of her population. The conflicts between IPRs and protecting the rights and traditional knowledge of indigenous communities are present in the Philippines also. Swanson et al (Chapter 14) traces the phases and movements, and legal reform effected in the Philippines to conform to its international obligations and protect the interests of indigenous communities. They summarize the three movements for IPRs occurring within the Philippines. The first movement concerns the creation of rights in biological and genetic resources, as required by membership of the CBD. The second movement concerns the standardization of existing IPR regimes, as required by membership of the World Trade Organization (WTO). The third movement concerns the reconciliation of the various rights in existence within the Philippines, by reason of the multiplicity of peoples and cultures within that country. This third movement provides the legal regime that is the basis for a case study on Community Intellectual Property Rights. This case study indicates that it is probably necessary to develop a combined/consistent system of IPR, but that it will be extremely difficult to complete such a task.

Some of these issues and conflicts are also discussed by Swiderska (Chapter 15) based on the work of the International Institute for Environment and Development (IIED) and research and indigenous partners in Peru, Panama, India, Kenya and China. The study draws on the collaborative project 'Protecting Community Rights over Traditional Knowledge: Implications of Customary Laws and Practices', and in particular the work of the NGO ANDES in Peru. Through participatory action-research the project is exploring the customary laws and practices of indigenous communities to inform the development of appropriate policies and mechanisms for the protection of traditional knowledge and bio-genetic resources at local, national and international level. It emphasizes the need to shift the dominant paradigms of access and benefit-sharing (ABS) and IPRs, which reflect 'western' laws and models, towards one based on respect for indigenous customary laws and worldviews and human rights. This will also strengthen the institutional basis for endogenous development. A key element of the approach is the recognition of the indigenous worldview that traditional knowledge, biodiversity, landscapes, cultural values and customary laws are inextricably linked elements of indigenous 'bio-cultural heritage'. The concept of 'Collective Bio-Cultural Heritage' and its application as a means to protect traditional knowledge, biodiversity and livelihoods are discussed. It also identifies policy challenges and recommendations for promoting the protection of 'Bio-cultural Heritage' on a wider scale.

Climate change, biodiversity and ecosystem services

Climate change is going to be a major factor driving species extinctions and degradation of ecosystems. While scientific knowledge about climate change and its effects has advanced considerably in the recent past, a lot of uncertainty still remains. It is having profound and long-term impacts on human welfare and adds yet another pressure on terrestrial and marine ecosystems that are already under threat from land use change, pollution, overharvesting and the introduction of alien species (SCBD, 2003). The Conference of the Parties to the CBD has highlighted the risks, in particular, to coral reefs and to forest ecosystems, and has drawn attention to the serious impacts of loss of biodiversity of these systems on people's livelihoods. Biodiversity management can contribute to climate change mitigation and adaptation and to combating desertification (SCBD, 2003). The UNFCCC calls for the conservation and enhancement of terrestrial, coastal and marine ecosystems as sinks for greenhouse gases. Thus there are significant opportunities for mitigating climate change, and for adapting to climate change while enhancing the conservation of biodiversity (SCBD, 2003). Understanding the vulnerabilities at different scales – local, regional and global – and of different species and communities will help human societies and governments to devise appropriate strategies to cope with the negative fallouts of climate change.

Against the background of increased global warming and expected adverse impacts on agriculture and livestock production, Kabubo-Mariara (Chapter 16) examines the impact of climate change on livestock production and choice of livestock biodiversity in Kenya, using household level data supplemented by long-term averages of climate data. The impact of climate change on livestock production is analysed using the Ricardian approach, while the decision to engage in livestock management and also choice among livestock biodiversity are analysed using probit models. The impact of different climate change scenarios predicted by atmosphere–ocean global circulation models and a special report on emissions scenarios on livestock production and also on the choice of livestock species are also examined. The results show that livestock production in Kenya is highly sensitive to climate change and there is a non-linear relationship between climate change and net livestock incomes. The predicted impacts of different climate change scenarios suggest that a combined impact of increased temperature and precipitation will result in reduced livestock values. Further, while the probability of engaging in livestock management to variations in annual temperature is U-shaped, the response to changes in precipitation is hill-shaped. The non-linear relationships observed suggest that farmers adapt their livestock management decisions to climate change. Evaluation of different climate change scenarios further suggests that warming leads to substitution between dairy and beef cattle, and also goats and other livestock instead of sheep. Warming also makes it less profitable to keep cattle, inducing a shift in favour of small ruminants.

Coastal regions and communities are most vulnerable to climate change and its consequences, which will impact on their livelihoods and quality of life. Molua (Chapter 17) assesses the potential impacts of climate change on coastal ecosystems in Southwestern Cameroon, in relation to the livelihood, food and income security of coastal communities. The coastal ecosystem in Cameroon encompasses some of the most extensive and biologically diverse tropical coastal and marine ecosystems in Africa. This rich and fragile ecosystem is stressed by rising population, unsustainable resource use, habitat change and degradation, pollution and the spread of invasive species. Current climate variation and potential climate change adds an external stress to the beleaguered coastal ecosystems. Changes associated with increased precipitation, sea level rise and changing wave patterns is already impacting the livelihoods of households in this region as reflected in declining productivity, seedling survival rates in mangroves, etc. The socio-economic characteristics and the adaptation choices of coastal communities in South Western Cameroon are analysed. Communities report changes in species composition that affect goods provided by mangroves – such as food, firewood and other NTFP. The further loss of protective and regulatory functions of coral reefs, mangroves, lagoons and estuaries leave coastal communities more vulnerable to extreme climatic events. Possible adaptation options and measures to cope with climate change impacts are also discussed.

References

Baillie, J. E. M., Hilton-Taylor, C., Stuart, S. N. (eds) (2004) *2004 IUCN Red List of Threatened Species – A Global Assessment*, IUCN, Gland, Switzerland and Cambridge, UK

Costanza, R., d'Arge, R., de Groot, R., Farber, S., Grasso, M., Hannon, B., Limburg, K., Naeem, S., O'Neill, R. V., Paruelo, J., Raskin, R. G., Sutton, P., van den Belt, M. (1997a) 'The value of the world's ecosystem services and natural capital', *Nature*, vol 387, 15 May, pp253–260

Costanza, R., d'Arge, R., de Groot, R., Farber, S., Grasso, M., Hannon, B., Limburg, K., Naeem, S., O'Neill, R. V., Paruelo, J., Raskin, R. G., Sutton, P., van den Belt, M. (1997b) 'Valuing ecosystem services: A response', Letters, *Regulation*, Fall, pp2–3

EC (2008) *The Economics of Ecosystems and Biodiversity*, An interim report, European Communities, Wesseling, Germany

Gowdy, J. M. (1997), 'The value of biodiversity: Markets, society, and ecosystems', *Land Economics*, vol 73, no 1, pp25–41

Gowdy, J. M. and McDaniel, C. N. (1995) 'One world, one experiment: Addressing the biodiversity–economic conflict', *Ecological Economics*, vol 15, pp181–192

Kinzig, A., Perrings, C., Scholes, B. (2007) 'Ecosystem services and the economics of biodiversity conservation', www.public.asu.edu/~cperring/Kinzig%20Perrings%20 Scholes%20(2007).pdf, downloaded on 1 July 2008

Millennium Ecosystem Assessment (2005) *Ecosystems and Human Well-being: Biodiversity Synthesis*, World Resources Institute, Washington, DC

Ninan, K. N. (1996) *Forest Use and Management in Japan and India: A Comparative Study*, VRF Series No. 286, Institute of Developing Economies, Tokyo, Japan

Ninan, K. N., Jyothis, S., Babu, P., Ramakrishnappa, V. (2007) *The Economics of Biodiversity Conservation – Valuation in Tropical Forest Ecosystems*, Earthscan, London

ODA (Overseas Development Administration) (1991) *Biological Diversity and Developing Countries – Issues and Options*, ODA, Natural Resources and Environment Department, London

Pagiola, S., von Ritter, K., Bishop, J. (2004) *Assessing the Economic Value of Ecosystem Conservation*, Environment Department Paper No. 101, Environment Department, World Bank, Washington, DC

Pearce, D. and Moran, D. (1994) *The Economic Value of Biodiversity*, Earthscan, London

Perrings, C. (2000) *The Economics of Biodiversity Conservation in Sub-Saharan Africa – Mending the Ark*, Edward Elgar, Cheltenham and Northampton

Secretariat of the Convention on Biological Diversity (2001) *The Value of Forest Ecosystems*, CBD Technical Series No. 4, Secretariat of the Convention on Biological Diversity (SCBD), Montreal

Secretariat of the Convention on Biological Diversity (2003) *Interlinkages Between Biological Diversity and Climate Change – Advice on the Integration of Biodiversity Considerations into the Implementation of the United Nations Framework Convention on Climate Change and its Kyoto Protocol*, CBD Technical Series No.10, Secretariat of the Convention on Biological Diversity (SCBD), Montreal

Secretariat of the Convention on Biological Diversity (2006) *Global Biodiversity Outlook 2*, Montreal

Smith, V. K. (1997) 'Mispriced planet?' in Perspectives, *Regulation*, Summer, pp16–17

Turner, W. R., Brandon, K., Brooks, T. M., Costanza, R., Da Fonseca, G. A. B. and Portela, R. (2007) 'Global conservation of biodiversity and ecosystem services', *Bioscience*, vol 57, no 10, pp868–873

World Wide Fund for Nature (2006) *Living Planet Report 2006*, World Wide Fund for Nature (WWF), Gland, Switzerland

www.earthtrends.wri.org/features/view_feature.php?fid=15&theme=5, last accessed 27 June 2008

www.esa.org/ecoservices/comm/body.comm.fact.ecos.html, last accessed 27 June 2008

1

BIODIVERSITY, ECOSYSTEM SERVICES AND VALUATION

2

Total Economic Valuation of Endangered Species: A Summary and Comparison of United States and Rest of the World Estimates

Leslie Richardson and John Loomis

Introduction

As biodiversity is becoming increasingly threatened in developed and developing countries alike, it is quite apparent that the situation needs to be analysed at the global level. The number of species classified as threatened or endangered is on the rise throughout the world and it is and will continue to be extremely important to quantify the many benefits these species provide people when considering conservation policies. The struggle between development issues, such as land use and population growth, and environmental issues, such as biodiversity conservation, continues to play a major role in the political realm, fuelling the need for a consistent measure of the benefits provided by habitat protection. Currently, one of the accepted methods used to quantify these benefits is the contingent valuation method (CVM), which employs the use of surveys outlining a hypothetical market or referendum in order to elicit people's willingness to pay (WTP) for the preservation of a particular species (Mitchell and Carson, 1989). It has been found that people are willing to pay a small portion of their income towards the protection of endangered or rare species for a variety of reasons. This willingness to pay measure represents the total economic value of the species, which consists of both recreational use and non-use values (existence and bequest values) placed on the species.

The contingent valuation method has been used by economists for over 30 years in the US and other developed countries as a means to quantify the monetary benefits of natural resources that are not priced in markets but nevertheless have considerable value, such as threatened and endangered species. While the use of CVM in developing countries is still relatively new, with the majority of studies published in the last 5–10 years, it is clearly on the rise. The difficulties that were assumed to come with trying to ask low-income respondents to pay a hypothetical portion of their income for the preservation of a natural resource can be overcome with careful survey design and implementation. Economists such as Dale Whittington have published articles addressing the most effective way to administer contingent valuation surveys in developing countries and how to handle problems that may arise (Whittington, 1998).

The benefits of biodiversity flow across national boundaries and its value will continue to play an important role in conservation decisions throughout the world. This makes it extremely important to find a set of 'standard practices' when using CVM in order to consistently apply it in countries with different economic, social or political situations, and then compare findings. The objective of this chapter is to review and synthesize the available literature on the economic value of rare, threatened and endangered species. We also perform a comparative analysis of the value of species in the US and the rest of the world and by type of CVM used.

Data sources

After searching various economic and scientific research databases, such as EconLit, JSTOR and Web of Science, 12 usable CVM studies valuing threatened and endangered species conducted outside of the US were found. A database of 31 usable CVM studies conducted in the US was assembled using these same sources. Full data on these 43 studies can be found in the appendix to this chapter. One goal of comparing the US studies to rest of the world studies, as well as studies conducted in developed countries to those conducted in developing countries, was to analyse the way the CVM was applied. While the socio-economic characteristics of the sampled population may differ greatly in studies that take place in different countries, the techniques used to elicit what value people place on a particular species share common features as follows:

*   Each study uses a representative random sample of people to survey, which minimizes sampling bias.
*   The survey given to respondents outlines the background of the threatened or endangered species and informs them of the change in the size of the species population they are valuing.

- Surveys use either a dichotomous choice, open-ended or payment card format.
- Surveys elicit information on the socio-economic characteristics of the respondent.
- Studies obtain a reasonable response rate.

These features represent the generally accepted guidelines to follow when conducting a contingent valuation survey. In looking at the 43 various studies from eight different countries, no marked differences were found in the way the CVM was applied. Knowing that each study, regardless of the country it was conducted in, used the same general approaches to elicit the WTP value for a particular species, allows us to compare these values. Using CVM studies valuing threatened and endangered species throughout the world, we can compare the total economic value (TEV) of individual endangered species, or groups of similar species. This allows us to look at differences in WTP values in developed versus developing countries, as well as to see if there are any overall differences in studies conducted in the US versus other countries. All WTP values were converted to US dollars in a 2006 base year using the consumer price index for comparability.

Results

Comparative valuation of groups of similar species

Our first comparison looks at the average TEV of groups of similar threatened or endangered species in studies conducted both in the US and in the rest of the world. In CVM studies, the surveys given to respondents to elicit the value they place on a particular species present the hypothetical payment as either an annual, recurring payment, or a single lump sum, one-time payment. Table 2.1 compares average WTP values in US versus rest of the world studies for different groups of similar species broken down into studies using annual versus lump sum payments. Unfortunately no studies valuing endangered fish were found outside of the US, so hopefully this will be an area of future research.

A few things stand out in Table 2.1. First, US studies using lump sum payments get very high average values for both marine mammals and birds. The average value of marine mammals is based on only one study with two estimates. The 1989 study by Samples and Hollyer surveyed Hawaii households to elicit a value for the monk seal and the humpback whale. The high value can be attributed to the fact that these species are two of the most charismatic marine mammals in the US, and have gained considerable attention over the years. The average value of the birds is based on only two studies, one of which values the

Table 2.1 *Average WTP values per household based on payment frequency (in 2006 US$)*

Payment frequency and species group	US studies	Rest of the world studies
Annual WTP		
Mammals	17	50
Marine mammals	40	72
Birds	42	44
Fish	105	–
Lump sum WTP		
Mammals	61	9
Marine mammals	203	23
Birds	209	–

Source: Appendix Tables 2.1 and 2.2.

bald eagle, a nationally symbolic species which would be expected to have a very high value placed on it. If we remove the bald eagle study, the value drops considerably to about US$32. Second, rest of the world studies using lump sum payments to value mammals get a much lower value than would be expected. This could be due to the fact that it is only based on four different types of mammals, three of which are smaller, less charismatic species: the water vole, red squirrel and brown hare.

Finally, even though there are no rest of the world studies using a lump sum payment to value birds and no studies valuing fish, a very striking pattern still stands out. Rest of the world studies in all three categories that elicit WTP using an annual payment have higher values on average than US studies using the same annual payment time horizon. Likewise, US studies that use a lump sum, one-time payment method have much higher WTP values on average than studies conducted outside the US. Although this could partly be due to other differences in study variables, there is a finding that could help explain this pattern. Many of the rest of the world studies were conducted in low income countries, or regions within a country. In a contingent valuation study on the Exxon Valdez oil spill, Carson et al (2003) point out that for lower income households especially, longer payment periods mean that budget constraints are less binding. This could lead to lower income respondents on average being willing to pay more in an annual payment scheme and less in a lump sum payment scheme.

Comparative valuation of individual species

This section shifts the focus from the average TEV of *groups* of similar species to the TEV of *individual* species in order to compare studies conducted in different countries to see if they get similar values for the same, or very similar species. This will allow us to account for specific study variables, such as the change in the size of the species population being valued, and if respondents are valuing a gain in the species or avoiding a loss. Since the socio-economic characteristics of respondents can differ greatly in various countries, it is also important to compare these values as a percentage of annual income (also converted to US dollars and 2006 as a base year for comparison).

Starting with mammals, we will look at the TEV of the wolf. The one study conducted outside the US surveyed Swedish households in 1993/1994 to elicit the value of the wolf in Sweden. The authors found that respondents were willing to pay on average about US$123 annually to avoid the loss of wolves in Sweden when faced with a dichotomous choice question format and US$63 annually when faced with an open-ended question format (Boman and Bostedt, 1999). Eight US studies valuing the gray wolf were found, but some are considerably different to the Swedish study because they surveyed visitors to a national park. The four studies that surveyed households used the dichotomous choice question format to elicit a value for the gray wolf. Three of these studies valued the reintroduction of gray wolves to a national park near surveyed households, and the fourth valued the avoidance of the further loss of gray wolves. Each study found a lump sum WTP value between US$20 and US$40 (USDOI, 1994; Duffield et al, 1993) with the fourth study, which is the most similar in survey parameters to the Swedish study, finding a value of US$23 (Chambers and Whitehead, 2003). It is reasonable to compare these values to the US$123 value found in the Swedish study using the same question format. One way to check if these values are statistically different is to examine the confidence intervals around these estimates to see if they overlap. While there is a fairly large confidence interval around the value in the Swedish wolf study, it is still not large enough to include the WTP values from the US studies that surveyed households. In addition, the mean income of respondents in all four US studies was higher than the mean income of respondents in the Swedish study, widening the gap between these estimates. Because the Swedish study involves asking annual WTP, the present value over several years would be even larger than the US lump sum amounts. So it appears that on average, for this particular species and holding as many variables constant as possible, the value placed on wolves in Sweden is much higher than the value placed on wolves in the US.

Next, turning to endangered marine mammals, there is one CVM study from Greece valuing the Mediterranean monk seal and one similar CVM study from the US valuing the northern elephant seal, both of which are members of the Phocidae ('true seals') family. The TEV of the Mediterranean monk seal was found by surveying local households in Mytilene, on the island of Lesvos, Greece in 1995 using an open-ended question format. Respondents were willing to pay US$24 every 3 months, about US$72 annually, to avoid further loss of the seal (Langford et al, 1998). The study in the US valuing the northern elephant seal surveyed California households in 1984 using a payment card question format and found that respondents on average were willing to pay US$35 annually to avoid further loss of the species (Hageman, 1985). The confidence intervals for these estimates do not overlap, showing that the values are statistically different. If we try to compare these values as a percentage of income, the difference becomes even more apparent. In the US study, the mean annual income of respondents, when adjusted to 2006 US$ is a rather high US$67,000. Although the mean income of respondents is not reported in the Langford et al (1998) study, the authors do point out that in terms of development, Mytilene at the time of the survey was somewhere between a developed city and a less developed settlement, characteristic of the islets across the Aegean. It is highly unlikely that the income of respondents was any higher than the average in Greece at that time, which was much lower than US$67,000. So again, it appears that the value placed on seals in Greece is higher than the value placed on seals in the US.

We will now look at another marine mammal, the sea otter. A study published in 1997 by White et al surveys households in North Yorkshire, Britain, and finds an average lump sum WTP of US$23 for a 25 per cent gain in the species population. A similar US study valuing the threatened California sea otter surveyed California households in 1984 and found an average annual WTP of US$40 to avoid further loss of the species (Hageman, 1985). Since the annual payment is greater than the lump sum payment, we can just look at the confidence intervals and since one estimate does not lie in the confidence interval of the other estimate, we can see that these values are significantly different. The change in population size being evaluated is larger in the US than in the British study, which hinders comparability between the two studies, however. These results suggest the value placed on the sea otter is higher in the US than in Britain.

In addition, we find two studies valuing the endangered sea turtle, one from the US and one from Australia. There is insufficient data on confidence intervals to formally state whether the difference in the values obtained are statistically significant but both studies surveyed households to find an annual WTP value for the respective sea turtle in each region using the dichotomous choice question format, allowing a general idea of the values to be discovered. In the US study, the economic value of the sea turtle is found to be about US$19 annually (Whitehead, 1991) while in the Australian study the value is found to be about US$43 annually (Wilson and Tisdell, 2007). Given the fact that WTP values between countries in the seal and sea otter cases varied by a factor of two and were statistically different, we suspected the sea turtle values would also be significantly different. A summary of these individual species comparisons can be found in Table 2.2.

Table 2.2 *Comparison of WTP values per household for a single species (in 2006 US$)*

Species	US studies	Rest of the world studies	Country	Significantly different?
Wolf	20–40	123	Sweden	Yes
Seal	35	72	Greece	Yes
Sea otter	40	23	Britain	Yes
Sea turtle	19	43	Australia	Not enough information

Source: Appendix Tables 2.1 and 2.2.

Comparison of developing versus developed countries

This section compares differences between studies in developing versus developed countries. Since we found only three studies conducted in developing countries, we will have to look at these on an individual basis. Two of the three studies value the endangered Asian elephant, one taking place in Sri Lanka and the other in India. The first study to be considered values the endangered elephant in Sri Lanka. This not only gives us insight into how people in developing countries versus developed countries value endangered species, but since the elephant is considered very symbolic in Sri Lankan culture, it is interesting to compare its value to a nationally symbolic species in the US, the bald eagle. A survey of households in Colombo, Sri Lanka in 2004 found that the value placed on the elephant ranges from about US$14.50 to US$17.50 annually, for various percentage gains and avoidance of losses in the species population. While this may not seem like a lot, the average income of respondents was only about US$1620 per year, meaning that respondents were willing to pay nearly 1 per cent of their annual income toward the preservation of this species (Bandara and Tisdell, 2005). If we compare this value as a percentage of income to the one other study conducted in a developing country, which valued the black-faced spoonbill in China, we find that respondents there were only willing to pay about 0.2 per cent of their annual income toward the preservation of this particular bird species (Jianjun et al, 2007).

Likewise, a study by Ninan et al (2007) values the threatened elephant in India, surveying households in Maldari village as well as Badaganasirada villagers in Uttar Kannada. While the nature of this CVM study differed slightly, it is again very interesting to see how a culturally important species is valued by the local community. The majority of respondents in these samples reported their willingness to pay for participation in an elephant conservation programme in terms of time, which was then converted into a dollar value based on the opportunity cost of their time in terms of forgone income. Given this marked difference in payment vehicle, these monetary values were not included in the tables of average WTP values due to concerns about commensurability. The value of the elephant in terms of income forgone is US$140 annually per household in

Maldari to avoid further loss of the species and US$60 annually per household in Uttar Kannada. This represents a large percentage of respondents' income, in the 10 per cent range, but this could be due to the way the value was elicited as an opportunity cost of time, a resource probably less constrained than income for many of these households.

Turning to US studies, there are three studies valuing the bald eagle, a nationally symbolic species in the US. The first study, published in 1987, surveys Wisconsin households and finds an average WTP value of roughly US$21 annually to avoid further loss of the species (Boyle and Bishop, 1987). The second study, published in 1991, surveyed New England households and finds an average WTP value of about US$45 annually to avoid further loss of the species when using the dichotomous choice format and $32 when using the open-ended format (Stevens et al, 1991). The third study, published in 1993, gets a considerably larger estimate. This is due to the fact that it surveys Washington visitors rather than households and values a 300 per cent gain in the species. The author finds an average lump sum WTP value for the bald eagle of about US$350 when using the dichotomous choice question format and US$245 for the open-ended question format (Swanson, 1993). Although the mean income of respondents was not reported in these studies, using the US Census averages for those regions, we find that for the two studies that surveyed households, respondents were only willing to pay about 0.05–0.07 per cent of their annual income. Visitors were willing to pay considerably more and although we don't have mean income data for respondents, if we take this value as a percentage of the average income of US residents at the time, we find that this value represents about 0.6 per cent of their income. Looking at the WTP as a percentage of income for other birds which are not nationally symbolic, we find that on average people are WTP about 0.1 per cent of their annual income toward the preservation of a species.

So, it appears that for studies in developing countries, people are willing to pay more as a percentage of income for nationally symbolic species than species that do not have symbolic significance. In the US, however, it appears that only visitors and not necessarily households are willing to pay, on average, more for nationally symbolic species than species without this significance. In addition, it seems that when it comes to nationally symbolic species, households in developing countries are willing to pay more as a percentage of income than households in the US to preserve habitat for these species.

Influence of CVM methodology on value estimates

An important difference in contingent valuation studies is the way the willingness to pay question is asked in the survey. It is common to pose the valuation question to respondents using either a dichotomous choice, or referendum format (would you be willing to pay $XX?) or an open-ended format (what is the largest amount you would be willing to pay?). While the National Oceanic and Atmospheric Administration (NOAA) Panel on contingent valuation in 1993 recommended using the referendum format because it tends to provide more reliable and accurate valuation than the open-ended format (Arrow et al, 1993), there has been considerable debate over the years as to which question format is more accurate. Brown et al (1996) summarize 11 studies which elicit hypothetical WTP values for public goods using both a dichotomous choice and open-ended format, and find that mean WTP values are consistently higher when the survey question is posed using the dichotomous choice format. In conducting their own survey, the authors find the same result and outline some possible explanations for this discrepancy. More recent studies find similar results.

In terms of our data, for US studies, if we separate those using the dichotomous choice format versus the open-ended format, we can see there is a considerable difference in the values obtained (studies using the payment card method are not included because there are too few studies using this question format). This is outlined in Table 2.3, with values broken down by groups of similar species that contain enough observations to compare differences. Due to the fact that the majority of studies used an annual payment frequency rather than a lump sum, one-time payment frequency, we will just look at annual WTP values in order to have a large enough sample to make generalizations.

Looking at Table 2.3, it is apparent that for CVM studies conducted in the US, those using the dichotomous choice question format, on average, get a higher WTP value than those using an open-ended question format, consistent with the current literature. Now we will turn to studies conducted outside the US to see if the same pattern emerges. The only species category that contains enough observations is mammals, so Table 2.4 outlines the average WTP values for mammals, again only looking at studies using annual WTP payment frequency.

Although Table 2.4 only looks at one category of species, the same pattern is clear, with studies using the dichotomous choice question format on average

Table 2.3 *US studies: Annual average WTP values per household based on question format (in 2006 US$)*

Payment frequency and species group	Dichotomous choice format	Open-ended format
Annual WTP		
Marine mammals	71	33
Birds	51	34
Fish	116	57

Source: Appendix Tables 2.1 and 2.2.

Table 2.4 *Rest of the world studies: Annual average WTP values per household based on question format (in 2006 US$)*

Payment frequency and species group	Dichotomous choice format	Open-ended format
Annual WTP		
Mammals	82	53

Source: Appendix Tables 2.1 and 2.2.

reporting higher WTP values than studies using the open-ended question format. Without actual cash validation studies, it is difficult to know which WTP elicitation format most closely matches the true WTP.

Conclusion

This analysis has raised a number of important issues in the valuation of threatened and endangered species. First, when comparing the total economic value for groups of similar species, we find that respondents in US studies seem to be willing to pay more on average for the conservation of a species than respondents in rest of the world studies when asked to pay a one-time, lump sum payment. However, US respondents would pay less than respondents in rest of the world studies when asked to pay an annual payment scheme. Second, when comparing values for similar individual species in studies conducted throughout the world, we find that these values are significantly different depending on the country where the study was conducted. As more studies valuing endangered species emerge in the future, it will be interesting to see if this trend continues. Third, in comparing studies conducted in developing versus developed countries, it seems that respondents in developing countries are, on average, willing to pay more as a percentage of income for the preservation of threatened or endangered species, especially for nationally symbolic species. There is a definite need in the literature for more contingent valuation studies on threatened and endangered species in developing countries, and hopefully this will be an area of future research.

Finally, looking at methodological issues, we find many similarities in CVM studies throughout the world. Values on average seem to be higher when respondents are presented with the dichotomous choice question format as opposed to the open-ended question format, regardless of where the study was carried out. In addition, while there were some differences in the values obtained in studies conducted in various countries, there were generally no major differences found in the way the methodology was applied. Nearly all studies use similar practices in the way the CVM is carried out, regardless of where the study takes place. This allows greater confidence and ease in comparing the TEV of endangered species throughout the world. This methodological consistency makes comparison of values around the world easier for prioritizing and ranking species conservation investments by international environmental and non-governmental organizations.

References

Arrow, K., Solow, R, Portney, P. R., Leamer, E. E., Radner, R., Schuman, H. (1993) 'Report of the NOAA Panel on Contingent Valuation', *Federal Register*, vol 58, pp4601–4614

Bandara, R. and Tisdell, C. (2005) 'Changing abundance of elephants and willingness to pay for their conservation', *Journal of Environmental Management*, vol 76, pp47–59

Bell, K. P., Huppert, D., Johnson, R. L. (2003) 'Willingness to pay for local Coho salmon enhancement in coastal communities', *Marine Resource Economics*, vol 18, pp15–31

Berrens, R. P., Ganderton, P., Silva, C. (1996) 'Valuing the protection of mini instream flows in New Mexico', *Journal of Agricultural and Resource Economics*, vol 21, no 2, 294–309

Boman, M. and Bostedt, G. (1999) 'Valuing the wolf in Sweden: Are benefits contingent on the supply?', *Topics in Environmental Economics*, pp157–174

Bowker, J. M. and Stoll, J. R. (1988) 'Use of dichotomous choice nonmarket methods to value the whooping crane resource', *American Journal of Agricultural Economics*, vol 70, pp372–381

Boyle, K. and Bishop, R. (1987) 'Valuing wildlife in benefit–cost analysis: A case study involving endangered species', *Water Resources Research*, vol 23, pp943–950

Brown, T. C., Champ, P. A., Bishop, R. C., McCollum, D. W. (1996) 'Which response format reveals the truth about donations to a public good?' *Land Economics*, vol 72, no 2, 152–166

Carson, R. T., Mitchell, R. C., Hanemann, M., Kopp, R. J., Presser, S., Ruud, P. A. (2003) 'Contingent valuation and lost passive use: Damages from the Exxon Valdez Oil Spill', *Environmental and Resource Economics*, vol 25, pp257–286

Chambers, C. and Whitehead, J. (2003) 'Contingent valuation estimate of the benefits of Wolves in Minnesota', *Environmental and Resource Economics*, vol 26, pp249–267

Cummings, R., Ganderton, P., McGuckin, T. (1994) 'Substitution effects in CVM values', *American Journal of Agricultural Economics*, vol 76, pp205–214

Duffield, J. (1991) 'Existence and non-consumptive values for wildlife: Application of wolf recovery in Yellowstone National Park', W-133/Western Regional Science Association Joint Session. Measuring Non-Market and Non-Use Values, Monterey, CA

Duffield, J. (1992) 'An economic analysis of wolf recovery in Yellowstone: Park visitor attitudes and values', in J. Varley and W. Brewster (eds), *Wolves for Yellowstone?* National Park Service, Yellowstone National Park

Duffield, J. and Patterson, D. (1992) 'Field testing existence values: Comparison of hypothetical and cash transaction values, benefits and costs' in B. Rettig (compiler) *Natural Resource Planning, 5th Report*, W-133 Western Regional Research Publication, Dept. of Agricultural and Resource Economics, Oregon State University, Corvallis, OR

Duffield, J., Patterson, D., Neher, C. (1993) 'Wolves and people in Yellowstone: A case study in the New Resource Economics', Report to Liz Claiborne and Art Ortenberg Foundation, Department of Economics, University of Montana, Missoula, MT

Ericsson, G., Kindberg, J., Bostedt, G. (2007) 'Willingness to pay (WTP) for wolverine *Gulo gulo* conservation', *Wildlife Biology*, vol 13 (Suppl. 2), pp2–12

Giraud, K., Loomis, J., Johnson, R. (1999) 'Internal and external scope in willingness-to pay estimates for threatened and endangered wildlife', *Journal of Environmental Management*, vol 56, pp221–229

Giraud, K., Turcin, B., Loomis, J., Cooper, J. (2002) 'Economic benefit of the protection program for the Stellar Sea Lion', *Marine Policy*, vol 26, pp451–458

Hageman, R. (1985) 'Valuing marine mammal populations: Benefit valuations in a multi-species ecosystem', Administrative Report LJ-85-22, Southwest Fisheries Center, National Marine Fisheries Service, La Jolla, CA

Hagen, D., Vincent, J., Welle, P. (1992) 'Benefits of preserving old-growth forests and the spotted owl', *Contemporary Policy Issues*, vol 10, pp13–25

Jakobsson, K. and Dragun, A. (2001) 'The worth of a possum: Valuing species with the contingent valuation method', *Environmental and Resource Economics*, vol 19, pp211–227

Jianjun, J., Zhishi, W., Xuemin, L. (2007) 'Valuing black-faced spoonbill conservation in Macao: A policy and contingent valuation study'. Manuscript Draft

King, D., Flynn, D., Shaw, W. (1988) 'Total and existence values of a herd of desert bighorn sheep', in *Benefits and Costs in Natural Resource Planning, Interim Report. Western Regional Research Publication* W-133, University of California, Davis, CA

Kontoleon, A. and Swanson, T. (2003) 'The willingness to pay for property rights for the giant panda: Can a charismatic species be an instrument for nature conservation? *Land Economics*, vol 79, no 4, pp483–499

Kotchen, M. and Reiling, S. (2000) 'Environmental attitudes, motivations, and contingent valuation of nonuse values: A case study involving endangered species', *Ecological Economics*, vol 32, pp93–107

Langford, I. H., Kontogianni, A., Skourtos, M. S., Georgiou, S., Bateman, I. J. (1998) 'Multivariate mixed models for open-ended contingent valuation data', *Environmental and Resource Economics*, vol 12, pp443–456

Layton, D., Brown, G., Plummer, M. (2001) *Valuing Multiple Programs to Improve Fish Populations*, Washington State Department of Ecology

Loomis, J. B. and Ekstrand, E. (1997) 'Economic benefits of critical habitat for the Mexican spotted owl: A scope test using a multiple-bounded contingent valuation survey.' *Journal of Agricultural and Resource Economics*, vol 22, no 2, pp356–366

Loomis, J. B. and Larson, D. (1994) 'Total economic values of increasing gray whale populations: Results from a contingent valuation survey of visitors and households', *Marine Resource Economics*, vol 9, pp275–286

Loomis, J., and White, D. (1996) 'Economic benefits of rare and endangered species: A summary and meta-analysis', *Ecological Economics*, vol 18, pp197–206

Mitchell, R. C. and Carson, R. T. (1989) 'Using surveys to value public goods: The contingent valuation method', *Resources for the Future*, Washington, DC

Ninan, K. N., Jyothis, S., Babu, P., Ramakrishnappa, V. (2007) *The Economics of Biodiversity Conservation: Valuation in Tropical Forest Ecosystems*, Earthscan, London and Sterling, VA

Olsen, D., Richards, J, and Scott, D. (1991) 'Existence and sport values for doubling the size of Columbia river basin salmon and steelhead runs', *Rivers*, vol 2, pp44–56

Reaves, D. W., Kramer, R. A. and Holmes, T. P. (1994) 'Valuing the endangered red cockaded woodpecker and its habitat: A comparison of contingent valuation elicitation techniques and a test for embedding', AAEA meetings paper

Rubin, J., Helfand, G. and Loomis, J. (1991) 'A benefit-cost analysis of the northern spotted owl', *Journal of Forestry*, vol 89, no 12, pp25–30

Samples, K. and Hollyer, J. (1989) 'Contingent valuation of wildlife resources in the presence of substitutes and complements', in: R. Johnson and G. Johnson (eds) *Economic Valuation of Natural Resources: Issues, Theory and Application*, Westview Press, Boulder, CO

Stanley, D. L. (2005) 'Local perception of public goods: Recent assessments of willingness-to-pay for endangered species', *Contemporary Economic Policy*, vol 2, pp165–179

Stevens, T., Echeverria, J., Glass, R., Hager, T., More, T. (1991) 'Measuring the existence value of wildlife: What do CVM estimates really show?' *Land Economics*, vol 67, pp390–400

Swanson, C. (1993) 'Economics of non-game management: Bald eagles on the Skagit River Bald Eagle Natural Area, Washington', PhD Dissertation, Department of Agricultural Economics, Ohio State University

Tanguay, M., Wiktor, L., Boxall, P. (1992) 'An economic evaluation of woodland caribou conservation programs in Northwestern Saskatchewan', Department of Rural Economy Project Report 95-01, University of Alberta

US Department of the Interior, Fish and Wildlife Service (1994) *The Reintroduction of Gray Wolves to Yellowstone National Park and Central Idaho, Final Environmental Impact Statement*. Helena, MT, pp421–427

White, P. C. L., Gregory, K. W., Lindley, P. J., Richards, G. (1997) 'Economic values of threatened mammals in Britain: A case study of the otter *Lutra lutra* and the water vole *Arvicola terrestris*', *Biological Conservation*, vol 82, pp345–354

White, P., Bennett, A., Hayes, E. (2001) 'The use of willingness-to-pay approaches in mammal conservation', *Mammal Review*, vol 31, no 2, pp151–167

Whitehead, J. (1991) 'Economic values of threatened and endangered wildlife: A case study of coastal nongame wildlife', in *Transactions of the 57th North American Wildlife and Natural Resources Conference*, Wildlife Management Institute, Washington, DC

Whitehead, J. (1992) 'Ex ante willingness to pay with supply and demand uncertainty: Implications for valuing a sea turtle protection programme', *Applied Economics*, vol 24, pp981–988

Whittington, D. (1998) 'Administering contingent valuation surveys in developing countries', *World Development*, vol 26, no 1, pp21–30

Wilson, C. and Tisdell, C. (2007), 'How knowledge affects payment to conserve an endangered bird', *Contemporary Economic Policy*, vol 25, no 2, pp226–237

Appendix Table 2.1 *US WTP studies – threatened and endangered species*

Reference	Survey date	Species	Gain or loss	Size of change	Willingness to pay (2006 US$)		CVM[a] method	Survey region	Sample size	Response rate	Payment vehicle
					Lump sum	Annual					
Bell et al (2003)	2000	Salmon	Gain	100%		138.64 91.55	DC	Grays Harbor, WA households	357	49.1%	Annual tax Annual tax
			Gain	100%		141.27 90.64		Willapa Bay, WA households	386	61.7%	Annual tax Annual tax
			Avoid loss	100%		57.99 47.70		Coos Bay, OR households	424	58.4%	Annual tax Annual tax
			Avoid loss	100%		91.99 28.39		Tillamook Bay, OR households	347	53.2%	Annual tax Annual tax
			Avoid loss	100%		134.00 87.84		Yaquina Bay, OR households	357	59.7%	Annual tax
Berrens et al (1996)	1995	Silvery minnow	Avoid loss	100%		37.77	DC residents	NM	726	64.0%	Trust fund
Bowker and Stoll (1988)	1983	Whooping crane	Avoid loss	100%		43.69	DC	TX and US households	316	36.0%	Foundation
		Whooping crane	Avoid loss	100%		68.55	DC	Visitors	254	67.0%	Foundation
Boyle and Bishop (1987)	1984	Bald eagle	Avoid loss	100%		21.21	DC	WI households	365	73.0%	Foundation

Study	Year	Species	Scenario	%				Population	N	%	Payment vehicle
Chambers and Whitehead (2003)	2001	Striped shiner	Avoid loss	100%		8.32	DC		352	56.1%	One-time tax
		Gray wolf	Avoid loss	100%	22.64		DC	Ely and St Cloud, MN households	723	42.0%	Increase state taxes
Cummings et al (1994)	1994	Squawfish	Avoid loss	100%		11.65	OE	NM	158	30.6%	
Duffield (1991)	1990	Gray wolf	Reintroduction		93.92		DC	Yellowstone National Park visitors	121	86.0%	Lifetime membership
Duffield (1992)	1991	Gray wolf	Reintroduction		162.10		DC	Yellowstone National Park visitors	189	46.6%	Lifetime membership
Duffield et al (1993)	1992	Gray wolf	Reintroduction		37.43		DC	ID, MT, WY households	335	69.6%	Lifetime membership
USDOI (1994)	1993	Gray wolf	Reintroduction		28.37		DC	ID, MT, WY households	345	69.6%	Lifetime membership
USDOI (1994)	1993	Gray wolf	Reintroduction		21.59		DC	ID, MT, WY households	157	27.3%	Lifetime membership
Duffield and Patterson (1992)	1991	Arctic grayling	Improve 1 of 3 rivers	33%	26.47		PC	US visitors			Trust fund
		Arctic grayling		33%	19.84		PC	US visitors			Trust fund
Giraud et al (1999)	1996	Mexican spotted owl	Avoid loss			68.84	DC	US households	688	77.1%	Trust fund
Giraud et al (2002)	2000	Steller sea lion	Avoid loss	100%		70.90	DC	AK and US households	1653	54.4%	Increase federal tax
Hageman (1985)	1984	Bottlenose dolphin	Avoid loss	100%		36.41	PC	CA households	180	63.6%	Increase federal tax
		Northern elephant seal	Avoid loss	100%		34.50	PC		174	21.0%	

Appendix Table 2.1 *US WTP studies – threatened and endangered species* (Cont'd)

Reference	Survey date	Species	Gain or loss	Size of change	Willingness to pay (2006 US$)		CVM method	Survey region	Sample size	Response rate	Payment vehicle
					Lump sum	Annual					
Hageman (1985)	1984	Grey-blue whale	Avoid loss	100%		45.94	PC	CA households	180	21.0%	Increase federal tax
		Sea otter	Avoid loss	100%		39.80	PC		174		
Hagen et al (1992)	1990	No. spotted owl	Avoid loss	100%		130.19	DC	US households	409	46.0%	Taxes and wood prices
King et al (1988)	1985	Bighorn sheep	Avoid loss	100%		16.99	OE	AZ households	550	59.0%	Foundation
Kotchen and Reiling (2000)	1997	Peregrine falcon	Gain	87.5%	32.27		DC	ME residents	206	63.1%	One-time tax
Layton et al (2001)	1998	E. WA/ Columbia R. Freshwater Fish	Gain	50%		210.84	CE	WA households	801	68.0%	Monthly payment (converted to annual)
		E. WA/ Columbia R. Migratory Fish	Gain	50%		146.57					
		W. WA/ Puget Sound Freshwater Fish	Gain	50%		229.31					
		W. WA/ Puget Sound Migratory Fish	Gain	50%		307.76					

Study	Year	Species	Measure	% change	Value	Method	Sample	n	Response rate	Payment vehicle
Loomis and White (1996)	1994	W. WA/ Puget Sound Saltwater Fish	Gain	50%	311.31					
		Salmon and steelhead	Gain	600%	79.53	DC	Clallam County, WA households	284	77.0%	Increase federal tax
		Salmon and steelhead	Gain	600%	98.41	DC	WA households	467	68.0%	
		Salmon and steelhead	Gain	600%	91.67	DC	US households	423	55.0%	
Loomis and Ekstrand (1997)	1996	Mexican spotted owl	Avoid loss		51.52	MB	US households	218	56.0%	
Loomis and Larson (1994)	1991	Gray whale	Gain	50%	23.65	OE	CA households	890	54.0%	Protection fund
		Gray whale	Gain	100%	26.53	OE	CA households	890	54.0%	
		Gray whale	Gain	50%	36.56	OE	CA visitors	1003	71.3%	Protection fund
		Gray whale	Gain	100%	43.46	OE	CA visitors	1003	71.3%	
Olsen et al (1991)	1989	Salmon and steelhead	Gain	100%	42.97	OE	Pac. NW households	695	72.0%	Electric bill
			Gain	100%	95.86	OE	Pac NW HH option		72.0%	
			Gain	100%	121.40	OE	Pac. NW anglers	482	72.0%	
Reaves et al (1994)	1992	Red-cockaded woodpecker	% chance of survival	99%	14.69	OE	SC and US households	225	53.0%	Recovery fund
				99%	20.46	DC		223	52.0%	
				99%	13.14	PC		234	53.0%	
Rubin et al (1991)	1987	No. spotted owl	% chance of survival	50%	38.61	OE	WA households	249	23.0%	Unspecified
				75%	39.99	OE				

Appendix Table 2.1 *US WTP studies – threatened and endangered species* (Cont'd)

Reference	Survey date	Species	Gain or loss	Size of change	Willingness to pay (2006 US$) Lump sum	Annual	CVM method	Survey region	Sample size	Response rate	Payment vehicle
Samples and Hollyer (1989)	1986	Monk seal	Avoid loss	100% 100%	165.80	60.84	OE DC	HI households	165	40.0%	Preservation fund
		Humpback whale	Avoid loss	100%	239.53						Money and time
Stanley (2005)	2001	Riverside fairy shrimp	Avoid loss	100%		28.38	PC	Orange County, CA households	242	32.1%	Annual tax
Stevens et al (1991)	1989	Wild turkey	Avoid loss	100%		11.38	DC	New England households	339	37.0%	Trust Fund
			Avoid loss	100%		15.36	OE	New England households			
		Atlantic salmon	Avoid loss	100%		10.00	DC	MA households	169	30.0%	Trust fund
		Atlantic salmon	Avoid loss	100%		11.12	OE				
		Bald eagle	Avoid loss	100%		45.21	DC	New England households	339	37.0%	Trust fund
Swanson (1993)	1989	Bald eagle	Avoid loss	100%			OE	WA visitors	747	57.0%	Membership fund
		Bald eagle	Increase in populations	300%	349.69	31.85	DC				
				300%	244.94		OE	WA visitors			
Whitehead (1991, 1992)	1991	Sea turtle	Avoid loss	100%		19.01	OE DC	NC households	207	35.0%	Preservation fund

Notes: [a] DC = dichotomous choice; OE = open ended; PC = payment card; CE = choice experiment.

Appendix Table 2.2 *Rest of the world WTP studies – threatened and endangered species*

Reference	Survey date	Species	Gain or loss	Size of change	Willingness to pay (2006 US$)		CVM method	Survey region	Sample size	Response rate	Payment vehicle
					Lump sum	Annual					
Bandara & Tisdell (2005)	2004	Asian elephant	Gain	25%		14.51	DC	Colombo, Sri Lanka HH	266	94.0%	Monthly tax (converted to annual)
			Gain	50%		14.95					
			Gain	75%		15.18					
			Avoid loss	25%		14.62					
			Avoid loss	50%		15.89					
			Avoid loss	75%		17.61					
Boman & Bostedt (1999)	1993	Wolf	Avoid loss	100%		122.80	DC	Swedish HH	1221	61.0%	Annual payment
						63.49	OE	Swedish HH	1072	53.6%	Annual payment
Ericsson et al (2007)	2004	Wolverine	Gain	37%		47.46	DC	Dalarna, Sweden HH	7376	67.0%	Annual tax
						46.07		Gävleborg, Sweden HH			
						49.50		Jämtland, Sweden HH			
						66.04		Västernorrland, Sweden HH			
						42.76		Västerbotten, Sweden HH			
						46.19		Norrbotten, Sweden HH			
						75.33		Rest of Sweden HH		57.0%	Annual tax
Jakobsson & Dragun (2001)	1996	Leadbeater's possum	Avoid loss	100%		71.14	DC	Victoria, Australia HH	210	32.0%	State tax
						33.86			190	29.0%	Donation to conservation org.

Appendix Table 2.2 *Rest of the world WTP studies – threatened and endangered species* (Cont'd)

Reference	Survey date	Species	Gain or loss	Willingness to pay (2006 US$)			CVM method	Survey region	Sample size	Response rate	Payment vehicle
				Size of change	Lump sum	Annual					
Jianjun et al (2007)	2005	Black-faced spoonbill				59.31	DC	Macao, China HH	137		Addition to water bill
						27.69	DC	Macao, China HH	135		Addition to water bill
Kontoleon & Swanson (2003)	1998	Giant panda	Gain	150%	4.80		PC	OECD country tourists	305	70.0%	Airport tax surcharge
			Gain	150%	10.38						
			Gain	150%	18.30						
Langford et al (1998)	1995	Mediterranean monk seal	Avoid loss	100%		71.59	OE	Mytiline, Lesvos, Greece HH	112	45.6%	Public fund
Ninan et al (2007)	2007	Asian elephant	Avoid loss	100%		161.67[b]	DC	Maldari, India HH	125		Opp. cost of time – participation in elephant conservation programme
						69.35[b]		Uttar Kannada, India	80		
Tanguay et al (1992)	1992	Woodland caribou	Avoid loss	100%		45.14	OE	SK, Canada HH	2054	51.2%	Annual trust fund
						51.29	OE				Annual trust fund
						99.48	DC				Annual trust fund
						107.15	DC				Annual trust fund

Study	Year	Species		%	Value 1	Value 2	Method	Location	Days	%	Payment
White et al (1997)	1996	Otter	Gain	25%	23.19		DC	N. Yorkshire, Britain HH	105	64.0%	Single addition to taxes
		Water vole	Gain	37.5%	14.48		DC	N. Yorkshire, Britain HH	105	64.0%	Single addition to taxes
White et al (2001)	1997	Red squirrel	Gain	37.5%	5.49		DC	N. Yorkshire, Britain HH	150	52.2%	Single addition to taxes
		Brown hare	Gain	100%	0.00		DC	N. Yorkshire, Britain HH	150	52.2%	Single addition to taxes
Wilson & Tisdell (2007)	2002	Golden-shouldered parrot				46.26	DC	Brisbane, Australia HH	119	58.0%	Campaign
		Tree kangaroo				45.62	DC				
		Hawksbill sea turtle				43.39	DC				

Notes: [a] DC = dichotomous choice; OE = open ended; PC = payment card; CE = choice experiment. [b] Originally valued in terms of time (days) of participation in an elephant conservation programme. Converted to dollars using opportunity cost of time in terms of forgone income.

3

The Economics of Fish Biodiversity: Linkages between Aquaculture and Fisheries – Some Perspectives

Clem Tisdell

Introduction

The development of aquaculture and the husbandry of terrestrial organisms generally, has helped to support a larger human population at a higher standard of living than would have been possible by depending solely on the gathering and capture of wild terrestrial organisms. The relative economic advantage of supplies from cultured organisms has meant that human dependence on economic supplies from wild stocks has largely been replaced by supplies from agriculture, animal husbandry and silviculture. As a result, there has been a loss of biodiversity in the wild and a change in the composition of the genetic stock of domesticated organisms for reasons that are well documented. Concerns have been raised that losses in the wild genetic stock and changes in the gene pool of domesticated species could result in lack of sustainable economic production from biological resources.

Practices in aquaculture that result in reduced biodiversity of wild fish stocks are summarized in Table 3.1 and the processes leading to a loss of wild fish biodiversity are also specified. The processes are quite varied and many involve adverse environmental externalities or spillovers. When such spillovers exist, fish farmers' costs of production do not reflect the full social cost of their production. Consequently, their economic behaviour is unlikely to be socially optimal unless it is regulated in a suitable manner by the government or collectively (Tisdell, 2005, ch 3). However, optimal regulation is difficult to achieve because of uncertainties, the transaction costs involved in social regulation and imperfections in political and social systems.

Trends in fish supplies from aquaculture versus supplies from wild catch

Terrestrial patterns in sources of food supplies from the wild compared to those from husbandry now appear to be repeating themselves in aquatic areas as

Table 3.1 *Aquaculture practices and their consequences for biodiversity loss*

Practice	Consequences
Translocation of fish species or varieties of fish with their accidental or deliberate release to the wild.	Loss of indigenous fish species and other wild species due to competition, habitat disturbance and so on. Examples include translocation of European carp, tilapia and trout.
Release (accidental or deliberate) of improved varieties of fish or transgenic varieties to the wild (Myhr and Dalmo, 2005).	May alter the genetic composition of the wild stock if they are sufficiently fit for survival in the wild and the releases are sufficient in number (cf. Muir, 2005).
Narrowing of the diversity of the genetic stock in aquaculture due to human selection of species and their varieties (Hulata, 2001).	The genetic diversity of farmed fish stock is often much less than the wild stock for which it is a substitute or replacement. Consider the example given by Stotz (2000) of scallops. Market extension and globalization are strong forces working in favour of reduced biodiversity of farmed organisms. The economic mechanisms resulting in this are varied but the operation of the economics of comparative advantage plays an important role. See Tisdell (2003a).
Appropriation of habitat and space of areas used by wild species for aquaculture and destruction or or significant alteration of habitat.	Wild species excluded or partly excluded from aquaculture areas. Loss of food sources, shelter and breeding areas.
Exploitation of wild aquatic fish and materials to provide food for aquaculture organisms	Because of the loss of food sources of wild fish and over harvesting of targeted species, loss of biodiversity in the wild may occur.
Use of chemicals and antibiotics in aquaculture may adversely affect local aquatic microfauna and macrofauna (Beardmore et al, 1997).	Possible loss of some such fauna with negative impacts on the food chain and potentially, therefore, on higher order species.
Intensive collection of seed for aquaculture ranching Movement of objects (biological and non-biological) over considerable distances for use in aquaculture.	May threaten wild stocks or alter the genetic composition of these. Accidental or incidental introduction of new pathogens, parasites or pests generally to new areas with biodiversity loss possible.

Note: Anderson (1985) argues that aquaculture adds to the supply of fish, reduces fish prices and, therefore, may have positive consequences for the conservation of wild stocks. While this is theoretically possible, it does not appear to have been so in practice. This can be attributed, in part to the processes outlined above. See Tisdell (2003b, ch 28).

aquaculture develops rapidly. In 1950, supplies of fish from aquaculture were negligible relative to the wild catch but in proportion to the wild catch they have increased exponentially in recent times. By 2004, they amounted to more than

60 per cent of the wild catch (Figure 3.1). An accelerating rate of growth in supplies of fish from aquaculture relative to that from the wild is evident beginning in the early 1970s.

Furthermore, since the late 1980s, aquaculture has been the sole source of the increase in global supplies of fish; production from the wild catch has been virtually stagnant since then (Figure 3.2). If the same pattern is followed as on land, one might expect supplies from the wild catch to fall eventually due to such factors as habitat loss as a result of the expansion of aquaculture. However, this displacement effect from the growth of aquaculture will probably be less marked than it has been on land from the expansion of agriculture. This is because it is likely to be more difficult (costly) for humans to transform or convert aquatic areas to farming than terrestrial areas. This suggests that habitat conversion, particularly in relation to marine areas, is likely to be less strong as a source of habitat loss, and consequently of biodiversity loss, than on land. Nevertheless it is still likely to be important as one of the sources of loss of wild fish biodiversity. Thus, the view stressed by Swanson (1994, 1997) that habitat conversion for human use is the major reason for loss of terrestrial biodiversity may also extend to aquatic biodiversity.

China is by far the largest producer of aquacultured fish in the world and aquaculture in China has developed earlier and on a greater scale than elsewhere in the world. Therefore, its experiences may provide a pointer to future global patterns as far as the development of aquaculture relative to captive fisheries is concerned. By 1983, China's production of fish from aquaculture had overtaken its wild catch. By 2004, China's supply of aquacultured fish was nearly two and a half times its wild catch (Figure 3.3). In such circumstances, one might expect such a massive expansion in aquaculture to have a negative impact on wild fish stocks and catches in China. Do trends in China's volume of wild catch provide any hint that this is so?

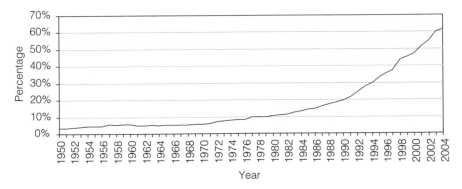

Figure 3.1 Global aquaculture production as a percentage of global wild catch, 1950–2004

Source: Based on FAO statistics – FishStat.

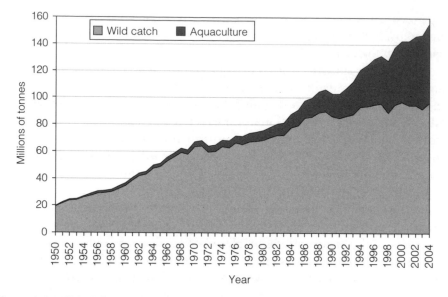

Figure 3.2 Global fish production, 1950–2004

Source: Based on FAO statistics – FishStat.

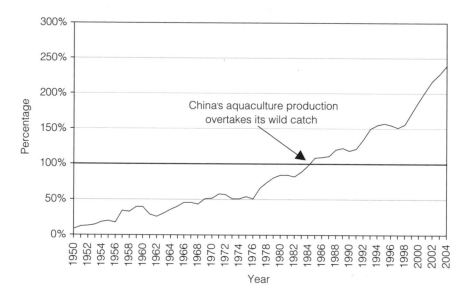

Figure 3.3 China's aquaculture production as a percentage of its wild catch, 1950–2004

Source: Based on FAO statistics – FishStat.

Figure 3.4 reveals that the volume of China's wild catch has been constant since about 1998 and that all growth in fish supplies in China has come from aquaculture. However, because an increasing share of China's fish catch has

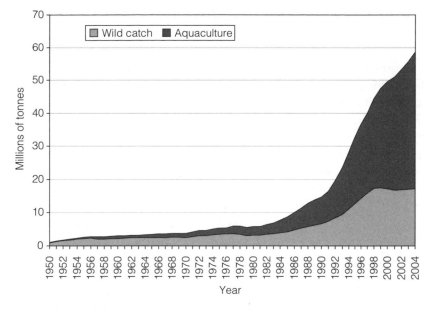

Figure 3.4 China's fish production, 1950–2004

Source: Based on FAO statistics – FishStat.

been obtained from distant water fishing, it can be inferred that China's domestic wild catch has been falling in recent years. Therefore, it is possible that the expansion of aquaculture in China has contributed to a decline in China's domestic catch of wild fish, even though it is unlikely to be the only influence on this reduction.

Even if sufficient data happened to be available, it would still be difficult to decompose the decline in China's domestic fish catch into its causal components. Influences could include price variations, reductions in available wild stocks of fish and increased operating costs involved in fishing. Furthermore, it is not only the development of aquaculture that is likely to have a negative impact on stocks of wild fish. The increase in water pollution and other environmental change brought about generally by China's rapid economic growth also have negative spillover effects on its domestic fish stocks.

The most common explanation given for falling wild catches is usually that increased catch effort pushes yield beyond its maximum sustainable level and consequently, yields begin to decline. However, this is only part of the explanation. Environmental changes which alter available habitat for wild fish stocks also play a role. Such adverse environmental impacts arise generally from the expansion of economic activity. They are not exclusively due to the development of aquaculture but as aquaculture expands, it can add significantly to these adverse environmental spillovers (Table 3.1).

Commercial and recreational fishing as a source of biodiversity loss in the wild

Both commercial and recreational fishing are capable of causing significant biodiversity loss. These effects can result in the extinction of individual species, and usually alter the composition of species in the natural population.

Two issues are involved. In the absence of 'ideal' social regulation of the fishing effort, catches of some species are liable to exceed their maximum economic yield and even their maximum sustainable biological yield. Second, particularly in the case of slowly reproducing species, such as large marine mammals, for example large whales, fishing efforts when open access exists is liable to drive targeted species to extinction. This nearly happened to blue whales in the past. They were probably only saved from extinction because controls on harvesting were eventually imposed by the International Whaling Commission. Some species of marine mammals, such as Stellar's sea cow, were harvested to extinction. Overharvesting can easily lead to extinction of some wild marine species, and has already done so.

However, it is too simplistic to believe that open access property is the sole reason for the extinction of species. As Clark (1976) has pointed out, maximization of commercial gain can result in the extinction of species even when they are private property and their owners are able to appropriate all the economic benefits from the ownership of the species. Furthermore, human-induced habitat change seems to account for the loss of many more wild species than the hunting or capture of them.

Incidental bycatch of commercial fisheries can also threaten vulnerable species. Much of the bycatch from fishing dies, or it is sometimes used to manufacture fishmeal. Marine birds, such as albatross are also at risk from some fishing procedures such as long-line fishing. Again, trawl fishing can damage benthic structures with adverse consequences for aquatic biodiversity.

It is also known that recreational fishing, which is popular in several higher income countries (Tisdell, 2003c; Hurkens and Tisdell, 2006), can have significant adverse impacts on aquatic biodiversity. Given the ecological impacts of recreational fishing, most higher income countries have been developing or have in place policies to regulate it, many of which are discussed by Hurkens and Tisdell (2006). Tisdell (2003c) considers the possibility that the development of fish farms for the purpose of recreational fishing could moderate the harvesting pressure of recreational fishers on wild stocks.

The utilization of wild fish stocks has been an important social issue in more developed countries. Arlinghaus et al (2002), drawing on European experience, argue that the dominant influences on the utilization of wild fish stocks have shown a cyclical pattern. In their sociological theory, they argue that at first those interested in fish for food and commercial use dominated social policy for the fisheries, and subsequently the dominant force was those interested in fish and aquatic areas for angling and recreation. These authors believe that the dominant force eventually will be those interested in fish and aquatic areas for the purpose of nature conservation. Their theory is discussed by Hurkens and Tisdell (2006) and related to policy developments in fisheries in The Netherlands and Australia.

Many complexities are involved in determining the stock of genetic material which should be conserved in the wild. Features which need to be taken into account include the total economic value of different species (see, for example, Ninan et al, 2007, pp8–9), the mixed good characteristics of some species, the economic consequences of economic interdependence between populations of species, and the priorities to be established (criteria to be agreed on) for saving different species from extinction. Other matters of relevance are the value of property rights in genetic material in providing an incentive for biodiversity conservation and the consequences of growing globalization and market extension for the conservation of biodiversity. These matters are analysed for example in Tisdell (2005, ch 5). In addition, the consequences of open access to natural resources and of common property for biodiversity conservation are important as is ranching and the farming of species and these activities are discussed, for example, in Tisdell (2005, ch 6). Additional factors affecting biodiversity are discussed in Ninan et al, (2007, ch 1).

Aquatic biodiversity and the resilience of productive ecosystems

It has been argued that the sustainability of yields from production requires ecosystems to be resilient (Conway, 1987). Furthermore, it has been claimed that the preservation of biodiversity in ecosystems is important for maintaining their resilience (Perrings et al, 1995). However, this may be too sweeping a generalization because some ecosystems possessing little biological diversity can be more resilient than extremely diverse systems because their component species are more adaptable (Tisdell, 1999, ch 4) Mackenzie (2006, p10) claims that it has never been proven that more biological diverse terrestrial systems are more resilient than less diverse ones. On the other hand, it could be true that if similar ecosystems in different geographical locations are compared, the ones which have more biodiversity intact would be more resilient.

Worm et al (2006) have recently provided evidence that ocean ecosystems possessing greater biodiversity are more productive and resilient than those with less biodiversity. They find that restoration of biodiversity in ocean ecosystems increases their productivity several fold and reduces significantly the vulnerability of their productivity. They find that genetic biodiversity provides more robustness and resilience in the exploitation of fish. They argue that the preservation of marine biodiversity provides many economically valuable ecosystem services.

Tisdell (2006) has argued recently that it is much more difficult to preserve marine biodiversity in developing countries compared to higher income ones for social and political reasons and that governments in developing countries are rarely in a position to extricate their countries from impending biodiversity loss and biological depletion in the wild. Furthermore, there seems to be scant prospect of aquaculture saving developing countries from this problem. In fact, its development, unless well managed, can exacerbate the problem, as for example the development of some forms of prawn (shrimp) farming has done.

Consequences of the development of aquaculture for the biodiversity of farmed fish

Expansion in aquaculture has come about both as a result of its extension and intensification and this expansion is continuing. Genetic 'improvements' in cultured fish and greater attention to human selection of species and strains of fish have contributed to the economics of expanding aquaculture. However, economic gains from genetic selection usually depend on the use of a narrow package of supporting inputs in the farming of selected organisms. For example, environmental conditions, nutrition, and so on, of improved varieties of fish may need to be carefully controlled to achieve high yields and satisfactory economic returns, as in the case, for example, of high-yielding rice varieties. Consequently, issues involving economic sustainability, variability of high yields and income distribution arise (Conway, 1987; Tisdell, 1999, ch 4).

To an ever increasing extent, human selection of genetic material is and has been replacing its natural selection. In addition, environmental changes brought about by humans are altering the global genetic stock by accelerating the extinction of some species, favouring others and creating a new array of environments capable of affecting the natural selection of organisms. It is difficult to know how these changes can be confidently assessed from an economic point of view.

Biodiversity of cultivated crops and domestic livestock has declined considerably in recent decades (see for example, Tisdell, 2003b). Because aquaculture has developed later than agriculture, it is still in an early exploratory stage of development and new aquatic species and strains are being continually trialled for farming. Therefore, it is possible that the genetic biodiversity of farmed fish stock will continue to rise for some time to come. Eventually, however, it is also likely that the biodiversity of this stock will decline, as has occurred in agriculture. This may primarily occur as a result of the economic sorting out of the species trialled.

Because human selection of genetic material has become so important, institutional arrangements for this selection have also become of increasing significance. Different types of institutional arrangements are likely to result in different types of selection and development of the domesticated genetic stock of fish and other species. For example, if private companies are able to have property rights in fish varieties, they are likely to want to conserve and develop genetic material from which they can appropriate the greatest economic benefit. Their selfish choices may displace other existing genetic assets and alter development paths in socially inferior ways. Consequently, the social benefits from human-controlled genetic change may be socially unsatisfactory. To what extent should genetic selection and development be the province of public bodies or international public organizations, such as WorldFish? What criteria should be applied to the human selection and development of genetic material?

Uncertainty about the economic benefits of alterations in fish biodiversity

Because the selection of genetic material involves decision making under uncertainty and because the economic costs of loss of biodiversity (or of genetic material) are uncertain and reduce future economic options, the question arises of how much and what types of biodiversity should be conserved in cultured stocks of species, such as fish species, and in wild stocks. Economists have no ready answer to this question.

We do know, however, that the development of aquaculture has already started to reduce genetic diversity in wild fish stocks. On the basis of experience with land-based farming, it is reasonable to predict that this process will continue with the further development of aquaculture. Furthermore, the genetic diversity of farmed fish may also eventually decline as has happened to crops and livestock. While economists are aware that a sustainability problem may emerge as a result of the genetic changes arising from farming, they are not able yet to provide a definitive economic valuation of the processes involved. They cannot confidently determine the very long-term economic consequences of genetic manipulation and change for farmed and wild fish. They cannot say whether the present economic benefits from genetic change are sufficient to outweigh the possible future costs, and whether future generations will be richer or poorer as a result of human impacts on our genetic stock. We don't know. We may never know until the future becomes the present, and then the situation will be irreversible. Should we take the risk? The answer does not depend solely on economics but is a major challenge for economists.

Some social scientists, including economists, favour the adoption of the precautionary principle. However, this leaves open the question of how much caution really should be shown in decision making. Also we should bear in mind that the presence of uncertainty does not rule out completely the possibility of rational decision. Even if uncertainty exists, some types of choices can be irrational in all the possible circumstances, and should not be made. Consequently, in making a rational decision, we should confine our choices to the non-inferior subset of possible choices. Loss of genetic material which is certain to make us worse off should naturally be avoided.

Concluding comments

It also seems probable that supplies of fish from aquaculture will continue to increase and supplies from the wild will probably fall. Marine areas are most likely going to be the main sources from which increased cultured supplies of fish will be obtained, given that freshwater is an increasingly scarce commodity.

Several mechanisms have been listed by which the development of aquaculture can reduce the biodiversity of wild fish stocks, although, as pointed out, it is not the only factor leading to a reduced genetic diversity of wild fish stocks. Furthermore, if the same pattern is followed as in the development of agriculture, the genetic diversity of stocks husbanded in aquaculture is likely to decline eventually. Nevertheless, because of the late development of aquaculture compared to agriculture, the biodiversity of stocks used in aquaculture may still rise, before declining. Many scientists are of the view that such a loss of biodiversity is likely to make it difficult to sustain the economic production of fish or cultivated organisms generally. While there is a real possibility, uncertainty makes it difficult to predict accurately the likely economic consequences of declining biodiversity.

Acknowledgements

I wish to thank Hemanath Swarna Nantha for research assistance. This is a revised and extended version of notes which were prepared for a mini-symposium organized by Dr Madan Dey as part of the 26th Conference of the International Association of Agricultural Economists held at Gold Coast, Australia, 12–18 August, 2006. I wish to thank Dr Dey and participants for their useful comments on that occasion.

References

Anderson, J. L. (1985) 'Market interaction between aquaculture and the common property commercial fishery', *Marine Resource Economics*, vol 2, pp1–24

Arlinghaus, R., Mehner, T., Coux, I. G. (2002) 'Reconciling traditional inland fisheries management and sustainability in industrialised countries, with emphasis on Europe', *Fish and Fisheries*, vol 3, pp261–316

Beardmore, J. A., Mair, G. C., Lewis, R. I. (1997) 'Biodiversity in aquatic systems in selection to aquaculture', *Aquaculture Research*, vol 28, pp829–839

Clark, C. W. (1976) *Mathematical Bioeconomics: The Optimal Management of Renewable Resources*, John Wiley, New York

Conway, G. R. (1987) 'The properties of agroecosystems', *Agricultural Systems*, vol 24, pp95–117

Hulata, G. (2001) 'Genetic manipulations in aquaculture: A review of stock improvement by classical and modern technologies', *Genetica*, vol 111, pp155–173.

Hurkens, R. and Tisdell, C. (2006) 'Ecological and socioeconomic features of recreational fishing and fishing policies: Review and case studies for The Netherlands and Australia', pp99–129 in R. Burk (ed.), *Focus on Ecology Research*, Nova Science Publishers, New York

McKenzie, D. (2006) 'Glimmer of hope for "doomed" fish', *NewScientist*, vol 192, no 2577, p10

Muir, J. (2005) 'Managing to harvest? Perspectives on the potential of aquaculture', *Philosophical Transactions of the Royal Society*, B 360, pp193–218

Myhr, A. E. and Dalmo, R. A. (2005) 'Introduction of genetic engineering in aquaculture: Ecological and ethical reflections for science and governance', *Aquaculture*, vol 250, pp542–554

Ninan, K. N., Jyothis, S., Babu, P., Ramakrishnappa, V. (2007) *The Economics of Biodiversity Conservation: Valuation in Tropical Forest Ecosystems*, Earthscan, London, UK and Sterling, VA

Perrings, C. A., Mäler K.-G., Folke, C., Holling, C. S., Jansson, B.-O (1995) *Biodiversity Conservation: Problems and Policies*, Kluwer, Dordrecht

Stotz, W. (2000) 'When aquaculture restores and replaces an overfished stock: Is the conservation of the species assured? The case of the scallop *Argopecten purpuratus* in Northern Chile', *Aquaculture International*, vol 8, pp237–247

Swanson, T. (1994) *The International Regulation of Extinction*, New York University Press, New York

Swanson, T. (1997) *Global Action for Biodiversity*, Earthscan, London

Tisdell, C. A. (1999) *Biodiversity, Conservation and Sustainable Development*, Edward Elgar, Cheltenham, UK and Northampton, MA

Tisdell, C. A. (2003a) 'Socioeconomic cases of loss of animal genetic diversity: Analysis and assessment', *Ecological Economics*, vol 45, pp361–376

Tisdell, C. A. (2003b) *Economics and Ecology in Agriculture and Marine Production*, Edward Elgar, Cheltenham UK and Northampton, MA

Tisdell, C. A. (2003c) 'Recreational fishing: Its expansion, its economic value and aquaculture's role in sustaining it', *Economies, Ecology and Economics*, Working Paper No. 93. The University of Queensland

Tisdell, C. A. (2005) *Economics of Environmental Conservation*, Edward Elgar, Cheltenham, UK and Northampton, MA

Tisdell, C. A. (2006) 'Poverty, political failure, and the use of open-access resources in developing countries', *Indian Development Review*, vol 4, pp441–450

Worm, B., Barbier, E. B., Beaumont, N., Duffy, J. E., Folke, C., Halpern, B. S., Jackson, J. B. C., Lotze, H. K., Micheli, F., Palumbi, S. R., Sala, E., Selkar, K. A., Stachowicz, J. J., Watson, R. (2006) 'Impacts of biodiversity loss on ocean ecosystems', *Science*, vol 314, pp778–790

4

Biodiversity Conservation in Sea Areas Beyond National Jurisdiction: The Economic Problem

Charles Perrings

Ecosystem-based management and the problem of scale

This chapter considers the problem of biodiversity conservation in the high seas. It starts from the assumption that the aim of conservation is the sustainable use of marine resources, and that this implies maintenance of the resilience of large marine ecosystems (LMEs). There are many threats to the resilience of such systems, including the effects of pollution on marine environments, the transmission of pests and pathogens in ballast water, bottom trawling that harms biodiversity in the substrate, seamounts and deep-water corals and the habitat disruption caused by the mining of seamounts for ferromanganese crusts, or hydrothermal vents for polymetallic sulphides (Pew Oceans Commission, 2003a; FAO, 2004; UN, 2004a). Of all threats, however, the greatest relate to the commercial exploitation of fish and other marine animals. This is the most frequently cited source of stress in marine systems (Jackson et al, 2001; Pauly et al, 2002; Myers and Worm, 2003; Hughes et al, 2005), with bycatch (Lewison et al, 2004), loss of habitat (Pandolfi et al, 2003; Pyke, 2004), climate change (Hughes et al, 2003) and the spread of pathogens (Harvell et al, 2004) being contributory factors. The linkage between changes in the relative abundance of species due to overexploitation and the resilience of marine ecosystems is often indirect, but has been shown for particular systems, for example coral reefs (Bellwood et al, 2004; McManus and Polsenberg, 2004; Hughes et al, 2005) and kelp systems (Stenek et al, 2002). Indeed, there appears to be a consensus among marine biologists that overexploitation of fisheries is significantly more important as an explanation of biodiversity loss than all other factors (Dulvy et al, 2003; Tittensor et al, 2006).

There is a similar consensus about the underlying social causes of overexploitation: the lack of effective institutions and governance mechanisms (Berkes et al, 2003; Hilborn et al, 2005). In the extreme, ineffective governance means that users have open access to the resource, where open access means that there is nothing to exclude users from the resource, and no incentive to conserve it. As H. Scott Gordon observed: 'most of the problems associated with the words "conservation" or "depletion" or "overexploitation" in the fishery are, in reality, manifestations of the fact that the natural resources of the sea yield no economic rent' (Gordon, 1954, p124): that is, they are not owned by anyone, and hence are free to all.

The resources at issue are those in the 'Area' – defined by the UN Convention on the Law of the Seas (UNCLOS) as the seabed and ocean floor beyond the limits of national jurisdiction.[1] Under UNCLOS, the 'Area' and its resources are defined to be the common heritage of mankind, the exploration and exploitation of which is, in principle, to be carried out for the benefit of mankind as a whole. At the same time, however, UNCLOS asserts the 'freedom of the High Seas' as a fundamental principle, and so enshrines open access. Moreover, since UNCLOS does not contain any provisions relating to the conservation or use of biodiversity, except where threatened by mining activities, exploitation of the biological resources of the high seas and the seabed is currently largely unconstrained by UNCLOS, although it is partially regulated by other multilateral agreements.

I am interested in challenges of regulating access in large marine ecosystems so as to protect their resilience: that is so as to maintain a desirable flow of ecosystem services over a range of environmental conditions. The resilience of marine ecological-economic systems has been analysed from a number of different perspectives. There is a rich literature on the resilience of specific ecological components of marine systems, especially coral reefs (Hughes, 1994; Pandolfi et al, 2003; Jackson et al, 2001; Hughes et al, 2003; Hughes et al, 2005) and kelp forests (Steneck et al, 2002; Steneck et al, 2004).

Particular mechanisms for changes in the level of marine resilience have also been explored, especially the impact of changes in species diversity on the level of functional redundancy across a range of systems (Diaz et al, 2003; Fonseca and Ganade, 2001). A parallel literature on the resilience or vulnerability of marine-based social systems has focused on properties of the system that allow responsiveness and adaptability to change (Folke et al, 2002; Berkes et al, 2003; Dietz et al, 2003; Folke et al, 2004), the quality of the feedback mechanisms between the social and ecological components of the system (Gunderson and Pritchard, 2002; Olsson et al, 2004), and the nature of the data required for management for resilience (Charles et al, 2001; Pitcher, 2001; Petraitis and Dudgeon, 2004). In all cases, resilience represents the capacity of the system to function over a range of environmental conditions, and may be measured by the effect of stresses and shocks on the value of ecosystem services.

The problem of biodiversity conservation for resilience is ultimately about the people who directly exploit the system. It involves two questions. What is the scope for establishing institutions with sufficient regulatory authority over international common pool resources to assure the resilience of the system? How can incentives be developed to encourage those accessing international common pool resources to

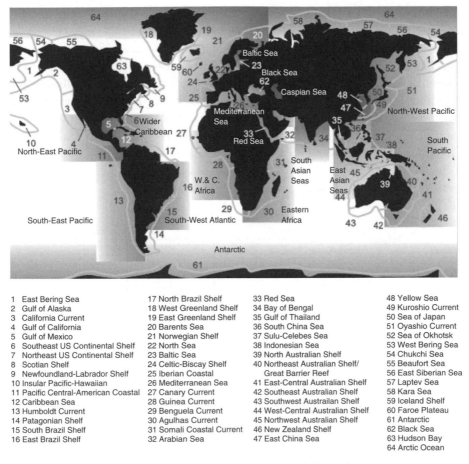

Figure 4.1 Regional seas and large marine ecosystems (LMEs)

1 East Bering Sea	17 North Brazil Shelf	33 Red Sea	48 Yellow Sea
2 Gulf of Alaska	18 West Greenland Shelf	34 Bay of Bengal	49 Kuroshio Current
3 California Current	19 East Greenland Shelf	35 Gulf of Thailand	50 Sea of Japan
4 Gulf of California	20 Barents Sea	36 South China Sea	51 Oyashio Current
5 Gulf of Mexico	21 Norwegian Shelf	37 Sulu-Celebes Sea	52 Sea of Okhotsk
6 Southeast US Continental Shelf	22 North Sea	38 Indonesian Sea	53 West Bering Sea
7 Northeast US Continental Shelf	23 Baltic Sea	39 North Australian Shelf	54 Chukchi Sea
8 Scotian Shelf	24 Celtic-Biscay Shelf	40 Northeast Australian Shelf/	55 Beaufort Sea
9 Newfoundland-Labrador Shelf	25 Iberian Coastal	Great Barrier Reef	56 East Siberian Sea
10 Insular Pacific-Hawaiian	26 Mediterranean Sea	41 East-Central Australian Shelf	57 Laptev Sea
11 Pacific Central-American Coastal	27 Canary Current	42 Southeast Australian Shelf	58 Kara Sea
12 Caribbean Sea	28 Guinea Current	43 Southwest Australian Shelf	59 Iceland Shelf
13 Humboldt Current	29 Benguela Current	44 West-Central Australian Shelf	60 Faroe Plateau
14 Patagonian Shelf	30 Agulhas Current	45 Northwest Australian Shelf	61 Antarctic
15 South Brazil Shelf	31 Somali Coastal Current	46 New Zealand Shelf	62 Black Sea
16 East Brazil Shelf	32 Arabian Sea	47 East China Sea	63 Hudson Bay
			64 Arctic Ocean

Source: Adapted from www.unep.org/regionalseas/Publications/RSP_Large_Marine.pdf.

use the resource sustainably? While much will be made of the weaknesses of a multilateral agreement, UNCLOS, that enshrines open access as a fundamental right, attention will also be paid to the merits of the regional seas programmes (Figure 4.1) and their role in supporting conservation goals, strengthening property rights and coordinating management actions at the level of LMEs (UN, 2004b).

Open access capture fisheries in the high seas

Although many of resources in LMEs are threatened by the weakness of existing regulatory institutions, this chapter focuses on the problem of fisheries. This is not the primary problem in all cases. A recent study of the socio-economic pressures on both regional seas and LMEs identified a number of activities that have the potential to disrupt ecosystem services aside from fisheries (Hoagland and Jin, 2006). For example, climate change may be the most important driving force in the Humboldt, Benguela, Iberian Coastal, Guinea, Canary and California Currents. At the other end of the spectrum, land-based pollution and eutrophication is the principal driver in the Black Sea. However, overfishing is implicated in many of the remaining LMEs, and is widely accepted to be the main driver of change in the US Northeast Shelf, the Yellow Sea and the East China Sea. By the measures identified by Hoagland and Jin (2006), these LMEs occur in the most heavily exploited regional seas (Figure 4.2). In all cases, overfishing is associated with poorly regulated access.

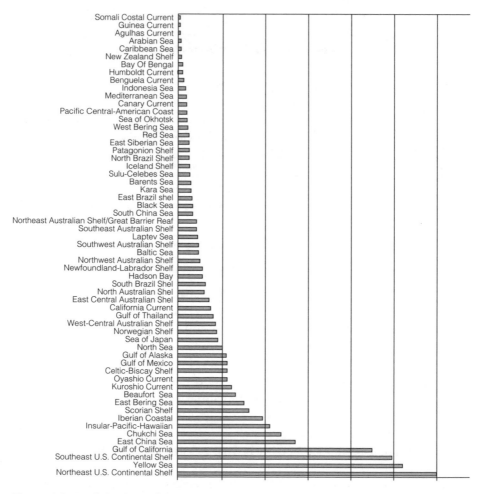

Figure 4.2 Exploitation of LMEs

Note: The MAI/SEI are indexes of marine activity and socio-economic activity respectively.
Source: Hoagland and Jin (2006).

The effect of open access on exploitation rates in fisheries is well understood. Fishers will increase their fishing effort up to the point at which the total cost of effort is equal to the total revenue, ignoring any effect that their activity has on future fish stocks. The result is that the level of effort/fishing capacity under open access will be strictly greater than the level of effort that would occur under either regulated access common property or private property. While open access does not necessarily lead to the extinction or local extirpation of a species, the probability of extinction or local extirpation of stocks is higher than under regulated access or well-defined property rights.

More recently, open access at the scale of the high seas has been argued to be problem in that it permits spatially sequential fishing patterns that increase the pressure on spatially separate stocks. Berkes et al (2005) argue that the sequential exploitation of stocks by fishing firms ('roving bandits') has significantly increased the pressure on all fisheries, in many cases leading to the collapse of individual fish stocks. They argue that this has been driven by growth in world demand for capture fisheries along with the difficulty of regulating new fisheries that are being exploited in this way. Small or localized stocks are fished out before fisheries managers are even aware that there is a problem. For species that are more widely distributed, the depletion of local stocks may be hidden by changes in the spatial pattern of harvest. In fact the spatial distribution of fishing effort is now reasonably well understood (Sanchirico and Wilen, 1999, 2005). The level of fishing effort in any one site depends on net rents per vessel obtainable in that site, and is sensitive to the strength of the dispersion of species between sites. What is not so clear is the implications of fishing effort over multiple sites for the stability of yields across the whole system. Nevertheless, there is a perception that open access at larger scales exacerbates the problem of open access at smaller scales.

The net effect of open access is a clear decline in yields in many of the world's major fisheries. Worm et al (2006) identified catches from 1950 to 2003 within all 64 LMEs[2] worldwide: the source of 83 per cent of global catches over the past 50 years. They reported that the rate of fisheries collapses in these areas (catches less than 10 per cent of the recorded maximum) has been accelerating, and that 29 per cent of fished species were in a state of collapse in 2003. Cumulative collapses affected 65 per cent of all species fished.

In areas beyond national jurisdiction, the most important developments in capture fisheries concern the epipelagic and deep-water species. There are a number of well documented examples of overexploitation followed by collapse in epipelagic and deep-water fisheries. The general picture is that while overall catches are still increasing in some sea regions, they are declining in 12 regions, and in 4 the decline has been very sharp. In the Northwest Atlantic, for example, total catches have declined by 50 per cent since 1968. In the Southeast Atlantic, they have fallen by 47 per cent since 1978, and in the Southeast Pacific by 31 per cent since 1994. In most cases this is ascribed to overfishing induced in part by rising demand for fish products, and in part by the ineffectiveness of mechanisms for the governance of the high seas (FAO, 2004).

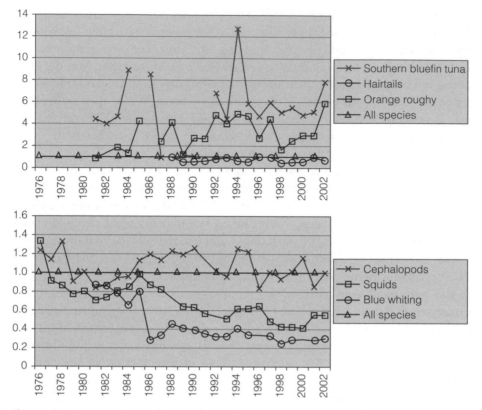

Figure 4.3 Export prices of oceanic species relative to prices of all species caught, 1976–2004, US$

Source: FAO, 2005a.

Overfishing of deep-water species[3] is a particular cause for concern. All are characterized by slow growth rates and late age at first maturity, which implies low sustainable yields (Garibaldi and Limongelli, 2002). Many have been exploited on a non-sustainable basis. In 2002, exports of oceanic species accounted for 10 per cent of the value of total exports of fish and fishery products. While the physical quantity of exports of oceanic species has increased by a factor of 5 since 1976, the real value of exports has increased by a factor of more than 10 (FAO, 2004). This is largely driven by rising prices for particular high-valued species such as southern blue finned tuna and orange roughy (see Figure 4.3). Export prices for many other oceanic species, particularly low-valued industrial species like blue whiting, have fallen relative to average export prices.

A second factor is the collapse of alternative fish stocks. Between the 1960s and the 1990s, for example, catch per unit effort in the East China Sea declined by a factor of 3, and within the coastal fisheries there had been a switch from large, high-valued, predator fish to smaller, low-valued planktivorous fish, and from mature to immature fish (FAO, 1997). At the same time the tightening of regulations within national jurisdictions has increased the attraction of fishing in the high seas where international law and management mechanisms are unable to operate effectively. The freedom to fish on the high seas means open access to deep-water fisheries, while the lack of any supranational authority means that there is no body with a mandate to enforce compliance with agreed conservation measures (FAO, 2004). The net effect is that the level of fishing effort committed to oceanic species, and to deep-water species in particular, has increased relative to the level of effort in other capture fisheries.

Deep-water fisheries have developed largely in the Pacific and the Atlantic, most of the growth occurring in the Atlantic (Figure 4.4). A particular problem associated with the development of this sector is the effect of bottom trawling on marine habitats, especially seamounts and cold-water and deep-water corals. This concern is strong enough that a number of countries have been pressing for a global moratorium on bottom trawling or at least for time-limited regional bans (UN, 2004b). Other important marine communities that are vulnerable to bottom fishing include slow growing cold-water corals that are associated with a rich diversity of flaura and fauna, including molluscs, sponges and crustaceans, that may be abundant in the corals but are extremely rare elsewhere. Although the science is very limited at the moment, many species of fish identified in particular deep-water corals appear to have an extremely limited distribution elsewhere.

Figure 4.4 shows indices of deep-water catches relative to the total marine catch over the last five decades and shows that the rate of growth of deep-water fisheries considerably exceeds that of marine capture fisheries as a whole.

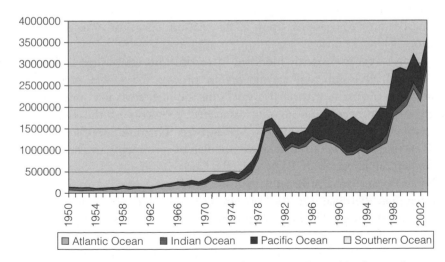

Figure 4.4 Landings of deep-water species by ocean, 1950–2004 (tonnes)

Source: FAO, 2005b.

The governance of LMEs

The main challenge to biodiversity conservation at the scale of the high seas derives from the open access to that comes with freedom of the high seas. Although there are a number of multilateral agreements related to fisheries in areas beyond national jurisdiction, there are few incentives to comply with the terms of those agreements and there is no supranational authority to enforce compliance. Fishers respond to the signals offered by international markets for marine goods and services that are generally incomplete, in the sense that they do not reflect the full cost of fishing activities, and that are actively distorted by the effect of national subsidies. Incomplete markets imply that there are effects that are not taken into account in market transactions, referred to as externalities. If such externalities are negative, as is the case in many of the indirect effects of fishing described above, then decisions based on market prices alone will lead to 'too much' fishing effort relative to the social optimum. Where fishers are subsidized, the position will be exacerbated.

All of these things militate against effective conservation of marine resources. Those who exploit the high seas and the seabed have little incentive to take account of the effects of their activities on marine biodiversity. The only constraints on the behaviour of resource users are voluntary. So, for example, the FAO Code of Conduct for Responsible Fisheries notionally applies to fishing firms, subregional, regional and global organizations, whether governmental or non-governmental, as well as those concerned with the management and development of fisheries. However, it is purely voluntary. Although there are four International Plans of Action agreed under the code, and although it embodies the 'Agreement to promote compliance with international conservation and management measures by fishing vessels on the high seas'[4] these do not create any legally binding obligations upon either nation states or non-governmental entities.

Open access is currently modified by institutions established to implement multilateral environmental agreements to protect the global commons and specific agreements to protect fish stocks on the high seas. The most important of these are the conventions and associated protocols of the Regional Seas Program and the Regional Fishery Management Organisations (RFMOs). The most encompassing of multilateral environmental agreements are the Convention on Biological Diversity (CBD), the UN Convention on the Law of the Sea (UNCLOS) and its instruments, the International Seabed Authority and the International Tribunal for the Law of the Sea. But there are many other agreements dealing with the conservation of marine biodiversity, ranging from species-specific instruments such as the North Atlantic Fur Seal Treaty or the International Commission for the Conservation of Atlantic Tuna (ICCAT), through instruments dealing with groups of species such as the International

Whaling Commission, to framework agreements such as the Antarctic Treaty which provides a framework for regulating the use of all marine and terrestrial resources south of the 60° latitude. Despite the existence of these agreements, however, the high seas are regarded as effectively unregulated (FAO, 2004).

Why is this? Beyond areas of national jurisdiction the CBD has nothing to say about particular species or assemblages of species. Instead it refers to activities and processes carried out under the jurisdiction or control of a signatory that have an impact on biological diversity. Because they have no jurisdiction over biodiversity located in areas beyond the limits of national jurisdiction, the signatories to the convention have no direct responsibility for its conservation and sustainable use. In these areas, therefore, the CBD requires signatories to cooperate to achieve the goals of the Convention, but there are no penalties for non-cooperation and no incentives to cooperate.

Because the vast majority of marine organisms occur in benthic ecosystems, and because the seabed is the focus of the UNCLOS, the CBD secretariat has requested UNCLOS to consider what can be done within its provisions to enhance the protection of benthic biodiversity. A major difficulty with this is that Article 87 of the Convention affirms the principle of the 'freedom of the High Seas', and specifically refers to the 'freedom of fishing'. There is a qualification to this – that freedoms should be exercised with due regard to the interests of others – but the implication of 'freedom of the High Seas' is that open access is enshrined as a fundamental principle of the Convention. The qualifications to the freedoms affirmed in Article 87 include a number relevant to fisheries. Specifically, they include a duty to cooperate with other states in the conservation and management of living resources (Article 118) and a duty to maintain or restore populations of harvested species at levels consistent with maximum sustainable yield (Article 119a). These obligations have not, however, been implemented, and freedom to fish on the high seas implies that many epipelagic and deep-water fisheries are effectively unprotected (FAO, 2004).

Agreements to protect fish stocks on the high seas include the 1993 FAO Compliance Agreement, the 1995 UN Fish Stocks Agreement, the 1995 FAO Code of Conduct for Responsible Fisheries,[5] and an International Plan of Action to Prevent, Deter and Eliminate Illegal, Unreported and Unregulated Fishing. The Compliance and Fish Stocks Agreements are both notionally binding, and do affect some heavily stressed fisheries. The Fish Stocks Agreement, for example, now extends over the high seas areas adjacent to the EEZs of 51 countries (UN, 2004b). The Code of Conduct and its Action Plans, on the other hand, are voluntary. There have been no studies of the effectiveness of the incentives involved in these instruments, but experience with analogous instruments in terrestrial systems suggests that they are seldom effective in conditions where the incentive to defect (the gains from non-compliance) are significant (Barrett, 1994, 2003).

There are currently 12 regional seas programmes (corresponding to the regional seas identified in Figure 4.1), each involving a specific convention and action plan. They reflect a regional seas strategy that has a number of objectives, including the use of regional partnerships to achieve conservation goals, to strengthen national property rights, to translate regional seas conventions into national legislation and to coordinate management actions at the regional level (UN, 2004b). The most important manifestation of regional coordination is the RFMO (Table 4.1), and much has been made of the potential role of RFMOs in addressing a range of problems. From an economic perspective, RFMOs and regional groupings generally are the appropriate level at which to manage environmental resources wherever the ecosystems concerned are regional in extent. In the case of straddling or migratory stocks, for example, the appropriate regional grouping will cover the sea areas within which those stocks move.

The conservation of such stocks is a regional public good, in the sense that it yields non-exclusive and non-rival benefits to people at a regional scale. In such cases the principle of subsidiarity indicates that the right level of governance is the regional level (Sandler, 2005). A recent (July 2006) example of this is that six countries (the Comoros, France, Kenya, Mozambique, New Zealand and the Seychelles) and the European Community have concluded an agreement on the management of fishing in the high seas in the South Indian Ocean. The South Indian Ocean Fisheries Agreement (SIOFA) is aimed at both conservation and sustainable use of fishery resources (other than tuna) in areas beyond national jurisdictions. The agreement requires signatories to implement joint management and conservation measures, to establish effective mechanisms to monitor fishing in the SIOFA, to report on fishing operations, including amounts of captured and discarded fish; to conduct inspections of ships visiting ports of the Parties to verify compliance with SIOFA, and to refuse landing privileges to those who do not comply; to undertake regular studies of the state of fish stocks and the impact of fishing on the environment and to determine which operators are allowed to fish in the SIOFA area.

In principle, matching political, economic and environmental domains should promote efficiency. By making sure that decisions reflect the interests of all relevant stakeholders, it is possible to ensure that resources will be allocated up to the point where the benefits to all interested parties just cover the costs of the allocation. Under UNCLOS, it was envisaged that regional groupings would assume a substantial role in the protection of fish stocks, especially in areas beyond national jurisdiction, in providing information and advice on the conservation needs in those areas and on the outer limits of the EEZs, and in implementing agreements.

Yet, as the FAO points out, UNCLOS does not confer any management authority on regional fishery bodies, and FAO considers many RFMOs are little different from open access regimes (FAO, 2004). Nevertheless, the RFMOs are still the preferred instrument for the regulation of fisheries in the high seas. The

Table 4.1 *Regional Fishery Management Organizations*

FAO bodies

APFIC	Asia-Pacific Fisheries Commission
CECAF	Fishery Committee for the Eastern Central Atlantic
CWP	Coordinating Working Party on Fishery Statistics
GFCM	General Fisheries Commission for the Mediterranean
IOTC	Indian Ocean Tuna Commission
RECOFI	Regional Commission for Fisheries (not yet in force)
SWIOFC	South West Indian Ocean Fishery Commission (not yet finalised)
WECAFC	Western Central Atlantic Fishery Commission

Non-FAO bodies

AAFC	Atlantic Africa Fisheries Conference
CCAMLR	Commission for the Conservation of Antarctic Marine Living Resources
CCSBT	Commission for the Conservation of Southern Bluefin Tuna
COREP	Regional Fisheries Committee for the Gulf of Guinea (not yet in force)
CPPS	South Pacific Permanent Commission
CTMFM	Joint Technical Commission for the Argentina/Uruguay Maritime Front
FFA	South Pacific Forum Fisheries Agency
IATTC	Inter-American Tropical Tuna Commission
IBSFC	International Baltic Sea Fishery Commission
ICCAT	International Commission for the Conservation of Atlantic Tuna
ICES	International Council for the Exploration of the Sea
IPHC	International Pacific Halibut Commission
IWC	International Whaling Commission
NAFO	Northwest Atlantic Fisheries Organization
NAMMCO	North Atlantic Marine Mammal Commission
NASCO	North Atlantic Salmon Conservation Organization
NEAFC	North-East Atlantic Fisheries Commission
NPAFC	North Pacific Anadromous Fish Commission
OLDEPESCA	Latin American Organization for the Development of Fisheries
PICES	North Pacific Marine Science Organization
PSC	Pacific Salmon Commission
SEAFO	South East Atlantic Fishery Organization (not yet in force)
SPC	Secretariat of the Pacific Community
SRCF	Sub-regional Commission on Fisheries
WCPFC	Western and Central Pacific Fisheries Commission (not yet in force)
WIOTO	Western Indian Ocean Tuna Organization

Source: UNEP (2006).

UN has urged states, through RFMOs, to prohibit destructive practices by vessels under their jurisdiction that have an adverse impact on marine ecosystems in areas beyond national jurisdiction, to address the impact of deep-sea bottom trawling, to comply with existing obligations and to implement the International Plan of Action to Prevent, Deter and Eliminate Illegal, Unreported and Unregulated Fishing adopted by the Committee on Fisheries of the FAO (UN, 2004b).

The main weakness of regional organizations of the kind discussed here is that they cannot effectively establish exclusive rights for member states (Barrett, 2003). Nevertheless, regional groupings are still the preferred solution to the open access issue in areas beyond national jurisdiction. A recent interdisciplinary review of the problem of the Arctic, for example, proposes that the Arctic Council take the lead in identifying the most important changes expected to occur, to establish whether it is possible to prevent or mitigate these changes if society acts now before the changes occur and to evaluate the costs and benefits of mitigation and to propose coordinated policies for arctic countries for mitigation (or adaptation to projected changes where mitigation is not a viable option (Chapin et al, 2005).

In the Arctic case, though, the forces that are driving local change are global in nature, and hence mitigation actions need to take place at a global level if they are to be effective. Indeed, the same paper notes that the global community has a vested interest in enhancing Arctic resilience precisely because the Arctic is biologically connected to the rest of the world through annual migrations of marine mammals and fish (Chapin et al, 2005). A similar concern has been expressed by the FAO over the effectiveness of regional approaches – that regional solutions may merely shift the problem from one marine area to another. This indicates the need for a global approach of the kind envisaged in the FAO Compliance Agreement (FAO, 2004). Indeed, some have argued that it implies the need for a Global Environmental Organisation analogous to the WTO (Esty, 2004).

Economic incentives under ecosystem-based management

International markets for marine resources, like other markets, are regulated by the General Agreement on Tariffs and Trade (GATT), along with a set of subsidiary agreements. These include the Agreement on Technical Barriers to Trade (TBT), which ensures that technical standards are not used as barriers to trade; the Agreement on the application of Sanitary and Phytosanitary Measures (SPS), which ensures that health and safety standards are not used to discriminate between countries with identical or similar conditions; and the Agreement on Subsidies and Countervailing Measures (SCM), which restricts the use of subsidies for, *inter alia*, fishery products. The market provides an effective negative feedback mechanism in which changes in harvest are reflected in changes in relative prices. The problem lies not with the market *per se*, but with the various factors that drive a wedge between the market price and the true value – the social opportunity cost – of marine resources. These include the lack of well defined property rights that result in open access. They also include the existence of subsidies and various other perverse incentives, all of which exacerbate the overcapacity created by open access. The various multilateral and regional agreements that exist attempt to impose restrictions on the activities of fishing entities that will reduce fishing pressure to sustainable levels, but the weakness of incentives to comply and the lack of penalties for non-compliance make them relatively ineffective.

It follows that the development of incentives for the sustainable use of marine resources requires measures that counteract the misleading signals of an imperfect set of markets. We are interested in incentives that encourage resource users to behave in ways that are consistent with the resilience of LMEs: that is to limit the stresses on LMEs to levels that leave those systems capable of operating over the expected range of environmental conditions. The traditional way of regulating behaviour has been by proscription of undesirable behaviours through so-called command and control mechanisms. This includes a range of access rules – close seasons, catch quotas, gear restrictions – and the like, along with more direct prohibitions on use. The incentives associated with rules of this kind comprise penalties or punishment for non-compliance with the regulation. Environmental and resource economists generally favour a set of mechanisms that more directly mimic the effect of market prices. This includes taxes, user fees and access charges or subsidies, grants and compensation packages. It also includes combined mechanisms that involve both a quantitative restriction and the used of market-based incentives.

Individual transferable quotas (ITQs) are the most common of the mixed mechanisms favoured by economists concerned with the exploitation of marine ecosystems. ITQs still rely on the protection offered by a physical limit on harvest (and on penalties for non-compliance with that limit). However, by permitting the development of a market they offer individual fishers an incentive to use the total allowable catch efficiently. Entry to the market is possible only if fishers buy quota from those already in the market, and each entrant will only buy permits up to the point where the marginal cost of the permit is equal to the expected marginal net benefit from the sale of the allowable catch. Since the expected marginal net benefits from sale of allowable catch will fall as the cost of harvest rises, and since the cost of harvest rises the more scarce the fish stocks, it follows that ITQ prices will be lower the more stressed the system is. In other words, the value of the asset (the quota) will fall if the resource is stressed. This in turn will serve as a disincentive to new entrants.

What ITQs do is to assign a property right to the resource. Assigning property rights to users has two important effects. One is that it encourages them to take the future consequences of their harvesting decisions into account since they themselves bear those future consequences. More particularly, it encourages them to include the 'user cost' of the resource in their harvesting decisions, and to try to protect the value of their asset. The second important effect is that property rights give the right holder the authority to exclude others from access to the resource. But the allocation of property rights does assume that there is an authority with the power to assign rights.

This is the principal justification for maritime countries' seizure of resources through the establishment and extension of exclusive economic zones (EEZs). By assuming the right to assign property to resources in the EEZs, maritime states have made it possible to create markets in those resources, and hence to change the incentives to resource users. So, for example, the Magnuson-Stevens Fishery Conservation and Management Act in the US (Public Law 94–265) authorizes both the use of transferable quota, and mandates action where fisheries are 'overfished'. The establishment and extension of EEZs has frequently (but not always) led to a reduction in pressure on stressed resources in those sea areas. In every case, however, it has also increased pressure on remaining open access resources.

Market-based incentives work by changing the cost to the resource user. If an incentive increases/reduces the cost of access to a resource it provides an incentive to reduce/increase the use of that resource. The degree to which resource users' behaviour changes depends on their elasticity of response – the higher the elasticity the greater the change in use caused by an incentive of given size. Response elasticities depend on the extent to which the user is locked into a particular pattern of behaviour and, since this typically depends on the time available for the response, elasticities also change over time. Empirically, it has been found that short-run elasticities are typically much lower than long-run elasticities. In other words, the change in resource use associated with a given increase in the cost of access will be greater the longer the time allowed for people to adjust their behaviour. In principle, incentives should be set so that the cost to resource users should reflect the social opportunity cost of the resource, that is its value to society. Where taxes or subsidies are the mechanism of choice, the optimum tax/subsidy is the difference between unregulated market prices and the true cost of resource use to society. Where market creation is the mechanism of choice, if property rights in the asset are well defined, the market price should converge on the true cost of the resource to society.

The problem with sea areas beyond national jurisdiction is that there is no sovereign authority with the right to assign property rights or to levy taxes, so it is not possible to use direct incentives of this kind. Moreover, the problem is made significantly worse by the widespread practice of subsidizing national fleets that exploit the resources of the high seas. Current subsidies to the fishing industry in different countries take various forms, including grants towards the cost of vessel construction or the cost of increasing the capacity of vessels, direct subsidies on the cost of production and marketing, and price support on fish and fish products. Subsidies are estimated at around 20 per cent of fisheries revenues worldwide, although the level of subsidies varies significantly by country. Japan, Russia, South Korea, Spain and Australia are frequently singled out for the direct subsidies offered to the industry, but many more countries indirectly subsidize fisheries (and other industries) through major inputs such as fuel. Indeed, many fisheries would not be financially viable without the subsidies. In all cases the effect of subsidies is to exacerbate the overfishing induced by open access. It follows that even if it is not possible to address the problem of open access to the high seas directly, it would be possible to reduce pressure on the resource by the removal of subsidies to national fishing fleets. While removal of subsidies is on the agenda for the Doha round of negotiations of the GATT this remains a stubborn problem.

Beyond the removal of subsidies, the only incentive system that will ultimately assure protection of marine resources is one that confronts users with the full social opportunity cost of their actions. Under an open access regime the negative effects on stocks of overexploitation are ignored in the market transactions of both producers and consumers. They are external to the market. Since the problem of externality lies in the incompleteness of markets – which leaves some effects of economic activities unaccounted for – it is not surprising that the solutions explored by economists have tended to focus on the assignment of property rights and the provision of information to make markets more complete, together with the elimination of policies that compound the problem.

The extension of national property rights over an increasing proportion of the sea area has brought the majority of the world's capture fisheries under national control. While this has led to an improvement in the management of fisheries in those areas – for the most part – it has also increased pressure on the remaining sea areas. This is reflected in the increasing volume and value of the world's oceanic fisheries. At the same time, improved scientific understanding of marine ecosystems has led to an awareness that overfishing and the incidental damage caused by bottom trawling is increasingly damaging to important marine systems, particularly seamounts and deep-water corals in sea areas beyond the limits of national jurisdiction. There are clearly no easy fixes to this problem. The fact that open access to the high seas is enshrined in UNCLOS remains a fundamental source of difficulty. Open access is an appropriate rule wherever natural resources are genuinely non-scarce. While the high seas were legitimately regarded as a non-scarce resource for centuries, it is no longer the case that marine resources are non-scarce, and open access is no longer an appropriate rule. The fact that there is no authority with responsibility for the high seas is also a fundamental source of difficulty, and one that is at least as intractable.

Biodiversity conservation investment

There are two areas where collective investment in biodiversity conservation in the high seas might usefully be increased: the first is the provision of information on changes currently taking place in marine ecosystems and global fisheries, and the implications of these changes for human well-being. The second is the development of mechanisms to support regional conservation agreements, including incentives to comply with regional agreements. Loreau et al (2006) have recently argued the need for a scientific body both to undertake routine monitoring and assessment of the world's biological resources, and to provide decision makers (especially at the international level) with timely information on research results on changes in biodiversity.

The mechanism for funding conservation as a global public good is the Global Environment Facility (GEF). It is currently the only mechanism by which the global community invests in natural capital stocks. Recent spending by the GEF on both biodiversity conservation and international waters has declined since 1999 (Table 4.2). Spending on international waters is largely accounted for by pollution clean-up, but the line item also includes projects that benefit marine biodiversity. Two foci of the international waters programme are unsustainable exploitation of fisheries and protection of fisheries habitats. In 2003 it stood at under US$80 million.

The GEF's budgeted funding for projects affecting sea areas beyond national jurisdiction has been increased to US$398 million for the period 2003–2006, restoring funding to the level of 1999, and it is expected to increase to US$189 million for the year 2007 (Clémençon, 2005). This is not currently based on any assessment of the global risks of damage to marine systems in waters beyond the limits of national jurisdiction, but by any criteria it is a very low level of investment in a resource that supplies the nutritional needs of a substantial part of the world's population.

One reason that global investment in marine biodiversity conservation is so low is the paucity of information on the economic importance of the goods and services deriving from marine ecosystems. Worm et al (2006) is one of a very few efforts to address this problem. There is scope for doing more. The CBD's Clearing House Mechanism and the FAO's Fishstat facilities are important contributions to the conservation and sustainable use of marine biodiversity, in that they provide a best shot solution to the information public good. The scientific effort in support of the regional seas programme is likewise an important source of information. However, few resources have been committed to developing a database on the derived value of ecosystems that are at risk. An expansion of the data generated or provided by these bodies to include estimates of the opportunity cost of damage to seamounts, deep-water corals and similar benthic systems would help identify the value of the resource to be protected through GEF resources.

Regional cooperation and coordination is a helpful way of addressing some of the least tractable issues in the provision of international public goods or the exploitation of international common pool resources, in that it addresses both the problem of large numbers of contracting parties and allows for repeated

Table 4.2 *GEF funding of global biodiversity conservation and international waters, 1999–2003 (US$ million)*

	Biodiversity	Biosafety	International waters	Total
1999	181.48		96.28	473.06
2000	182.75		47.43	453.20
2001	185.30		74.53	469.59
2002	79.35	7.19	80.11	340.98
2003	120.79	2.00	79.60	514.36

Source: Clémençon (2005).

renegotiation (Barrett, 2005). But regional public goods have their own problems. One is the difficulty of funding regional initiatives. National public goods are funded by nation states and the multilaterals and the GEF exists to fund global initiatives, but regional initiatives are frequently ignored (Sandler, 2005). In principle, the GEF funds only the incremental cost of providing global public goods – that is, the difference between the cost of provision of the public good and the local benefits it offers. In practice GEF funding covers more than just the incremental costs of conservation projects, but it does not apply to conservation whose benefits are largely local or regional. Hence marine conservation efforts whose benefits largely accrue exclusively to a particular group of countries are not eligible.

To address this problem, it is important to identify the different levels at which conservation benefits accrue, and to use this information to develop a hierarchical funding structure. Application of the incremental cost principle implies at least three levels of funding: national, regional and global. Nation states should carry a share of the cost of conservation projects with wider benefits, and the GEF and other global sources should cover the global costs. At the regional level Sandler has suggested both that regional development banks be engaged in the provision of regional public goods, and that regional trade pacts be engaged in the process (Sandler, 2005).

A separate problem at both regional and global levels is enforcement and compliance. Taking ICCAT as an example, although countries have agreed to conserve the tuna that pass through their EEZs, none has an incentive to do so. Moreover, the conservation incentive is even weaker in the high seas. Not only does a reduction in fishing effort leave more fish for others to catch, but also by increasing profitability it provides non-signatories to the Fish Stocks Agreement with an incentive to enter the fishery. At the same time the vessels of compliant countries themselves have an incentive either to withdraw from the agreement or to ignore the agreed catch levels. ICCAT has adopted trade restrictions as penalties against both non-participants and non-complying states, but since there are fewer than 40 signatories those who are not in compliance are easily able to evade those sanctions (Barrett, 2005).

Although many common pool resource problems are in the nature of a prisoner's dilemma, if cooperation and coordination are capable of yielding a net benefit to the contracting parties to an agreement, then it may be possible to design the agreement such that it is self-enforcing. This is not always true, and the form of the agreement will be sensitive to the particular conditions of the resource, the markets and the institutions within which the contracting parties operate. Many agreements have failed to deliver net benefits (Sandler, 1997), frequently because they fail to include an appropriate set of incentives to comply with its terms (Barrett, 2003). An important element of the research needed to support marine biodiversity conservation is accordingly an evaluation of the incentives offered by the agreements governing the conservation of both fish stocks and the resources of the seabed.

Concluding remarks

The bottom line is that open access to the high seas and the public good nature of conservation activities in the high seas make it hard both to coordinate and enforce conservation efforts in areas beyond national jurisdiction. Yet ecosystem-based management (EBM) in LMEs will be ineffective in the absence of coordination between the nation states exploiting those systems. The brightest signs currently lie in two areas. The first is the fact that many countries do have a direct interest in the conservation of biodiversity within their own jurisdiction, and that the effectiveness of these efforts can be significantly enhanced if there is coordination of effort in areas beyond national jurisdiction. This provides a positive incentive to explore the benefits of coordination. It does not solve the problem of illegal, unreported and unregulated fishing by private interests, but it provides countries with an incentive to coordinate actions regionally. Given this, there is scope for the development of agreements whose net benefits to members make them self-enforcing.

The second (related) source of hope is that marine biodiversity conservation in areas beyond national jurisdiction may be a threshold public good, implying that the effectiveness of individual conservation efforts depends on a minimum level of collective conservation. Certainly, the fact that there appears to be a consensus amongst marine scientists that marine biodiversity conservation requires that around 30 per cent of sea areas be protected supports the notion. The reason that this is a source of hope is that it reduces the problem posed by free-riding. The more countries that commit to collective action to conserve LMEs as productive assets, the fewer will be the number that free-ride on the conservation efforts of others. This also increases the incentive for those with the deepest pockets (the US in the Pacific and the EU in the Atlantic) to underwrite conservation activities beyond their national jurisdictions. Taken together, these two areas of hope give reason to believe that it is possible to develop both self-enforcing regional agreements to coordinate conservation actions that go beyond the RFMOs, and the resources to make regional coordination effective.

Ultimately, the development of incentives to protect the resilience and hence sustainability of fisheries in sea areas beyond national jurisdiction depends on the introduction of access charges that reflect the user cost of the resource. These resources are part of the common wealth of humanity, and their use has a cost. That cost should be factored into the investment and harvesting decisions of private fishing firms and national governments alike. The introduction of access charges or royalties payable to the United Nations, as representative of the collective interest of humanity, may be some way off, but it is what must ultimately happen. The alternative is progressively more aggressive claims to sea areas beyond national jurisdiction by extension of the Exclusive Economic Zones. While this has created at least some of the necessary conditions for the efficient management of marine resources, it remains a fundamentally inequitable solution to the problem.

Notes

1. National jurisdiction includes both territorial waters and exclusive economic zones (EEZs). Most signatories of UNCLOS as well as the majority of non-signatories claim territorial sea of 12 nautical miles or less, together with a contiguous zone of 24 nautical miles. However, most coastal states also claim an exclusive economic zone of up to 200 nautical miles. A small number of states – mostly non-signatories of UNCLOS – claim territorial waters beyond 12 miles (UN, 2004a).

2. They define LMEs to be large (>150,000 km^2) ocean regions reaching from estuaries and coastal areas to the seaward boundaries of continental shelves and the outer margins of the major current systems.

3. These include hairtail, orange roughy, oreos, alfonsinos, cusk eels and brotulas, Patagonian toothfish, Pacific armourhead, sablefish, Greenland halibut, morid cods and various species of Scorpaenidae. Away from seamounts, Gadiformes are the most commonly exploited deep-water species. A number of deep-water species, such as blue whiting – which accounts for around half of all deep-water catches – are caught for reduction into fishmeal.

4. www.ecolex.org/en/treaties/treaties_fulltext.php?docnr=3105&language=en

5. The code exhorts nation states to: conserve aquatic ecosystems, recognizing that the right to fish carries with it an obligation to act in a responsible manner; promote the interests of food security, taking into account both present and future generations; prevent overfishing and excess capacity; base conservation and management decisions on the best scientific evidence available, taking into account traditional knowledge of the resources and their habitat; apply the precautionary approach; develop further selective and environmentally safe fishing gear, in order to maintain biodiversity, minimize waste, catch of non-target species, etc.; maintain the nutritional value, quality and safety in fish and fish products; protect and rehabilitate critical fisheries habitats; ensure fisheries interests are accommodated in the multiple uses of the coastal zone and are integrated into coastal area management; ensure compliance with and enforcement of conservation and management measures and establish effective mechanisms to monitor and control activities of fishing vessels and fishing support vessels; exercise effective flag State control in order to ensure the proper application of the Code; cooperate through subregional, regional and global fisheries management organizations; ensure transparent and timely decision-making processes; conduct fish trade in accordance with the principles, rights and obligations established in the WTO Agreement; cooperate to prevent disputes, and resolve them in a timely, peaceful and cooperative manner, including entering into provisional arrangements; promote awareness of responsible fisheries through education and training, as well as involving fishers and fishfarmers in the policy formulation and implementation process; ensure that fish facilities and equipment are safe and healthy and that internationally agreed standards are met; protect the rights of fishers and fish workers, especially those engaged in subsistence, small scale and artisanal fisheries; promote the diversification of income and diet through aquaculture. www.fao.org/figis/servlet/static?xml=CCRF_prog.xml&dom=org

References

Adger, W. N., Hughes, T. P., Folke, C., Carpenter, S. R., Rockström, J. (2005) 'Social-ecological resilience to coastal disasters', *Science*, vol 309, pp1036–1039

Barrett, S. (1994) 'The biodiversity supergame', *Environmental and Resource Economics*, vol 41, pp111–122

Barrett, S. (2003) *Environment and Statecraft: The Strategy of Environmental Treaty-making*, Oxford University Press, Oxford

Barrett, S. (2005) *Managing the Global Commons*, Background working paper for the Task Force on Global Public Goods, Stockholm, Sweden

Bellwood, D., Hughes, T., Folke, C. Nyström, M. (2004) 'Confronting the coral reef crisis', *Nature*, vol 429, pp827–833

Berkes, F., Colding, J., Folke, C. (eds) (2003) *Navigating Social-ecological Systems: Building Resilience for Complexity and Change*, Cambridge University Press, Cambridge

Berkes, F., Hughes, T. P., Steneck, R. S., Wilson, J. A., Bellwood, D. R., Crona, B., Folke, C., Gunderson, L. H., Leslie, H. M., Norberg, J., Nyström, M., Olsson, P., Österblom, H., Scheffer, M., Worm, B. (2005) 'Globalization, roving bandits, and marine resources', *Science*, vol 311, pp1557–1558

Chapin, F. S., Hoel, M., Carpenter, S. R., Lubchenco, J., Walker, B., Callaghan, T. V., Folke, C., Levin S., Mäler, K.-G., Nilsson, C., Barrett, S., Crépin, A.-S., Danell, K., Rosswall, T., Starrett, D., Xepapadeas, A. (2005) *Building Resilience and Adaptation to Manage Arctic Change*, Beijer Institute Working Papers, Stockholm

Charles, A., Boyd, H., Lavers, A., Benjamin, C. (2001) *A Preliminary Set of Ecological, Socio-economic and Institutional Indicators for Nova Scotia's Fisheries and Marine Environment*, Saint Mary's University, Environmental Studies, Halifax

Clémençon, R. (2005) 'What future for the global environment facility?', *Journal of Environment and Development*, vol 15, no 1, pp50–74

Copeland, B. R. (2000) 'Trade and environment: Policy linkages', *Environment and Development Economics*, vol 54, pp405–432

Costanza, R., Andrade, F., Antunes, P., van den Belt, M., Boersma, D., Boesch, D., Catarino, F., Hanna, S., Linburg, K., Low, B., Molitor, M., Pereira, J. G., Rayner, S., Santos, R., Wilson, J., Young, M. (1998) 'Principles for sustainable governance of the oceans', *Science*, vol 281, pp198–199

Costello, C. and McAusland, C. (2003) 'Protectionism, trade, and measures of damage from exotic species introductions', *American Journal of Agricultural Economics*, vol 85, pp964–975

Diaz, S., Symstad, A. J., Stuart Chapin, F. III., Wardle, D. A., Huenneke, L. F. (2003) 'Functional diversity revealed by removal experiments', *Trends in Ecology and Evolution*, vol 18, pp140–146

Dietz, T., Ostrom, E., Stern, P. C. (2003) 'The struggle to govern the commons', *Science*, vol 302, pp1907–1912

Dulvy, N. K., Sadovy, Y., Reynolds, J. D. (2003) 'Extinction vulnerability in marine populations', *Fish and Fisheries*, vol 4, pp25–64

Esty, D. (2004) *Sustainable Management of the Global Natural Commons*, Background working paper for the Task Force on Global Public Goods, Stockholm, Sweden

FAO (1997) *Review of the State of World Fishery Resources: Marine fisheries*, FAO Fisheries Circular No. 920 FIRM/C920, Rome

FAO (2004) *The State of World Fisheries and Aquaculture*, FAO Fisheries Department, FAO, Rome

FAO (2005a) *FISHSTAT Plus: Fisheries commodities production and trade 1976–2002 dataset*, Fishery Information, Data and Statistics Unit, FAO, Rome

FAO (2005b) *FISHSTAT Plus: Capture production 1950–2004 dataset*, Fishery Information, Data and Statistics Unit, FAO, Rome

Folke, C., Carpenter, S., Walker, B., Scheffer, M., Elmqvist, T., Gunderson, L., Holling, C. S. (2002) 'Resilience and sustainable development: Building adaptive capacity in a world of transformations', *Ambio*, vol 31, pp437–440

Folke, C., Carpenter, S., Walker, B., Scheffer, M. (2004) 'Regime shifts, resilience and biodiversity in ecosystem management', *Annual Review of Ecology and Systematics*, vol 35, pp557–581

Fonseca, C. R. and Ganade, G. (2001) 'Species functional redundancy, random extinctions and the stability of ecosystems', *Journal of Ecology*, vol 89, pp118–125

Gaines, S. D., Gaylord, B., Largier, J. L. (2003) 'Avoiding current oversights in marine reserve design', *Ecological Applications*, vol 131, ppS32–S46

Garibaldi, L. and Limongelli, L. (2002) *Trends in Oceanic Captures and Clustering of Large Marine Ecosystems: Two Studies Based on the FAO Capture Database*, FAO Fisheries Technical Paper, no. 435. FAO, Rome

Gordon, H. S. (1954) 'The economic theory of a common property resource: The fishery', *Journal of Political Economy*, vol 62, no 2, pp124–142

Gundersen, L. H. and Pritchard, L. (eds) (2002) *Resilience and the Behavior of Large-scale Systems*, Island Press, Washington, DC

Harvell, D., Aronson, R., Baron, N., Connell, J., Dobson, A., Ellner, S., Gerber, L., Kuris, K. A., McCallum, H., Lafferty, K., McKay, B., Porter, J., Pascual, M., Smith, G., Sutherland, K., Ward, J. (2004) 'The rising tide of ocean diseases: Unsolved problems and research priorities', *Frontiers in Ecology and the Environment*, vol 2, pp375–382

Hastings, A. and Botsford, L. W. (2003) 'Comparing designs of marine reserves for fishery and biodiversity', *Ecological Applications*, vol 131, ppS65–S70

Hilborn, R., Orensanz, J. M., Parma, A. M. (2005) 'Institutions, incentives and the future of fisheries', *Philosophical Transactions of the Royal Society of London, Series B*, vol 360, pp47–57

Hoagland, P. and Jin, Di. (2006) *Accounting for Economic Activities in Large Marine Ecosystems and Regional Seas*, UNEP Regional Seas Reports and Studies no. 181, Nairobi, UNEP

Hughes, T. P. (1994) 'Catastrophes, phase-shifts, and large-scale degradation of a Caribbean coral-reef', *Science*, vol 265, no 5178, pp1547–1551

Hughes, T. P., Baird, A. H., Dinsdale, E. A., Moltschaniwskyj, N. A., Pratchett, M. S., Tanner, J. E., Willis, B. L. (2000) 'Supply-side ecology works both ways: The link between benthic adults, fecundity and larval recruits', *Ecology*, vol 81, pp2241–2249

Hughes, T. P., Bellwood, D. R., Connolly, S. R. (2002a) 'Biodiversity hotspots, centres of endemicity, and the conservation of coral reefs', *Ecology Letters*, vol 5, pp775–784

Hughes, T. P., Baird, A. H., Dinsdale, E. A., Harriott, V. J., Moltschaniwskyj, N. A., Pratchett, M. S., Tanner, J. E., Willis, B. L. (2002b) 'Latitudinal patterns in larval recruitment: Detecting regional variation using meta-analysis and large-scale sampling', *Ecology*, vol 83, pp436–451

Hughes, T. P., Baird, A. H., Bellwood, D. R., Card, M., Connolly, S. R., Folke, C., Grosberg, R., Hoegh-Guldberg, O., Jackson, J. B. C., Kleypas, J., Lough, J. M., Marshall, P., Nyström, M., Palumbi, S. R., Pandolfi, J. M., Rosen, B., Roughgarden, J. (2003) 'Climate change, human impacts, and the resilience of coral reefs', *Science*, vol 301, pp929–933

Hughes T. P., Bellwood, D. R., Folke, C., Steneck, R. S., Wilson, J. (2005) 'New paradigms for supporting the resilience of marine ecosystems', *Trends in Ecology and Evolution*, vol 20, no 7, pp380–386

Jackson, J. B. C., Kirby, M. X., Berger, W. H., Bjorndal, K. A., Botsford, L. W., Bourque, B. J., Bradbury, R. H., Cooke, R., Erlandson, J., Estes, J. A., Hughes, T. P., Kidwell, S., Lange, C. B., Lenihan, H. S., Pandolfi, J. M., Peterson, C. H., Steneck, R. S., Tegner, M. J., Warner, R. R. (2001) 'Historical overfishing and the recent collapse of coastal ecosystems', *Science*, vol 293, pp629–638

Lewison, R. L., Crowder, L. B., Read, A. J., Freeman, S. A. (2004) 'Understanding impacts of fisheries bycatch on marine megafauna', *Trends in Ecology and Evolution*, vol 19, pp598–604

Loreau, M., Oteng-Yeboah, A., Arroyo, M. T. K., Babin, D., Barbault, R., Donoghue, M., Gadgil, M., Häuser, C., Heip, C., Larigauderie, A., Ma, K., Mace, G., Mooney, H. A., Perrings, C., Raven, P., Sarukhan, J., Schei, P., Scholes, R. J., Watson, R. T. (2006) 'Diversity without representation', *Nature*, vol 442, pp245–246

McAusland, C. and Costello, C. (2004) 'Avoiding invasives: Trade related policies for controlling unintentional exotic species introductions', *Journal of Environmental Economics and Management*, vol 48, pp954–977

McManus, J. W. and Polsenberg, J. F. (2004) 'Coral–algal phase-shifts on coral reefs: Ecological and environmental aspects', *Progress in Oceanography*, vol 60, pp263–279

Margolis, M., Shogren, J., Fisher, C. (2005) 'How trade politics affect invasive species control', *Ecological Economics*, vol 523, pp305–313

Meester, G. A., Mehrotra, A., Ault, J. S., Baker, E. K. (2004) 'Designing marine reserves for fishery management', *Management Science*, vol 50, pp1031–1043

Myers, R. A. and Worm, B. (2003) 'Rapid worldwide depletion of predatory fish communities', *Nature*, vol 423, pp280–283

Nyström, M. and Folke, C. (2001) 'Spatial resilience of coral reefs', *Ecosystems*, vol 4, pp406–417

Nyström, M., Folke, C., Moberg, F. (2000) 'Coral reef disturbance and resilience in a human-dominated environment', *Trends in Ecology and Evolution*, vol 15, pp413–417

Olsson, P., Folke, C., Berkes, F. (2004) 'Adaptive co-management for building resilience in social–ecological systems', *Environmental Management*, vol 34, pp75–90

Pandolfi, J. M., Bradbury, R. H., Sala, E., Hughes, T. P., Bjorndal, K. A., Cooke, R. G., McArdle, D., McClenachan, L., Newman, M. J. H., Paredes, G., Warner, R. R., Jackson, J. B. C. (2003) 'Global trajectories of the long-term decline of coral reef ecosystems', *Science*, vol 301, pp955–958

Pauly, D. and Maclean, J. (eds) (2003) *In a Perfect Ocean: The State of Fisheries and Ecosystems in the North Atlantic Ocean*, Island Press, Washington, DC

Pauly, D., Christensen, V., Guenette, S., Pitcher, T. J., Sumaila, U. R., Walters, C. J., Watson, R., Zeller, D. (2002) 'Towards sustainability in world fisheries', *Nature*, vol 418, pp689–695

Perrings, C., Williamson, M., Dalmazzone, S. (eds) (2000) *The Economics of Biological Invasions*, Cheltenham, Edward Elgar

Petraitis, P. S. and Dudgeon, S. R. (2004) 'Detecting alternative stable states in marine communities', *Journal of Experimental Marine Biology and Ecology*, vol 300, pp343–371

Pew Oceans Commission (2003a) *America's Living Oceans: Charting a Course for Change*, Summary Report, Pew Oceans Commission, Arlington, Virginia

Pew Oceans Commission (2003b) *Socioeconomic Perspectives on Marine Fisheries in the United States*, Staff Paper, Pew Oceans Commission, Arlington, Virginia

Pitcher, T. J. (2001) 'Fisheries managed to rebuild ecosystems? Reconstructing the past to salvage the future', *Ecological Applications*, vol 11, pp601–617

Pyke, C. R. (2004) 'Habitat loss confounds climate change impacts', *Frontiers in Ecology and the Environment*, vol 2, pp171–182

Roberts, C. M. (2002) 'Deep impact: The rising toll of fishing in the deep sea', *Trends in Ecology and Evolution*, vol 175, pp242–245

Roberts, C. M., Andelman, S., Branch, G., Bustamante, R. H., Castilla, J. C., Dugan, J., Halpern, B. S., Lafferty, K. D., Leslie, H., Lubchenko, J., McArdle, D., Possingham, H. P., Ruckelshaus, M., Warner, R. R. (2003) 'Ecological criteria for evaluating candidate sites for marine reserves', *Ecological Applications*, vol 131, ppS199–S214

Sanchirico, J. and Wilen, J. E. (1999) 'Bioeconomics of spatial exploitation in a patchy environment', *Journal of Environmental Economics and Management*, vol 37, pp129–150

Sanchirico, J. and Wilen, J. E. (2005) 'Optimal spatial management of renewable resources: Matching policy scope to ecosystem scale', *Journal of Environmental Economics and Management*, vol 501, pp23–46

Sandler, T. (1997) *Global Challenges*, Cambridge University Press, Cambridge

Sandler, T. (2005) *Regional Public Goods and Regional Cooperation*, Background working paper for the Task Force on Global Public Goods, Stockholm, Sweden

Steneck, R. S., Graham, M. H., Bourque, B. J., Corbett, D., Erlandson, J. M., Estes, J. A., Tegner, M. J. (2002) 'Kelp forest ecosystems: Biodiversity, stability, resilience and future', *Environmental Conservation*, vol 29, pp436–459

Steneck, R. S., Vavrinec, J., Leland, A. V. (2004) 'Accelerating trophic-level dysfunction in kelp forest ecosystems of the Western North Atlantic', *Ecosystems*, vol 7, pp323–332

Tittensor, D. P., Worm, B., Myers, R. A. (2006) 'Macroecological changes in exploited marine systems', in J. D. Witman and K. Roy (eds) *Marine Macroecology*, University of Chicago Press, Chicago, IL

United Nations (2004a) *Oceans and the Law of the Sea: Report of the Secretary-General*, Fifty-ninth session Item 51 a, UN A/59/62, New York

United Nations (2004b) *Oceans and the Law of the Sea: Report on the work of the United Nations Open-ended Informal Consultative Process on Oceans and the Law of the Sea at its fifth meeting*, UN A/59/122, New York

United Nations Environment Program (UNEP) (2006) *Ecosystems and Biodiversity in Deep Waters and High Seas*, UNEP Regional Seas Report and Studies No. 178, Nairobi

UNEP/RSP and NOAA LME Partnership, Holland, D., Sanchirico, J. N., Curtis, R., Hicks, R. L. (2004) 'An introduction to spatial modeling in fisheries economics', *Marine Resource Economics*, vol 191, pp1–6

Vitousek, P. M., Aber, J. D. Howarth, R. W., Likens, G. E., Matson, P. A., Schindler, D. W., Schlesinger, W. H., Tilman, D. G. (1997) 'Human alteration of the global nitrogen cycle: Sources and consequences', *Ecological Applications*, vol 7, pp37–750

Worm, B., Barbier, E. B., Beaumont, N., Duffy, J. E., Folke, C., Halpern, B. S., Jackson, J. B. C., Lotze, H. K., Micheli, F., Palumbi, S. R., Sala, C., Selkoe, K. A., Stachowicz, J. J., Watson, R. (2006) 'Impacts of biodiversity loss on ocean ecosystem services', *Science*, vol 314, pp787–790

Appendix

Appendix Table 4.1 *Export value of fisheries by region, 1976–2004 (US$ million)*

	Europe	Asia	N. America	S. America	Africa	Ex USSR	Oceania
1976	2,931,738	2,393,063	1,424,705	521,018	346,388	198,774	164,238
1977	3,525,078	2,950,233	1,730,841	644,816	352,263	203,976	252,509
1978	4,019,737	3,475,541	2,661,025	821,100	411,313	245,461	294,532
1979	4,898,728	4,154,689	3,010,405	1,044,724	516,928	310,979	401,250
1980	5,504,223	4,276,826	3,113,863	1,247,574	539,326	307,916	525,070
1981	5,312,498	4,598,818	3,363,764	1,264,760	683,499	257,435	524,274
1982	4,865,144	4,550,710	3,251,291	1,403,291	647,449	229,438	571,377
1983	5,045,302	4,691,028	3,165,527	1,298,814	700,043	368,698	599,617
1984	4,865,442	4,979,272	3,103,768	1,415,457	691,521	369,544	666,214
1985	5,326,762	5,141,271	3,386,653	1,488,896	766,958	383,908	637,851
1986	7,126,099	6,977,583	4,337,335	1,875,847	1,082,996	587,079	760,932
1987	9,008,950	8,796,355	5,257,842	2,069,680	1,154,044	637,287	885,763
1988	9,708,404	10,321,021	5,827,131	2,311,837	1,224,505	799,633	1,128,829
1989	9,926,098	10,328,208	5,853,471	2,556,237	1,266,176	718,407	1,072,137
1990	12,070,748	11,178,541	6,523,954	2,572,511	1,482,710	933,448	1,100,226
1991	12,817,246	12,081,375	6,793,702	3,217,566	1,603,943	818,566	1,296,239
1992	13,971,245	12,760,521	6,830,676	3,534,320	1,580,982	–	1,436,910
1993	13,762,817	14,217,190	6,544,381	3,679,735	1,618,901	–	1,451,582
1994	15,875,713	16,572,764	6,872,484	4,574,184	2,239,456	–	1,616,571
1995	17,259,387	17,650,951	7,563,439	5,185,418	2,612,887	–	1,860,386
1996	18,787,612	17,194,460	7,446,544	5,294,365	2,515,466	–	1,822,617
1997	18,227,849	18,013,487	6,996,354	6,082,924	2,515,041	–	1,868,997
1998	19,110,446	16,309,222	6,573,956	5,115,631	2,764,000	–	1,644,197
1999	19,485,783	17,005,247	7,362,754	5,015,781	2,530,312	–	1,830,208
2000	18,803,284	19,169,122	7,822,161	5,226,585	2,742,838	–	1,886,810
2001	19,149,473	19,023,287	7,972,218	5,756,191	2,842,442	–	1,794,812
2002	20,602,121	19,596,410	8,090,203	5,306,475	3,120,524	–	1,892,566
2003	23,381,762	20,701,841	8,692,707	5,908,466	3,247,393	–	1,911,955
2004	26,500,666	24,013,533	9,313,260	6,547,098	3,245,741	–	2,108,313

Source: FAO fishery statistics: www.fao.org/fishery/statistics.

5

Making the Case for Investing in Natural Ecosystems as Development Infrastructure: The Economic Value of Biodiversity in Lao PDR

Lucy Emerton

Introduction: Biodiversity as a key component of development investments

Biodiversity contributes directly to poverty reduction in at least five key areas: food security, health improvements, income generation, reduced vulnerability and ecosystem services (Koziell and McNeill, 2002). Conservation is therefore key to achieving the Millennium Development Goals (MDGs). Biodiversity does not only link to MDG 7, the 'environmental sustainability goal', but also provides a strong source of support to the development and poverty reduction targets that are outlined in the other MDGs concerned with hunger, education, gender, child mortality, maternal health and disease. Biodiversity loss and natural ecosystem degradation pose a significant barrier to the achievement of the MDG targets for 2015, and may ultimately undermine any progress that is made towards meeting them (Millennium Ecosystem Assessment, 2005).

Although biodiversity underpins socio-economic well-being – and despite the fact that conservation brings large payoffs in terms of development and poverty reduction (Deverajan et al, 2002) – the linkages between biodiversity, poverty reduction and economic development are often overlooked. In all too many cases 'conservation' goals are seen as being distinct from (and sometimes even as being in conflict with) 'development' goals. A choice or a trade-off is posed between investing in biodiversity and investing in poverty reduction and basic development infrastructure.

This chapter contends that economic and development concerns, and especially the targets towards global poverty reduction that are articulated in the MDGs, cannot in reality be separated from the need to conserve and sustainably use biodiversity – in relation to policy formulation, to funding decisions and to on-the-ground implementation. Failing to understand that biodiversity offers a basic tool for alleviating poverty, and forms a key component of investments in development infrastructure, leads to the risk of incurring far-reaching economic and development costs – especially for the poorest and most vulnerable sectors of the world's population.

This chapter provides concrete examples of the linkages between biodiversity and the economy in Lao PDR. It articulates the economic contribution that biodiversity makes to local livelihoods and national development indicators, and in particular underlines its value for the poorest and most vulnerable groups in the country. The chapter also describes how, over the last decade, both domestic and overseas funding to biodiversity has declined dramatically in Lao PDR. At the same time, many of the policy instruments that are being used in the name of promoting development have acted to make conservation financially unprofitable and economically undesirable. The case of Lao PDR illustrates a situation, and highlights an apparent paradox, that is also found in many other parts of the world. If biodiversity has such a demonstrably high economic and livelihood value, especially for the poorest, then why is it persistently marginalized by the very economic policies and funding flows that are tied to strengthening livelihoods, reducing poverty and achieving sustainable socio-economic development?

The Case of Lao PDR

Lao PDR is among the most forested countries in Asia, and in biodiversity terms ranks as one of the richest in the region (Nurse and Soydara, 2002). It is estimated that almost half of Lao PDR's land area, or 11.6 million hectares, is under forest (Department of Forestry, 1992). Some of the highest rates of diversity and endemism for aquatic species in the world have been recorded in the rivers, water bodies and other natural and constructed wetlands that are estimated to cover just under 945,000ha or 4 per cent of Lao PDR. With the exception of a small number of introduced fish used for aquaculture, almost all of the fish caught in Lao PDR are indigenous species. The country contains important agrobiodiversity. Indigenous crop and livestock varieties and their genetic diversity play an important role in agricultural production. Lao PDR lies within the primary centre of origin and domestication of Asian Rice, *Oryza sativa L.* More than 13,000 samples of cultivated rice have been collected in the country, including wild species such as *Oryza ranulata*, *O. nivara* and *O. rufipogon*, along with spontaneous interspecific hybrids between wild and cultivated rice. The majority of livestock originate from stock domesticated within Lao PDR or in nearby China and Vietnam, and can be considered to be indigenous or traditional breeds (MAF, 2001).

Perhaps unsurprisingly, the human population of Lao PDR is also characterized by an extremely high economic dependence on biodiversity. Alongside rice farming, biological resources underpin the majority of Laotians' livelihoods – more than 80 per cent of the country's 5.5 million people live in rural areas, and depend largely on harvesting wild plant and animal products for their day-to-day subsistence and income (Emerton et al, 2002b).

Despite – or perhaps because of – the conservation significance of Lao PDR's wild species and ecosystems, and the high economic reliance on them, biodiversity loss is becoming a major problem. During the 1980s reduction in national forest area was estimated at between 100,000–200,000 hectares per year or about 1 per cent of the 1981 forest area (MAF, 1990). Estimates of deforestation in the latter part of the 1990s range between 0.3 per cent and 2 per cent of the national forest area per year (World Bank et al, 2001). Overfishing is rapidly depleting aquatic biodiversity, wetlands and water bodies are being degraded due to upstream water diversion and on-site land reclamation. The proportion of rice production in Lao PDR made up of indigenous varieties has been decreasing over time, as improved cultivars and introduced varieties have become more common and have been promoted by government agricultural extension agencies and donor projects. In 1993 it was estimated that less than a tenth of rainfed lowland area was grown to improved varieties. By 2000 more than 70 per cent of the area in some provinces along the Mekong River Valley was planted with improved varieties, and all of the dry season irrigated rice was composed of introduced or improved varieties – today only upland fields are planted wholly with traditional varieties (NAFRI, 2000).

Although the causes of biodiversity loss in Lao PDR are multiple and complex, one important reason that biodiversity is being allowed – and in some cases even being encouraged – to decline is that it is undervalued in national economic statistics and development decision making. For this reason, investments in conservation are accorded a low priority both by central government and by the foreign donors who provide large amounts of funding to national development budgets. In particular little importance is attached to local-level and non-market biodiversity benefits, including local livelihood values.

For example, according to official statistics, the forest sector contributed only 3 per cent of gross domestic product (GDP) in 2000 – representing a real GDP of US$4.3 million or nominal GDP of US$52.5 million (IMF, 2002). This figure is based almost wholly on estimates of formal-sector timber output, including gross revenues from commercial round log harvesting of up to US$50 million (World Bank et al, 2001) and government timber revenues of approximately US$11.6 million (IMF, 2002). These figures, and commercially marketed biodiversity output, however, represent just the tip of the iceberg in economic terms. Lao PDR's biodiversity is actually worth many times this amount, but the bulk of this value is comprised of household-level benefits that never appear in formal markets and therefore remain largely invisible to economic decision makers and planners. Because biodiversity is undervalued and, in the light of urgent and pressing needs for socio-economic development, many policy makers see little economic gain from conserving or investing in biodiversity and perceive little economic cost associated with its degradation and loss.

The value of biodiversity at a local level: Nam Et and Phou Loei Protected Areas

Lao PDR's network of protected areas covers more than 29,000 km^2, and lies at the core of national efforts to conserve biodiversity The 4200km^2 Nam Et-Phou Loei (NEPL) Protected Area, located in the northeast of the country, is considered to have particular global and national conservation significance (Robichaud et al, 2001), and harbours among the highest faunal biodiversity of any protected area in northern Lao PDR (MAF and IUCN, 1998; WCS, 1998).

NEPL lies mainly in Vienthong District, which is located in Houaphan Province of the Northern Region of Lao PDR. Overall the Northern Region has the highest prevalence of poverty in the country, and poverty rates are greatest in Houaphan Province. Three-quarters of the population were classified as poor in 1998 with an equivalent 2002 per capita GDP of just US$204 as against a national average of some US$350 (UNDP, 2002). Other socio-economic indicators such as infant mortality rate, access to safe water and medical facilities also lie far below the national average (Table 5.1), underlining the fact that there are few basic services or infrastructure in the area around NEPL.

NEPL's resources provide a wide range of products that are used for income and subsistence by the 24,000 residents of Vienthong District who live in or beside the protected area. Forest use includes harvesting wild products for food, medicines, fodder, house construction and handicrafts production. Over 40 species of trees, 15 bamboos, 6 palms, 34 wild vegetables, 12 wild fruits, 7 grasses, 4 vines, 56 medicinal plants and 13 mushrooms have been identified as being used by local villagers (MAF and IUCN, 2001), and birds, snakes, frogs, fish, porcupine, barking deer and wild pigs are all regularly consumed as food. In total, it is estimated that 165kg of wild plant products and 141kg of wild meat are consumed each year at the household level (Schlemmer, 2001), that almost all of domestic energy and construction needs are sourced from the protected area, as well as the bulk of livestock fodder and pasture, human medicines and raw materials for crafts and utility items (Emerton et al, 2002a).

Table 5.1 *Socio-economic indicators for Houaphan Province, Lao PDR*

Indicators	Houaphan	Lao PDR
Per capita GDP index	56	100
% poor	74.6	38.6
Decline in poverty rate 1992–1998	1.0	3.1
Infant mortality rate	125	104
Access to safe water (% households)	1.8	15.1
Hospital more than 8 hours away (% households)	36	8

Source: Provincial statistics, UNDP, 2002.

Unsurprisingly, the economic value of biological resource utilization for villages in Viengthong District is significant. For almost all households living close to NEPL, wild species contribute a high proportion of household income and subsistence – an average of almost US$500 a year, or some 40 per cent of household livelihoods. Subsistence-level consumption (mainly for food, medicines and building) accounts for almost three-quarters of this value, while approximately a quarter is earned as cash income from selling forest products.

There are notable differences in socio-economic status between the households who live in and adjacent to NEPL, with richer households generally having higher levels of food self-sufficiency, benefiting from a much greater range (and level) of subsistence and income-earning opportunities, and being able to access more and better quality farming land. There is a corresponding variation in the types, overall values and relative importance of forest product use between households. In particular, there is a clear relationship between the relative wealth or poverty of individual households, the level and value of forest use, and livelihood dependence on biodiversity.

Households can be differentiated according to access to productive assets which can be taken as proxies for wealth, including rice surplus/deficit, cropped area, and livestock numbers. These measures are chosen to reflect indicators emphasized in the Lao PDR Participatory Poverty Assessment (ADB, 2001) and Interim Poverty Reduction Strategy Paper (Government of Lao, 2001), which identify degree of rice self-sufficiency as the primary determinant of poverty, livestock ownership as the primary indicator of wealth, and lack of arable land as a secondary condition of poverty.

According to all of these socio-economic and poverty indicators, both the richest and the poorest households consistently harvest biological resources to a much higher annual value than other sectors of the population (Figure 5.1). The absolute value of wild resource use is highest for the richest and poorest categories of households. Yet whereas richer households focus primarily on higher-value and market commodities, the high forest values accruing to poorer households reflects their reliance on forest products for subsistence and home consumption, and sales of low-value wildlife and NTFP due to the absence of alternative sources of income. Although valuable in absolute terms, forest resources do not form the main component of richer households' production. As poverty levels rise, so forest products make a progressively greater economic contribution to livelihoods. Wild resources contribute 50–60 per cent of the livelihoods of the poorest households, who face critical and recurrent rice deficits, have access to little or no crop land, and own few or no livestock.

Thus, like many other forests in the country, NEPL plays an essential role in meeting the gap between the level of basic subsistence and income that a rapidly growing human population require to survive, and that which the government is currently able to afford to provide. Reflecting this role, in 2000 the annual worth of protected area (PA) resource use for Viengthong villages was equal to the total

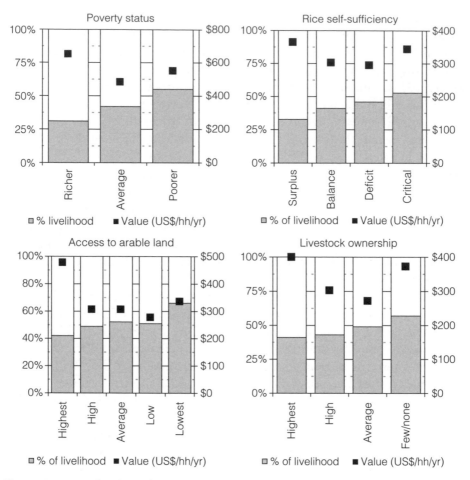

Figure 5.1 Contribution of PA resources to household livelihoods

Source: Emerton, 2006.

recorded economic output for the District, and on a per capita basis was more than double the entire annual development expenditures made by central government and donors in Houaphan Province each year (UNDP, 2002).

Biodiversity values in the national economy

At the national level, non-timber forest products alone are thought to comprise nearly half of household subsistence and cash income (Foppes and Ketpanh, 2000). Rice, much of it indigenous varieties, contributes two-thirds of household calorie intake (NAFRI, 2000), wild foods provide up to 80 per cent of non-rice food consumption by weight (Clendon, 2001), and fish and other aquatic animals comprise 30–50 per cent of protein consumption (Coates, 2002). More than three-quarters of the population, and many businesses and enterprises, rely on woodfuel as their primary energy source to an annual value of more than US$6.5 million a year, use of natural forest wood for house construction is worth more than US$13 million, and commercial non-timber forest product exploitation is thought to generate gross revenues of more than US$46 million, including US$32 million in export earnings (Emerton et al, 2002b).

Such figures have major implications for national economic and development processes. Far from being a minor component of Lao PDR's national and local economies, biodiversity may in fact be one of the most important sources of economic production and consumption in the country. Clearly, national statistics have miscalculated the economic value of biodiversity in the Lao PDR economy. They have also underestimated the importance of biodiversity to some of the country's key development goals. So, for example, analysis of the full value of biodiversity shows that it contributes, directly or indirectly, three-quarters of per capita GDP, more than 90 per cent of employment, almost 60 per cent of exports and foreign exchange earnings, just under a third of government revenues and nearly half of foreign direct investment inflows (Figure 5.2).

At the same time, biodiversity degradation and loss poses real threats to economic development and poverty reduction. The Lao PDR economy has

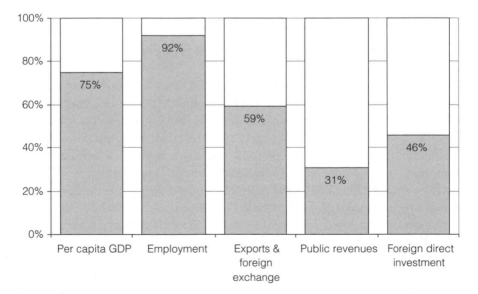

Figure 5.2 Contribution of biodiversity to national economic and development indicators

Source: Emerton et al, 2002b.

experienced rapid growth rates, in excess of 6 per cent over the last decade. Agricultural output has grown by 5.2 per cent over the last 5 years, the industrial sector by 10 per cent and services by 6.8 per cent. The incidence of poverty has fallen by over 13 per cent since 1993, and per capita GDP has increased almost threefold since 1985. Interest rates have fallen, exchange rates remained stable and inflation held down, the trade balance has improved and private sector investment has grown rapidly. Overall the national economy has performed well, and gives a positive picture of economic growth prospects for the country.

Closer analysis of this encouraging economic picture, however, raises causes for concern. While the national economy is undoubtedly growing, there are also signs of biodiversity loss. Forest area has declined, wetlands have decreased and wildlife numbers have fallen. Land degradation and resource depletion are occurring, and other renewable and non-renewable natural resources are being rapidly depleted. Biodiversity degradation and loss is, however, not just an ecological issue, it is also incurring high economic and development costs. Already vulnerable and with limited sources of income, employment and foreign exchange, these are economic costs that the Lao PDR economy can ill afford to bear. Most rural communities in Lao PDR depend on biological resources for their livelihoods, and are hit hardest by biodiversity degradation. Biodiversity loss impacts the most on the poorest and most vulnerable sectors of the population, whose livelihood bases are already limited and insecure, who lack alternatives sources of income and subsistence and who are least able to bear these social and economic costs.

Biodiversity investments: Recent trends

Undervaluation of Lao PDR's biodiversity is not just a hypothetical or statistical issue – it also has serious consequences for economic policy and practice. Most basically, it has meant that conservation has been given a low priority in economic planning, continues to receive extremely little funding, and often faces discriminatory signals from the policies, markets and prices which are used to manipulate the economy and to influence economic behaviour.

Even though there exist some positive economic incentives for conservation in Lao (such as reduced land taxes on stabilized land use and reforestation, exemptions on turnover tax for forestation activities, and release from the reforestation component of timber tax against replanting), biodiversity continues to be marginalized by many of the economic policy instruments that are being used to support other sectors. For example a wide range of implicit subsidies favour land clearance for farming, including the provision of preferential credit to agriculture, minimum farmgate prices, relatively lower tax rates and reduced trade duties on agricultural products and inputs. Sustainable biodiversity-based activities are not subject to such special treatment. The relative profitability of agriculture vis-à-vis conservation is enhanced still further by exemptions on agricultural land tax for newly cleared land in both mountain and lowland areas, and on newly established industrial orchards. Within the logging sector below-market royalties are also thought to promote excessive demand, and tax variation between different timber products encourage the use of only premium quality logs and encourage wastage in harvesting (World Bank et al, 2001).

Biodiversity and ecosystem conservation also tends not to be considered to be a priority when public budgets are formulated or donor funds are released. Recurrent allocations to the national, provincial and district government agencies mandated with environmental management and conservation remain extremely low compared to other departments. The share of forestry and wildlife in the government Public Investment Programme has fallen by more than a half over the last decade, from 7.5 per cent in 1991 to just 3.6 per cent in 2000 (MEPF, 1991; World Bank, 1997).

Donor assistance provides a major source of budgetary support to Lao PDR: it is estimated that over three-quarters of outlays for the Public Investment Programme are financed from foreign sources (World Bank, 1997). Over the last decade there has been a dramatic decline in donor funding to the environment and to biodiversity conservation (Figure 5.3), even though overall aid inflows have increased considerably (more than doubling from just over US$150 million in 1990 to around US$400 million today). After rising steadily for much of the 1990s, funding to protected areas and biodiversity conservation has fallen dramatically since 2000 from a figure of more than US$18 million to just US$7 million in 2006. As a proportion of all environment funding, which itself has decreased dramatically, the share given over to biodiversity has declined from more than half in 1996 to just 15 per cent in 2006 (Emerton, 2006). Today, little foreign or domestic funding is available for biodiversity conservation in Lao PDR.

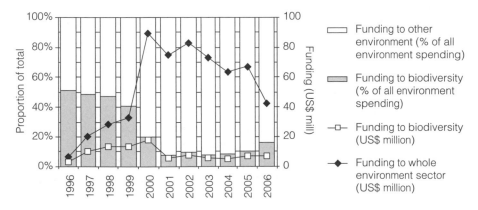

Figure 5.3 Trends in donor funding to environment and biodiversity in Lao PDR, 1996–2006

To a large extent this trend can be explained by a shift in the targeting of aid towards activities which are concerned directly with poverty alleviation. This shift coincides with a reorientation of government policy and donor assistance strategies to poverty reduction and the Millennium Development Goals, in line with the 2001 Interim Poverty Reduction Strategy and the Fifth Five Year Socio-Economic Development Plan (SEDP) for 2001–2005. For the main part, biodiversity conservation is not considered by either foreign donors or by the Lao PDR government to contribute directly to poverty alleviation. It is therefore now accorded a low priority in public budgets, and in the country assistance strategies of bilateral and multilateral donors to Lao PDR.

Conclusions: The returns to investing in natural ecosystems as development infrastructure

The close linkages that exist between biodiversity conservation, poverty reduction and socio-economic development in Lao PDR also hold in many other parts of the world. Other countries also face similar constraints to conservation. Economic and development decision makers frequently undervalue biodiversity, both in terms of its overall economic worth as well as in the way that it contributes to national and local development processes.

The case of Lao PDR illustrates that, contrary to such misperceptions, biodiversity often generates very high – and quantifiable – economic benefits. At the site level, Protected Areas such as Nam Et-Phou Loei make a demonstrable contribution to the country's primary socio-economic development goals. Not only do they underpin local subsistence and income but they also fill the gap between the goods and services that a poor and rapidly growing human population require to survive, and that which the government is currently able to afford to provide. At the macroeconomic level, biodiversity in Lao PDR provides a foundation from which to generate national income, employment, foreign exchange earnings, public sector revenues and inflows of investment funds. Yet, until existing conditions change, investments in conserving biodiversity are a critical component of poverty alleviation strategies.

The case of Lao PDR makes the point that failing to invest in the natural capital that is biodiversity and natural ecosystems is not only short-sighted in economic terms, but the costs, losses and forgone values that result may ultimately undermine many of the gains from other efforts at development and poverty reduction. In contrast, if ecosystems are recognized as assets which yield a flow of services that are required for equitable and sustainable development and poverty alleviation, the human, social and financial capital that is required to sustain them (and which they, in turn, sustain) also needs to be allocated to their upkeep. In order to ensure their productivity and continued support to human development, ecosystems need to be maintained and improved to meet both today's needs as well as intensifying demands and pressures in the future — just like any other component of infrastructure.

A key question is, therefore, how to find ways of stimulating investment in natural ecosystems as a core component of development and poverty reduction infrastructure. A shift in paradigm is required – moving from approaches that fail to factor in ecosystem costs and benefits, to those which recognize and invest in them as valuable and productive assets that are of particular importance for the poorest. Continuing to omit considerations of ecosystems as key components of development infrastructure may ultimately undermine many of the goals that so much time, effort and funds are being channelled into: to reduce poverty, and provide cost-effective, equitable and sustainable development for all.

Acknowledgements

The information and results presented in this paper are based on work carried out in Lao PDR between 2001 and 2007 under the project 'A Review of Protected Areas and their Role in the Socio-Economic Development of the Four Countries of the Lower Mekong Region' International Centre for Environmental Management (ICEM) and IUCN, in collaboration with the National Mekong Committee Secretariat; Science, Technology and Environment Agency; Department of Forest Resource Conservation; and the Nam Et-Phou Loei Integrated Conservation and Development Project) and the Lao PDR National Biodiversity Strategy and Action Plan (GEF-UNDP, in collaboration with the Science, Technology and Environment Agency of the Government of Lao PDR). The former relied heavily on data collected via a socio-economic survey carried out by Viengthong District Office in June 2001. Particular acknowledgement is due to these institutions and to the individuals involved in the research, including S. Bouttavong, L. Kettavong, O. Philavong, S. Manivong, S. Sivannavong and K. Thanthatep.

References

ADB (2001) *Technical Assistance to the Lao PDR for Participatory Poverty Monitoring and Assessment*, TAR LAO 33362, Asian Development Bank, Manila

Clendon, K. (2001) *The Role of Forest Food Resources in Village Livelihood Systems: A Study of Three Villages in Salavan Province, Lao PDR*, Non-Timber Forest Products Project in Lao PDR, Department of Forestry, Ministry of Agriculture and Forestry and IUCN, Vientiane

Coates, D. (2002) *Inland Capture Fishery Statistics of Southeast Asia: Current Status and Information Needs*, RAP Publication No. 2002/11, Asia-Pacific Fishery Commission, Food and Agriculture Organization of the United Nations, Bangkok

Department of Forestry (1992) *Forest Cover and Land Use in Lao PDR: Final Report on the Nationwide Reconnaissance Survey*, Lao-Swedish Forestry Programme, Department of Forestry, Ministry of Agriculture and Forestry, Vientiane

Devarajan, S., Miller, J., Swanson, E. (2002) *Goals for Development: History, Prospects, and Costs*, Policy Research Working Paper 2819, Office of the Vice President, World Bank, Washington, DC

Emerton, L. (2006) *Trends in Donor Funding to Protected Areas: A Case Study of Lao PDR*, Paper prepared for Working Group on Economic Aspects of Biodiversity, OECD, Paris

Emerton, L., Philavong, O., Thanthatep, K. (2002a) *Nam Et-Phou Loei National Biodiversity Conservation Area, Lao PDR: A Case Study of Economic and Development Linkages*, IUCN, Regional Environmental Economics Programme, Karachi

Emerton, L., Bouttavong, S., Kettavong L., Manivong, S., Sivannavong, S. (2002b) *Lao PDR Biodiversity: Economic Assessment, National Biodiversity Strategy and Action Plan*, Science, Technology and Environment Agency, Vientiane

Foppes, J. and Ketphanh, S. (2000) 'Forest extraction or cultivation? Local solutions from Lao PDR', Paper presented at Workshop on the Evolution and Sustainability of 'Intermediate Systems' of Forest Management, FOREASIA, 28 June–1 July, Lofoten

Government of Lao PDR (2001) *Interim Poverty Reduction Strategy Paper*, Government paper prepared for the Executive Boards of the International Monetary Fund and the World Bank, Vientiane

IMF (2002) *Lao People's Democratic Republic: Selected Issues and Statistical Appendix*, IMF Country Report No. 02/61, International Monetary Fund, Washington, DC

Koziell, I. and McNeill, C. (2002) *Building on Hidden Opportunities to Achieve the Millennium Development Goals: Poverty Reduction through Conservation and Sustainable Use of Biodiversity*, IIED London and UNDP Equator Initiative New York

MAF (1990) *Lao PDR Tropical Forestry Action Plan (First Phase)*, Ministry of Agriculture and Forestry, Vientiane

MAF (2001) *Masterplan Study on Integrated Agricultural Development in Lao People's Democratic Republic*, Ministry of Agriculture and Forestry, Vientiane

MAF and IUCN (1998) *Project Document: Integrated Biodiversity Conservation and Community Development in Nam Et-Phou Loei National Biodiversity Conservation Areas*, Lao PDR. Ministry of Agriculture and Forestry and IUCN, Vientiane

MAF and IUCN (2001) *Progress Report: Integrated Biodiversity and Conservation and Community Development in Nam Et – Phou Loei PAs*, Lao PDR. Ministry of Agriculture and Forestry and IUCN – The World Conservation Union, Vientiane

MEPF (1991) *Policy Framework for Public Investment Programme*, Ministry of Economy, Planning and Finance, Vientiane

Millennium Ecosystem Assessment (2005) *Ecosystems and Human Well-being: Synthesis*, Island Press, Washington, DC

NAFRI (2000) *Collection and Classification of Rice Germplasm from the Lao PDR Between 1995–2000*, National Rice Research Programme and Lao-IRRI Biodiversity Project, National Agriculture and Forestry Research Institute, Vientiane

Nurse, M. and Soydara, V. (2002) *Lessons Learned in Collaborative Management for the Sustainable Use of Non Timber Forest Products in Lao PDR*, IUCN, Lao PDR Country Office, Vientiane

Robichaud, W., Marsh, C., Southammakoth, S., Khounthikoummane, S. (2001) *Review of the National Protected Area System of Lao PDR*, Lao-Swedish Forestry Programme, Division of Forest Resources Conservation and IUCN, Vientiane

Schlemmer, G. (2001) *Integrated Biodiversity and Conservation and Community Development in Nam Et – Phou Loei PAs, Lao PDR: Community Livelihoods Analysis*, Ministry of Agriculture and Forestry and IUCN, Vientiane

UNDP (2002) *Lao PDR Human Development Report (2001)*, Advancing Rural Development, United Nations Development Programme, Vientiane

WCS (1998) *A Wildlife and Habitat Survey of Nam Et and Phou Louey National Biodiversity Conservation Areas, Houaphanh Province, Lao PDR*, Centre for Protected Areas and Watershed Management (CPAWN)/Wildlife Conservation Society (WCS) Co-operative Program, Department of Forestry, Ministry of Agriculture and Forestry, Vientiane

World Bank (1997) *Lao PDR Public Expenditure Review: Improving Efficiency and Equity in Spending Priorities*, World Bank Country Operations Division, East Asia and Pacific Regional Office, Washington, DC

World Bank, Sida and Government of Finland (2001) *Lao PDR Production Forestry Policy: Status and Issues for Dialogue*, Volume I: Main Report. World Bank, Sida and Government of Finland, Vientiane

6

Non Timber Forest Products and Biodiversity Conservation: A Study of Tribals in a Protected Area in India

K. N. Ninan

Introduction

Non Timber Forest Products (NTFPs) are important from an economic, social, cultural and ecological viewpoint. Apart from providing subsistence, income and employment to tribals and indigenous communities, they are also high-value internationally traded products estimated at US$11 billion a year (Simpson, 1999; SCBD, 2001; Shanley et al, 2002). Although NTFP values may not compete well with land conversion values, their importance arises more in the context of the role they play in supporting local community incomes (SCBD, 2001). Some NTFPs also have significant cultural value as totems, incense and other ritual items (www.cifor.org). Whether extraction of NTFPs is compatible with biodiversity conservation or not is widely debated. While some (cf. Peters et al, 1989) suggest that NTFP extraction is financially viable and ecologically sustainable, others point to its adverse social and ecological consequences (cf. Arnold and Perez, 2001; SCBD, 2001). In view of its significance, this paper seeks to analyse the economics of NTFPs and the economic values appropriated by tribals in a protected area in India, and their value preferences for biodiversity conservation. The Nagarhole National Park (NNP) located in the Western Ghat region in South India, which is one of the 25 biodiversity hotspots in the world, is the setting for the study (Myers 1988, Myers et al, 2000). The NNP is rich in flora and fauna including several endangered species. The biodiversity of the national park is facing threats and immense pressure due to anthropogenic and other factors. In addition, there are tribal settlements both within and on the periphery of the park who depend on the park for NTFPs and other benefits.

Objectives

In the light of the above, the specific objectives of the chapter are as follows:

1   To estimate the economic values of NTFPs appropriated by the tribal households of NNP.
2   To estimate the net benefits from NTFPs derived by the tribal households both excluding and including the external costs of wildlife conservation, i.e. wildlife damage costs and defensive expenditures to protect against wildlife attacks.
3   To estimate the NTFP benefits obtained by the total local community from the Nagarhole National Park
4   To analyse the local tribal community's willingness to accept (WTA) compensation and relocate outside the national park and the socio-economic and other factors influencing their 'yes' or 'no' responses.

Data and methodology

The study is based on a sample survey of 100 tribal households selected from three sets of tribal hamlets, that is, those residing within the NNP, on the park fringe and a rehabilitated village on the park's periphery. Tribal hamlets were selected purposively and then cluster sampling was used whereby all the households within the selected hamlet were surveyed. Data were collected in the year 2000 through a detailed structured schedule comprising two parts, a socio-economic survey and a contingent valuation method (CVM) survey. For the CVM study, the discrete choice method that seeks simple 'Yes' or 'No' answers to an offered bid is used. The discrete choice method was preferred over other methods (e.g. open-ended method) because of its inherent advantages – for example this method would make it easier for villagers to react to the questions; households could respond keeping some budget or constraint in view, that is to say, the upper bounds on bids could be controlled; also this method minimizes any incentive to strategically over-state or under-state willingness to pay (WTP)/willingness to accept (WTA) (Loomis, 1988; Moran, 1994). Dichotomous choice methods require the use of parametric (typically logit or probit) probability models relating 'Yes' or 'No' responses to relevant socio-economic and other variables. Opportunity cost method and cost–benefit appraisal have been used to estimate the benefits from NTFPs. Logit model has been used for the contingent valuation analysis.

NTFP benefits

Like most forest communities, the tribal communities of Nagarhole depend on the NNP for a variety of goods and services, and especially for NTFPs

(Ninan et al, 2007). These NTFPs provide subsistence, income and employment for the tribals. Before analysing our data, it would be useful to review the various cross country estimates of the economic values of NTFPs and their limitations.

Economic value of NTFPs: A review

Estimates of the economic values derived from NTFP extraction show wide variation across regions, forest sites and communities. Reviews by Godoy et al (1993) and SCBD (2001) covering a cross section of countries observed the net economic values from NTFP extraction to vary widely between US$1 and US$420 per ha per year with a median value of US$50 per ha per year. These wide variations in the estimates of NTFP values are due to differences in the methodology and assumptions employed to estimate the economic value of NTFPs, biological and economic diversity of areas studied, NTFP products valued, etc. It is, however, not clear whether the various estimates from different studies conducted between 1981 and 2000 are expressed in terms of constant US dollars to make them comparable, or in current prices. Godoy et al (1993) cite several limitations of the studies reviewed by them. First and foremost they failed to make a clear distinction between two types of quantities being valued viz., the inventory or stock quantity of the forest resource, and the flow, that is the actual quantity of forest resources extracted. While some researchers have valued the inventory and others the flow, still others have valued both. The two are, of course, interrelated. Overharvesting of forest resources (actual flows) will affect the stock of forest resources, which in turn will impact on the potential flow of forest goods (SCBD, 2001). The SCBD (2001) review makes a clear distinction btweeen the various estimates of NTFP values in terms of the stock of goods, potential and actual flows. While in terms of the stock concept, the gross or net benefits from NTFPs across countries and regions varied from US$377 to US$787 per ha per annum, in terms of the flow concept (potential or actual flows) these values ranged between US$0.3 and US$188 per ha per annum. Earlier studies are also not clear as to whether the estimates provided by them are gross or net values. From an economic standpoint, it is the net economic value (i.e. gross value minus costs) that is relevant, since it is this factor which provides the necessary incentive to extract NTFPs. Further, while most studies have either valued only the flora or only the fauna, a proper and full assessment of the economic values derived from NTFP extraction should value both the flora and fauna harvested from the forests. The prices used to value the NTFPs is another issue which has received inadequate attention. It is suggested that while NTFPs that are marketed ought to be valued at the selling prices, those retained for consumption need to be valued at forest gate or local market prices. In the case of NTFPs that are not traded or for which prices are not available, the price of a close substitute may be used to value such NTFPs. Alternatively, what users of the products are willing to pay for the NTFP in question, as revealed through a contingent valuation survey is also recommended. Moreover, a proper economic valuation of NTFPs should correct for taxes and subsidies or use shadow prices including estimating the externalities of extracting NTFPs (Godoy et al, 1993). For instance, extraction of NTFPs deprive the wild animals of their food sources; in turn this may lead them to search for alternate food sources in human settlements and habitations resulting in their causing damage to agricultural crops, property, livestock and at times even human life. These externalities of NTFP extraction need to be accounted for while estimating the net benefits from NTFP extraction. In estimating the cost of NTFP extraction some researchers have used the country's official wage rate as an estimate of the unprotected rural wages. But a proper economic valuation should use the wages that people actually pay or wages prevalent at the local level (Godoy et al, 1993). Moreover, harvesting, consumption or sale of NTFPs occur at different time periods and hence discounting of the values derived from NTFPs is essential. The sustainability of NTFP extraction is another aspect which has been relatively neglected in the studies reviewed (Godoy et al, 1993; SCBD, 2001). To top it most studies are also not clear as to what they mean by non timber forest products. While some exclude fuelwood from the purview of NTFPs, others include it (Ninan et al, 2007). In our analysis NTFPs are taken to also include fuelwood, but excludes timber, sawn timber, etc.

Estimates of NTFP values

Keeping in view the above, in our survey information was elicited on both the flora and fauna collected by the sample tribal households from the NNP, prices realized and quantities retained for self-consumption, etc. To estimate the economic values of the NTFPs, the selling prices quoted by the tribal households have been used to value those NTFPs that were marketed (including that portion retained for self-consumption); in those cases where the tribal households have not reported any price, the forest gate or local market prices have been used. In the case of those NTFPs that are wholly retained for self-consumption prices quoted by the tribal households or when these were not furnished the forest gate or local market prices have been used. For certain NTFPs, such as wild edible tubers, green leaves, mushrooms and bush meat for which prices are not available or known, the price of a close substitute has been used. In the case of medicinal plants where the tribal respondents were unable to disclose the quantity collected, and there were problems in valuing them, the opportunity cost of labour time spent collecting medicinal plants has been used to value them. Although the most scientific way to value the NTFPs is to identify, count, weigh and measure them as they enter the village each day (cf. Godoy et al, 1993) over all the seasons of the forest cycle, if not over the entire year, due to resource and time constraints most researches such as ours are based on single point time surveys, which rely on

Table 6.1 *Summary of the various NTFP benefits appropriated by the local tribals of Nagarhole from Nagarhole National Park*

Benefits derived from Nagarhole National Park	Valuation method	Value of NTFP benefits derived by sample Nagarhole Tribal Households in Rs per household per annum (1999 prices)
Fuelwood	Market based valuation. The local market price of fuelwood was Rs0.85 per kg at 1999 price	1689.3
Bamboo and tender bamboo shoots	Market based valuation. The price of bamboo in the local market was Rs40 per pole and of tender bamboo shoots Rs2 per kg	750.0
Honey and honey wax	Market based valuation. The price of honey was Rs40 per kg and of honey wax about Rs47 per kg in the local market	635.3
Wild edible tubers	Market based valuation. The price of a close substitute, that is, cassava (tapioca) has been used for valuation. The price of tapioca was Rs2.5 per kg in the local market	378.0
Wild edible green leaves	Market based valuation. The price of a close substitute, vegetable leaves, in the local market has been used for valuation, i.e. Rs2 per kg	316.8
Wild edible mushrooms	Market based valuation. The price of a close substitute, domestic mushroom, has been used for valuation. The price of mushrooms was about Rs16.58 per kg in the local market	254.7
Wild meat (Bush meat)	Market based valuation. The price of a close substitute, mutton, has been used for valuation. The price of mutton was Rs100 per kg in the local market	207.0
Fibre	Market based valuation. The local market price of the close substitute of fibre, thin coir rope, has been used to estimate the value. Value of thin coir rope was Rs30 per kg at 1999 price	149.8
Wild edible fruits and nuts	Market based valuation. The local price was around Rs5 per kg	103.2
Tree seeds	Market based valuation. Forest department's price for tree seeds was Rs9 per basket of 10kgs at 1999 price. One basket contains approximately 10kg of seeds	87.3
Gooseberry	Market based valuation. The local market price of gooseberry was around Rs5 per kg	84.3
Gum	Market based valuation. The average local market price of gum was around Rs30 per kg	26.5
Medicinal plants	Opportunity cost of labour time spent for collection has been used	8.9
TOTAL		4691.0

the recall method to estimate the quantity and value of the NTFPs collected and consumed or marketed. In doing so care has to be taken during the survey so that no item is omitted or under- or overestimated as well as account for the seasonal availability and collection of NTFPs. In our survey, a structured household questionnaire was used to collect details of NTFPs collected, consumed and/or sold by the tribal respondents. The respondents were asked to furnish details of all NTFPs collected during the preceding 30 days; and, in the case of certain NTFP food items, over the preceding week. These figures were then used to extrapolate and arrive at the economic values derived by the tribals from NTFP collection per year. Care has been taken at this stage also to account for the seasonal availability of most forest products.

A summary of the NTFPs extracted and the economic values derived by the sample tribal households from the NNP are furnished in Table 6.1. As is evident, fuelwood followed by honey, wild edible tubers, tree seeds and bush meat are the major items collected by the sample tribal households from the NNP.

Net NTFP benefits

To estimate the benefits derived by the sample tribal households from NNP, the stream of NTFPs benefits must to be converted into present value terms. For this purpose, the cash flow of benefits is summed over a time period of 25 years. This does not seem unreasonable considering that more than 25 years after NNP was notified as a national park (in 1975), the tribals continue to appropriate NTFPs from the park. This also assumes that the forest is used sustainably and there is no bar on the local tribals from limited use of the forest. In this case the cash flows will constitute the benefits derived by the tribals from NNP. However, the Indian Wildlife (Protection) Act of 1972 prohibits any human use of national parks in which case the benefits estimated need to be considered as the forgone benefits of biodiversity conservation borne by the tribals of Nagarhole. The cash flow of NTFP benefits derived by the sample tribal households from NNP are estimated using three alternate discount rates, 8, 10 and 12 per cent, so as to check the robustness of our estimates. For assessing costs, we have taken into account the time spent by the tribals for collecting NTFPs as well as the seasonal nature and duration of the availability and collection of different NTFPs. Further certain items are collected jointly (e.g. fuelwood and fodder) and this factor has also been taken note of while estimating costs so as to avoid double counting. The estimated time spent for collecting NTFPs has been imputed at the minimum wage forgone by the tribals for working in nearby coffee estates, that is, Rs40 per humanday. Using this information, the net present values (NPVs) of the NTFP benefits derived by the sample tribal households from NNP is presented in Table 6.2.

Table 6.2 *NPV of NTFP benefits derived by sample tribal households of Nagarhole from Nagarhole National Park in Rs per household for cash flows summed up over 25 years at 1999 prices*

Tribal villages/hamlets	Discount rate %	NPV of benefits derived from NTFP		
		Food items	Non-food items	Total
		(Rs per household)		
Nagapura	8	12,908.9	12,052.0	24,960.9
(Rehabilitated	10	10,976.7	10,248.2	21,224.9
village on park periphery)	12	9484.6	8855.1	18,339.7
Dammanakatte	8	17,342.1	37,865.8	55,207.9
(Village on park	10	14,746.5	32,198.3	46,944.8
boundary)	12	12,741.9	27,821.3	40,563.2
Villages inside	8	20,321.9	34,094.2	54,416.1
the National Park	10	17,280.2	28,991.2	46,271.4
	12	14,931.2	25,050.2	39,981.4
All villages/hamlets	8	16,954.9	25,471.7	42,426.6
	10	14,417.1	21,659.3	36,076.4
	12	12,457.3	18,715.0	31,172.3

As evident, the NPVs of the NTFP benefits derived by the sample tribal households from the NNP is positive and significant. Taking all tribal households as a whole it is seen that the NPVs of total NTFP benefits realized by the tribals for cash flows summed up over 25 years at 1999 prices varies from over Rs31,172 to Rs42,426 per household using alternate discount rates. Non-food items constitute the dominant share of NTFP benefits appropriated by the tribal households residing within the national park, and on the Park's boundary (i.e. Dammanakatte), whereas among the Nagapura tribals the share of food items in total NTFP benefits is slightly higher than non-food items. If forests are used unsustainably this will impact on the benefits by reducing expected benefits and also increase the costs of collection such as more time being needed to spend to collect NTFPs, etc.

One approach suggested by Markandya and Pearce (1987 vide Godoy et al, 1993) to adjudge whether NTFP extraction rates are sustainable or not is to estimate the value of NTFPs after adjusting the cost of extraction by adding a depletion premium based on the expected rate of extraction (Godoy et al, 1993). The alternate approach is to do a sensitivity analysis of the estimate of net benefits from NTFP extraction which is attempted here. A sensitivity analysis using alternate assumptions indicates that if the expected benefits were to reduce by 50 per cent, and costs rise by a similar proportion, the NPVs will decline sharply to just around Rs9967 per household at 12 per cent discount rate (Table 6.3).

Table 6.3 *Sensitivity analysis of the NPV of NTFP benefits derived by the sample tribal households of Nagarhole from the Nagarhole National Park in Rs per household for cash flows summed up over 25 years at 1999 prices*

Assumption made	Discount rate %	NPVs of benefits derived from NTFPs		
		Food items	Non-food items	Total
		(Rs per household)		
Benefits	8	12,027.0	17,881.1	29,908.1
reduced by 25%	10	10,226.9	15,204.8	25,431.7
	12	8836.7	13,137.9	21,974.6
Cost rise by	8	16,265.7	24,249.1	40,514.8
25%	10	13,831.2	20,619.6	34,450.8
	12	11,951.0	17,816.7	29,767.7
Benefits	8	11,337.9	16,658.5	27,996.4
reduced by	10	9640.9	14,165.1	23,806.0
25%, and costs rise by 25%	12	8330.4	12,239.6	20,570.0
Benefits	8	5721.0	7845.2	13,566.2
reduced by	10	4864.7	6671.0	11,535.7
50%, and costs rise by 50%	12	4203.4	5764.2	9967.6

NTFP benefits and externalities

In assessing the net NTFP benefits one needs to account for the externalities of NTFP extraction. As stated earlier, extraction of NTFPs from the national park deprives the wild animals of their food sources, leading them to search for alternative food sources in human settlements and agricultural lands resulting in their causing damage to crops, property, livestock and humans. Extraction of NTFPs thus give rise to negative externalities in the form of wildlife damages to crop and property of NTFP extractors and third parties. The sample tribal households reported wildlife damage costs of over Rs101 per household during 1999–2000. However, it is not only the NTFP extractors who are affected by the negative externalities of NTFP extraction but also third parties. In our study, for instance, the sample households of Maldari, a coffee growing village bordering NNP, reported wildlife damage costs and defensive expenditures to protect against attacks from wildlife. It could be argued that NTFP extraction by the tribals of Nagarhole not only affected them but also third parties such as the coffee growers of Maldari. These external costs need to be accounted for while estimating the net benefits from NTFP extraction. Table 6.4 presents the estimates of net NTFP benefits derived by the sample tribal households of Nagarhole both excluding and including these external costs. It is interesting to

Table 6.4 *Net NTFP benefits excluding and including external costs*

Item	Net NTFP benefits		
	Excluding external costs[a]	Including external costs borne by sample tribal households (i.e. NTFP extractors)[b]	Including external costs borne by sample tribal households and third parties[c]
	Rs per household per year		
Undiscounted values	3974.5	3873.3	−510.7
Discounted values at the following discount rates:	Rs per household (for cash flows summed up over 25 years at 1999 prices)		
8%	42,426.6	41,346.3	−4371.6
10%	36,076.4	35,157.8	−3717.3
12%	31,172.3	30,378.6	−3212.0

Notes: [a] External costs refers to wildlife damage costs and defensive expenditures to protect against wildlife attack.

[b] Net NTFP benefits here is calculated after deducting costs of extraction plus the external costs (wildlife damage costs) borne by the sample tribal households (i.e. NTFP extractors) from gross NTFP benefits.

[c] Net NTFP benefits here is calculated after deducting costs as above plus also the external costs (i.e. wildlife damage costs and defensive expenditures) borne by a third party, viz., the sample households of Maldari, the coffee growing village, which is close to the Nagarhole National Park boundary in Kodagu district of Karnataka State.

note that even after including these external costs borne by the sample tribal households, that is, the NTFP extractors, the net NTFP benefits are positive and high. But most interesting is that if the external costs borne by a third party (i.e. coffee growers of Maldari) are also added to costs the net NTFP benefits turn negative (Rs−510.7 per household per year or Rs−3212 at 12 per cent discount rate for cash flows summed up over 25 years). It is thus clear that although from the perspective of the tribals, NTFP extraction yields positive and high returns, when the negative externalities of NTFP extraction borne by third parties are also taken into account the net NTFP benefits turn negative.

Estimate of NTFP benefits for Nagarhole National Park

To estimate the economic value of NTFPs appropriated from NNP we need to extrapolate the benchmark values obtained from our survey and generalize for the park as a whole, as well as convert these values from per household to per hectare terms. This is also to facilitate comparison of our estimate with those of other studies. However, in undertaking such an exercise, one faces a number of problems. One is how appropriate it is to generalize based on the benchmark values obtained from a small area of forest to wider areas or the entire forest. The benchmark values may not necessarily be typical of the entire forest. The second is that in order to estimate the NTFP values on a per hectare basis, we need to know the park catchment area that is accessible and used by the tribals and local people for appropriating NTFPs. Typically NTFP values ought to be higher in more accessible forest areas, and lower in less accessible areas as the costs of extraction rise when higher distances need to be covered for extracting NTFPs. SCBD (2001) lists other problems: that in a hypothetical world where the whole forest was exploited for NTFPs, prices and hence profitability of NTFP production should fall; failure to define whether the values in question relate to the stock of goods and services or their potential or actual flows; failure to account for post-harvest losses, etc.

In order to extrapolate the benchmark values and arrive at the estimated total value of NTFPs extracted by the population as a whole, we need information about the number of households within and on the periphery of the National Park. As per a World Bank document (World Bank, 1996) there are about 1550 households residing within the NNP and 14,779 households residing in the periphery of NNP that is a total of 16,329 households over which the benchmark values need to be extrapolated. However, NTFP extraction rates would vary across forest sites and regions and the benchmark values may not adequately reflect the NTFP values appropriated by the population as a whole. Another important question is regarding the park catchment area that is accessible and from which the tribals and locals extract NTFPs. This becomes all the more complicated when the villages and human settlements are not clustered or concentrated in any particular part of the national park or protected area but spread widely across the park and its surroundings, as is the case in our study area. In the NNP there are tribal settlements spread across the core and non-core zones of the park and almost all round the park's periphery. Zeroing in on any particular figure to represent the park catchment area thus becomes all the more difficult. Keeping this in mind in our study, the NTFPs values obtained from the tribal hamlets located within the NNP have been used to extrapolate and generalize for the 1550 households living within NNP. The NTFP values of Nagapura have been used to generalize for all the households in the periphery of the national park. Using the above procedure, the total NTFP values aggregated over all households living within and around the NNP works out to about Rs48.20 million excluding external costs, and Rs46.40 million when the external costs (i.e. wildlife damage costs) borne by the NTFP extractors are included. The external costs borne by coffee growers is not included due to lack of information on the coffee growers in the Park's vicinity. Moreover, these external costs will vary depending on the distance and location of the coffee estates from the park boundary, etc. The estimated values then need to be converted to a per hectare

Table 6.5 *Estimated net NTFP benefits from Nagarhole National Park in Rs and US$ per hectare per year*

Assumed park catchment area as % to total national park area[a]	Net NTFP benefits[b]	
	excluding external costs	Including external costs incurred by NTFP extractors
	Rupees per ha per year	
10	7492.1	7212.4
25	2996.8	2884.9
50	1498.4	1442.5
	US$ per ha per year[c]	
10	174.0	167.5
25	69.6	67.0
50	34.8	33.5

Notes: [a] Park catchment area refers to that proportion of the national park area that is assumed to be accessible and used by the households living within and on the periphery of the Nagarhole National Park for NTFP extraction.
[b] External costs refers to wildlife damage costs.
[c] The figures in Indian Rupees has been converted into US Dollar terms by using the exchange rate of 1US$ = Rs43.0552 in 1999.

basis. Keeping in view the limitations mentioned earlier, a range of values is estimated based on alternative assumptions, namely, that 10, 25 or 50 per cent of the national park constitutes the park catchment area from which the tribals and locals can access and harvest NTFPs. The NTFP values expressed in terms of Rs and US$ per ha per year are presented in Table 6.5. As is evident, the NTFP values after including the external costs borne by the NTFP extractors for NNP vary from over Rs1442 to Rs7212 per ha per year (or US$33.5–167.5 per ha per year) depending on the assumptions made regarding the park catchment area. Interestingly our estimates fall within the range of NTFP values of US$1–188 per ha per year indicated by the various studies reviewed in SCBD (2001).

Valuing local tribal community's preferences for biodiversity conservation

The fact that the national park is a major source of livelihood for the tribal communities living within and on the periphery of the national park poses a serious challenge for biodiversity conservation efforts. Although the government had initiated a programme for the rehabilitation of tribals living inside protected areas by offering them a compensation package to relocate outside protected areas, out of around 1550 households residing within the NNP only 50 tribal households accepted the rehabilitation package at the time of our survey.

An obvious question that arises is why many of the tribal households have not accepted the package and moved out of the forest. Leaving aside the institutional hurdles in the rehabilitation programme, we tried to capture what determines the probability of their accepting the compensation and rehabilitation package offered by the government. To study this we conducted a contingent valuation survey. The CVM survey was conducted as per the guidelines of the NOAA panel such as pre-testing of questionnaires, sufficient sample size, etc. Those tribal households who had not accepted the offer were asked to state whether they are ready to play a major role in biodiversity conservation by expressing their willingness to accept the rehabilitation package offered by the government and leave the park so as to provide a better habitat for the wildlife. The respondents were given a dichotomous choice of answering 'yes' or 'no' to the question.

To estimate the valuation function, the 'yes' or 'no' responses were regressed on a number of socio-economic variables. In addition to age, literacy status, sex, and household size of the respondents, we included variables to represent the income from NTFPs, coffee employment and forest employment, and whether the respondents were staying within the core zone of the NNP or outside. It was hypothesized that although the state or Forest Department would desire that all human settlements within the national park should be relocated outside the park limits, official concern and pressure is likely to be more on those tribals residing within the core zone of the national park. Hence, the attitude of the tribals residing within the core zone of the park may differ from those residing in the non-core zone. Due to space constraints, the summary statistics of the variables used to model the valuation function is not presented here.

Table 6.6 presents the results of the estimated equation using logit maximum likelihood estimates. As evident, the dummy variable for households living inside or outside the core zone of the national park is negative and statistically significant. This implies that the probability of the respondent to say 'Yes' to the WTA question is less when the respondent is from the core zone of the national park. Further, people having more income from employment in coffee estates and forest employment are less inclined to move out of the forest. This could be due to their fear about losing their employment in the coffee estates and forest if they are rehabilitated outside the forest. Alternatively this indicates that they are not fully convinced about the economic activities that they could undertake after rehabilitation. Although the tribal households derive considerable NTFP benefits from the national park, it is perplexing to note that the coefficient for the variable income from NTFPs has a positive sign, albeit not statistically significant. It may be noted that extraction of NTFPs from protected areas is illegal as per the Indian Wildlife (Protection) Act of 1972, which may also explain as to why the respondents are more concerned about losing the income from employment in coffee estates and forest in case they have to relocate outside the national park. The estimated model is highly significant with a likelihood ratio test of the hypothesis that the seven coefficients are zero based on a chi-square value of 12.51. The Pseudo R^2 is 0.20, which is a good fit for cross-section data.

Table 6.6 *Maximum likelihood estimates using logit model of WTA compensation (rehabilitation package) by sample tribal households of Nagarhole National Park and relocate outside the park*

Variable	MLE coefficients	Standard error	–ratio
Constant	−0.0834	1.869	−0.045
Age of the respondent	0.008	0.30	0.270
Dummy for the sex of the respondent[a]	0.639	0.780	0.819
Dummy for the literacy status of the respondent[b]	0.490	0.779	0.629
Household size of the respondent	0.040	0.326	0.123
Dummy for households living inside and outside the core zone of the national park[c]	−1.379***	0.736	−1.873
Income of the respondent from work in coffee estates and forest employment per year	−0.00006***	0.00003	−1.784
Net income from NTFP marketed per year	0.003	0.002	1.342
Log likelihood value	−24.857		
LR Chi squared (7)	12.51		
Significance level of Chi square	0.0849		
Pseudo R²	0.2011		
No. of observations	59		

Notes: *** Statistically significant at 10 per cent level of significance.

[a] 1 for male, 0 for female.

[b] 1 for literate, 0 for illiterate.

[c] 1 for households living inside the core zone of the park, 0 for households living outside the core zone of the park.

Conclusion

The analysis indicates that the tribal households of Nagarhole derive considerable NTFP benefits from the Nagarhole National Park. They collect NTFPs for meeting their subsistence needs and also earn income. Even after including external costs (i.e. wildlife damage costs) the net NTFP benefits derived by the sample tribal households (i.e. the NTFP extractors) are quite high and significant. However, when the external costs borne by third parties (i.e. coffee growers in our case) are also included, these net NTFP values turn negative. In other words, although from the viewpoint of the NTFP extractors harvesting of NTFPs is viable even after including the external costs borne by them, from the society's viewpoint this is not so. The estimated NTFP values (after including external costs borne by NTFP extractors only) appropriated from the NNP using alternate assumptions regarding the park's catchment area that is accessed by the tribals for harvesting NTFPs averages about Rs1442 to over Rs7212 or US$33.5–167.5 per ha per year. The analysis shows that although the forgone benefits of NTFPs for the tribal communities are high, the tribal communities still have a positive attitude towards the conservation of NNP. The logit analysis shows that the probability of saying 'Yes' to the WTA question is less if the tribals are residing within the core zone of the national park, and also if they have higher income from employment in coffee estates and the forest. The study suggests improving the incentive structure in order to obtain the support and participation of tribals in biodiversity conservation strategies.

References

Arnold, J. E. M. and Perez, M. R. (2001) 'Can non-timber forest products match tropical forest conservation and development objectives?', *Ecological Economics*, vol 39, pp437–447

Godoy, R., Lubowski, R., Markandya, A (1993) 'A method for the economic valuation of non-timber tropical forest products', *Economic Botany*, vol 47, no 3, pp220–233

Loomis, J. B. (1988), 'Contingent valuation using dichotomous choice models', *Journal of Leisure Research*, vol 20, no 1, pp46–56

Moran, D. (1994) 'Contingent valuation and biodiversity: Measuring the user surplus of Kenyan protected areas', *Biodiversity and Conservation*, vol 3, pp663–684

Myers, N. (1988) 'Threatened biotas: "hotspots" in tropical forests', *The Environmentalist*, vol 8, no 3

Myers, N., Mittermeier, R. M., Mittermeier, C. G., da Fonseca, G. A. B., Kent, J. (2000) 'Biodiversity hotspots for conservation priorities', *Nature*, vol 403, 24 February, pp853–858

Ninan, K. N., Jyothis, S., Babu, P., Ramakrishnappa, V. (2007) *The Economics of Biodiversity Conservation – Valuation in Tropical Forest Ecosystems*, Earthscan, London

Peters, C. M., Gentry, A. H., Mendelsohn, R. O. (1989) 'Valuation of an Amazonian rainforest', *Nature*, vol 339, no 29, pp655–656

SCBD (2001) *The Value of Forest Ecosystem*, CBD Technical Series No.4, Secretariat of the Convention on Biological Diversity, Montreal, Canada

Shanley, P., Pierce, A. R., Laird, S. A., Guillen, A. (eds) (2002) *Tapping the Green Market – Certification and Management of Non-Timber Forest Products*, People and Plants Conservation Series, Earthscan, London

Simpson, R. D. (1999) 'The price of biodiversity', *Issues in Science and Technology*, Online, vol 15, Spring, www.issues.org/15.3/simpson.htm, accessed 30 October 2008

World Bank (1996) *India Eco-Development Project*, Project Document, Global Environment Facility, South Asia Dept. II, Agriculture and Water Division, Report No. 14914-IN

7

National Parks as Conservation and Development Projects: Gauging Local Support

Randall A. Kramer, Erin O. Sills and Subhrendu K. Pattanayak

Introduction

As the rate and scale of tropical forest exploitation has increased, governments and environmental organizations have shown increasing interest in establishing and expanding national parks to protect biodiversity, provide recreation and produce a variety of environmental services. About a tenth of the world's 90,000 parks and reserves are located in tropical biomes where they cover 5.3 million km² (Chape et al, 2003). Many of the protected areas established in tropical countries over the past century followed the US model of preserving pristine ecosystems with no allowance for use of the resources within park boundaries (van Schaik and Rijksen, 2002). In the 1970s, dissatisfaction with this traditional park model led to the United Nations Educational, Scientific and Cultural Organization (UNESCO) Man and the Biosphere Program, which promoted the idea of integrating conservation and development in single projects (Batisse, 1982). Since the 1980s, many of the parks established with international funding and assistance have followed the integrated conservation and development project (ICDP) model, which links biological resource conservation with economic development initiatives to benefit local populations. From the conservation perspective, a key motivation for these projects is to build local support for parks, but this has been difficult to quantify and evaluate. In this chapter, we consider the contingent valuation method as a way to gauge local support for ICDPs in two Indonesian parks.

Because ICDPs are complex, experimental and costly, it is not surprising that many have fallen short of their goals (Brandon and Wells, 1992; Kramer et al, 1997b; Terborgh, 1999; Wells et al, 1999; Wells and McShane, 2004). Proponents of ICDPs argue that a key ingredient for successful protected areas is the involvement and participation of local communities (Dixon and Sherman, 1990). In fact, it is argued that the protection of a park's biological resources will only be possible if local people have a stake in the park (Furze et al, 1996). Yet, designing effective conservation programmes that involve local people is exceedingly difficult given the complex interactions of policy, social systems and ecosystems that characterize the park management setting (Brandon et al, 1998; Muller and Albers, 2004; Garnett et al, 2007). Programme design could benefit from a better understanding of local perceptions regarding parks and proposed ICDPs (Borrini-Feyerabend, 1995; West and Brockington, 2006).

Contingent valuation is a survey-based stated preference method, which asks people directly how much they are willing to pay for a good or service that is not traded in markets. It has been widely used to assign economic values to changes in the level of environmental goods, such as improvements or reductions in endangered species habitat, water quality and visibility in the US and Europe. The contingent valuation method (CVM) is used to value levels of environmental goods that do not currently exist, complex proposed changes in environmental goods, and environmental goods that are not directly used but are valued for their mere existence. CVM has been controversial, especially because of potential biases that could result from respondents either not taking the question seriously (hypothetical bias) or responding strategically to influence pricing or public funding decisions that may be based on the study (strategic bias). Rigorous reviews of the literature have suggested that these biases can be mitigated through careful implementation of best practice protocols (Carson et al, 2001). Some analysts have argued that CVM is a fundamentally democratic method of quantifying environmental values, because it is based on responses from a representative sample of all concerned citizens (Pearse and Holmes, 1993). Motivated by the cost of new CVM studies, recent research has focused on the comparability (benefits transfer) of CVM results across commodity descriptions, study sites and evaluation methods (Shreshtha and Loomis, 2001; Carson et al, 2001; Smith et al, 2002; Lindhjem and Navrud, 2007).

CVM was used in this study because:

1   we could draw on 30 years of experience with the method, including extensive literature on optimal survey design and methods of analysis;
2   the product (a park as a development project) is typically not bought and sold and thus has no market price that would reveal values for the ICDP;
3   CVM provides quantitative estimates of the extent of support in concrete monetary terms and thus is potentially more informative than alternative question formats such as Likert scale or binary opinions;
4   use of a structured survey instrument allowed a large number of households and communities to be included in the study;
5   CVM provides a way to aggregate opinions of the diverse components of an ICDP;
6   we can contribute to the small but growing literature testing the applicability of CVM to developing countries.

While CVM is well established in the literature, there are still significant questions about its validity in different contexts. Most relevant to our case, Adamowicz et al

(1998) discuss the use of CVM to measure the value of forest resources to indigenous people, raising cautions about the influence of sacred values, the potential for satiation, variations in property rights and difficulties in aggregating from individual to group values. Boxall and Beckley (2002) discuss possible adjustments to CVM for application in developing countries. For example, Shyamsundar and Kramer (1996) measure WTP in rice rather than money, because rice is a common instrument of barter in Madagascar. Whittington (1998) describes the challenges and opportunities presented by survey research – including CVM – in developing countries. Recognizing both the potential and the concerns with CVM, we consider here whether it is a useful tool for gauging local support for ICDPs.

A number of studies in developing countries have quantitatively evaluated preferences for parks, or for conservation of biodiversity more generally, within the economic framework of CVM. Shyamsundar and Kramer (1996) examine attitudes of rural residents towards a proposed park in Madagascar. They find that degree of dependence on collection activities and attitudes towards buffer zones are statistically associated with a willingness to accept (WTA) compensation for restricted use as defined in the CVM survey.

Other applications of CVM have focused on either the general population or residents of major urban centres. Hadker et al (1997) use a stated preference approach to gauge the support of urban residents for a nearby national park in India. They find that years of residence in the area, a 'green' attitude index and perceptions about the services provided by the park are positively correlated with WTP. In a contingent valuation study of Taiwanese wetlands, Hammitt et al (2001) find substantial support among local residents for protecting the wetlands. Based on WTP values, which are correlated with income, knowledge and respondent characteristics, the authors determine that the results bracket the amount that the government paid to finally purchase the wetlands for protection. Adams et al (2007) examine support for a state park in the Atlantic Coastal Forest among residents of one of Latin America's largest cities, São Paulo. Nearly 40 per cent of the respondents objected to the CVM question about how much they would be willing to pay via a monthly tax on their water bill. Among the respondents who accepted this scenario, WTP was most strongly determined by income. Studies that employ CVM to evaluate support for the conservation of particular biomes or species in developing countries include Amirnejad et al (2006) on forests in Iran, Bandara and Tisdell (2003) on elephants in Sri Lanka, and Turpie (2003) on the fynbos ecosystem in South Africa. In most of these studies, the authors conclude that CVM provides useful summary indicators of household preferences, if not precise estimates of non-market values, and that the strength of household preferences would justify increased public investment in protected areas and other biodiversity conservation measures.

In this chapter, we examine local support for two ICDPs established in Indonesia in the late 1990s. The Siberut National Park on Siberut Island in Sumatra and the Ruteng Nature Recreation Park on Flores Island in Nusa Tenggara Timur were established as part of an Asian Development Bank project for biodiversity conservation. The parks are components of ICDPs intended to build local support for conservation and to improve economic well-being in impoverished areas. Our objective is to gauge local support for the ICDPs by analysing responses to a survey question about willingness to pay an annual household fee to support park activities.[1] We identify correlates of support that explain differences within and across the ICDPs, and consider whether the patterns of support at one site can be generalized to help gauge support at a second site without implementing another full household survey.

Case study

The Biodiversity Conservation Project in Flores and Siberut

Financed by the Asian Development Bank and the government of Indonesia, this project aimed to improve the management of two protected areas and to strengthen the government institutions responsible for protected areas in Indonesia (Asian Development Bank, 1992).[2] The project was implemented over a 6-year period by the national parks authority of the Ministry of Forestry. A key feature of the project design was linking protected area management with the socio-economic development of surrounding communities through ecologically benign income generating activities. Expected benefits from the parks were of two types: income generating activities and environmental services. The income generating activities included agroforestry systems and other forms of agricultural and forestry enterprises in surrounding buffer zones for the benefit of local communities. There were also potential market benefits through ecotourism. The environmental services included biodiversity, regulation of the quality and flows of water, and reduced carbon emissions due to avoided deforestation. Our analyses of individual products and services confirmed that forest conservation can benefit local populations (Pattanayak and Kramer, 2001; Pattanayak, et al, 2003; Pattanayak et al, 2004; Pattanayak and Butry, 2005; Pattanayak and Wendland, 2007). However, in a review of ICDPs throughout Indonesia conducted several years after our study, the Flores and Siberut project was deemed unsuccessful in achieving many of its conservation and development goals (Wells et al, 1999).

Siberut Park

Siberut Island is the largest of the Mentawai islands located off the west coast of Sumatra. Because of its unique indigenous culture, large number of endemic species, and concern and conflict over development issues on the island, Siberut has received much international attention over the past 30 years (Caldecott, 1996). In 1981, the island was declared a Man and the Biosphere Reserve under the UNESCO Man and the Biosphere (MAB) programme (Ministry of Forestry, 1995a).

The Siberut National Park was established in 1993, encompassing a total of 190,500ha, nearly half of Siberut Island. Much of the island is remote and relatively undisturbed rainforest. Because the island has been isolated from mainland Sumatra since the mid-Pleistocene, it has a high degree of floral and faunal endemism, including four primate species (Kloss Gibbon *Hylobates klossii*, Mentawai Langur *Presbytis potenziani*, Mentawai Pig-tailed Macaque *Macaca pagensis* and the Pig-tailed Langur *Simias concolor*).

Siberut is home to about 20,000 indigenous people known as the Mentawai who depend on the forests for swidden agriculture, hunting and gathering and sago harvesting. Of all the Mentawai Islands, the traditional culture is strongest on Siberut, with social organization around clan councils or *rumah adats*, and with rituals and taboos controlling land clearance, hunting and other resource use. To earn cash income, the people harvest rattan from throughout the island, including the park (Sills, 1998a). Under the ICDP, management of the Siberut protected area and buffer zone was intended to enable a continuation of traditional lifestyles and to generate important local economic benefits through new agricultural, agroforestry and tourism enterprises (Ministry of Forestry, 1995a). More recent projects have taken a similar approach (e.g. Siberut Conservation Project, 2005).

Modern health care on Siberut is largely limited to the two main towns, and malaria, tuberculosis and pneumonia are widespread. Transportation on the island is by foot, canoes or speedboats, as there are no roads outside the two major towns. In the 1990s, a small-scale tourism industry developed on the island, catering to young, foreign, budget-oriented tourists interested in experiencing the traditional Mentawai culture (Ministry of Forestry, 1995a; Sills, 1998b). More recently, surf tourism has developed in southern Siberut, and a non-governmental organization associated with the surf industry has provided immunizations, mosquito nets and other health supplies in several rural communities (SurfAid International, 2004).

Ruteng Park

Located some 1500 miles to the east of Siberut, Ruteng Park is in a rugged section of Flores Island. The park consists of seven volcanic ridges and varies in elevation between 900 and 2400 metres. Nearly two-thirds of the slopes are steeper than 40 per cent (Ministry of Forestry, 1995b). The mountain chain forms a critical watershed for the population of the district capital Ruteng and for surrounding agricultural areas (Pattanayak and Kramer, 2001). Established as a Nature Recreation Park in 1993, the park has 32,000ha of protected forest, with limited production activities allowed, and 56,000ha of buffer zone. The Ruteng site contains some of the best submontane and montane forest left from the increasingly fragmented forests on Flores. There are a number of endemic species known to occur in the Ruteng mountains, including cave bats and the Komodo rat (*Komodomys*). Other wildlife in the park includes monkeys, wild boar, civets, Asian cobras and Russel's vipers.

Most local people are indigenous Manggarai inhabitants, with approximately 13,650 living in the buffer zone. The Manggarai are agriculturalists, with major crops including coffee, vanilla, cloves, timber and fruit trees, rice, corn and cassava. Many farmers also raise livestock. There is a substantial logging community, which derives almost all of its income from cutting trees in government forests including the Ruteng Park. The health status of the population is generally poor, with an infant mortality rate of 52 per 1000 (Ministry of Forestry, 1995b). There is a modest amount of tourism in the area centred on the Manggarai culture and on natural sites. Under the ICDP, the management plan for Ruteng Park emphasized the development of nature-based tourism inside the park, the provision of ecological services (drought mitigation) outside the park, and the development of new agroforestry enterprises in the buffer zone (Ministry of Forestry, 1995b).

Conceptual framework

Households in Siberut and Ruteng consume a variety of goods purchased in the market and self-produced, including products collected from the forests within the parks. In a simplified model, we can think of households combining their labour and limited capital with available agricultural land and natural resources to produce subsistence and market goods. In Ruteng, households generate cash income by selling a variety of agricultural crops including rice and coffee. The main cash generator in Siberut is rattan. Households also value leisure and non-material goods such as spiritual ceremonies, which may require inputs from the forest. It is not possible a priori to determine if households will be supportive of the establishment of ICDPs. The projects may improve the households' ability to produce material and non-material goods by stabilizing natural resource stocks and ecosystem functions. The ICDPs restrict certain extractive activities (e.g. logging and hunting), while supporting the expansion of others (e.g. tourism). ICDPs are – by definition – multifaceted, and involve new services and economic activities, all within a novel approach to park management. In many cases, it is impractical to individually measure and sum the local impacts of all project components. Thus, we take the approach of measuring the total net contribution of all project components to individual households. This is one basis for local support of the parks.

From an economic perspective, the value of these contributions (positive or negative) to a household can be measured as WTP for the ICDP. This WTP is defined as the payment, equivalent to a change in income that leaves the household just as well off with the park as it was without the park. A positive WTP suggests that a household would vote in favour of establishing the park. We chose to query households about a specific monetary contribution using established CVM techniques – rather than elicit general indicators of support – because we believe that this process is more likely to convince households to carefully consider the worth of the park relative to other economic activities and options that compete for household resources and generate utility. Thus, we use the CVM as a mechanism to gauge local support for parks in order to inform planning for the ICDPs.

Empirical methods

Approximately 1000 households from the communities in and around the parks were administered socio-economic questionnaires in 1996. Interviewers were recruited from local universities and underwent several days of training. The survey instruments included detailed questions on demographic characteristics and the value of various commodities and services provided by the parks. The survey instruments were refined through a process that included review by local experts, focus groups and pre-tests. The interviews took approximately one hour per household, and in most cases, were conducted with male household heads. The authors were part of the questionnaire and study design, as well as the training and monitoring team. Households were selected from the total population in a stratified, random sampling scheme to reflect the population weights of the various villages in the park and buffer zones. In Siberut, households were selected from 35 villages, while in Ruteng, households were interviewed in 48 village clusters.

At the time of the survey, both parks had been officially established, and non-governmental organizations had conducted environmental education programmes to inform local people about the parks and planned ICDP activities. However, few conservation and development activities had been carried out. In both surveys, respondents were provided a detailed description of park activities that would come about if the management plans were fully implemented. In Siberut the households were told that there would be some restrictions on hunting and logging, but the park would provide schools, health care clinics and promote new income generating activities. In Ruteng, the respondents were told that the park would restrict fuelwood collection, timber harvesting and hunting, but it was likely that streams would be cleaner and wildlife would be more abundant. Tourism, reforestation and extension services for new income generating activities were also included in the description of both parks.

After describing these activities, the interviewers asked whether the household would benefit from the park. Households who indicated that they would be better off were then asked their maximum willingness to pay an annual household fee to support the park activities.[3] The magnitude of that WTP is an indicator or index of support for the parks. As discussed above, the query about a specific monetary contribution encourages households to carefully consider the contributions of the park relative to other demands on their income. Thus, the WTP stated by the household is an important indicator of the degree to which they would support the park, given implementation of the activities described in the survey.

Not all households stated a positive WTP. Other possibilities were to not respond, to state zero WTP or to indicate that the household would be worse off with the park. Rather than attempting to model these potentially overlapping categories as separate responses, we consider whether or not a household states a positive WTP (SUPPORT) and account for this 'self-selection' process in our WTP model using the Heckman two-step method (Heckman, 1979). Explicitly modelling this decision avoids the potential bias that would result from dropping non-respondents (and others who do not state positive WTP) if the determinants of non-response are related to the determinants of WTP (Strazzera et al, 2003a).[4] The probability of indicating support for the park is modelled as a function of a set of observable variables (x) and a random error term (u) with a normal distribution. The variables in x include characteristics of the survey process (Q), household socio-economic status (H) and survey site (R). The probability of indicating positive support (Support = 1) is therefore given by Equation (1), where β are coefficients to be estimated.

$$\text{Prob}\{\text{Support=1}\} = \int_{-\infty}^{\beta'x} \phi(t)dt = \Phi(\beta'x) \tag{1}$$

The second stage of our model is an ordinary least squares regression of WTP on R, H, Q, household use of the forest (F), attitudes towards the park (A) and the inverse Mills ratio ($\lambda = \varphi(\beta x)/\Phi(\beta x)$) calculated from the first stage (see Equation (2)). The inverse Mills ratio tests and corrects for self-selection bias. That is, by including the inverse Mills ratio, we can interpret the coefficients of the other independent variables as the marginal effects of those factors on support for the ICDP in the population as a whole, and we can calculate the mean and median WTP of that population.[5]

$$\text{LNWTP} = \alpha + \beta R + \beta H + \beta Q + \beta F + \beta A + \beta \lambda + \varepsilon \tag{2}$$

For the dependent variable, we use the natural log of WTP (LNWTP), which is appropriate for distributions truncated at zero and with long upper tails. The predicted LNWTP (excluding the error term) may represent a lower bound on WTP, following the logic of Schulze et al (1996) and Smith et al (1997). The error term ε is due both to our inability to completely specify the function, and to the fact that respondents themselves may not be entirely sure of their WTP, especially for an unfamiliar good such as an ICDP.

The average WTP differs significantly across the two sites. By estimating a pooled model, we can investigate alternative explanations for this difference. First, WTP may be driven by different factors at the two sites, or the same factors (explanatory variables) may have different effects at the two sites. Interaction terms between DRuteng and all other independent variables (labelled as I + variable name) allow us to test for such differences in marginal effects across sites. Wald tests are used to test the statistical significance of the sum of each variable and its interaction term, to determine which variables have a significant effect in Ruteng. Second, the factors themselves may be at different levels at the two sites (e.g. wealth may be systematically higher in one site). Third, the coefficient on the site variable (DRuteng = 1 for Ruteng, 0 for Siberut) is a test for different levels of WTP at the two sites, after controlling for all of the factors in the model. Thus, the pooled model allows us to investigate whether differences in WTP between the two sites are due to (1) different relationships between the people and the parks as reflected in statistically significant coefficients on interaction terms; (2) different characteristics (i.e. different mean vectors of explanatory variables) of the populations that shift their expected benefits and/or ability to pay; and/or (3) some fixed difference between the two sites captured in the coefficient on the site variable DRuteng).

One reason for our interest in the stability of the WTP function across the two sites is that it would be useful to generalize findings from a given site to new parks. This would avoid the expensive and time-consuming process of conducting a new survey with CVM questions for each park. Average household characteristics are often available, for example from previous surveys or government census. We investigate whether these average values for a new park can be combined with a function estimated from a household survey at a study site to predict local support for an ICDP at the new park.[6] Consider first a scenario in which we had conducted a household survey in Siberut and were now faced with the task of estimating support for the Ruteng ICDP, using only secondary data on average population characteristics in Ruteng. In this case, we estimate a model of WTP using the survey data from Siberut. We then 'transfer' that model to Ruteng, using the estimated coefficients from Siberut and the mean values from Ruteng to calculate a 'transferred LNWTP' for Ruteng. To determine whether the transferred WTP estimate is close to actual WTP, we first estimate a model to predict LNWTP using the actual data from Ruteng. Taking multiple draws of the Ruteng data, we calculate the 'transferred LNWTP' (from the Siberut function) and the predicted LNWTP (from the Ruteng function) at the mean of the explanatory variables from each draw of the data. To evaluate our ability to predict levels of support in the entire population, we also calculate predicted and transferred LNWTP assuming $\lambda = 0$ (i.e. no self-selection) for each draw of the data. We then compare the distributions of transferred LNWTP and predicted LNWTP based on 100 different draws of the data.[7]

Results

Of the 995 households interviewed, 659 (66 per cent) indicated positive support for the parks.[8] The other 336 households either said that they would require compensation for the park (38), reported zero WTP (60) or simply did not respond (238).⁹ A higher percentage of households in Ruteng than in Siberut indicated support: 79 per cent in Ruteng and 54 per cent in Siberut. Among those who indicated positive support, the mean WTP is also significantly higher in Ruteng (mean Rp.4623, st.dev 7928) than in Siberut (mean Rp.1799, st. dev 3072). At the 1996 exchange rate of Rp.2200 to the US dollar, these may both appear to be trivial amounts to western readers, but the mean total annual cash expenditure in these areas was less than one million rupiah per household.

To investigate the reasons for the substantial variation in WTP both within and across sites, we turn to the explanatory variables suggested in Equation (2). Table 7.1 reports the mean and standard deviation of socio-economic, forest use and attitudinal variables for the sample of 970 households who responded to all of the questions used in the subsequent analysis. Based on *t*-tests at the 5 per cent level of significance, the mean values of all household characteristics except for expenditures are significantly different across parks, suggesting one possible explanation for different levels of WTP. For example, support may be more widespread and systematically higher in Ruteng because of less dependence on the park for timber, rattan and hunting. If these differences in household

Table 7.1 *Descriptive statistics for households at each park site*

Variable	Definition	Siberut (N=478)		Ruteng (N=492)	
		Mean (standard deviation)			
AGE	Age of household head	36.14	(10.17)	39.05	(11.86)
ILLNESS	Health index (# of illnesses)	2.75	(2.59)	5.25	(3.28)
EXPEND	Annual cash expenditures in Rupiah	984,505	(1,292,565)	998,533	(1,406,130)
WEALTH	Wealth index (count of durable possessions)	0.57	(0.22)	0.12	(0.19)
LAND	Hectares of land under cultivation	2.99	(3.71)	1.19	(1.06)
KMDIST	Km from nearest town	20.8	(9.24)	14.3	(8.14)
DLONGRES	Long-time resident of village (1=yes, 0=no)	0.80	(0.40)	0.89	(0.31)
DHUNT	Hunt mammals (1=yes, 0=no)	0.40	(0.49)	0.19	(0.40)
DTIMBER	Harvest timber (1=yes, 0=no)	0.23	(0.42)	0.53	(0.22)
DRATTAN	Harvest rattan (1=yes, 0=no)	0.64	(0.48)	0.49	(0.22)
DPROTECT	Believe park is necessary to protect ecosystems (1=yes, 0=no)	0.85	(0.36)	0.35	(0.48)

Note: 1. Dummy variable names start with 'D'.

characteristics – rather than some difference in the underlying benefits function – are the primary reason for differences in WTP, then benefits transfer between the two parks would be feasible. To evaluate the underlying function (the relationship between the characteristics and WTP), we turn to a multivariate model of WTP.

The estimation results of the two-stage selection model of LNWTP are reported in Table 7.2.[10] The signs and statistical significance of the coefficients in our econometric model of willingness to pay indicate that demand for the ICDP project has considerable theoretic and intuitive basis. For example, households who live further from trading centres (have greater need for ICDP assistance) are willing to pay more, while households who are long-term residents of their current village (have less need for ICDP assistance) are willing to pay less. Households who harvest timber (and thus would bear greater costs of the park project) are willing to pay less. However, just as important to note are variables that do not have a significant impact. Contrary to expectations, harvesting rattan and hunting mammals do not have a statistically significant impact on WTP, even though these activities are likely to be regulated by the ICDP.

Turning to the interaction terms, the effects of wealth, cash expenditures, illness and opinions on protecting ecosystems are all significantly different in Ruteng than in Siberut. A Wald test indicates that illness is only statistically significant in Siberut, perhaps because health care is a less important element of the Ruteng ICDP and therefore was not mentioned in its description. Wealthier households with higher cash expenditures are willing to pay more only in Ruteng. Households with higher cash expenditures were actually willing to pay less in Siberut, possibly because they felt less need for park assistance. Finally, Ruteng households who believe the park is necessary to protect ecosystems are actually willing to pay less, perhaps because they do not believe that they should have to pay for this public good provided by the parks.

Two survey variables are also significant. Households who did not respond to earlier questions about the value of commodities provided by the parks are willing to pay more in Siberut and willing to pay less in Ruteng. This could reflect differences in the relevance of the specific commodity offered in the earlier question. The date of the interview also has an effect in Siberut; this may reflect regional patterns, because interviewers moved systematically from village to village during the survey period. This type of geographic pattern would be captured more effectively by the distance variable in Ruteng, where it is measured more precisely due to differences in administrative structures (smaller size *desas* in Ruteng). Finally, the Ruteng site variable (DRuteng) has a statistically significant coefficient, indicating that, all else being equal, households in Ruteng have a lower WTP for the ICDP.

The mean LNWTP for the 659 respondents used in the second stage estimation reported in Table 7.2 is 7.15 (WTP = Rp.1274). The negative coefficient on lambda (the inverse Mills ratio) suggests that contrary to expectations, households with higher WTP are less likely to respond to the

Table 7.2 *Model of support for the park (Two stage selection model – dependent variable is LNWTP for Park)*

	Coefficient	Std.Err.	T-ratio	P-value
ONE	8.388	0.982	8.542	0.000
DLONGRES	−0.397	0.192	−2.069	0.039
DHUNT	−0.137	0.161	−0.852	0.394
DTIMBER	−0.314	0.153	−2.046	0.041
DRATTAN	−0.029	0.156	−0.185	0.853
WEALTH	−0.201	0.317	−0.633	0.526
LN(EXPEND)	−0.098	0.053	−1.842	0.065
LAND	−0.034	0.024	−1.447	0.148
ILLNESS	0.126	0.034	3.708	0.000
DPROTECT	0.178	0.221	0.807	0.420
LN(KMDIST)	0.306	0.170	1.794	0.073
DNORES	0.982	0.396	2.477	0.013
DATE	−0.081	0.033	−2.473	0.013
INT-DLONGRES	0.425	0.303	1.401	0.161
INT-DHUNT	−0.043	0.251	−0.170	0.865
INT-DTIMBER	0.241	0.360	0.669	0.503
INT-DRATTAN	0.243	0.346	0.701	0.483
INT-WEALTH	1.166	0.530	2.199	0.028
INT-LNEXP	0.239	0.078	3.066	0.002
INT-LAND	0.031	0.073	0.424	0.671
INT-ILLNESS	−0.108	0.041	−2.629	0.009
INT-DPROTECT	−0.445	0.270	−1.649	0.099
INT-LNKMDIST	−0.173	0.200	−0.865	0.387
INT-DNORES	−1.542	0.284	−5.438	0.000
INT-DATE	0.064	0.036	1.777	0.075
DRUTENG	−2.489	1.226	−2.030	0.042
LAMBDA	−1.335	0.393	−3.398	0.001

Notes:
1. Loglikelihood = −1017.526, Akaiki Information Criterion = 3.27, *N* = 639.
2. Site indicator is DRUTENG, which is 1 for Ruteng, 0 for Siberut households. Variable names beginning with 'INT-' are interaction terms with DRUTENG. Survey variables are NORES (1 if did not respond to survey questions about WTP for other park commodities) and DATE (day of interview). LAMBDA is the inverse Mills ratio, calculated from a probit model of the probability of expressing positive support for the park, as a function of EXPEND, LAND, LNKMDIST, DATE, NORES, DRUT and three dummies for particular interviewing teams (all significant at the 10% level) and LNAGE (statistically insignificant). Interaction terms were not significant in this model. It predicts 79% of responses correctly, and has a Veall-Zimmerman pseudo-r-squared of 45%.
3. Chi-Squared Statistics for Wald tests of significance of sum of variable and its interaction term with DRUTENG: DLONGRES: 0.014; DHUNT: 0.867; DTIMBER: 0.05; DRATTAN: 0.478; WEALTH: 5.147; LNEXP: 4.676; LAND: 0.002; ILLNESS: 0.614; DPROTECT: 2.967; DLNDIST: 1.247; NORES: 5.537; DATE: 0.702.

question (cf Dolton and Makepeace, 1987; Nicaise, 2001; Strazzera et al, 2003b). The mean LNWTP predicted by this model for the entire population is 7.79 (9 per cent higher LNWTP, but nearly twice as high WTP). Some households who would benefit from and hence support the ICDP may be hesitant to reveal their support in the survey, due to their limited means, or limited experience with the cash economy. For example, the first stage of the model suggests that households with greater cash income and land are more likely to respond, but the second stage suggests that these households actually have lower WTP. This could be interpreted as a protest against the survey process: households who most need the ICDP object to being asked to pay for it. Thus, understanding the WTP of non-respondents is critically important to gauging support for the parks.

The significant coefficients on the Ruteng site variable and several of the interaction terms suggest that generalizing WTP from one park to the next will not be straightforward. To further explore this issue, we test benefit transfer under the counterfactual that we had complete survey data from one park and only mean values of household characteristics from the other park. Based on 100 random draws of the data, we first estimate the same model as in Table 7.2 for each site separately, excluding the Ruteng site variable and interaction terms. Next, we multiply the estimated coefficients by the mean household characteristics from the other site (and the sample average values for survey variables), again based on 100 random draws of the data. These two steps provide 100 estimates of 'transferred' mean LNWTP for each park, using only its mean characteristics and a model of WTP transferred from the other park. We compare this to the 'predicted' mean LNWTP estimated with full information from the park of interest.

Consider first the mean LNWTP for the respondents, or those households who stated positive WTP in the survey (respondents). The median for Siberut households is 6.65, with a 90 per cent confidence interval of 6.64–6.67. The transferred LNWTP (based on a model estimated just with data from Ruteng) is significantly higher at 7.3, and the confidence intervals do not overlap (see Table 7.3). The LNWTP transferred to Ruteng using a function estimated only with data from Siberut (6.99) is significantly lower than the raw data on LNWTP (median = 7.55) collected in Ruteng. Again, the confidence intervals do not overlap.

The selection model also allows us to predict LNWTP for the entire population, as reported in the last two rows of Table 7.3. The models estimated for Siberut consistently have a significant negative coefficient on LAMBDA, which results in a much higher transferred LNWTP for the population than for respondents in Ruteng. In contrast, there is less consistent evidence of selection bias in Ruteng, which means that the transferred LNWTP for the Siberut *population* is similar to the transferred LNWTP for the Siberut *respondents*. In general, transferred values for the populations are more accurate (closer to the predicted values) than the transferred values for only the respondents. In fact, the only benefits transfer that could be considered accurate even at the 75 per cent level is

Table 7.3 *Predicting support at new parks*

	Transferred LNWTP	Predicted LNWTP
	Median (90% confidence interval)	
Siberut – respondents	7.3 (7.24–7.37)	6.65 (6.64–6.67)
Ruteng – respondents	6.99 (6.94–7.09)	7.55 (7.53–7.56)
Siberut – population	7.35 (7.27–7.42)	7.66 (7.64–7.7)
Ruteng – population	7.82 (7.77–7.88)	7.47 (7.43–7.49)

Notes:
1. Medians and 90% confidence intervals are based on 100 draw bootstrapping. Medians are reported because {median(logWTP)}={log(medianWTP)}, but means are close to the medians for these distributions.
2. Respondents are those open supporters of the parks who indicated positive WTP, with $\lambda = \varphi/\Phi$. Population includes all respondents to the survey (representative of population), with $\lambda = 0$. Transferred LNWTP is calculated from model estimated at other park (100 times, with different draws of the data), using only the means of household characteristics from park of interest (using 100 draws of the data). Predicted LNWTP is just the median of the stated WTP from the park of interest for respondents (with the mean calculated 100 times based on random draws of that data), and is based on model parameters and explanatory variable means from the park of interest (estimated 100 times) for the population.
3. Individual park models use same specification as pooled model, except for exclusion of DRUTENG and interaction terms. Estimation results are available from the authors.

the transferred value from the Ruteng model to the Siberut population. These tests suggest that one of the key difficulties with predicting values at new sites is the inherent selection bias in reported WTP when there is significant non-response.

Conclusions

Integrated conservation and development projects have been a key element of global and national strategies to protect the environment without compromising rural development. Supported by a large number of multilateral and bilateral aid agencies and NGOs, ICDPs are fundamentally based on the concept of gaining local support for parks. This challenges researchers to accurately gauge this local support and understand its variation across households. In principle, contingent valuation is a promising method for meeting this challenge. Our examination of support for two new parks in Indonesia provides mixed evidence on the effectiveness of CVM in this context.

Economists developed the contingent valuation method in order to understand and quantify preferences for non-market public goods, such as ICDPs. CVM relies on the direct evaluations of those affected, rather than inferring values from their behaviour. In this sense, it is a democratic and participatory method. Unlike ordinal or binary opinion survey questions, CVM encourages respondents to make their evaluations in the context of limited budgets and competing demands. The method produces an estimate of household 'willingness to pay', which is a conceptually robust measure of the expected welfare change resulting from the provision (or change in provision) of a public good. We claim that this welfare change, represented by WTP, is a useful gauge of local support for an ICDP. As discussed by others (notably Adamowicz et al, 1998) and corroborated by our results, it is not the only determinant of expressed support, perhaps particularly so in traditional, semi-subsistence societies such as Siberut and Ruteng.

In our case studies of parks in Siberut and Ruteng, nevertheless, we find several encouraging results. In a multivariate regression model (Table 7.2), we find expected correlation between WTP and households characteristics, such as illness in Siberut and wealth in Ruteng. Other variables that we expected to be related to WTP, such as rattan harvest and hunting, were statistically insignificant, which could reflect the net effect of maintaining forest (a benefit to those who rely on forest products) but restricting access (a cost to those same households). The correlation of WTP and survey variables suggests that future research should collect information that will allow survey effects (such as date of interview) to be distinguished from regional characteristics (such as remoteness). Collectively these suggest some caution in interpreting CVM results to gauge support for ICDPs. Clearly, survey methodologies such as CVM should be complemented by more in-depth, ethnographic studies of how local communities' lifestyles and livelihoods are impacted by ICDP projects so as to better understand the dynamics of local support.

While 35 years of research on CVM has resulted in many refinements to the method, the cost of implementing a survey remains a major drawback. This is at the heart of current interest in the transferability of CVM results to new sites, based on mean characteristics of those sites rather than entirely new surveys. We evaluate this possibility, first by jointly modelling the WTP for the Ruteng and Siberut ICDPs. We find evidence for three possible reasons for different levels of support: different means of explanatory variables, a statistically significant coefficient on the site indicator and some statistically significant interaction terms (Tables 7.1 and 7.3). The statistically significant coefficients suggest that transfer may be difficult, and in fact we find that the transferred and actual value come moderately close (overlapping 75 per cent confidence interval) for only one site, and only after we account for the fact that not all respondents indicated positive support. Clearly, further research on this topic is merited, with particular attention to the non-response (self-selection) issue.

Given that local support is considered the central advantage of ICDPs over traditional parks, the information provided by CVM surveys is critical. We find that two-thirds of households in Siberut and Ruteng support the proposed ICDPs, in the concrete sense of being willing to pay some positive amount.

While we would not suggest designing a tax or fee structure based on these results, we do contend that they provide a more informative and more complete measure of support than simply asking households whether they are in favour of the ICDPs or their various components. In particular, we show how support varies across households, including estimating support by households who chose not to respond. The heterogeneity in support indicates that ICDP managers should carefully target and tailor their activities to take advantage of existing support and change conditions so as to gain new support. While further research and great care in interpreting results are clearly needed, we believe that the contingent valuation method could prove broadly useful in efforts to turn national parks into conservation *and* development projects.

Acknowledgements

The authors thank Sahat Simunjuntak, Mariyanti Hendro and Frans Dabukke for facilitating our study, and K. N. Ninan, Clem Tisdell and John Loomis for helpful comments. We also thank our interviewers and respondents.

Notes

1. This analysis was part of a larger study 'Economics of Biodiversity Conservation in Indonesia: Protected Areas on Flores and Siberut Islands', conducted by Duke University in cooperation with the Indonesian Directorate General of Forest Protection and Nature Conservation (Kramer et al, 1997a). The larger study examined several of the economic impacts of conserving biodiversity and habitat in Siberut National Park and Ruteng Nature Recreation Park.
2. The Asian Development Bank loaned US$25 million for the project.
3. Open-ended contingent valuation questions are generally believed to provide a more conservative estimate of WTP than the most popular alternative question format, called dichotomous choice or referendum format (Schulze et al, 1996; Smith et al, 1997).
4. A reviewer suggested that an alternative approach to modelling the response data would be the extended spike model of Kriström (1997). We did not use such an approach due to the small number of non-positive responses to the CV questions.
5. The inverse Mills ratio is $\lambda = \varphi(\beta x)/\Phi(\beta x)$ for households who indicate positive support (households who self-select into responding), while for others it is $\lambda = -\varphi(\beta x)/(1-\Phi(\beta x))$ (Greene, 1993). The significance of the coefficient on the inverse Mills ratio, using the standard error corrected for pre-estimation, is the test for self-selection. The model assumes that the error terms in the first (u) and second (ε) stage are distributed bivariate normal.
6. This approach follows the 'benefits transfer' literature in the analysis of benefits of environmental protection under resource and time constraints by combining a pre-estimated benefits function and its regression coefficients – estimated for a site

(study site) with values of regressors from another site (policy site) to assess policy benefits (Smith, 1992; Downing and Ozuna, 1996; Kirchhoff et al, 1997).

7.   Using the same specification as the pooled model, we first estimate the model using only the Siberut survey data, noting the predicted LNWTP at the means of the explanatory variables in Siberut. We then calculate the 'transferred LNWTP' using the coefficients estimated from this Siberut model and the mean household characteristics from Ruteng. Second, we estimate the model using only the Ruteng survey data, note the predicted LNWTP for Ruteng, and calculate the 'transferred LNWTP' for the mean household in Siberut. By repeatedly drawing random samples of the data, estimating the function, finding the predicted mean LNWTP for the study site, and calculating the transferred mean LNWTP for the other site, we can obtain distributions of actual (predicted) LNWTP and transferred LNWTP. We summarize the results with medians rather than means, because median(LNWTP) = ln(median WTP). With earlier specifications of the model, we drew 1000 random samples from the data, and the results were not qualitatively different than findings based on 100 random draws.

8.   It should be noted that this degree of support was measured in the early days of the project based on expectations of benefits. The assessment by Wells et al (1999) conducted several years later, suggests that these expected benefits were not fully realized.

9.   We exclude three respondents who reported WTP greater than Rp.80,000, which was over a third higher than the value of the next highest WTP. We did not attempt to model responses from households who indicated that the ICDP would be a net cost to them, because of the small number (38) of these responses, many of which were very large. In contrast to the WTP case, willingness to accept (WTA) is not bounded by income, making it difficult to distinguish protests from true reports of WTA.

10.   Our focus is on the distribution of support in the population as a whole. If the goal were to estimate actual donations to the ICDP, we would focus on the net effect of explanatory factors on the probability of expressing support (as captured in the inverse Mills ratio) and the level of support. Levels of cash expenditures, land under cultivation, and survey variables such as response to earlier questions and date of interview, do not have significant net effects when considering their influence in both stages of the model. We do not present these combined marginal effects, because we are not arguing for actually collecting fees from households, but rather for using CVM as a means to understand local support for ICDPs.

References

Adamowicz, W., Beckley, T., Hatton-Macdonald, D., Just, L., Luckert, M., Murray, E., Phillips, W. (1998) 'In search of forest resource values of indigenous peoples: Are nonmarket valuation techniques applicable?', *Society and Natural Resources*, vol 11, pp51–66

Adams, C., Seroa da Motta, R., Ortiz, R. A., Reid, J., Ebersbach Aznar, C., de Almeida Sinisgalli, Paulo, A. (2007) 'The use of contingent valuation for evaluating protected areas in the developing world: Economic valuation of Morro do Diabo State Park,

Atlantic Rainforest, Sao Paolo State (Brazil)', *Ecological Economics*, vol 66, no 2–3 pp359–370

Amirnejad, H., Assareh, S. M. H., Ahmadian, M. (2006) 'Estimating the existence value of north forests of Iran by using a contingent valuation method', *Ecological Economics*, vol 58, pp665–675

Asian Development Bank (1992) 'Appraisal of the biodiversity conservation projects in Flores and Siberut in Indonesia', LAP: IN023154, Manila

Bandara, R. and Tisdell, C. (2003) 'Comparison of rural and urban attitudes to the conservation of Asian elephants in Sri Lanka: Empirical evidence', *Biological Conservation*, vol 110, pp327–342

Batisse, M. (1982) 'The Biosphere Reserve: A tool for environmental conservation and management', *Environmental Conservation*, vol 9, pp101–111

Borrini-Feyerabend, G. (1995) *Collaborative Management of Protected Areas: Tailoring the Approach to the Context*, IUCN, Social Policy Unit, Gland, Switzerland

Boxall, P. C. and Beckley, T. (2002) 'An introduction to approaches and issues for measuring non-market values in developing economies', in B. Campbell and M. Luckert (eds), *Uncovering the Hidden Harvest: Valuation Methods for Woodland and Forest Resources*, Earthscan, London

Brandon, K. and Wells, M. (1992) 'Planning for people and parks: Design dilemmas', *World Development*, vol 20, pp557–570

Brandon, K., Redford, K. H., Sanderson, S. (1998) *Parks in Peril: People, Politics, and Protected Areas*, Island Press, Washington, DC

Caldecott, J. (1996) *Designing Conservation Projects*, Cambridge University Press, Cambridge

Carson, R. T., Flores, N. E., Meade, N. F. (2001) 'Contingent valuation: Controversies and evidence', *Environmental and Resource Economics*, vol 19, pp173–210

Chape, S., Blyth, S., Fish, L., Fox, P., Spalding, M. (compilers) (2003) *United Nations List of Protected Areas*, IUCN, Gland, Switzerland

Dixon, J. A. and Sherman, P. B. (1990) *Economics of Protected Areas: A New Look at Benefits and Costs*, Island Press, Washington, DC

Dolton, P. J. and Makepeace, G. H. (1987) 'Interpreting sample selection effects', *Economics Letters*, vol 24, pp373–379

Downing, M. and Ozuna, T. (1996) 'Testing the reliability of the benefit function transfer approach', *Journal of Environmental Economics and Management*, vol 30, pp316–322

Furze, B., De Lacy, T., Birckhead, J. (1996) *Culture, Conservation and Biodiversity*, John Wiley, New York

Garnett, S. T., Sayer, J. A., du Toit, J. (2007) 'Improving the effectiveness of interventions to balance conservation and development: A conceptual framework', *Ecology and Society* [Online] URL: www.ecologyandsociety.org/vol12/iss1/art2/, accessed 30 June 2008

Greene, W. H. (1993) *Econometric Analysis*, Macmillan Publishing Company, New York

Hadker, N., Sharma, S., David, A., Muraleedharan, T. R. (1997) 'Willingness-to-pay for Borivili National Park: Evidence from a contingent valuation', *Ecological Economics*, vol 21, pp105–122

Hammitt, J., Liu, J., Liu, J. (2001) 'Contingent valuation of a Taiwanese wetland', *Environment and Development Economics*, vol 6, no 2, pp259–268

Heckman, J. J. (1979) 'Sample selection bias as a specification error', *Econometrica*, vol 47, no 1, pp153–161

Kirchhoff, S., Colby, B., LaFrance, J. (1997) 'Evaluating the performance of benefit transfer: An empirical inquiry', *Journal of Environmental Economics and Management*, vol 33, pp75–93

Kramer, R. A., Pattanayak, S., Sills, E., Simanjuntak, S. (1997a) *The Economics of the Siberut and Ruteng Protected Areas: Final Report, Directorate General of Forest Protection and Nature Conservation*, Government of Indonesia, Biodiversity Conservation Project in Flores and Siberut, Asian Development Bank Loan No. 1187-INO, 109 pages

Kramer, R. A., van Schaik, C., Johnson, J. (eds) (1997b) *Last Stand: Protected Areas and the Defense of Tropical Biodiversity*, Oxford University Press, Oxford

Kriström, B. (1997) 'Spike models in contingent valuation', *American Journal of Agricultural Economics*, vol 79, pp1013–1023

Lindhjem, H. and Navrud, S. (2007) 'How reliable are meta-analyses for international benefit transfers?' *Ecological Economics*, vol 66, no 2–3, pp 425–435

Ministry of Forestry, Directorate General of Forest Protection and Nature Conservation (1995a) *Siberut National Park Integrated Conservation and Management Plan*, Volumes 1–3, Biodiversity Conservation Project in Flores and Siberut, ADB Loan No. 1187-INO (SF), Jakarta, Indonesia

Ministry of Forestry, Directorate General of Forest Protection and Nature Conservation (1995b) *Ruteng Nature Recreation Park Integrated Conservation and Management Plan*, Volumes 1–3, Biodiversity Conservation Project in Flores and Siberut, ADB Loan No. 1187-INO (SF), Jakarta, Indonesia

Muller, J. and Albers, H. J. (2004) 'Enforcement, payments, and development projects near protected areas: How the market setting determines what works where', *Resource and Energy Economics*, vol 26, pp185–204

Nicaise, I. (2001) 'Human capital, reservation wages and job competition: Heckman's lambda re-interpreted', *Applied Economics*, vol 33, pp309–315

Pattanayak, S. K. and Butry, D. T. (2005) 'Spatial complementarity of forests and farms: accounting for ecosystem services', *American Journal of Agricultural Economics*, vol 87, no 4, pp995–1008

Pattanayak, S. K. and Kramer, R. A. (2001) 'Worth of watersheds: A producer surplus approach for valuing drought mitigation in Eastern Indonesia', *Environment and Development Economics*, vol 6, pp123–146

Pattanayak, S. K. and Wendland, K. J. (2007) 'Nature's care: Diarrhea, watershed protection, and biodiversity conservation in Flores, Indonesia', *Biodiversity Conservation*, vol 16, pp2801–2819

Pattanayak, S. K., Sills, E. O., Mehta, A. D., Kramer, R. A. (2003) 'Local uses of parks: Uncovering patterns of household production from forests of Siberut, Indonesia', *Conservation and Society*, vol 1, pp209–222

Pattanayak, S. K., Sills, E. O., Kramer, R. A. (2004) 'Seeing the forest for the fuel', *Environment and Development Economics*, vol 9, pp155–179

Pearse, P. and Holmes, T. (1993) 'Accounting for nonmarket benefits in southern forest management,' *Southern Journal of Applied Forestry*, vol 17, pp84–89

Schulze, W., McClelland, G., Waldman, D., Lazo, J. (1996) 'Source of bias in contingent valuation', in D. J. Bjornstad and J. R. Kahn (eds), *Contingent Valuation of Environmental Resources: Methodological Issues and Research Needs*, Brookfield, Edward Elgar, VT

Shrestha, R. K. and Loomis, J. (2001) 'Testing a meta-analysis model for benefit transfer in international outdoor recreation', *Ecological Economics*, vol 39, pp67–83

Shyamsundar, P. and Kramer, R. A. (1996) 'Tropical forest protection: An empirical analysis of the costs borne by local people', *Journal of Environmental Economics and Management*, vol 31, pp129–144

Siberut Conservation Project (2005) URL: www.siberutisland.org/, last accessed March 2008

Sills, E. (1998a) 'Options for Estimating and Influencing Local Collection of Forest Products: Case Study of Rattan from Siberut National Park', *Proceedings of the 1998 Southern Forest Economics Workshop*, R. Abt and K. Lee (eds), USDA Forest Service, Research Triangle Park

Sills, E. (1998b) 'Ecotourism as an integrated conservation and development strategy: econometric estimation of demand by international tourists and impacts on indigenous households in Indonesia', Dissertation, Duke University

Smith, J., Mourato, S., Veneklaas, E., Labarta, R., Reategui, K., Sanchez, G. (1997) 'Willingness to pay for environmental services among slash-and-burn farmers in the Peruvian Amazon: Implications for deforestation and global environmental services', CSERGE Working Paper, London

Smith, V. K. (1992) 'On separating defensible benefit transfers from "smoke and mirrors"', *Water Resources Research*, vol 28, pp685–694

Smith, V. K., Van Houtren, G. and Pattanayak, S. K. (2002) 'A benefit transfer via preference calibration: "Prudential algebra" for policy', *Land Economics*, vol 78, pp132–152

Strazzera, E., Genius, M., Scarpa, R., Hutchinson, G. (2003a) 'The effect of protest votes on the estimates of WTP for use values of recreational sites', *Environmental and Resource Economics*, vol 25, pp461–476

Strazzera, E., Scarpa, R., Calia, P., Garrod, G., Willis, K. (2003b) 'Modelling zero values and protest responses in Contingent Valuation Surveys', *Applied Economics*, vol 35, no 2, pp133–138

SurfAid International (2004) *Annual Report*, Padang, Indonesia

Terborgh, J. (1999) *Requiem for Nature*, Island Press, Washington, DC

Turpie, J. K. (2003) 'The existence value of biodiversity in South Africa: How interest, experience, knowledge, income and perceived level of threat influence local willingness to pay', *Ecological Economics*, vol 46, pp199–216

Van Schaik, C. P. and Rijksen, H. D. (2002) 'Integrated conservation and development projects: Problems and potential', in J. Terborgh et al (eds), *Making Parks Work: Strategies for Preserving Tropical Nature*, Island Press, Washington, DC

Wells, M. P. and McShane, T. (2004) 'Integrating protected area management with local needs and aspirations', *Ambio*, vol 33, Royal Swedish Academy of Sciences.

Wells, M., Guggenheim, S., Khan, A., Wardojo, W., Jepson, P. (1999) 'Investing in Biodiversity: A review of Indonesia's integrated conservation and development projects', World Bank, Washington, DC, July

West, Paige and Brockington, D. (2006) 'An anthropological perspective on some unexpected consequences of protected areas', *Conservation Biology*, vol 20, no 3, pp609–616

Whittington, D. (1998) 'Administering contingent valuation surveys in developing countries', *World Development*, vol 26, pp21–30

2

INCENTIVES AND INSTITUTIONS

8

Payments for Ecosystem Services: An International Perspective

Jeffrey A. McNeely

Introduction

The Millennium Ecosystem Assessment (MEA) offers a productive framework for communicating environmental issues more effectively to decision makers, through a broader consideration of the benefits of ecosystems for people (MEA, 2005). These so-called 'ecosystem services' include:

- *Provisioning services*: Goods produced or provided by ecosystems, such as food, freshwater, fuelwood and genetic resources.
- *Regulating services*: The benefits obtained from regulation of ecosystem processes, such as the regulation of pollinators, climate, diseases, nutrients and extreme natural events.
- *Cultural services*: The non-material benefits from ecosystems, including spiritual, recreational, aesthetic, inspirational and educational benefits. In many ways, these cultural services help to define who we are as citizens of our respective countries.
- *Supporting services*: The services necessary for the production of the other ecosystem services, and include soil formation, nutrient cycling, primary production, carbon sequestration and so forth.

The approach taken by the MEA implies that ecosystem services have value to people, which in turn implies that these ecosystem services have an *economic* value which can be internalized in economic policy and the market system. Some of these services are relatively easy to quantify, which facilitates the estimation of their economic value and the development of appropriate market incentives. Others are more abstract, but are nonetheless valuable. For example, developing a market for non-use values (such as existence value) can be extremely challenging, especially when a lack of resource tenure discourages people from caring about biodiversity. Current markets often are imperfect, so this chapter will describe some new approaches to building efficient markets for ecosystem services.

All ecosystem services are supported by biodiversity, which includes the full range of genes, populations, species, communities and ecosystems. The MEA did not consider biodiversity conservation to be an ecosystem service on its own. Nonetheless, conserving biodiversity provides many values because genes, species, habitats and ecosystems support the provision of numerous services, such as producing trees, enabling genetic resources to continue evolving and providing attractions for the tourism industry. However, the multiple relationships between biodiversity and ecosystem services remain only partially understood and is an area of active research (Cardinale et al, 2006).

Together, the ecosystem services contribute to the constituents of human well-being, which include security, basic material for a good life, health, good social relations and the ability to make choices on how to live one's life. This model demonstrates to decision makers how important ecosystem services, and the biodiversity that supports them, are for all aspects of human development. Ecosystem services also underlie virtually all of the Millennium Development Goals approved by the governments of the world at the 2000 Millennium Summit (Millennium Project, 2005), although this link has not yet been clearly stated.

The concept of ecosystem services also implies that those who are providing the services (in the past, often as a public good) deserve to be compensated when they manage ecosystems to deliver more services to others. Payment of conservation incentives can reward forest managers and farmers for being good stewards of the land, and ensure that payments are made by those who are receiving benefits. Similarly, those who degrade ecosystems and reduce the supply of ecosystem services should be expected to pay an appropriate level of compensation for the damage they cause, in line with the Polluter Pays Principle.

People who live close to nature know better than anyone that a healthy, resilient ecosystem is essential for a productive and profitable ecosystem. Basing the conservation of ecosystem services on economic incentives recognizes the capacity of managers to care for the land, and it supports practices that may not necessarily provide the greatest short-term financial return, but pay off in the longer term. With appropriate incentives, rural people can become land managers as well as commodity producers, ensuring that areas under their control are sustainably managed to provide multiple ecosystem benefits.

Values of ecosystem services

Assessing the economic values of ecosystem services remains very much a work in progress (Boyd and Banzhaf, 2005). However, some detailed estimates have been made, and a few of these are presented here. In the relatively small US state of Massachusetts, the annual value of non-market ecosystem services is over US$6.3 billion annually, in addition to the US$1.9 billion from marketed ecosystem services. Saltwater wetlands were found to have extremely high value per unit area.[1]

The value of pollination services has not been estimated at a global level, but some indications are available. For example, the value of pollination to alfalfa seed growers in the Canadian prairies is estimated to be 35 per cent of annual crop production (Blawat and Fingler, 1994), amounting to a value of about US$8 million per year. The value of native pollinators to the agricultural economy of the US is estimated to be in the order of at least US$4.1 billion per year (Southwick and Southwick, 1992). In Costa Rica, forest-based pollinators increased coffee yields by 20 per cent within one kilometre of forest, and improved coffee quality as well. Pollination services from two forest fragments of 46ha and 111ha yielded a benefit of US$60,000 per year for one Costa Rican farm (Ricketts et al, 2004).

A 1994 independent study of the water catchment of Melbourne, Australia, found that the value of clean fresh water outweighs that of the timber in the forest. It showed that extending the current harvest rotation from 80 to 200 years would deliver benefits of US$81 million, while shorter 20-year rotations would decrease the benefits derived from the catchment by US$525 million and require building a US$250 million water treatment works. These figures clearly indicate the value of maintaining forests in Australia. More details on water values can be found in Emerton and Bos (2004).

The value of carbon sequestration in forests has received considerable attention (for example, Swingland, 2003). The value of the tropical forests contained in ten tropical countries was estimated at US$1.1 trillion on the basis of carbon stored, using the then-current rate of US$20 for a one-ton unit of carbon dioxide (rather high: the first buyers in Asia offered $4–7 per ton).[2] Lubowski et al (2005) concluded that about a third of the US target under the Kyoto Protocol (if it had ratified) could be cost-effectively achieved by forest-based carbon sequestration. At a global scale, some US$11.3 billion worth of carbon credits were traded on the international market in 2005.

Most ecosystem services have been seen as public goods that benefit large groups of people and resist private ownership. A major challenge is to align private incentives with the public interest. For detailed references on payments for ecosystem services, see Pennington (2005). A useful valuation website is www.naturevaluation.org.html.

Markets for ecosystem services

Over the past 10 years or so, markets and other payments for forest ecosystem services have emerged in many parts of the world (Wunder, 2005; Pagiola et al, 2005). For example, Landell-Mills and Porras (2002) identified 287 initiatives for forest ecosystem service payments; 61 of these were specifically associated with watersheds. The emergence of these markets has been driven by frustration with traditional government regulatory approaches, growing recognition of the limits of the contributions that protected areas can make to conserving biodiversity, the demands of society for ecologically sound and sustainably grown products, and the need of forest-based industries to find additional revenue sources to remain competitive. The expectation is that such markets can contribute to forest protection and restoration and become a sustainable source of new income for the forest-dependent poor who occupy a large share of the world's forests (Scherr et al, 2005).

This chapter discusses four categories of market and payment schemes:

1   eco-labelling of forest or farm products, an indirect form of payment for ecosystem services;
2   open trading under a regulatory cap or floor, such as carbon trading or mitigation banking;
3   user fees for environmental and cultural services, such as hunting licenses or entry to protected areas;
4   public payment schemes to private forest owners to maintain or enhance ecosystem services, such as 'conservation banking' and watershed protection.

Eco-labelling

Many certification schemes are being used as an incentive for both producers and consumers. Perhaps the best established is the Forest Stewardship Council, which has been working for well over a decade (see www.fsc.org). Over the past decade, some 50 million hectares in more than 60 countries have been certified according to FSC standards. Several thousand products have been produced using Forest Stewardship Council (FSC) certified wood and carry the FSC trademark. Using consultative processes, it sets international standards for responsible forest management and accredits independent third-party organizations who are authorized to certify forest managers and forest product producers to FSC standards. Its trade mark provides international recognition to organizations that support responsible forest management and allows consumers to recognize products that have been responsibily produced. The FSC membership includes a wide range of social, community and indigenous peoples groups as well as responsible corporations (such as IKEA), development aid agencies and other public organizations. In several countries, companies have formed 'buyers groups' that have committed themselves to selling only independently certified timber and timber products. The FSC-labelling scheme is preferred by at least some buyers groups in Japan, the UK, The Netherlands, Belgium, Austria, Switzerland, Germany, Brazil and the US. Other forest labelling schemes are also in operation, such as the Programme for the Endorsement of Forest Certification Schemes (PEFC)[3] and regional initiatives based on the international forestry management standard ISO 14001.

Organic products have long been labelled, and the organic movement, through its International Federation of Organic Agriculture Movements (IFOAM), is seeking to ensure that organic farming is also biodiversity-friendly.[4] The global organic market was worth US$27.8 billion in 2004 and is expected to reach US$133.7 billion by 2012, with the greatest growth in China (although credible certification remains a limitation). Other eco-friendly labels are also being used; for example, shade-grown coffee has a market of US$5 billion in the US alone.[5]

Carbon sequestration and trading

The most widespread of the marketed ecosystem services is carbon sequestration. Forests, grasslands and other ecosystems remove carbon dioxide from the atmosphere through the storage of carbon as part of the process of photosynthesis. A reasonably prosperous industry has been established in trading 'certified emission reductions' within the Clean Development Mechanism (CDM) of the Kyoto Protocol or 'verified carbon emission reductions' (CERs) outside of the Kyoto regime (see, e.g. Swingland, 2003). The carbon market is substantial, with 64 million metric tons of carbon dioxide equivalent exchanged through projects (most transactions intended for compliance with the Kyoto Protocol) from January to May 2004, nearly as much as during the whole year 2003 (78 million tons) (Lecocq, 2004). Japanese companies are the largest market buyers, with 41 per cent of the 2003–2004 market, and Asia is the largest seller of emission reduction projects, accounting for 51 per cent of the volume supplied.

The Kyoto-compliant carbon emission offset market is expected to grow to a minimum of 15 million tons of carbon dioxide in 2008–2012 (Scherr et al, 2005). The European Union Emissions Trading Scheme began in 2005, with futures and spot contracts trading on several exchanges across Europe; it is used mostly by the high-emission power and steel sectors. The European carbon market is now being linked to CDM projects in Asia, including Asia Carbon Global activities in China, India, Vietnam and Indonesia. It is not clear how these payments are affecting forest carbon sequestration. The International Emissions Trading Association (TETA) is a useful source of information on these issues.[6]

Carbon taxes also affect forest management. Joining several other countries that have already imposed a carbon tax, the Ministry of the Environment in Japan unveiled a plan on 25 October 2005 for a carbon tax aimed at curbing global warming. The tax will be levied on carbon contained in fossil fuels, with the tax amounting to 2400 Yen per ton of carbon contained in fuels. It is not clear how the funds raised will be used to address global warming, but many hope that this will include carbon sequestration projects affecting forests.[7]

At the Ninth Conference of Parties of the Climate Change Convention in 2005, a group known as the Tropical Forest Coalition, consisting of Papua New Guinea, Costa Rica and several others, proposed that Parties explore potential new mechanisms to encourage conservation of *existing* forests under the UNFCCC. Parties agreed to discuss this potential further, and it is widely recognized that conservation of old-growth forests is the most cost-effective means of sequestering carbon (and keeping it sequestered). Avoided deforestation is likely to become a significant area of discussion for the post-Kyoto efforts to reduce (or at least stabilize) atmospheric carbon dioxide.

Payments for cultural services

Among the many cultural services ecosystems support are the provision of scenic beauty and other aesthetic values that contribute to recreation, tourism and a sense of identity of place to those who have long lived in a particular locality. One mechanism to finance scenic beauty is through entrance fees to protected areas, a 'user pays' market approach. Numerous other ways of paying for protected areas are discussed in Quintela et al (2004) and at the website of the Conservation Finance Alliance.[8]

Rural people may require government-supported payments to encourage them to protect habitats or endangered species (Fox and Nino-Murcia, 2005). However, payments to protect habitats come not only from government – for example, highway departments that need to offset habitat loss due to road building – but also from private developers who need to offset habitat loss arising from residential, commercial or industrial development. The main role of government in these cases is to regulate offsets so as to ensure that the policy goal of no net loss of habitat is being met, and that the 'exchange rate' uses the proper currency (for example, not just area, but also ecosystem function and habitat for key species).

Species conservation banking – the creation and trading of 'credits' that represent biodiversity values on private land – is about a decade old. In the US, for example, some 76 properties are identified as conservation banks but only 35 of these have been established under a Conservation Banking Agreement approved by the US Fish and Wildlife Service (USFWS) (Fox and Nino-Murcia, 2005). The 35 'official' conservation banks cover 15,987ha and support more than 22 species listed under the US Endangered Species Act. Financial motives drove the establishment of 91 per cent of the conservation banks, and a majority of for-profit banks are breaking even or making money. With credit prices ranging from US$7000 to US$325,000 per hectare, banking agreements offer financial incentives that compete with development and provide a business-based argument for conserving habitat. Although the bureaucracy of establishing an agreement with the USFWS was burdensome, nearly two-thirds of bank owners reported that they would set up another agreement given the appropriate opportunity. Increasing information sharing, decreasing the time to establish agreements (currently averaging 2.18 years), and reducing bureaucratic challenges can further increase the amount of private property voluntarily committed to banking. While many ecological uncertainties remain, conservation banking can offer at least a partial solution to the conservation versus development conflict over biodiversity.

The International Habitat Reserve Programme (IHRP) is a system of institutional arrangements that facilitates conservation contracting between national or international actors and individuals or groups that supply ecosystem services. An IHRP involves a contract that specifies that the outside agents will make periodic payments to local actors if a targeted ecosystem remains intact or if target levels of wildlife remain in the ecosystem (Ferraro, 2001).

Watershed protection

Another very well known ecosystem service is watershed protection, often linked to forests. Watershed services are far more numerous and complex than is usually appreciated, and provide numerous kinds of benefits to people, including the rural poor (Dyson et al, 2003). A partial list includes:

- provide water for consumptive uses, such as drinking water, agriculture, domestic uses and industrial uses;
- non-consumptive uses such as hydropower generation, cooling water and navigation;
- water storage in soils, wetlands and flood plains to buffer floods and droughts;
- control of erosion and sedimentation, which can have effects on productive aquatic systems;
- maintain a flow of water required to enable river dynamism, riparian habitats, fisheries and water management systems for rice cultivation and fertilization of flood plains;
- maintain mangroves, estuaries and other coastal ecosystems that may require fresh water infusions;
- control of the level of groundwater tables, potentially preventing adverse effects on agriculture by keeping salinity far below the surface;
- maintenance of water quality that may have been reduced through inputs of nutrients, pathogens, pesticides, fertilizers, heavy metals or salinity;
- support for cultural values including aesthetic qualities that support tourism and recreational uses as well as supporting traditional ways of life and providing opportunities for adapting to changing conditions.

The services provided by forests protecting watersheds overlap with many other ecosystem services, indicating the synergies that can be realized through improved management of forest systems. Many of these services have market values, while others have non-market values that are nonetheless significant.

Many countries in various parts of the world are developing mechanisms for collecting payments for watershed protection. Of just a few that could be quoted:

- *Brazil*: A water utility in Sao Paulo pays 1 per cent of total revenues for the restoration and conservation of the Corumbatai watershed. The funds collected are used to establish tree nurseries and to support reforestation along riverbanks.
- *Costa Rica*: A hydropower company pays US$10 per ha/year to a local conservation NGO for hydrological service in the Peñas Blancas watershed. In the town of Heredia, the drinking water company earmarks a portion of water sales revenue for reforestation and forest conservation.
- *Ecuador*: Municipal water companies in Quito, Cuenca and Pimampiro impose levies on water sales, which are invested in the conservation of upstream areas and payments to forest owners (Landell-Mills and Porras, 2002).
- *Lao PDR*: The Phou Khao Khouay Protected Area currently receives 1 per cent of the gross revenues from a downstream hydropower dam, and the proposed Nam Theun 2 hydropower project is expected to provide over US$1 million per year for the management of the Nakai-Nam Theun Protected Area.
- *Japan*: The Kanagawa Prefectural Assembly adopted an ordinance in October 2005 that will impose an additional residence tax to be used exclusively for protecting water sources, with the funds going to projects aimed at conserving and restoring forests and rivers. The new tax will be introduced in April 2007 and continue for five years.[9]
- *Colombia*: In the Cauca valley, water user associations have assessed themselves additional charges and used the revenue to finance conservation activities in their watershed areas (Echevarria, 2002).

IUCN has just begun a 3-year project in Vietnam (with USAID funding) to design and initiate a payment for an environmental services scheme for Don Nai watershed/Cat Tien National Park. Payment for ecosystem services will include partnerships with Coca Cola (for water payments) and Masterfoods/Snickers (for payments for shade/organic grown cocoa).

The value of watershed services will depend on:

- maintaining the integrity of ecosystem functions or processes that support the watershed protection service;
- the scale at which the benefits from watershed protection have economic significance;
- the effectiveness of the institutional arrangements that have been put in place to ensure provision and access, including such issues as land secure tenure (Tognetti et al, 2005).

Payments for watershed services are often politically popular, as the value of water is well recognized. Regular information on recent developments in this field is available from an online paper, *Flows*.[10] Linking watershed protection services with improved livelihoods is the objective of a project carried out by IIED in London.[11]

A non-marketed value: Protection against extreme natural events

Recent human disasters caused by extreme natural events, including the 2004 Indian Ocean tsunami, and the 2005 Kashmir earthquake, have demonstrated the value of intact ecosystems in reducing the impact of such extreme natural events on human well-being. In the case of the tsunami, intact coral reefs and mangroves greatly reduced the negative impact of the tsunami on people (Danielsen et al, 2005); and in Kashmir, slopes that remained forest-covered suffered far less landslide damage than those where forests had been willfully overexploited.

The value of ecosystem services to protect human well-being against the implications of such extreme natural events is seldom quantified as no market exists for them, but the implications in terms of human fatalities, economic disruptions, and social disruptions carry a very real cost: in the two events mentioned above, human fatalities totalled over 300,000 and the economic costs of restoration exceed US$5 billion. Such costs need to be better quantified and incorporated in decision making that affects ecosystem functioning. These costs were externalized in Kashmir and along the coasts of the Indian Ocean, to the great detriment of the people living there. One element in the payment for ecosystem services, therefore, is to avoid expenditures that lead to ecosystem destruction or degradation.

Building markets for forest ecosystem services

As seen above, many systems of paying for ecosystem services are supported by taxes. The US Conservation Reserve Program is funded through general tax revenue. Costa Rica's National Fund for Forest Financing (FONAFIFO), a programme of payments for ecosystem services that includes protection of watersheds, is in part funded by a fuel tax, with the remainder funded through payments from beneficiaries; for example, tourism agencies pay for biodiversity and landscape beauty, and foreign energy companies purchase carbon offsets. Watershed management in Colombia is partly funded through a 6 per cent tax on the revenue of large hydroelectric plants (Tognetti et al, 2005).

In New South Wales, Australia, the Forest Department has initiated an Environmental Services Scheme that compensates landowners through credits for multiple benefits of forests, including biodiversity, carbon sequestration, soil conservation and protection of water quality that offsets the rise in salinity levels (State Forests of New South Wales, 2004).

In support of the implementation of the Millennium Development Goals, the World Bank and the Organisation for Economic Co-operation and Development (OECD) have promoted environmental fiscal reform (EFR), stressing that poverty reduction and improved environmental management go hand in hand. They advocate a range of taxation or pricing instruments that can raise revenue while simultaneously furthering environmental goals. This is achieved by providing economic incentives to correct market failures in the management of natural resources and the control of pollution (World Bank, 2005). They believe that EFR can mobilize revenue for governments, improve environmental management practices, conserve resources and reduce poverty. EFR includes a wide range of economic instruments, including:

- taxes on natural resource use (for example, forestry and fisheries) that will reduce the inefficient exploitation of publicly owned or controlled natural resources that results from operators paying a price that does not reflect the full value of the resources they extract;
- user charges or fees and subsidy reform that will improve the provision and quality of basic services such as water, while providing incentives to reduce any unintentional negative environmental effects arising from inefficient use;
- environmentally related taxes that will make polluters pay for the 'external costs of their activities and encourage them to reduce these activities to a more socially desirable level'.

Payment for environmental services may also have some hidden dangers. For example, if payments for ecosystem services become commonplace, this may risk eroding the sense of an environmental duty of caring for natural resources and managing them sustainably. It may even discourage private investment in the environment by creating the impression that environmental stewardship is the duty of governments rather than individuals (Salzman, 2005). Other potential dangers to consider include rent-seeking behaviour, where certain individuals may exaggerate their potentially negative impacts on ecosystem services in the hopes of gaining greater compensation. Others are concerned that at least some subsidies may pay the recipients for precisely the behaviour that the subsidies are seeking to overturn. Payments for ecosystem services also need to be provided equitably, so that those who are already providing an ecosystem service are paid as well as those who are expected to change their behaviour to come into conformity with the provision of the service (for example, watershed protection). But in any case, the establishment of an appropriate system of payments for ecosystem services will certainly change the perception of rural people about how they should manage their land.

The issue of payment for ecosystem services is still in its infancy, and further experimentation and research is required involving interdisciplinary teams of economists, ecologists and entrepreneurs to determine what ecosystem functions support the provision of specific benefits, how their key parameters can be measured or estimated, and how efficient economic incentives can be created to encourage the sustainable supply of ecosystem services.

Capturing the willingness to pay

As with any ecosystem service, it is essential to establish an enabling framework for any transactions that include payments. The ecosystem services are provided by those who own or manage the ecosystem. The markets for ecosystem services often work through an intermediary who issues certificates for the ecosystem services, with a verifier who controls and monitors the sustainable management of the ecosystem providing the services. The buyer of certificates from the intermediary is the source of financial resources into the system. The intermediary plays a critical role in managing the transaction, although of course it is also possible for the owner or manager of the ecosystem to provide the services directly to the buyer and to receive the funding immediately.

Formal legislation is not always necessary. For example, most certification is voluntary yet it seems to work relatively well and meets a market demand. And in the case of carbon, at least, the Kyoto Protocol provides a supporting policy framework.

The certificates that are issued can represent units such as hectares of the ecosystem that is providing the service, tons of carbon being sequestered, area of crops being pollinated, cubic metres of clean water being provided, or amount of certified timber being produced. A system of certificates for ecosystem services may enable them to be traded, as carbon sequestration certificates now are on the market in many parts of the world.

Institutions supporting payments for ecosystem services

A group of international organizations, including IUCN, has formed an international working group composed of leading experts from forest and energy research institutions, the financial world and environmental NGOs that is dedicated to developing markets for some of the ecosystem services provided by forests. Known as the Katoomba Group, it seeks to address key challenges for developing markets for the ecosystem services discussed above. It builds on the knowledge and experience of network members in the fields of establishing new market institutions, developing strategies for pricing and marketing, and monitoring the effects of such measures.

Serving as a source of ideas on ecosystem markets and providing strategic information on them, the Katoomba Group provides a service where providers and beneficiaries of ecosystem services can work together to capture the benefits associated with ecosystem services.[12] It has also established a global information service to report on developments in new ecosystem service-based markets.[13]

Not everyone supports 'conservation banking', if it is used to offset damage to old-growth forests. While money to support thinly stretched conservation activities is always welcome, some worry that even the best-managed habitat 'banks' can seldom supply the range of services provided by the ecosystems whose destruction they are meant to offset. Many habitats may simply be irreplaceable, and for these it is often best to establish and effectively manage classic protected areas (which now cover about 12 per cent of the world's land area); but even these areas can be seen to provide multiple ecosystem services that can be valued.

An essential element to the effective functioning of any market is access to information. Generating a market for ecosystem services will require knowledge about the values and functions of the various services. One effort to provide such information is the Conservation Commons.[14] It is a cooperative effort of non-governmental organizations, international and multilateral organizations, governments, academia and the private sector, to improve open access to data, information and knowledge related to the conservation of biodiversity, including ecosystems. It encourages organizations and individuals to ensure open access to the data, information, expertise and knowledge related to the conservation of biodiversity, which can also contribute to a market for ecosystem services.

Conclusions

Forest ecosystem services have four major market characteristics:

1   Payments have grown dramatically over the past decade and are especially significant to low-income producers. Some ecosystem services are not yet linked to significant commodities, but instead support niche markets for products of special value to a narrow range of buyers. Scherr et al (2005) estimate the annual value of direct payments through ecosystem markets in tropical countries is in the order of hundreds of millions of US dollars, while indirect payments via eco-labelled products such as certified timber generates several billion dollars per year.
2   Markets for forest ecosystem services are expected to grow quickly over the next 20 years. The potential for increased demand for watershed services is immense, providing significant opportunities for increased payments. The growth of these markets can generate new forms of financing and open up new opportunities for non-extractive management regimes for forest ecosystems.
3   Governments play a critical role as the direct buyers of many ecosystem services and catalysts for many private sector direct payment schemes. Since many ecosystem services are public goods, government intervention may be required to establish a market. This may entail directly paying for a service,

establishing property rights or establishing regulations that set caps and govern trading schemes.

4 Ecosystem service payments will usually cover only a modest share of the costs of good forest management, but this contribution can be important in improving the way forests are managed. The prices of ecosystem services are not yet sufficient to justify forest conservation in areas with moderate to high opportunity costs for the land. Even so, these payments can have a disproportionate catalytic effect on forest establishment and management (Scherr et al, 2005).

In order to enable payments for ecosystem services to become a significant part of rural economies, several strategic policy issues need to be addressed. These include:

- Property rights and national legal frameworks are required to enable ecosystem service markets to develop. Such steps are often politically contentious and costly, yet they are fundamental to establishing payment schemes of any type.
- Markets for ecosystem services will contribute substantially to poverty alleviation only if proactive efforts are made to recognize rights and establish markets that will provide equal access to low-income producers of forest ecosystem services (Landell-Mills and Porras, 2002). Rules governing the market tend to be set by the more powerful sectors of society who have the capital and capacity to invest in designing the rules, thereby marginalizing the rural poor who most require assistance to be brought into the market.
- New market institutions are needed to reduce transaction costs and financial risks. It is often helpful to provide intermediaries between buyers, sellers, investors, certifiers and other key groups in the value chain.
- Information about ecosystem service markets is scarce and the capacity to assess and develop markets is currently limited. Few national, provincial or local government entities have access to the information needed to shape policy on market design. Realizing the potentials of ecosystem service markets will require leading organizations to fill these knowledge gaps.

This chapter has briefly introduced the vast topic of payments for ecosystem services. Applying the principles and examples outlined here to the specific needs of any specific country will require information and analysis, policy support and political will. The result will be better-managed forests and more prosperous rural people: comprehensive, harmonious and sustainable development.

Acknowledgements

Joshua Bishop, Senior Economics Advisor at IUCN, generously shared his information and insights on payment for ecosystem services. Lucy Emerton, from

IUCN's Asia Regional Office, also provided useful insights. I would like to send a special thanks to Sara Scherr at Ecoagriculture Partners for her advice and input on both this chapter and many other aspects of sustainable forest use. Nadine McCormick helped with editorial support and Wendy Price provided secretarial support. Andrew Laurie, Xie Yan and Wang Sung helped me to make my perspectives more relevant to China.

Notes

1. www.massaudubon.org/losingground.
2. http://news.mongabay.com/2005/1129-rainforests.html.
3. www.pefc.org.
4. www.ifoam.org.
5. For more on certification, see www.certificationwatch.org.
6. www.ieta.org.
7. www.japanfs.org/db/database.cgi?cmd=dp&num=1256&dp=data_e.html.
8. www.conservationfinance.org.
9. www.japanfs.org/db/database.cgi?cmd=dp&num=1253&dp=data_e.html.
10. www.flowsonline.net.
11. www.iied.org/forestry/research/projects/water.html.
12. www.katoombagroup.org.
13. www.ecosystemmarketplace.com.
14. www.conservationcommons.org.

References

Blawat, P. and Fingler, B. (1994) *Guidelines for Estimating Cost of Production: Alfalfa Seeds. Manitoba Agriculture*, Winnipeg, Manitoba, Canada

Boyd, J. and Banzhaf, H. S. (2005) 'Ecosystem services and government accountability: The need for a new way of judging nature's value', *Resources*, Summer

Cardinale, B. J., Srivastava, D. S., Emmett Duffy, J., Wright, J. P., Downing, A. L., Sankaran, M., Jouseau, C. (2006) 'Effects of biodiversity on the functioning of tropic groups and ecosystems', *Nature*, vol 443, pp989–992

Danielsen, F., Sørensen, M. K., Olwig, M. F., Selvam, V., Parish, F., Burgess, N. D., Hiraishi, T., Karunagaran, V. M., Rasmussen, M. S., Hansen, L. B., Quarto, A., Suryadiputra, N. (2005) 'The Asian tsunami: A protective role for coastal vegetation', *Science*, vol 310, pp643–644

Dyson, M., Bergkamp, G., Scanlon, J. (eds) (2003) *Flows: The Essential of Environmental Flows*. IUCN, Gland, Switzerland

Echevarria, M. (2002) *Water User Associations in the Cauca Valley: A Voluntary Mechanism to Promote Upstream–downstream Cooperation in the Protection of Rural Watersheds.* FAO, Rome

Emerton, L. and Bos, E. (2004) *Value: Counting Ecosystems as Water Infrastructure*. IUCN, Gland, Switzerland

Ferraro, P. J. (2001) 'Global habitat protection: Limitations of development interventions and a role for conservation performance payments', *Conservation Biology*, vol 5, no 4, pp990–1000

Fox, J. and Nino-Murcia, A. (2005) 'Status of species conservation banking in the United States', *Conservation Biology*, vol 19, no 4, pp996–1007

Godoy, R., Wilkie, D., Overman, H., Cubas, A., Cubas, G., Demmer, J., McSweeney, K., Brokaw, N. (2000) 'Valuation of consumption and sale of forest goods from a Central American rainforest', *Nature*, vol 406, pp62–63

Kevan, P. G. and Phillips, T. P. (2001) 'The economic impacts of pollinator declines: An approach to assessing the consequences', *Conservation Ecology*, vol 5, no 1, pp8, www.consecol.org/vol5/iss1/art8/

Landell-Mills, N. and Porras, I. T. (2002) *Silver Bullet or Fool's Gold? A Global Review of Markets for Forest Environmental Services and Their Impact on the Poor*, IIED, London

Lecocq, F. (2004) *State and Trends of the Carbon Market 2004*, World Bank, Washington, DC

Lubowski, R. N., Plantinga, A. J., Stavins, R. N. (2005) *Land-use Change and Carbon "Sinks": Economic Estimation of the Carbon Sequestration Supply Function Resources for the Future*, Resources for the Future, Washington, DC

MEA (2005) Millennium Ecosystem Assessment. *Synthesis Report*, Kuala Lumpur, Malaysia. Also available at www.maweb.org

Meinzen-Dick, R. S. and Bruns, B. R. (eds) (2000) *Negotiating Water Rights*, Intermediate Technology Publications and the International Food Policy Research Institute, London

Millennium Project (2005) *Investing in Development: A Practical Plan to Achieve the Millennium Development Goals*, Earthscan, London

Pagiola, S., Arcenas, A., Paltais, G. (2005) 'Can payments for ecosystem services help reduce poverty? An exploration of the issues and the evidence to date from Latin America', *World Development*, vol 33, no 2, pp237–253

Pennington, M. (2005) *Payments for Ecosystem Services: Annotated Bibliography*, Winrock International, Little Rock, AK

Perrot-Maître, D. and Davis, P. (2001) *Case Studies: Developing Markets for Water Services from Forests*, Forest Trends, Washington DC. Also available at www.foresttrends.org/resources/pdf/casesWSofF.pdf

Quintela, C., Thomas, L., Robin. R. (eds) (2004) *Building a Secure Financial Future: Finance and Resources*, IUCN, Gland, Switzerland

Ricketts, T. H., Daly, G. C., Ehrlich, P. R., Michener, C. D. (2004) 'Economic value of tropical forest to coffee production', *PNAS*, vol 101, no 34, pp12579–12582. Also available at www.pnas.org/cgi/doi/10.1073/pnas.0405147101

Salzman, J. (2005) 'The promise and perils of payments for ecosystem services', *International Journal of Innovation and Sustainable Development*, vol 1, no 1/2, pp5–20

Scherr, S., White, A., Kaimowitz, D. (2004) *A New Agenda for Forest Conservation and Poverty Reduction: Making Markets Work for Low-income Producers*, Forest Trends, Washington, DC

Scherr, S., White, A., Khare, A. (2005) *Current Status and Future Potential of Markets for Ecosystem Services of Tropical Forests: An Overview*, Forest Trends, Washington, DC. Also available at www.foresttrends.org/whoweare/ publications.htm

Southwick, E. E. and Southwick, L. (1992) 'Economic value of honey bees in the United States', *Journal of Economic Entomology*, vol 85, no 3, pp621–633

State Forests of New South Wales (2004) Environmental Services Scheme. www.forest.nsw.gov.au/env_services/ess

Swingland, I. R. (ed.) (2003) *Capturing Carbon and Conserving Biodiversity: The Market Approach*, Earthscan, London

Tognetti, S. S., Aylward, B., Mendoza, G. F. (2005) 'Markets for Watershed Services', in M. Anderson (ed.), *Encyclopedia of Hydrological Sciences*, John Wiley and Sons, UK

Whitten, S., Salzman, J., Shelton, D., Proctor, W. (2003) 'Markets for ecosystem services: Applying the concepts', paper presented at the 47th Annual Conference of the Australian Agricultural and Resource Economics Society, Fremantle

World Bank (2005) *Environmental Fiscal Reform: What Should be Done and How to Achieve it*, IBRD, Washington, DC

Wunder, S. (2005) 'Payments for ecosystem services: Some nuts and bolts', *CIFOR Occasional Paper*, vol 42, pp1–24

9

Developing Mechanisms for *In Situ* Biodiversity Conservation in Agricultural Landscapes

Unai Pascual and Charles Perrings

Introduction

The most important anthropogenic cause of agrobiodiversity loss is rapid land use and land cover change (LUCC) and the subsequent transformation of habitats (MEA, 2005). In agricultural landscapes LUCC usually takes the form of land development. Most land development at the landscape level stems from the decentralized economic decisions of economic agents, including small-scale farmers, agribusiness and governments at different scales. The ecological causes and effects of such landscape transformations are increasingly well understood and documented, especially with regard to deforestation and desertification in developing regions (Lambin et al, 2001; Perrings and Gadgil, 2003). In agricultural landscapes, one impact of LUCC that is attracting increasing attention is the alteration of the flow of ecosystem services that are mediated by biodiversity (MEA, 2005; Perrings et al, 2006). This has significant implications for biodiversity conservation strategies in agro-ecosystems.

Agrobiodiversity is not a fixed asset that every person experiences similarly. Since it is experienced contextually, it is socially constructed (Rodríguez et al, 2006). There are differences in the way that social groups identify and value biodiversity-based services. Nevertheless, agrobiodiversity change can be seen as an investment/disinvestment decision made in the context of a certain set of preferences, 'value systems', moral strictures, endowments, information, technological possibilities, and social, cultural and institutional conditions. An important starting point for science is therefore to understand (1) how biodiversity supports the production of the ecosystem services; and (2) how those services are valued by different social groups.

From an economic perspective, biodiversity change is most obviously a problem wherever it yields negative net benefits. More generally, it is a problem wherever it is socially inefficient (given social distributional priorities). In most cases, this reflects market failures that are due to the existence of externalities (incomplete property rights) and the public-good nature of conservation. That is, there exists a wedge between individual agents' perceived net benefits from LUCC actions and those realized by the community that is affected by those same actions (Swanson, 1998; Perrings, 2001; MEA, 2005). Part of the problem in understanding the social value of biodiversity change is that while some of the opportunity costs of conservation or forgone benefits from land development are easily identified, there remain important gaps in the understanding of both the on- and off-farm benefits of agrobiodiversity conservation.

In many cases a preservation-centred strategy that involves allocating valuable resources (e.g. land) towards maximum *in situ* biodiversity conservation will not be socially efficient. The cost, in terms of the forgone food and fibre production, of allocating an additional hectare of land for conservation, is often larger than the additional conservation benefits. The 'optimal' intensification debate reflects this fact (Green et al, 2005). Such a debate would be enriched if scientists were able to identify the complex relationships between land management options, biodiversity impacts, changes in ecological services and their values (Perrings et al, 2006).

LUCC and concomitant agrobiodiversity effects depend on the social, economic and institutional conditions that frame economic agents' decisions. In this context, institutions encompass formal rules (e.g. laws, constitutions) and informal constraints (norms of behaviour, self-imposed codes of conduct) that govern land users' behaviour. They can also be referred to as 'rules in use' (North, 1990) as the ones found in markets. In this vein, decentralized decisions regarding the desired level of *in situ* planned agrobiodiversity, for example crop and livestock genetic diversity (Vandermeer and Perfecto, 1995; Jackson et al, 2007) usually depend on conditions in the relevant food, fuel and fibre markets (Smale et al, 2001). Market signals affect farmers' private land use decisions by fixing the private net benefits of their individual actions, given their risk aversion and rate of time preference.

One type of agrobiodiversity that is reasonably well understood is genetic diversity of cultivars and breeds (Smale et al, 2001). Since the social insurance benefits of higher levels of crop genetic diversity are not rewarded in many current markets, farmers have little private incentive to conserve genetic diversity (Perrings, 2001). The most profitable decision is frequently to grow only a few crop varieties, and not to invest in conservation of the varieties that are less 'favoured' by the market.

The problem, in this case, lies both in the public-good nature of conservation, and the fact that there are no markets for off-site ecosystem services that depend on on-farm agrobiodiversity. A good is catalogued as public if it does not exhibit rivalry and excludability characteristics. Biodiversity is non-rival as one individual's use of biodiversity does not affect another individual's use of it, that is, individuals can be equally satisfied simultaneously by the fact that biodiversity is conserved. It is generally non-excludable because it is impossible or very difficult to exclude or prevent someone from benefiting from its conservation. In the case of genetic diversity, farmers who maintain *in situ* crop genetic diversity are essentially conserving a global public good and thus they can be seen as net subsidizers of modern agriculture and food consumers worldwide. However, global institutions are not in place to provide compensation for generating such global benefits. Indeed, one reason for the profitability of modern specialized agriculture is that it is free-riding on those farmers who are investing in such genetic diversity. The net result is that global crop genetic diversity is being rapidly reduced, since the custodians of the global genetic portfolio are uncompensated by current international markets, and there are no corrective policies or mechanisms in place. For other types of agrobiodiversity, for example at the community and landscape level, the situation is even more complex because inventories and functions are so much more difficult to assess.

The fundamental causes of agrobiodiversity loss, therefore, lie in the institutional or meso-economic environment that mediates farmers' decentralized decisions. This chapter discusses such institutional (meso-economic) dimensions of *in situ* agrobiodiversity change in the context of a framework that identifies: (1) the forces at play at the microeconomic (farm economy) and meso-economic (market/institutional) level leading to (dis)investment in biodiversity within agricultural landscapes; and (2) the economic consequences of biodiversity change at the individual and social level. This allows us to discuss mechanisms that can help align the social and private values of biodiversity conservation.

The main focus of this chapter is agrobiodiversity and its effects on the multiple services that agriculture provides to society, especially those related to the provision of foods and fibres within agricultural landscapes. The impacts of agriculture on wild species without apparent agricultural value, their habitats and their contribution to other non-agriculturally related ecosystem services are not emphasized. The scope is purposefully limited, and the chapter is organized as follows: the next section addresses institutional failures at the micro-, meso- and macro-scales. In the following section we discuss the private and social value of agrobiodiversity conservation. The subsequent section then addresses the two main stages in market creation: capture and sharing of conservation benefits. We consider various nascent and potentially fruitful incentive mechanisms that can recreate decentralized markets to foster agrobiodiversity conservation. A final section recapitulates the main points and draws out the implications for the conservation of agrobiodiversity.

The drivers of agrobiodiversity change

Farmers' agrobiodiversity choices reflect a number of factors aside from the market prices, including the social, political and cultural conditions in which they operate. These are generally exogenous to the farmers own decisions (Lambin et al, 2001), but are strongly influenced by policy at the national and international levels. The problem we consider is the interaction between microeconomic (decentralized) farmers' decisions and meso- and macroeconomic/institutional factors.

At the micro-scale, the household, family farm or agribusiness constitutes an institution itself with its own behavioural 'rules' that impinge on LUCC decisions. In the case of farm households, if the internal rules are such that there is intra-household gender discrimination, the species to be conserved may be determined by gender dominance. In many African drylands, for example, women favour planting for fuelwood and men for fruit trees, because it is the women who tend to collect fuelwood, while men control cash income generated by selling fruit in the market. This helps to explain why, even as the sources of fuelwood continue to recede in many African countries, fruit trees are often planted (Dasgupta, 2000). This is an example of institutional failure at the household level.

At the macroeconomic level, institutional or policy failures are often more evident and their effects more far-reaching. Macroeconomic institutions include both national and international policies. Many of these affect the incentives facing individual farmers. One clear example of institutional failure at the macroeconomic level lies in the perverse agricultural production subsidies, tax breaks and price controls that not only make a biodiversity-based agriculture uncompetitive, but that have systematically distorted farm-level decisions in both developed and developing countries for decades (Tilman et al, 2002). At the beginning of the century, subsidies paid to the agricultural sectors of OECD countries averaged over US$324 billion annually (about one-third the global value of agricultural products in 2000) (Pearce, 1999).

Consider the following illustrative examples from Sudan (Barbier, 2000) and Indonesia (Tomich et al, 2001). Barbier (2000) analysed the impact of distortionary macroeconomic price policies affecting the 'gum arabic' (Acacia senegal) agroforestry system in Sudan. It is planted in bush-fallow rotation and intercropping farming systems. The gum produced by the tree is traditionally exported for manufacturing industries. Additionally, gum arabic provides ecological services such as the provision of fodder for livestock, fuelwood and it offers an important regulatory ecological function against desertification, as it serves as a windbreak for dune fixation. Indeed, given the potentially high financial returns to the gum arabic coupled with its important environmental benefits, this land use system seems to be ideal in arid regions. But as Barbier (2000) notes, in recent decades, macroeconomic policies by the Sudanese government, largely based on distortionary (overvalued) exchange rates and export policies, for example high export taxes, have meant that the rate of return to farmers for producing gum arabic has declined relative to its alternative competitive annual cash crops, such as sesame and groundnuts, and even to staple crops such as sorghum and millet. This is a compelling reason for farmers to disinvest in gum arabic stands in agroforests.

Tomich et al (2001) report that research into rubber agroforestry systems shows that extensively managed agroforests provide greater biodiversity benefits than intensive rubber tree plantations, but that at the current real producer price of rubber, relative to the minimum wage rate, returns to farm labour are 70 per cent higher in intensive plantation systems than agroforestry. Once distortionary prices, including tax and subsides for rubber production, are eliminated, however, labour returns to rubber production in extensive agroforestry systems outweigh its alternative plantation returns by 30 per cent.

Other important macro-level institutions that affect both micro- and meso-economic institutional contexts include the intergovernmental organizations (World Bank, International Monetary Fund, United Nations Development Programme) and international agreements (the General Agreement on Tariffs and Trade, the Sanitary and Phytosanitary Agreement and the International Plant Protection Convention). In some cases, they affect agrobiodiversity by limiting the choice of management strategy or technology used by farmers. In others, they work by encouraging the diffusion of new technologies or by dispersing new crop varieties, bio-control agents, pests and pathogens (Perrings, 2005). As in the case of direct subsidies, these indirect influences on farmers' decisions change the private returns on farm investments, often in ways that discourage agrobiodiversity conservation. Amongst other effects of the incentives offered directly and indirectly by such institutions are the loss of forest and wetland habitat, the devegetation of watersheds, the loss of soil and aquatic biodiversity through the application of pesticides, nitrogen and phosphorous, the depletion of many beneficial pollinators and pest predators (Scherr and McNeely, 2008), and the introduction of invasive species (Mooney et al, 2005).

The solution is to 'fix' these incentives – to realign the mismatch between the private interests of farmers and those of society at large – although markets do not operate in a vacuum. Their operation relies on other supporting institutions including those that shape the regulatory environment. Hence, correcting for market failures is a necessary but not sufficient condition for readdressing agrobiodiversity loss. Investing in adequate (effective, stable and resilient) institutions that allow markets to operate is also necessary to create favourable conditions that can lead farmers to further invest in biodiversity conservation in a decentralized and voluntary fashion.

An additional problem is that biodiversity is a public good, and as with other public goods, will be underprovided if left to the market. Even if relative prices were fixed to reflect the social opportunity cost of biodiversity, there would still be an incentive to free-ride on the conservation efforts of others. Nevertheless, it is clear that correcting many of the perverse incentives facing farmers requires that the policy maker understands the value of agrobiodiversity. It is important, therefore, to link the process of valuation with the creation of new effective and efficient institutions for conservation. At the same time, it is important that the valuation of biodiversity is linked to delivery of appropriate incentives to farmers. For example, the benefits to peasant households from conserving off-farm agrobiodiversity in forest margins needs to cover the costs in terms of forgone timber extraction revenues or the income that could accrue by converting such forest land to agricultural production for food security.

Economic valuation and the development of markets for biodiversity are potentially effective providing that they achieve (1) *demonstration*; (2) *capture*; and (3) *sharing* of biodiversity benefits especially taking into account the communities that face the opportunity costs of conservation (OECD, 2005). Demonstration refers to the identification and measurement of biodiversity values as the benefits from conserving it may not always be evident. It is the exercise of identifying the valuation pathways. This is a non-trivial task and much research is still needed (Opschoor, 1999; Jackson et al, 2007).

Capture, in turn, is the process of appropriating the demonstrated and measured biodiversity values in order to provide incentives for its conservation. This is achieved by regulations and markets to allow for such values to be made explicit and channelled from the beneficiaries (society as demander) to those who bear the cost of conservation (farmers as suppliers). For example, a niche market for 'biodiversity-friendly' products would channel the revenues to those farmers that certify the production of such 'green' outputs in order to compensate them for the forgone higher earnings from a privately more rewarding alternative land use. The market, in this case, may internalize the biodiversity values through price premiums creating positive incentives towards biodiversity conservation decisions.

Lastly, effectiveness ultimately depends on whether the benefits of the provision of the public good (conservation of biodiversity) are distributed to those who ultimately bear the costs of conservation. Following the above example, the price premium of the certified biodiversity-friendly products would need to be channelled back to the producers. This is not a trivial task, as often a disproportionate part of the price premium can be off-channelled to traders and middlemen (Bacon, 2005). At a global level, another example is that of the *free-prior consent* and *benefit sharing agreement* clauses imposed by the UN Convention of Biological Diversity with regard to bioprospection endeavours regarding plant genetic resources (ten Kate and Laird, 1999). This necessitates effectively asserting the property of bio-resources and genetic resources in particular to the source country (c.f. United Nations Convention on Biological Diversity (UNCBD) Article 15: Access to Genetic Resources).

Understanding the social value of agrobiodiversity

To demonstrate the value of agrobiodiversity, science can assist in (1) assessing the functional role of species in their crop- and non-crop habitats; (2) identifying the biotic and abiotic components of agro-ecosystem structures that support the provision of ecological services at the landscape level; and (3) assessing the contribution of such ecological functions to human well-being. The challenge is to translate such ecological interdependencies into tangible ecological services that can be valued from an anthropocentric perspective (Perrings et al, 2006). Here we address some of these complex issues by providing a conceptual framework of the links between agrobiodiversity as a stock (S), the provision of flows of ecosystem services (F) and the 'total economic value' (V) that this generates to society.

Figure 9.1 illustrates such linkages in stylized way. It also shows the links between values and well-being at both individual and social levels. Since existing markets fail to align the social and private values of agrobiodiversity through LUCC, policies are needed to correct for such market failure. A feedback loop exists between policies, LUCC and agrobiodiversity at the landscape level. The dotted arrows represent links that are difficult to appreciate and that need to be investigated further.

The framework in Figure 9.1 illustrates the complex links between biodiversity levels (stocks, S), flows of ecological services (F) and economic values (V) in agricultural landscapes leading to LUCC and policies that aim at aligning the private and social values of agrobiodiversity. The ecological system governing the interaction between on- and off-farm biodiversity stocks within agricultural landscapes provides

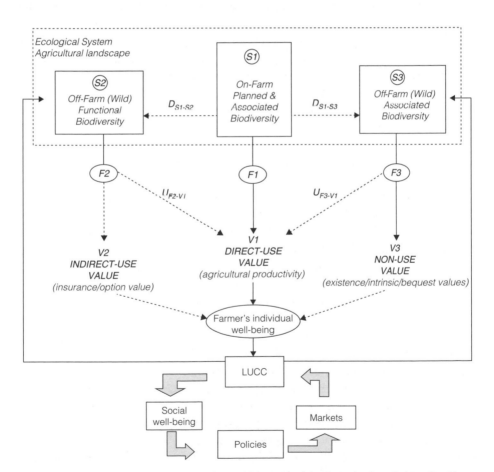

Figure 9.1 A framework of the linkages between biodiversity levels (stocks, S), flows of ecological services (F) and economic values (V) in agricultural landscapes

the flow of ecological services that benefits individual land users and society at large. Individual land users compare the directly perceived benefits of conservation and the opportunity costs in order to decide about their privately (decentralized) optimal land use and the level of (dis)investment in biodiversity. This in turn affects social well-being and policies are sought to change such perceived net benefits.

The direct 'instrumental value' of agrobiodiversity

Managed on-farm biodiversity can be represented as a stock or economic asset (S1). The asset represents the mix of species and communities that supply a flow of ecological services on-farm (F1) that can directly benefit farmers by maintaining or enhancing agricultural productivity. This is achieved, for example, by the control of on-farm *destructive biota*, such as weeds, insect pests and microbial pathogens (Swift and Anderson, 1993).

When on-farm biodiversity supports the productivity of crops by enhancing yields or substituting for the use of purchased capital inputs, such as pesticides, such biodiversity has an instrumental or 'use-value' for farmers (V1). Usually, V1 is more apparent and relatively more important in small-scale farming in resource-poor areas where access to capital inputs (e.g. irrigation and agrochemicals) is constrained, and where biodiversity is often managed to regulate pests and diseases, soil formation and nutrient recycling (Altieri, 1999). An example is that of the meso-American shifting cultivation 'milpa' system in which maize/squash/bean polycultures are more stable than monocultures (Altieri, 1999). This is reflected in the S1~F1~V1 link in Figure 9.1. If farmers are able to conserve such biodiversity, and if this permits them to stabilize and enhance agricultural income (V1), then this strategy can be viewed as sustainable (Conway, 1993).

Different crop mixes at the plot level and the diversity of uncoordinated individual agricultural management strategies creates a mosaic of agrobiodiversity at the landscape level. In this process, there are effects of changes in on-farm planned biodiversity (S1) on off-farm functional diversity (S2) at the landscape level. For example, the amalgamation of agricultural fields tend to produce homogeneous farmed landscapes leaving only a fragmented non-crop habitat that affects both the off-farm functional (S2) and associated (S3) diversity (Bélanger and Grenier, 2002; Benton et al, 2002; Tscharntke et al, 2005). We refer to this as a *downward* (or *forward*) biodiversity effect that links decentralized farmers' decisions and landscape level agrobiodiversity. This relationship is depicted in Figure 9.1 with the dotted arrows D_{S1-S2} and by D_{S1-S3}. The ecological-economic problem is to identify the mosaic of connected habitats that best supports both farm production (F1) and its value to farmers (V1) and the supply of off-farm ecosystem services (F2 & F3) that support off-farm values (V2 & V3).

There are also *upstream* (or *backward*) biodiversity effects. There is increasing evidence of the positive effect of off-farm biodiversity on on-farm productivity. Often this is associated with off-farm landscape level generalist species (S2) that provide pollination and biological control services against pests and invasive species. This is depicted by the dotted arrow U_{F2-V1}. In this case, the flow of ecological services provided by off-farm functional species (S2) generates an indirect use value to farmers – it can provide financial savings to farmers. For example, Kremen et al (2002) show that more intensive agricultural land management relative to less intensive systems, such as organic farming, increases the cost of pollination to farmers. In another study, Ricketts et al (2004) estimate the economic cost of the reduction of pollination services originating from off-farm forest habitats to coffee production in a Costa Rican farm to be in the order of US$60,000/year. This would be an approximate figure as neither of these studies considers the increased income generated by converting the neighbouring forest habitat to agriculture. Similarly, the loss of off-farm pollinators and pest predators increases the cost to farmers of pest and disease control (Symondson et al, 2002). At the same time, habitat fragmentation increases the risk of invasion by unwanted destructive off-farm species at the landscape level (Östman et al, 2003; Perrings, 2005).

Finally, we should note that transboundary landscape effects also affect upstream linkages (depicted by the dotted arrow U_{F3-V1}). Off-farm biodiversity at regional and even global scales can affect the long-run productivity of local agricultural systems. One well-known example is the relationship between the diversity of insectivorous birds, some of which migrate from tropical forests in Latin America to Canadian boreal forests, and which help to regulate the productivity of forest stands by controlling the destructive population of spruce budworms (*Choristoneura fumiferana*) (Holling, 1988).

The indirect use value of agrobiodiversity: The insurance hypothesis

While economists have long been aware that biodiversity has an 'indirect' value through the provision of regulating ecosystem services (Barbier, 1989), there have been few attempts to estimate this value for particular systems. Within the present framework, possibly the most important value of off-farm functional diversity (S2) stems from its role as an insurance mechanism (F2) (Folke et al, 1996; Loreau et al, 2002; Baumgärtner, 2007).

Ecologists argue that over small scales (e.g. the crop-field level) an increase in on-farm species richness and the diversity of overlapping functional groups of species enhances the level of functional diversity, which, in turn, increases ecological stability (Tilman et al, 1996) and resilience (Holling, 1988, 1996). In this sense, resilience refers to the size of perturbation that is required to transform a system from one state to a different state, and is frequently increasing in the number of species that are apparently 'redundant' under one set of environmental conditions, but that perform important functions under different environmental conditions (Holling, 1988; Peterson et al, 1998). Further, following Carpenter et al (2001), resilience of an adaptative agro-ecosystem would be determined primarily by: (1) the amount of disturbance that the system can absorb and still remain within the same state or domain of attraction; (2) the degree to which the system is capable of self-organization, *versus* the lack of organization, or organization forced by external factors; and (3) the degree to which the system can build and increase the capacity for learning and adaptation.

For instance, in biodiversity-poor intensive agricultural systems that depend on increasing use of artificial inputs, the agricultural system can be locked into a narrow range of agricultural technologies. At one level this can make the system more stable in the sense that there is less variation in the producer's economic activities following minor perturbations, but, conversely, it may also reduce the capacity of that system to absorb greater environmental or economic shocks, such as sudden and unexpected commodity price changes. By eliminating options towards productive diversification, a reduction in agrobiodiversity may also lock farmers into obsolete agricultural technologies (Perrings, 1998).

It follows that maintaining a wider portfolio of technological and natural resource-based options in agricultural systems is likely to maintain or enhance the capacity to respond to short-run shocks and stresses in constructive and creative ways. Various recent studies have analysed the contribution of crop diversity to the mean and variance of agricultural yields and farm income (Smale et al, 1998; Widawsky and Rozelle, 1998; Schläpfer et al, 2002; Di Falco and Perrings, 2003, 2005; Birol et al, 2006). One main conjecture is that risk averse farmers use crop diversity in order to hedge their production and income risks, especially when affected by changing market conditions. Hence, off-farm biodiversity through its insurance mechanism (F2) can provide an important insurance value to farmers (F2-V2) and productivity enhancing services (this is a *backward* linkage, U_{F2-V1}). To the individual farmer, however, the insurance effect may not generally be enough to justify conservation when there is ample access to improved artificial capital inputs, for example fertilizers, improved seeds, etc. The insurance value is thus better perceived and exploited in agricultural landscapes that are mainly associated with agroforestry and agroecological production systems. In addition, the insurance value can be associated with the idea of 'option value', reflected in the important efforts to maintain *ex-situ* genetic resource conservation (Jackson et al, 2007).

The infrastructure value of agrobiodiversity

Similarly, while there has been recognition of the value of biodiversity in underpinning ecosystem functioning and processes, which is sometimes referred to as 'primary' (Turner and Pearce, 1993), 'infrastructure' (Costanza et al, 1997) or 'contributory' (Norton, 1986) value, there have been few attempts to estimate this. This is partly due to the difficulty of capturing the interaction between species, and more generally the functional links between on- and off-farm biodiversity.

Economists first modelled this by assigning species the status of 'intermediate inputs' (Crocker and Tschirhart, 1992) due to their role in supporting more directly other productivity-enhancing species. The same idea can be generalized to say that species have value deriving from their indirect role in the production of valuable goods and services that is conditional on the state of the environment. So, for example, the derived value of members of a functional group of species, each of which performs differently in different environmental conditions, will vary with those conditions. Species that appear to be redundant in some conditions, will still have value depending on the likelihood that the conditions in which they do have value will occur in the future (Loreau et al, 2002). This translates easily into the idea that the cost of species deletion becomes the cost of the alternative ways of securing the same productivity outcome, as long as those species contribute to the productivity of the agricultural ecosystem.

Lastly, it should also be pointed out that besides biodiversity's effect on productivity (F1) and stability/resilience (F2), associated off-farm biodiversity (S3) can also provide other benefits to society, for example cultural and recreational (F3). For instance, in industrialized countries where natural habitats are scarce, there are important landscape values of farmland (V3), that typically consist of the benefits derived from the scenic beauty generated by a rural landscape such as open fields, orchards and herds of livestock grazing in green meadows (OECD, 1993; Cobb et al, 1999). The implication of the realization of such values in the EU, for example, has spurred renewed emphasis on the role of multifunctional agriculture to secure such recreational and non-instrumental social values and has provided impetus for the design and implementation of novel agri-environmental policies (Hodge, 2000).

From demonstration to capturing and sharing the benefits of agrobiodiversity conservation

There are compelling reasons to devise and implement incentive mechanisms for agrobiodiversity conservation. Incentives can be categorized into two main groups: (1) moral suasion, regulation and planning, for example by preventing specific land management practices or by designating conservation zones within agricultural landscapes, known as agroecological 'no take' zones resembling nature reserves and parks; and (2) market creation for agrobiodiversity conservation given the power of decentralized land use decisions.

Market creation stems from a simple but powerful idea, that is that markets can be devised to signal the opportunity cost to local land users of agricultural practices that affect agrobiodiversity either positively or negatively. Ideally, such incentives need to address the above mentioned *forward* and *backward* agrobiodiversity linkages and, thus, work at the landscape level. But this implies that such incentives may affect the livelihoods of large numbers of farmers. This adds a further layer of responsibility to public agencies to be aware of the distributional implications of alternative incentive measures.

Markets can take different forms. One is for interested 'buyers' such as firms and NGOs to purchase land use rights or permits. For instance once a logging permit is obtained, a conservation NGO may decide not to extract timber but instead to conserve the land for its biodiversity. More specifically, within agricultural landscapes 'use rights' include rights of access to particular biological resources, for example game, fish and non timber forest products, or other goods and services that may be associated with biodiversity, such as those associated with organic agricultural products.

Land use rights are currently being extended to enable voluntary contractual arrangements between farmers and off-farm users of ecosystem services that are affected by actual farm management. Here we discuss the potential of using markets in conjunction with land use rights for agrobiodiversity conservation at the landscape level focusing on various relatively nascent mechanisms that allow the capture and distribution of conservation values: (1) 'payments/rewards for environmental services', P(R)ES; (2) direct compensation payments (DCP); (3) transferable development rights (TDRs); and (4) auction contracts for conservation (ACCs).

Payments/rewards for environmental services

P(R)ES are voluntary transactions, not necessarily of a financial nature, in the form of compensation flows for a well-defined environmental service (ES), or land use likely to secure it. The notion of 'rewards' is used to acknowledge that transactions from beneficiaries to providers may not need to be based on a financial flow. It can also involve in-kind transactions that may include a myriad of valuable goods and services from the beneficiaries point of view, which can take intangible forms in diverse situations, such as knowledge transfer. P(R)ES is paid/rewarded by the beneficiaries and shared by the providers of the ES after eventually securing such compensation. The latter conditionality element frames such schemes under the *'Provider Gets Principle'* (Hodge, 2000).

P(R)ES are often designed to address problems related to the decline in some environmental services, such as the provision of water, soil conservation and carbon sequestration by upland farmers who manage forest lands in upper watersheds. In essence, such compensations are intended to internalize the positive externalities generated by upland farmers who can maintain the flow of valuable services that benefit lowland farmers or urban dwellers. However, a key obstacle in the successful implementation of P(R)ES arises at the value 'demonstration' stage, especially due to the scientific uncertainties underpinning the linkages between alternative land uses and the provision of the targeted environmental services.

Regarding the effectiveness of the capture and sharing of the benefits, recent evidence identifies various necessary conditions, including the need: (1) to clarify the level of excludability and rivalry of such ES by beneficiaries and providers; (2) of a sufficient demand or aggregate the willingness to pay for such services by the potential beneficiaries; (3) to delineate and enforce property rights surrounding land use and ES; and (4) of investments in social capital to foster collective action and cohesion between the providers and beneficiaries of ES (Pagiola et al, 2004; Rosa et al, 2004; Tomich et al, 2004; van Noordwijk et al, 2005; Wunder, 2005). Note that property rights regimes in natural resource management comprise a structure of rights to resources, rules under which those rights are exercised, and duties bound by both those who possess the right(s) and those who do not. As Bromley (1992, p2) puts it, '[p]roperty *is not* an object but rather is a social relation that defines the property holder with respect to something of value ... against all others'. In this context, Costa Rica is one of the few examples where an elaborate, nationwide PES programme is in place. Under this programme only farmers with property rights to land can be paid for the environmental conservation they provide (Pagiola, 2002).

A recent illustrative example of the potential effectiveness and flexibility of P(R)ES programmes is that of the RUPES approach: *Rewarding Upland Poor for Environmental Services*. RUPES is a partnership of the International Fund for Agricultural Development (IFAD), the World Agroforestry Centre (ICRAF) and a partnership of local, national and international partners.[1] RUPES aims to conserve environmental services at the global and local levels while at the same time support the livelihoods of the upland poor in Asia. So far, the main focus has been on Nepal, the Philippines and Indonesia and the environmental services mostly include water flow and quality from watersheds, biodiversity protection and carbon sequestration. Regarding the demonstration, capture and sharing of benefits, the preliminary learning stock from the ongoing various RUPES experiences, includes the following (van Noordwijk et al, 2005):

(i) *Demonstrating values* through scientific evidence of the link between ES and benefits under various land practices: In one RUPES site, Lake Singkarak in Sumatra, Indonesia, a major conclusion from an hydrological assessment conducted by ICRAF has been that reforesting the watershed may not significantly change the water inflows into the lake, which is originally what the local hydro-electrical company (the local ES buyer) is most interested in. This has implied questioning the (*a priori*) rationale for rewarding reforestation initiatives. Instead, the appraisal has identified water quality in the lake and the multiple sources of pollution as more important issues that would benefit both the hydro-electrical company and the local communities within the watershed.

(ii) *Capturing benefits* by identifying the potential beneficiaries/buyers: The RUPES experience is showing that localized buyers are more easily identifiable for effective partnership than regional or even global buyers. This implies that besides water conservation services, which may be more tangible for potential local buyers such as hydropower companies, biodiversity conservation and/or carbon sequestration pose more challenges given the difficulty to quantify the values that may justify a payment/reward for their sustained provision. In addition, identifying the providers of such services is also more elusive, due to their global public nature.

(iii)   *Sharing* benefits by creating an enabling environment for sustaining the ES agreements by identifying potential institutional constraints: In this case, RUPES acknowledges that both property rights, especially when *de facto* (non *de jure*) rights for resource control are prevalent, and social capital, which helps to foster collective action at the local community level, are the two foremost important enabling factors.

Direct compensation payments (DCP)

A variant of P(R)ES, is the approach based on *direct compensation payments* (DCP) for 'takings' of landowners' private land out of production and into conservation (Swart, 2003). While theoretically sound in principle, there are important issues to be considered. First, similar to other incentive mechanisms, the identification of the level of the efficient compensation payments to landowners requires the demonstration of an objective measure of its conservation value on both biological and economic grounds. Second, the change in decentralized behaviour needs to be sustained into the future, which requires longer-term political commitment. Third, there is a more subtle but more problematic issue at play. It involves the existence of asymmetric information between landowners and the compensating government agency. This informational problem can create perverse incentives that reduce the effectiveness of the compensation mechanism (Innes et al, 1998). For instance, if landowners expect a compensation payment which is lower than the present value of the benefit stream arising from developing the landholding, they have a motive to develop their holdings in the 'first period', that is before being compensated in a subsequent period. This would have potentially negative effects on biodiversity conservation. But from the landowners' viewpoint, it reduces the risk of losing the land through the government's 'takings' for conservation purposes.

Furthermore, even when the exact compensation is foreseen by landowners, that is, the compensation coincides with the forgone expected agricultural revenues, they may still have the incentive to develop their land further by over-investing, for example added intensification, before any compensation is offered. This is because the market value of their property may increase due to such investments and such market value is what the government is guaranteeing as full compensation.

Thus, landowners' strategic behaviour exploiting existing information asymmetries, can seriously undermine the effectiveness of DCP mechanisms. One solution would be to offer relatively high (more than full) compensation to owners of underdeveloped (and hence biodiversity richer) land property compared to over-developed property owners as this counters the perverse intensification strategy through overinvestment. However, as Innes et al (1998) note, this strategy could significantly increase the public implementation bill, thus undermining its attractiveness from a cost-efficiency perspective.

Transferable development rights (TDRs)

An interesting and cost-effective way to resolve the perverse incentives arising from DCPs is the use of *transferable (land) development rights* (TDRs). TDRs extend the longstanding 'agro-ecological zoning' schemes, which aim to direct development to areas of high productivity potential and to restrict agricultural land use in ecologically significant and sensitive areas. However, such zoning programmes do not allow for any substitutability between plots in meeting overall conservation goals. By providing a market-like alternative to the DCPs, flexibility in achieving conservation goals can be introduced. In this vein, the main advantage of a TDR is that it can, in principle, encourage conservation on lands with low agricultural opportunity costs, while providing appropriate incentives to the affected landholders (Panayotou, 1994; Chomitz, 1999).

In contrast to DCP, each landowner is issued tradable development permits by the government agency at an initial period. Subsequently, landowners hold the right to either develop/intensify their landholding. However, to develop that fraction of land a landowner needs to either use one of the development permits (s)he holds or buy it from other landowners, who upon selling it can no longer develop their land fraction and instead must give it up for conservation. In this case, the government can share the cost of the 'takings', that is compulsory government land acquisition, with the landowners themselves.

Two main types of TDR programmes exist at the landscape level: the single and dual zoning programme. The former is similar to permit systems such as those used in transferable fishing quotas or pollution control. After the initial allocation of quotas, anyone within the programme area may buy or sell the permits. An application of this type of such TDRs programme has been used to control soil degradation through erosion in the Lake Tahoe Basin (Johnston and Madison, 1997). The dual zone system instead explicitly designates both (permit) sending and receiving areas. This allows, for example, for new land use restrictions to be imposed on the sending zone that is more ecologically sensitive, upon obtaining additional information about its higher conservation value and assigning TDRs to compensate for such additional restrictions. Usually, tight restrictions are also imposed on the receiving zone so as to increase the demand for TDRs (Chomitz, 1999).

One of the forerunners of the TDR mechanism is Brazil. While some initiatives have been proposed, the implementation is still under discussion. The basic idea is to give the opportunity for Brazilian agricultural land owners not complying with the National Forest Code (Law number 4771 approved on 15 September 1965) to buy forest reserves in other areas, normally in close proximity to his/her property. However, a fully operational market for forest reserves is still to be implemented. Two examples are the National Provisionary Measure (Medida Provisória, Number 21666-67, approved on 24 August 2001), which amends the Forest Code and in the State of Sao Paulo (State Decree number 50889, approved on 16 June 2006).

For agrobiodiversity conservation, the effectiveness of the TDR scheme relies on whether the objective is to conserve certain habitats within the landscape due to having unique biodiversity characteristics, or if larger tracks of contiguous habitats are necessary for off-farm biodiversity. When the landscape is highly homogeneous, and the goal is to conserve a specified 'amount' of habitat within the landscape, regardless of its configuration, a single zone system may be more appropriate.

While there is a theoretically attractive incentive mechanism, few rural TDR programmes exist. This is possibly due to the political barriers. In fact, as with any tradable permit scheme, the initial allocation of permits is a sensitive issue that may have large distributional consequences (Chomitz, 1999). In addition, transaction costs also need to be taken into account as setting up TDRs may involve substantial administrative and legal (monitoring and enforcement) costs.

Auction contracts for conservation (ACC)

One other way to achieve a desired level of supply of agrobiodiversity conservation at the landscape level by private landowners is by applying a competitive bidding or auction mechanism. An auction is a quasi-market institution with an interesting feature, that is, it has a 'cost revealing' advantage compared to P(R)ES and DCP and can, in principle, be incorporated into a TDR system. In fact, the cost-revelation feature provides an edge to generate important cost savings to governments. This is especially so when significant information asymmetry between farmers and conservation agencies exist regarding (1) the real opportunity cost of conservation; and (2) the ecological significance of the natural assets existing in farmlands. While the former is often better known by farmers themselves, the latter is normally better known by environmental experts (Latacz-Lohmann and Van der Hamsvoort, 1997). As discussed above, such information asymmetries become a potent reason for missing agrobiodiversity conservation markets. The idea is to use auctions to reveal the hidden information needed to recreate voluntary conservation contracts between landholders and the government.

In essence, landholders submit bids to win conservation contracts from the government. But, while the latter prefers low bids, landowners need to submit bids that at least cover the opportunity cost of carrying out conservation activities on their farms. The problem is that information of such opportunity costs are often better known by farmers than by the government and they are also likely to be farmer-specific.

Stoneham et al (2008) provides a recent small-scale pilot case study of an auctioning system for biodiversity conservation contracts in Victoria, Australia, known as *BushTender*. The ACC involved 98 farmers from which 75 per cent obtained government contracts to conserve remnant vegetation on their farms, after all farmers submitted sealed bids associated with their nominated conservation action plans. The selection of the farmers who won the contract was based on ranking the relative cost-effectiveness of each proposed contract. This involved weighting each private bid against the associated potential ecological impacts at the landscape level. Given a public budget of $400,000, contracts with bids that averaged about $4600 were allocated and specified in management agreements over a 3-year period. In total the contracts covered 3160ha of habitat on private land.

Stoneham et al (2008) have estimated that the *BushTender* mechanism has provided 75 per cent more biodiversity conservation compared to a fixed-price payment scheme (or DCP). In addition, they contend that given the relatively few enforcement costs in their pilot study, this ACC has interesting cost-effective properties. The pilot case study shows that it is possible to recreate the supply side of a market for agrobiodiversity conservation.

All P(R)ES, DCP, TDPs and ACC share an important characteristic for successful market creation, and that depends on the provision of good and accurate information at the demonstration, capture and sharing stages. If it is not possible, or it is very costly, to convey clear and credible information about the nature of the services derived from biodiversity, then the perception by the demanders as to how much they are willing to pay for such services would be distorted. Moreover, it would be naive to champion market creation for biodiversity conservation if other supporting institutions are lacking. Furthermore, in general, if markets for agrobiodiversity are recreated without proper institutional and regulatory back-up, then the social costs of such policies may well outweigh the benefits from conservation (Barrett and Lybbert, 2000).

In a second-best world where information is elusive, most policy initiatives pragmatically focus on ensuring that institutions are developed so as to keep future options open (Tomich et al, 2004). In fact, most conservation policies are aimed at developing flexible and open institutions that can mitigate the negative effects of intensification in agro-ecosystems, without foreclosing future (de)intensification options.

Conclusions

In this chapter we have discussed the institutional issues involved in the creation of market-like mechanisms for agrobiodiversity conservation. Since the causes of farmers' decisions to 'disinvest' in agrobiodiversity as an asset lie in the incentives offered by current markets and other institutions, the solution lies in corrective institutional design. We interpret changes in agrobiodiversity as the product of explicit or implicit decentralized farm-level decisions whose effects include both farm and landscape level changes in a range of ecosystem services. The solution is to develop mechanisms that provide a different set of incentives.

We close with two observations. The first is that the importance of interdisciplinary research on biodiversity in both traditional and modern agro-ecosystems is recognized as a prerequisite for the development of more effective agrobiodiversity conservation regimes (Jackson et al, 2005; Perrings et al, 2006). In order to evaluate the social consequences of agricultural practices that cause the local extirpation of species, the fragmentation of habitats or the change in the relative abundance of species, we need to better understand three interconnected aspects: (1) the role of biodiversity in agro-ecosystem functioning and processes; (2) the way that changes in functioning and processes affect ecosystem services; and (3) the impact of changes in services on the production of goods and services that are directly valued by people on- and off-agricultural landscapes.

The sustainability of agricultural landscapes may involve a continuum of existing farm management systems from modern, intensive, mechanized, high-input, high-output systems at one end to traditional, extensive, labour-intensive, low-input, low-output systems at the other. Since the unit of analysis is the landscape, it may even be possible that an effective strategy is to have an extreme combination of highly intensive agriculture combined with low intensively managed areas (Green et al, 2005; Dorrough et al, 2007). Since the effects of such strategy can be different in landscapes that still contain wilderness areas, such in tropical forest margins, and in already ecologically impoverished agro-ecosystems, further collaborative research between ecologists and economists is identified as a high priority. In addition, often the alternative to intensification frequently involves encroachment on ever more marginal land and the destruction and fragmentation of ever more scarce habitat. But intensification that ignores the costs of a change in the mix of species in the system may be even more harmful. The point is, though, that this is an empirical question and that the research needed to identify the optimal mosaic has yet to be done. Alongside this point of view is the ongoing effort to advocate in favour of a biodiversity-based agriculture that can be managed in a way that can still produce high yields.

The second observation is that in a sector where the impact on biodiversity is in the hands of billions of independent landholders, management of agrobiodiversity by direct centralized control is not an option. What is important is that independent decision makers take into account the true social costs and benefits of their actions. For example, farmers who maintain production of drought or disease resistant crops or livestock confer social benefits (in terms of averting expenditures on famine relief) that are seldom reflected in the prices they receive. Whether this implies taxation of the high-risk components or subsidy of the low-risk components depends on local circumstances and the international trading regime. In other words, the effectiveness of alternative mechanisms for changing farmers' decisions is also an empirical question. While it may be possible to identify the social opportunity cost of alternative farm management strategies, the best method for inducing socially optimal behaviour depends on understanding not just the responsiveness of farmers and consumers, that is the relevant elasticities, but also the role of the social, cultural and institutional environment.

As in the EU, in many parts of the world, perverse subsidies are being morphed into direct compensation payments to providers of the non-marketed agrobiodiversity services or used to convert the overhead costs of setting up direct (e.g. DCP) or/and indirect incentive schemes (e.g. P(R)ES, TDR and ACC). While there is considerable advantage in removing the perverse incentive effects of historic subsidies, few of the current agricultural reforms are based on a serious valuation of the social opportunity cost of agrobiodiversity loss, and fewer still involve an appraisal of the allocative effects of the new payment schemes. Sensible design of market-like mechanisms for agrobiodiversity conservation requires both.

Acknowledgements

We would like to thank Kamal Bawa, George Brown, Louise Jackson, Danilo Igliori, Andreas Kontoleon, Esti Orruño, Per Stromber, Tom Tomich and Meine van Noordwijk for useful comments and suggestions to previous drafts of this chapter. We also extend out thanks to two anonymous referees.

Note

1. Some of the insights reflected here come from personal communication with Meine van Noordwijk, Tom Tomich and ICRAF personnel involved in RUPES programme in Sumatra, Indonesia.

References

Altieri, M. A. (1999) 'The ecological role of biodiversity in agroecosystems', *Agriculture Ecosystems and Environment*, vol 74, pp19–31

Bacon, C. (2005) 'Confronting the coffee crisis: Can fair trade, organic and specialty coffees reduce small-scale farmer vulnerability in Northern Nicaragua?', *World Development*, vol 33, pp497–511

Barbier, E. B. (1989) *The Economic Value of Ecosystems*, 1-Tropical Wetlands. Gatekeeper No LEEC 89-02. London Environmental Economics Centre (LEEC), London

Barbier, E. B. (2000) 'The economic linkages between rural poverty and land degradation: Some evidence from Africa', *Agriculture Ecosystems and Environment*, vol 82, pp355–370

Barrett, C. B. and Lybbert, T. J. (2000) 'Is bioprospecting a viable strategy for conserving tropical ecosystems?', *Ecological Economics*, vol 34, pp293–300

Baumgärtner, S. (2007) 'The insurance value of biodiversity in the provision of ecosystem services', *Natural Resource Modelling*, vol 20, no 1, pp86–127

Bélanger, L. and Grenier, M. (2002) 'Fragmentation increased along a gradient from traditional dairy agriculture to more intensive cash crop agriculture', *Landscape Ecology*, vol 17, pp495–507

Benton, T. G., Bryant, D. M., Cole, L., Crick, H. Q. P. (2002) 'Linking agricultural practice to insect and bird populations: A historical study over three decades', *Journal of Applied Ecology*, vol 39, pp673–687

Birol, E., Smale, M., Gyovai, Á. (2006) 'Using a choice experiment to estimate farmers' valuation of agricultural biodiversity on Hungarian small farms', *Environment and Resource Economics*, vol 34, no 4, pp439–469

Bromley, D. (1992) 'The commons, common property and environmental policy', *Journal of Environmental and Resource Economics*, vol 2, no 1, pp1–17

Carpenter, S., Walker, B., Anderies, J., Abel, N. (2001) 'From metaphor to measurement: Resilience of what to what?', *Ecosystems*, vol 4, pp765–781

Chomitz, K. E. (1999) 'Transferable development rights and forest protection: An exploratory analysis', paper prepared for the Workshop on Market-Based Instruments for Environmental Protection. July 1999. John F. Kennedy School of Government, Harvard University

Clark, C. W. (1990) *Mathematical Bioeconomics*, Wiley, New York

Cobb, D., Dolman, P., O'Riordan, T. (1999) 'Interpretations of sustainable agriculture in the UK', *Programme Human Geography*, vol 23, pp209–235

Conway, G. R. (1993) 'Sustainable agriculture: The trade-offs with productivity, stability and equitability', in E. B. Barbier (ed.), *Economics and Ecology: New Frontiers and Sustainable Development*, Chapman and Hall, London, pp45–65

Costanza, R., d'Arge, R., de Groot, R., Farber, S., Grasso, M., Hannon, B., Limburg, K., Naeem, S., O'Neill, R. V., Paruelo, J., Raskin, R. G., Sutton, P., van den Belt, M. (1997) 'The value of the world's ecosystem services and natural capital', *Nature*, vol 387, pp253–260

Crocker, T. D. and Tschirhart, J. (1992) 'Ecosystems, externalities, and economics', *Environment and Resource Economics*, vol 2, pp551–567

Dasgupta, P. (2000) 'Entry on valuing biodiversity', in S. Levin, G. C. Daily, J. Lubchenco, D. Tilman (eds), *Encyclopedia of Biodiversity*, Academic Press, London

Di Falco, S. and Perrings, C. (2003) 'Crop genetic diversity, productivity and stability of agroecosystems. A theoretical and empirical investigation', *Scottish Journal of Political Economy*, vol 50, pp207–216

Di Falco, S. and Perrings, C. (2005) 'Crop biodiversity, risk management and the implications of agricultural assistance', *Ecological Economics*, vol 55, pp459–466

Dorrough, J., Moll, J., Crosthwaite, J. (2007) 'Can intensification of temperate Australian livestock production systems save land for native biodiversity?', *Agriculture, Ecosystems and Environment*, vol 121, no 3, pp222–232

Folke, C., Holling, C. S., Perrings, C. (1996) 'Biological diversity, ecosystems and the human scale', *Ecological Applications*, vol 6, pp1018–1024

Green, R. E., Cornell, S. J., Scharlemann, P. W., Balmford, A. (2005) 'Farming and the fate of wild nature', *Science*, vol 307, pp550–555

Hodge, I. (2000) 'Agri-environmental relationships and the choice of policy mechanism', *World Economy*, vol 23, pp257–273

Holling, C. S. (1988) 'Temperate forest insect outbreaks, tropical deforestation and migratory birds', *Memoirs of the Entomological Society of Canada*, vol 146, pp21–32

Holling, C. S. (1996) 'Engineering resilience versus ecological resilience', in P. Schulze (ed.), *Engineering Within Ecological Constraints*, National Academy, Washington, DC, pp31–44

Innes, R., Polasky, S., Tschirhart, J. (1998) 'Takings, compensation and endangered species protection on private lands', *Journal of Economic Perspectives*, vol 12, pp35–52

Jackson, L. E., Bawa, K., Pascual, U., Perrings, C. (2005) 'AgroBIODIVERSITY: a new science agenda for biodiversity in support of sustainable agroecosystems', DIVERSITAS report. N. 4

Jackson, L. E., Pascual, U., Hodking, T. (2007) 'Utilizing and conserving agrobiodiversity in agricultural landscapes', *Agriculture Ecosystems and Environment*, vol 121, no 3, pp196–210

Johnston, R. and Madison, M. (1997) 'From landmarks to landscapes: A review of current practices in the transfer of development rights', *Journal of American Planning Association*, vol 63, pp365–378

Kremen, C., Williams, N. M., Thorp, R. (2002) 'Crop pollination from native bees at risk from agricultural intensification', *Proceedings of the National Academy of Sciences of the United States of America*, vol 99, pp16812–16816

Lambin, E. F., Turner, II B. L., Geist, H. J., Agbola, S., Angelsen, A., Bruce, J. W., Coomes, O., Dirzo, R., Fischer, G., Folke, C., George, P. S., Homewood, K., Imbernon, J., Leemans, R., Li, X., Moran, E. F., Mortimore, M., Ramakrishnan, P. S., Richards, J. F., Skånes, H., Steffen, W., Stone, G. D., Svedin, U., Veldkamp, T., Vogel, C., Xu, J. (2001) 'The causes of land-use and land-cover change: Moving beyond the myths', *Global Environmental Change*, vol 11, pp261–269

Latacz-Lohmann, U. and Van der Hamsvoort, C. (1997) 'Auctioning conservation contracts: A theoretical analysis and an application', *American Journal of Agricultural Economics*, vol 79, pp407–418

Loreau, M., Naeem, S., Inchausti, P., Bengtsson, J., Grime, J. P., Hector, A., Hooper, D. U., Huston, M. A., Raffaeli, D., Schmid, B., Tilman, D., Wardle, D. A. (2002) 'Biodiversity and ecosystem functioning: Current knowledge and future challenges', *Science*, vol 294, pp804–808

Millennium Ecosystem Assessment (MEA) (2005) *Ecosystems and Human Well-being: Biodiversity Synthesis*, World Resources Institute, Washington, DC

Mooney, H. A., Mack, R. N., McNeely, J. A., Neville, L. E, Schei, P. J., Waage, J. K. (eds), (2005) *Invasive Alien Species: A New Synthesis*, Island Press, Washington, DC

North, D. C. (1990) *Institutions, Institutional Change and Economic Performance*, Cambridge University Press, Cambridge

Norton, B. G. (1986) 'On the inherent danger of undervaluing species', in B. G. Norton (ed.), *The Preservation of Species*, Princeton University Press, Princeton

Organisation for Economic Co-operation and Development (OECD) (1993) *What future for Our Countryside? A Rural Development Policy*, OECD, Paris

OECD (2005) *Handbook of Market Creation for Biodiversity: Issues in Implementation*, OECD, Paris

Opschoor, J. H. (1999) 'Making the benefits of biodiversity conservation visible and real: Institutional aspects in a biodiversity research programme', *Environment and Development Economics*, vol 4, pp204–214

Östman, O., Ekbom, B., Bengtsson, J. (2003) 'Yield increase attributable to aphid predation by ground-living polyphagous natural enemies in spring barley in Sweden', *Ecological Economics*, vol 45, pp149–158

Pagiola, S. (2002) 'Paying for water services in Central America: Learning from Costa Rica', in S. Pagiola, J. Bishop, N. Landell-Mills (eds), *Selling Forest Environmental Services: Market-based Mechanisms for Conservation and Development*, Earthscan, London

Pagiola, S., Agostini, P., Gobbi, G., de Haan, G., Ibrahim, M., Murgueitio, E., Ramirez, E., Rosales, M., Ruiz, J. P. (2004) 'Paying for biodiversity conservation services in agricultural landscapes', Environment Department Paper no. 96, World Bank, Washington, DC

Panayotou, T. (1994) 'Conservation of biodiversity and economic development: The concept of transferable development rights', *Environment and Resource Economics*, vol 4, pp91–110

Pearce, D. W. (1999) *Economics and Environment: Essays on Ecological Economics and Sustainable Development*, Edward Elgar, Cheltenham

Perrings, C. (1998) 'Resilience in the dynamics of economy–environment systems', *Environment and Resource Economics*, vol 11, pp503–520

Perrings, C. (2001) 'The economics of biodiversity loss and agricultural development in low income countries', in D. R. Lee and C. B. Barrett (eds), *Tradeoffs or Synergies? Agricultural Intensification, Economic Development and the Environment*, Wallingford, CAB International, pp57–72

Perrings, C. (2005) 'Mitigation and adaptation strategies for the control of biological invasions', *Ecological Economics*, vol 52, pp315–325

Perrings, C. and Gadgil, M. (2003) 'Conserving biodiversity: Reconciling local and global public benefits', in I. Kaul, P. Conceicao, K. le Goulven, R. L. Mendoza (eds), *Providing Global Public Goods: Managing Globalization*, Oxford University Press, Oxford, pp532–555

Perrings, C., Barbier, E. B., Brown, G., Dalmazzone, S., Folke, C., Gadgil, M., Hanley, N., Holling, C. S., Mäler, K.-G., Mason, P., Panayotou, T., Turner, R. K. (1995) 'The economic value of biodiversity', in V. Heywood and R. Watson (eds), *Global Biodiversity Assessment*, Cambridge University Press, Cambridge, pp823–914

Perrings, C., Jackson, L., Bawa, K., Brussaard, L., Brush, S., Gavin, T., Papa, R., Pascual, U., de Ruiter, P. (2006) 'Biodiversity in agricultural landscapes: Saving natural capital without losing interest', *Conservation Biology*, vol 20, pp263–264

Peterson, G., Allen, C. R., Holling, C. S. (1998) 'Ecological resilience, biodiversity, and scale', *Ecosystems*, vol 1, pp6–18

Ricketts, T. H., Daily, G. C., Ehrlich, P. R., Michener, C. D. (2004) 'Economic value of tropical forest to coffee production', *Proceedings of the National Academy of Sciences, USA*, vol 101, pp12579–12582

Rodríguez, L.C., Pascual, U., Nemeyer, H. M. (2006) 'Peasant communities' cultural domain and the local-use value of plant resources: The case of Opunta Scrublands in Ayacucho, Peru', *Ecological Economics*, vol 57, pp30–44

Rosa, H., Kandel, S., Dimas, L. (2004) 'Compensation for environmental services and rural communities: Lessons from the Americas', *International Forest Review*, vol 6, pp187–194

Scherr, S. J. and McNeely, J. A. (2008) 'Biodiversity conservation and agricultural sustainability towards a new paradigm of "ecoagriculture" landscapes', *Philosophical Transcripts of the Royal Society. B*, vol 363, pp477–494

Schläpfer, F., Tucker, M., Seidl, I. (2002) 'Returns from hay cultivation in fertilized low diversity and non-fertilized high diversity grassland', *Environment and Resource Economics*, vol 21, pp89–100

Smale, M., Hartell, J., Heisey, P. W., Senauer, B. (1998) 'The contribution of genetic resources and diversity to wheat production in the Punjab of Pakistan', *American Journal of Agricultural Economics*, vol 80, pp482–493

Smale, M., Bellon, R. M., Aguirre Gomez, J. A. (2001) 'Maize diversity, variety attributes, and farmers' choices in Southeastern Guanajuato, Mexico', *Economic Development and Cultural Change*, vol 50, pp201–225

Stoneham, G., Chaudhri, V., Strappazzon, L., Ha, A. (2008) 'Auctioning biodiversity conservation contracts', in A. Kontoleon, U. Pascual, T. Swanson (eds), *Biodiversity Economics*, Cambridge University Press, Cambridge

Swanson, T. (ed.) (1998) *The Economics and Ecology of Biodiversity Decline: The Forces Driving Global Change*, Cambridge University Press, Cambridge

Swart, J. A. A. (2003) 'Will direct payments help biodiversity?', *Science*, vol 299, p1981

Swift, M. J. and Anderson, J. M. (1993) 'Biodiversity and ecosystem function in agroecosystems', in E. Schultze and H. A. Mooney (eds), *Biodiversity and Ecosystem Function*, Springer, New York, pp57–83

Symondson, W. O. C., Sunderland, K. D., Greenstone, M. H. (2002) 'Can generalist predators be effective biocontrol agents?', *Annual Review of Entomology*, vol 47, pp561–594

ten Kate, K. and Laird, S. A. (1999) *The Commercial Use of Biodiversity – Access to Genetic Resources and Benefit-Sharing*, Earthscan, London

Tilman, D., Wedin, D., Knops, J. (1996) 'Productivity and sustainability influenced by biodiversity in grasslands ecosystems', *Nature*, vol 379, pp718–720

Tilman, D., Reich, P., Knops, J., Wedin, D., Mielke, T., Lehman, C. (2001) 'Diversity and productivity in a long-term grassland experiment', *Science*, vol 294, pp843–845

Tilman, D., Cassman, K. G., Matson, P. A., Naylor, R., Polasky, S. (2002) 'Agricultural sustainability and intensive production practices', *Nature*, vol 418, pp671–677

Tomich, T. P., van Noordwijk, M., Budidarsono, S., Gillison, A., Kusumanto, T., Murdiyarso, D., Stolle, F., Fagi, A. M. (2001) 'Agricultural intensification, deforestation, and the environment: Assessing tradeoffs in Sumatra, Indonesia', in D. R. Lee and C. B. Barrett (eds), *Tradeoffs or Synergies? Agricultural Intensification, Economic Development and the Environment*, CAB International, Wallingford, UK, pp221–244

Tomich, T. P., Thomas, D. E., van Noordwijk, M. (2004) 'Environmental services and land use change in Southeast Asia: From recognition to regulation or reward?', *Agriculture Ecosystems and Environment*, vol 104, pp229–244

Tscharntke, T., Klein, A. M., Kruess, A., Steffan-Dewenter. I., Thies, C. (2005) 'Landscape perspectives on agricultural intensification and biodiversity ecosystem service management', *Ecological Letters*, vol 8, pp857–874

Turner, R. K. and Pearce, D. W. (1993) 'Sustainable economic development: Economic and ethical principles', in E. B. Barbier (ed.), *Economics and Ecology: New Frontiers and Sustainable Development*, Chapman & Hall, London

van Noordwijk, M., Poulsen, J. G., Ericksen, P. L. (2004) 'Quantifying off-site effects of land use change: Filters, flows and fallacies', *Agriculture Ecosystems and Environment*, vol 104, pp19–34

van Noordwijk, M., Kuncoro, S., Martin, E., Joshi, L., Saipothong, P., Areskoug, V., O'Connor, T. (2005) 'Donkeys, carrots, sticks and roads to a market for environmental services: Rapid agrobiodiversity appraisal for the PES – ICDP continuum, 2005', paper presented at the DIVERSTIAS First Open Science Conference, Oaxaca, November

Vandermeer, J. and Perfecto, I. (1995) *Breakfast of Biodiversity: The Truth about Rainforest Destruction*, Food First Books, Oakland, CA

Widawsky, D. and Rozelle, S. D. (1998) 'Varietal diversity and yield variability in Chinese rice production', in M. Smale (ed.), *Farmers, Gene Banks, and Crop Breeding. Economic Analyses of Diversity in Wheat, Maize, and Rice*, Kluwer, Boston, pp159–172

Wunder, S. (2005) 'Payments for environmental services: Some nuts and bolts', *CIFOR Occasional Papers*, Centre for International Forestry Research. Bogor Barat, Indonesia

10

Institutional Economics and the Behaviour of Conservation Organizations: Implications for Biodiversity Conservation

Clem Tisdell

Introduction

Drawing mostly on aspects of new institutional economics, this chapter examines institutional factors that may influence the behaviour of non-governmental conservation bodies and considers their implications for biodiversity conservation. Principal-and-agent problems are shown to be relevant, the question of rent capture is discussed, and several influences on selection by non-governmental organizations (NGOs) of focal species for their conservation efforts (such as whether they favour species that are more human-like, or charismatic or which could generate significant local impact on incomes via tourism generation) are considered. The competitive efficiency of NGOs in securing funding for promoting the conservation of different species, as well as the possible impact of this competition on the extent of conservation of biodiversity, is examined using analysis based on the theory of games. It is doubtful if this type of competition is efficient in promoting biodiversity conservation to the extent achievable. Furthermore, the theory outlined indicates that the conservation strategies adopted by NGOs may not be cost-effective. However, drawing on views presented by Hagedorn (1993), it is argued that the role of conservation NGOs should not be assessed solely on their economic efficiency but the political acceptability of their contributions to policy should also be taken into account, as well as other factors. A multidimensional approach is required to assess the role of such bodies in society. Furthermore, even if the actions of NGOs are not perfect in conserving biodiversity, it may not be possible to create institutions that give superior results.

So far, there appears to have been little application of institutional economics to the behaviour of non-governmental organizations (NGOs), such as conservation organizations, although there have been attempts by political scientists and sociologists to adopt institutional approaches to wildlife conservation as pointed out, for example, by Haas (2004). However, it seems likely that the theories, for example, of Niskanen (1971) about the behaviour of bureaucracies, aspects of the theory of games, theories of group behaviour as outlined by Olson (1965), Simon's views on administrative man (Simon, 1961) and the new institutional economics championed by Williamson (1975, 1986) would be applicable. In addition, some aspects of old or traditional institutional economics appear to be relevant.

The purpose of the article is to explore the relevance of institutional economics to the behaviour of conservation organizations and to assess the predicted performance of such organizations in pursuing their conservation goals, giving examples where possible, and to consider factors that may restrict the ability of their strategies to conserve biodiversity. The objective of the exercise is to explore theoretical possibilities as a first step towards further analysis and possible empirical work.

Conservation bodies are usually concerned with 'ensuring' the supply of environmental goods and avoiding the production of public environmental bads. The goods (or bads) concerned are usually shared by a considerable number of persons either partially or completely in contrast to private goods. These are commodities for which markets are missing or partially missing. Nevertheless, the goods involved are not necessarily pure public goods or pure public bads. Many are mixed goods (Tisdell, 2005, pp113–118). The activities of NGOs often generate social conflict in the case of mixed goods. This is because NGOs may try to limit or restrict the exploitation of these resources by those who want to use them as a private good. The aim of the NGO is to benefit those who obtain utility from the resources as a collective good. For example, the efforts by Greenpeace and other organizations to stop whaling by the Japanese benefits those who collectively value the free existence of whale populations but brings Greenpeace into conflict with Japanese whalers and Japanese consumers of whale meat. Even when public goods or bads are involved there can be social resentment. For example, some members of the public may believe that NGOs lobby for excessive public funding of conservation projects in some cases.

The methods that NGOs use to contribute to the supply of public or quasi-public conservation goods are varied. They may, for instance, raise funds from the public (or their members) to directly provide the good, for example a protected area; try to convince private individuals to supply the good and assist them to do so, and lobby governments to provide funds for the NGO's conservation efforts or persuade the government directly to supply the focal environmental good of interest to the NGO.

The Yellow-eyed Penguin Trust (YEPT) in New Zealand, for example, has as its prime goal the conservation of the yellow-eyed penguin (YEP) *Megadyptes antipodes*, which is listed by the International Union for the Conservation of Nature (IUCN) as an endangered species. To pursue its mission, the Trust raised funds initially from the public and was subsequently also able to obtain some funding from the New Zealand government. This funding continues and the

Trust has also obtained funding from some private companies. The Trust disseminates information about the conservation status of the YEP, engages directly in programmes to conserve it and has acquired a limited amount of land for the purpose of directly protecting this species. As well, it encourages landholders to covenant land (that is, ocean shore areas) suitable for the conservation of the YEP, gives landholders advice on the conservation of the YEP on their land, and so on. It also conducts research, has a small permanent staff and makes use of local volunteers in its activities. It is able to exert some political pressure on government to ensure that its policies do not threaten the survival of the YEP. Thus, it performs all of the types of functions mentioned above.

While many conservation NGOs combine all these functions, not all do. Some, for example, do not directly supply any environmental goods but merely act as political pressure groups, trying to influence public policy by lobbying and by the strategic dissemination of information. The Australian Liberal-National Party government while in power in the early part of this decade moved to reduce public funding for the latter type of institutions.

Consider in turn how the objectives of conservation NGOs may be influenced by institutional factors, the relevance of the bounded rationality of individuals to the activities of these NGOs, and consider how efficient they are likely to be in pursuing conservation objectives. This will be followed by a broader assessment of the social value of these organizations and some discussion of the relevance of traditional institutional economics to the evolution of conservation NGOs.

Institutional factors and the objectives of conservation NGOs

Conservation NGOs, especially large ones, are liable to be influenced by principal-and-agent problems of the type outlined, for example, by Perloff (2004, pp689, 722). Emphasis on the importance of principal-and-agent problems in large organizations is by no means new. For instance, Berle and Means (1932) emphasized its importance in public corporations. They argued that shareholders have only limited control over the behaviour of the managers of public companies. This subsequently became the basis of many theories of the behaviour of business firms. It was argued that managerial goals modify the behaviour of business firms (Tisdell and Hartley, 2008, ch. 7). The members of conservation NGOs may be unable or unwilling to exert control over their administrators and employees for similar reasons (mostly the transaction costs involved) to those observed in the case of large public corporations. National and international NGOs may be particularly prone to the agency problem. Many members may find it too costly to attend annual general meetings and participate in decision making by the NGO. The problem is likely to be less acute in the case of locally based community NGOs.

The larger the size and the greater the geographical spread of a conservation NGO, the more likely are agency problems to be present. The more likely too is its management to be in the hands of staff, many of whom may not be members of the NGO, or who may place their personal interest above that of rank-and-file members. The agency problem implies that managers or staff of NGOs have some scope to pursue their own goals as distinct from those of the NGO.

Given the theory of bureaucracy as outlined by Niskanen (1971), and similar managerial theories of the behaviour of large public companies (Penrose, 1959; Marris, 1964) managers (staff) of a conservation NGO might be primarily interested in the growth of their organization and/or in obtaining sufficient funding to ensure its continuing existence. While some rank-and-file members of the NGO may also want this, the NGO's managers may be more inclined to compromise the conservation objectives of the NGO to obtain increased funds for their NGO.

They may, for example, form alliances with bodies mainly interested in economic development, either to obtain funds directly from these bodies or via a joint approach to government for funds. The reason given for the alliance by the NGO's executive might be that with the alliance the conservation NGO will have some influence on the nature of development but without the alliance it has none. Therefore, compromise is necessary to ensure that developers take some account of conservation. The extent to which this is really the case and how much compromise is necessary to ensure conservation influence is unclear. However, Figure 10.1 may help to illustrate some of the issues.

In Figure 10.1, curve ABCD indicates the amount of funding that a conservation NGO can expect as a function of the degree to which it is prepared to compromise its conservation goals as measured by an indicator in the range

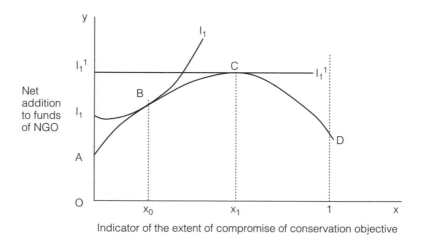

Indicator of the extent of compromise of conservation objective

Figure 10.1 Compromise of conservation goals as an option for a conservation NGO

$0 \leq x \leq 1$. This figure shows that the NGO can increase its funding by engaging in some compromise but will lose funds if it is too compromising. Probably in most cases, D is lower than A because a conservation NGO that is too compromising will lose its credibility as a conservation organization.

If the managers of NGOs act as Niskanen-type bureaucrats, they will favour the degree of compromise shown by x_1 because this maximizes the funds available to the NGO. In effect, their indifference curves would be a series of horizontal lines of which $I_1^1 I_1^1$ indicates one such curve. If the members of the NGO are strongly committed conservationists, they may, however, favour no compromise and prefer situation A. Their preferences would be indicated by a series of vertical indifference curves (not shown) with situations further to the left being favoured. In large organizations, however, it is possible that situation C rather than A will prevail if the bureaucrats are merely interested in the amount of funding obtained for their organization. Because of agency problems, members of the NGO may not be able to control a large NGO's managers effectively. Of course, particularly in smaller and more localized NGOs where members can exert greater control over management, management may be unable to deviate so far from the conservation goals of the principals of the NGO. In moderately sized NGOs, it is possible that the 'effective' indifference curves are like those represented by $I_1 I_1$ in Figure 10.1. This results in a degree of compromise corresponding to x_0 because the actions of the NGO's managers are restricted by its members. The situation has some similarities to that outlined by Williamson (1964) when developing the theory of the behaviour of managers in public companies.

Rent capture and conservation alliances

When public demand for conservation goods grows rapidly, this growth may generate possible rents for those engaged in the facilitation of their provision. An interesting question is who captures these rents? In some cases, it may be executives in conservation NGOs but it can also be public servants and to a lesser extent academics. Consider the following case.

The Australian Conservation Foundation (ACF), (a large conservation NGO in Australia) formed an alliance with the National Farmers' Federation (NFF, a peak farmers' pressure group) in 1989 to promote the Landcare Programme. The aim of this project was to encourage farmers to take more care of their land for conservation purposes. As a result of their joint approach to the Australian Government, these NGOs were able to achieve a large amount of government funding for the project, the Landcare Programme, which is still continuing. Possibly the interest of the ACF in the project was to extend its range of influence and that of the NFF was to create a more favourable impression of the role of farmers in conservation. Since participation in the programme by farmers was voluntary and subsidized by the government, it was clearly quite acceptable to farmers. Whether or not the ACF itself expected to obtain more funding from the government or ensure continuing support for its funding from the government as a result of its decision is unclear but it is possible. The ACF obtains some funds from the government and private contributions to this NGO are tax deductible.

This alliance was very favourable to the Australian Liberal-National Party government, which wanted to partially privatize Telstra, a state-owned telecommunications enterprise. This plan was unpopular with farmers who feared that rural telecommunications services might suffer as a result of a partial privatization of this state enterprise. As a 'carrot' to farmers, the Australian government announced that it would partially fund its support for Landcare from the funds obtained by the partial sale of Telstra. This move helped to placate farmers and was looked on favourably by conservationists.

The ACF gained virtually no control over the Landcare Programme. Most funds for the programme are channelled through government departments, mainly the Department of Agriculture, Fisheries and Forestry and are administered by the government. It is possible that public servants have captured most of the rents and the ACF obtained little, if any of those. Considerable red tape (transaction costs) appears to be involved in making an application for community funding under the programme and government bureaucrats may now be the main beneficiaries. The 'red tape' involved helps to keep public servants in employment. A further problem is that with strict accountability rules in the public service, much of the red tape may be difficult to eliminate. Thus, the original alliance between the ACF and the NFF has evolved in a way which may not have been fully envisaged by the partners when they proposed the Landcare Programme.

Similar issues seem to have arisen in relation to the European Unions' reformed Common Agricultural Policy (CAP). CAP has been reformed and continues to be reformed so that it is more environmentally friendly but the transaction costs involved in the new policy seem to be very high even though the actual transfers to civil servants for administering the scheme are not known. Although the WWF (Worldwide Fund for the Conservation of Nature) was invited to participate in the planning of the reformed scheme, it declined; possibly because it was afraid of being compromised.

Note that environmental NGOs are not being blamed for 'rent' capture by public servants. They may, however, be used strategically by public servants in the process of rent capture as 'pawns' in the game. If the public demands greater supplies of a particular environmental good, this provides scope for public administrators to capture a substantial portion of the public funding of policies to bring about that supply. Mechanisms for examining cost-effective public administration appear to be weak. For example, the public (and even politicians) may have limited access to information about the activities of public administrators and market-type competitive mechanisms do not apply.

Social influences on the selection by NGOs of focal species for conservation efforts – factors restricting the diversity of species favoured

Conservation NGOs may favour the promotion of a narrow range of species of wildlife for conservation. Metrick and Weitzman (1996, 1998) suggest that these are likely to be species that are more charismatic than others and of which the members are larger in size. It has also been claimed that humans like to favour the conservation of species that are more human-like than others (Plous, 1993; DeKay and McClelland, 1996; Gunnthorsdottir, 2001) presumably because humans have greater empathy for these. This suggests a preference for mammals over other taxa and probably species with eyes placed forward on the skull.

While there is some support for these views (Tisdell et al, 2006), the situation is more complex than appears at first sight because there seems to be a high degree of social support for the survival of some non-mammalian species, such as some species of turtles (Tisdell et al, 2005). In line also with the views of traditional institutionalists, there is evidence that social attitudes of individuals to the survival of different species of wildlife are to a large extent socially (culturally) conditioned (Tisdell et al, 2006). Furthermore, if portrayals of species (e.g. in folk tales and stories, cartoons) repeatedly emphasize or exaggerate the human-like appearance or qualities of species, they may alter human attitudes to them. Again, humans may prefer species that seem soft and cuddly – children prefer such objects. Some writers, therefore, argue that conservation NGOs excessively focus their conservation efforts on the conservation of charismatic species to the neglect of other species, for example keystone species, which may be very important in relation to the maintenance of biodiversity.

In their defence, some conservation bodies argue that without an emphasis on flagship and charismatic species, they would collect a much smaller amount of funds which would adversely affect their overall conservation impact. Even though the outcome may not be optimal, it is the best attainable outcome, in the view of some NGOs, given the social circumstances. Furthermore, some of the species may be umbrella species and thus their conservation could result in the conservation of other valued species. This is because conservation of the habitat of the focal umbrella species also incidentally conserves other species.

Of course, not all conservation NGOs focus their activities on a single species. Some use charismatic species for fund-raising purposes but are engaged in broader conservation activities. WWF uses a single species to symbolize the WWF, namely the giant panda. It seems to be quite common for NGOs in their drives for donations to use a single charismatic species that has emotional appeal to the public. In some cases, the funds collected by the NGOs are 'fungible' and help conserve species that are not highlighted by NGOs in their promotion campaigns. There is little doubt that some conservation organizations exploit charismatic wildlife species to obtain funds for the organization itself. For example, an Australian study of funding for the conservation of the koala and the northern hairy-nosed wombat found that, although the koala was not endangered, funding for its conservation was much greater than for the critically endangered hairy-nosed wombat (Tisdell and Swarna Nantha, 2007). Reasons could be that the koala is better known to the public, it is regarded as more human-like and it is a mixed economic good whereas, at this time, the northern hairy-nosed wombat is a pure public good and is less well known.

The koala is a mixed economic good because it is a private good in koala parks and zoos and is widely used as an icon for promotional purposes. Campaigns 'to save' the koala are likely to be supported by owners of koala parks and zoos, possibly partly to buy moral worthiness. In part, there may be bias of conservation bodies in favour of species that are mixed goods. By contrast, the northern hairy-nosed wombat is a pure public good (Tisdell and Swarna Nantha, 2007). It is confined to a forest reserve where scientists are trying to increase its population. It is not allowed in zoos or private collections, and the public is excluded from the reserve containing its remnant population.

Sometimes conservation NGOs directly conserve mixed economic goods or quasi-public goods themselves by relying on economic exclusion possibilities. For example, the Otago Peninsula Trust in New Zealand is instrumental in protecting a colony of the Northern Royal Albatross *Diomedea sanfordi* at Taiaroa Head. This species is listed by the IUCN as endangered. Visitors pay to see this albatross colony at relatively close range (Tisdell, 1990, ch. 7; Higham, 2001). The colony nests at this site. Their payments constitute the major source of funds for this NGO and in recent years the Trust has been able to obtain a financial surplus from operations of its Royal Albatross colony, which it has used to subsidize other conservation activities (Otago Peninsula Trust, 2005). Similarly, the Mareeba Wetland Foundation manages a wetland wildlife reserve in the Atherton Tablelands in Northern Queensland. A substantial amount of its funds are obtained from visitors to this wetland who pay to enter this reserve, which conserves a number of wild species in a natural setting. In both cases, components of the conserved commodity for which exclusion is possible help finance the organizations involved.

Some conservation bodies may favour conservation projects that have a substantial and demonstrable local positive economic impact. This may help to generate local positive economic and other support for the NGO. However, conservation projects that have greatest local economic impact may not necessarily be those of greatest economic value. They may not, for example, maximize net social welfare – for instance, as estimated by the use of social cost–benefit analysis (Tisdell, 2006a).

This raises a social dilemma. Suppose, for example, that there are two species, A and B, that could be conserved in a local area by a similar level of investment but that funds are sufficient to conserve only one and their conservation is mutually exclusive. A social choice must be made about which one to conserve. If A is conserved, the net total economic value (TEV) of this is estimated to be

$1 million and local income of $0.5 million is predicted to be generated. On the other hand, conservation of species B is estimated to yield a net TEV of $2 million but only generate $0.1 million in income locally. If net TEV is to be maximized, the project to conserve B is the optimal social choice but if local economic impact is to be the deciding factor, conservation of species A would be the appropriate social choice.

It is then a question of deciding what the appropriate social rules are. If the local community is, for example, very poor, it is possible that there would be a preference for the project that conserves species A. But what if the local community is rich? Should income transfers be made to the local community if this community is poor and it is decided to conserve species B? If so, how should these be made?

Bounded rationality and the operation of conservation NGOs

Individuals are undoubtedly limited in their rationality, their knowledge and the span of their attention (Simon, 1961). Conservation NGOs, by their communication, help focus individuals' attention on objects to be conserved. This may reduce their attention to other objects given that the attention spans of individuals are limited. Thus, the supply of public goods or quasi-public goods promoted by NGOs may be favoured by targeted members of the public. It is by no means certain that the composition of the transmitted information is ideal, even if an ideal can be defined for the transmission of such information.

In the case of wildlife conservation, provision of information by NGOs may be focused on species that are estimated to generate the greatest public financial support for the NGO. These may not, however, be the most valuable species to conserve.

Furthermore, there might be more emphasis than is socially desirable on species likely to suffer a decline in their existing population than on those for which an increase in their existing population is desirable. Results from psychological economics indicate that individuals are willing to pay more to avoid the loss of a valued commodity than to pay for an equivalent gain. This has been called the status quo or endowment effect (Knetsch, 1989; Kahneman et al, 1991; Tversky and Kahneman, 1991). In general, individuals will be willing to pay more to avoid the loss of a species, the more imminent the loss is believed to be and the greater are the perceived adverse consequences of the loss. This may entice some conservation NGOs to exaggerate the degree of endangerment of their focal species and the extent of the adverse consequences of that loss (Tisdell, 2006b). They hope as a result to marshal greater public action to conserve the species or secure more funds for the NGO. The public may not find it economic to scrutinize carefully the truth of statements made by NGOs.

As in the lemons' case (Akerlof, 1970), there is also a risk that dishonest NGOs or inefficient ones may collect funds from the public to help conserve wildlife species by supplying misleading information to the public. Information is asymmetric in this case. With increasing use of the internet, this problem may increase. However, one reviewer suggested that this may not happen because the internet may be used to check on those NGOs that request donations via websites. In practice, this is optimistic because significant online fraud occurs.

The efficiency of conservation NGOs in fund-raising and how their competition may narrow the diversity of species supported for conservation

It seems likely that conservation NGOs vary considerably in the competency with which they carry out their missions because they appear to be less subject to competitive discipline than business firms. However, they must receive adequate funding to survive and/or contributions of voluntary services. They do not seem to be subject to the discipline of possible takeovers by raiding companies as many businesses are, nor to the discipline imposed by bankers as many businesses are in some countries, for example Germany.

The question arises of just how efficient the organizational structures of individual conservation NGOs in promoting biodiversity conservation are and just how efficient is the whole array of extant NGOs in doing this. To what extent should such bodies be decentralized? What is the best organizational form for NGOs to achieve their mission? Is, for example, a U-form (unitary form) or an M-form (multidivisional form) best (Williamson, 1986)? Should they have a peak-type of organization to represent their interests nationally and internationally, such as the IUCN? Hagedorn (1993) suggests that governments (politicians) prefer to deal with peak civil organizations because this reduces their political transaction costs. This suggests that NGOs are more likely to influence government policy if they have a peak organization.

Sometimes, conservation NGOs duplicate the activities of one another, do not engage in coordinated action with one another and may forgo scale economies as a result. On the other hand, larger scales of operations may have drawbacks because of managerial 'slippage' and greater knowledge deficiencies in larger organizations as well as a reduced sense of belonging by individuals contributing to the activities of the conservation body.

Some simple game theory models can be used to illustrate the point: conservation NGOs in following their own self-interest may fail to promote biodiversity and, by competing, reduce the total net funds available to them collectively or even in some cases, individually. Suppose two conservation NGOs, A and B, each has two alternative strategies: promote species 1 or promote species 2. The net funds that they have donated depends upon which species they promote.

There are several possibilities that can be illustrated by matrices. One possibility is illustrated in Table 10.1. The pay-offs in the body of the matrix indicate the funds that the NGOs obtain for promoting the conservation of the different species, say in millions of dollars. Imagine that in the absence of support by NGOs to promote their conservation, each of the species will disappear. However, assume that if a minimum of $2 million is spent on fostering the conservation of an individual species, it will survive.

If each NGO's motive is to maximize its funds, then both will promote species 2. Consequently, species 1 receives no support and disappears but species 2 survives because the total promotional effort to save it equals $5 million. If the NGOs had been less selfish and had adopted either the contribution of strategies (A_1, B_2) or (A_2, B_1) both species would have survived and collectively their funds would have been greater. Nevertheless, the outcome (A_2, B_2) prevails and forms a Nash equilibrium. The result is not, however, Pareto suboptimal for the players as it would be in the prisoners' dilemma case. Note that if 6 is replaced by 2.7 in the matrix in Table 10.1, this would still result in the NGOs only promoting the conservation of species 2 if they follow their self-interest and once again; this results in a Nash equilibrium. This is an even more inefficient outcome than in the previous case because not only is there failure to achieve the maximum attainable level of biodiversity conservation but the overall cost of achieving the amount of biodiversity conservation obtained is higher than when more species are conserved. If either of the strategies (A_1, B_2) or (A_2, B_2) are adopted, both species are conserved at an overall cost of $4.7 million but when strategy (A_2, B_2) is adopted, only one species is conserved at the overall cost of $5 million.

If we assume that the goal of the NGOs is to maximize the number of species conserved subject to the attainable set of collective possibilities, it can be seen that there is a failure to achieve this in the above cases. From this point of view, there is collective organizational inefficiency. Furthermore, the collective costs of achieving a given degree of biodiversity is not necessarily minimized, as is evident from the second example. The goals of the NGOs are not always pursued in a manner that minimizes the collective cost of achieving a particular biodiversity outcome. In other words, the strategies of NGOs may not be collectively cost-effective. This indicates the presence of a type of economic inefficiency.

Table 10.1 *Matrix used to illustrate the incentives of NGOs to concentrate on the promotion of the same species and the possible shortcomings of this*

		NGO B	
		Promote species 1 (B₁)	Promote species 2 (B₂)
NGO A	Promote species 1 (A₁)	(2, 2)	(2, 6)
	Promote species 2 (A₂)	(6, 2)	(2.5, 2.5)

Table 10.2 *Matrix to show a prisoners' dilemma type problem and failure of NGOs to promote biodiversity*

| | | NGO B | |
		Promote species 1 (B₁)	Promote species 2 (B₂)
NGO A	Promote species 1 (A₁)	(2, 2)	(2, 6)
	Promote species 2 (A₂)	(6, 2)	(0.75, 0.75)

A Pareto suboptimal case (for NGOs) is illustrated in the matrix in Table 10.2. In the case shown there, both players (NGOs) acting in their selfish interest promote species 2. They obtain $0.75 million each as a result. This is Paretian suboptimal outcome from their point of view and the total promotional expenditure of $1.5 million is insufficient to save species 2. Neither species is saved, even though it is possible to save both by selecting either of the strategies (A₁, B₂) or (A₂, B₁). Once again, there is inefficiency in achieving the collective goal of maximizing biodiversity conservation. This is not to say that all Nash solutions in the prisoners' dilemma case will result in failure to save all the focal species. For instance, if in Table 10.2 the pay-offs corresponding to (A₂, B₂) were (1.5, 1.5), the total promotional effort for species 2 is $3 million. Thus, species 2 survives (but not species 1) given the assumption that an expenditure of $2 million is required to ensure the survival of a species. Nevertheless, in both cases, the selfish actions of NGOs result in less biodiversity conservation than is attainable.

A third related case can also be envisaged. This is illustrated by Table 10.3. In this case, the self-interest of each of the NGOs is to coordinate their strategies so that they do not accidentally promote the same species. If both NGOs promote species 1 it will survive, but not species 2. If both promote species 2, neither species will survive. This is based on the assumption (stated above) that each species requires a promotional expenditure of a minimum of $2 million to survive.

However, we should not conclude that duplication of effort by NGOs to conserve species is always unfavourable to conservation. For example, if effort is spread over many species, threshold levels of expenditure for the survival of only a few species may be reached. By concentrating conservation efforts on fewer species,

Table 10.3 *Matrix to illustrate a coordination problem for NGOs*

| | | NGO B | |
		Promote species 1 (B₁)	Promote species 2 (B₂)
NGO A	Promote species 1 (A₁)	(2, 2)	(3, 3)
	Promote species 2 (A₂)	(3, 3)	(0.75, 0.75)

it is possible that thresholds for the conservation of a larger number of species might be attained and greater biodiversity conserved. Again, however, there may not be social mechanisms to ensure that NGOs achieve the socially desired balance.

How should the (social) role of conservation NGOs be assessed?

The above discussion raises the issue of what is the appropriate way to assess the social role of conservation NGOs. Given the views of Hagedorn (1993), it would seem inappropriate to assess NGOs purely from an economic efficiency point of view; or in terms of the terminology he uses on the basis of the quality of their decisions. In his view, attention should also be given to the political legitimacy and the political acceptability of their policy proposals. He is critical of the fact that agricultural economists have concentrated on the economic efficiency or quality of decisions by institutions or policies and have neglected the political sustainability of decision-making processes or proposals.

If the most efficient policy alternatives are not politically acceptable, then they are irrelevant from a practical point of view. Proposed polices or institutional structures should be assessed taking into account both efficiency and political acceptability factors. For example, in Figure 10.2 the set bounded by OABCD may correspond to all policies that can address a particular social issue. A policy corresponding to point C would be the most efficient but not the most acceptable

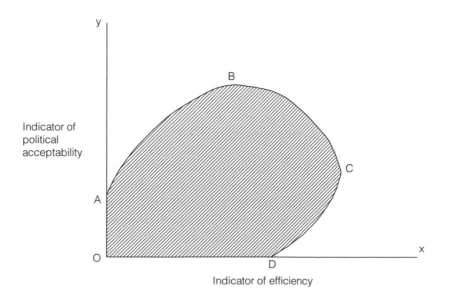

Figure 10.2 Efficient institutions and policies may not always be politically acceptable

politically. The politically most acceptable one corresponds to point B. Should society choose point B or C or some point on the segment between these points? The policy corresponding to point C may maximize net social benefit using traditional cost–benefit analysis (CBA) but that corresponding to B may give a distribution of benefits that makes it relatively more acceptable.

Another point to consider is that although an institutional structure does not provide the most efficient solution to a social problem, it may still have net benefits and no other feasible political alternative may be available. Thus, conservation NGOs may make a positive contribution to the supply of public or quasi-public conservation goods, a contribution that would not be made in their absence. Their contribution seems to be a positive one even though not perfect. Furthermore, no other workable institutional arrangements may be possible that will do a better job of filling conservation gaps. To be more specific in relation to biodiversity conservation, even if conservation NGOs are not as effective nor as efficient in promoting biodiversity conservation as they could be, their net contribution may be positive and superior institutional arrangements may not be possible.

An additional factor to bear in mind is that conservation NGOs are a part of civil society. They may, therefore, act as useful counters to the power of the state, and they provide separate sources of information and expertise. This is valued in itself by those that favour open societies (Popper, 2002).

Again, another positive social contribution of conservation NGOs (and other NGOs) is that they provide extra avenues for individuals to 'belong' to society. Most NGOs rely on volunteers and donations from individuals to function. They provide an alternative to the workforce for the social recognition of individuals. They can help counter social alienation and build community spirit. The importance of this type of sociological (social) contribution of conservation NGOs has been documented by Buchan (2007) by means of case studies. This all suggests that institutions need to be assessed from a multidimensional point of view.

Concluding comments

The analysis in this article is exploratory in the sense it applies behavioural theories mostly developed by new institutional economists to outline possible behaviours of conservation NGOs and assess the consequences of these behaviours. It was claimed that the administrators of NGOs may pursue goals different to those of rank-and-file members due to principal–agent phenomena and differing goals of the stakeholders. This is liable to result in some compromise of conservation goals by administrators of NGOs. Financial considerations may lead many conservation NGOs to concentrate on supporting a limited set of species for conservation (for example, charismatic ones) and they may take advantage of bounded rationality and asymmetry of information to bias the information they provide to the public. Application of game theory suggests that the competitive behaviour of conservation NGOs is less effective in promoting biodiversity conservation than it could be. It can result in fewer species being saved by the activities of an NGO than is attainable given their available strategies. Inefficiency can therefore arise in this case. Furthermore, the cost of conserving whatever species are conserved may be higher than it need be.

It could, however, be argued that the role of conservation NGOs in society should be assessed from a broader angle. For example, the political role of such institutions may need to be taken into account as well as their role in facilitating social activities. There is as yet no easy way to assess the social value of these multidimensional attributes.

This chapter has applied new concepts in economics, such as those developed in new institutional economies, to help analyse the behaviour of conservation NGOs and has shed light on the economic and social issues raised by the development of these organizations. The analysis should be regarded as suggestive rather than definitive.

When considering the evolution of conservation NGOs and the types of missions or objectives they pursue, it is probably wise to study also cultural factors and changes in social values (see Tisdell et al, 2006) as suggested by traditional economic institutionalists. This is because prevailing values held in societies alter with the passage of time. To some extent, NGOs may contribute to this change. However, to a large extent, changes in social values are likely to be exogenous to individual NGOs. As these values change, some new NGOs may arise with missions that reflect the new set of values, some existing NGOs may disappear and other existing NGOs may reform their goals in order to survive financially. There is considerable scope for studying the dynamics of such change but this has not been attempted here.

Many complexities are involved in determining the stock of genetic material which should be conserved in the wild. Features that need to be taken into account include the total economic value of different species (see, e.g. Ninan et al, 2007, pp8–9), the mixed good characteristics of some species, the economic consequences of economic interdependence between populations of species, and priorities have to be established (criteria have to be agreed on) for saving different species from extinction. Other matters of relevance are the value of property rights in genetic material in providing an incentive for biodiversity conservation and the consequences of growing globalization and market extension for the conservation of biodiversity. These matters are analysed for example in Tisdell (2005, ch. 5). In addition, the consequences of open access to natural resources and of common property for biodiversity conservation are important, as is ranching and farming of species and these are discussed for example in Tisdell (2005, ch. 6). Additional factors affecting biodiversity are discussed in Ninan et al (2007, ch. 1).

Acknowledgements

This is a revised version of a paper presented at a colloquium of the Institute of Resource Economics, Humboldt University of Berlin in February, 2007. I wish to thank participants for their useful suggestions, Dr Volker Beckmann for his particular contribution and Dr Martina Padmanabhan and Jes Weigelt for their detailed comments on the earlier version of this paper. The usual *caveat* applies.

References

Akerlof, G. (1970) 'The market for lemons: Quality, uncertainty and the market mechanism', *The Quarterly Journal of Economics*, vol 84, pp488–500

Berle, A. A. and Means, G. C. (1932) *The Modern Compensation and Private Property*, Harcourt Brace, New York

Buchan, D. (2007) *Not Just Trees in the Ground: The Social and Economic Benefits of Community-led Conservation Projects*, WWF – Wellington, New Zealand

DeKay, M. L. and McClelland, G. H. (1996) 'Probability and utility components of endangered species preservation progress', *Journal of Environmental Psychology: Applied*, vol 2, pp60–83

Gunnthorsdottir, A. (2001) 'Physical attractiveness of an animal species as a decision factor for its preservation', *Anthrozoös*, vol 14, pp204–216

Haas, T. C. (2004) 'Ecosystem management via interacting models of political and ecological processes', *Animal Biodiversity and Conservation*, vol 27, pp231–245

Hagedorn, K. (1993) 'Institutions and agricultural economics', *Journal of Economic Issues*, vol 27, pp849–886

Higham, J. E. S. (2001) 'Managing ecotourism at Taiaroa Head Royal Albatross Colony', in Myra Shackley (ed.), *Flagship Species: Case Studies in Wildlife Tourism Management*, International Ecotourism Society, Burlington, VT, pp17–29

Kahneman, D., Knetsch, J. L., Thaler, R. H. (1991) 'The endowment effect, loss aversion, and status quo bias', *Journal of Economic Perspectives*, vol 5, pp193–206

Knetsch, J. L. (1989) 'The endowment effect and evidence of non-reversible indifference curves', *The American Economic Review*, vol 79, pp1277–1284

Marris, R. (1964) *The Economic Theory of 'Managerial' Capitalism*, Macmillan, London

Metrick, A. and Weitzman, M. L. (1996) 'Patterns of behaviour in endangered species preservation', *Land Economics*, vol 72, pp1–16

Metrick, A. and Weitzman, M. L. (1998) 'Conflicts and choices in biodiversity preservation', *The Journal of Economic Perspectives*, vol 12, pp21–34

Ninan, K. N., Jyothis, S., Babu, P., Ramakrishnappa, V. (2007) *The Economics of Biodiversity Conservation: Valuation in Tropical Forest Ecosystems*, Earthscan, London and Sterling, VA

Niskanen, W. (1971) *Bureaucracy and Representative Government*, Aldine, Chicago

Olson, M. (1965) *The Logic of Collective Action*, Harvard University Press, Cambridge, MA

Otago Peninsula Trust (2005) *34th Annual Report of the Otago Peninsula Trust*, Dunedin, New Zealand

Penrose, E. (1959) *The Theory of the Growth of the Firm*, Basil Blackwell, Oxford

Perloff, J. M. (2004) *Microeconomics*, 3rd edn. Pearson Addison Wesley, New York and London

Plous, S. (1993) 'Psychological mechanisms in the human use of animals', *Journal of Social Issues*, vol 49, pp11–52

Popper, K. (2002) *The Open Society and its Enemies*, 5th edn, Routledge, London

Simon, H. (1961) *Administrative Behavior*, Macmillian, New York

Tisdell, C. A. (1990) *Natural Resources, Growth and Development*, Praeger, New York

Tisdell, C. A. (2005) *Economics of Environmental Conservation,* 2nd edn. Edward Elgar, Cheltenham and Northampton, MA

Tisdell, C. A. (2006a) 'Valuation of tourism's natural resources', in L. Dwyer and P. Forsyth, (eds), *International Handbook on the Economics of Tourism*, Edward Elgar, Cheltenham and Northampton, MA, pp359–378

Tisdell, C. A. (2006b) 'Knowledge about a species' conservation status and funding for its preservation: Analysis', *Ecological Modelling*, vol 198, pp515–519

Tisdell, C. and Hartley, K. (2008) *Microeconomic Policy: A New Perspective*, Edward Elgar, Cheltenham and Northampton, MA

Tisdell, C. and Swarna Nantha, H. (2007) 'Comparison of funding and demand for the conservation of the charismatic koala with those for the critically endangered wombat, *Lesiorhinus kreffti*', *Biodiversity and Conservation*, vol 16, pp1261–1281

Tisdell, C., Wilson, C., Swarna Nantha, H. (2005) 'Association of public support for the survival of wildlife species with their likeability', *Anthrozoös*, vol 18, pp160–174

Tisdell, C., Wilson, C., Swarna Nantha, H. (2006) 'Public choice of species for the "Ark": Phylogenetic similarity and preferred wildlife species for survival', *Journal for Nature Conservation*, vol 14, pp97–105, 266–267

Tversky, A. and Kahneman, D. (1991) 'Loss aversion in riskless choice: A reference-dependent model', *Quarterly Journal of Economics*, vol 106, pp1039–1061

Williamson, O. E. (1964) *The Economics of Discretionary Behavior: Managerial Objectives in a Theory of the Firm*, Prentice-Hall, Englewood Cliffs, NJ

Williamson, O. E. (1975) *Markets and Hierarchies: Analysis and Antitrust Implications*, The Free Press, New York

Williamson, O. E. (1986) *Economic Organizations: Firms, Markets and Policy*, Wheatsheaf, Brighton

3

GOVERNANCE

11

An Ecological Economics Approach to the Management of a Multi-purpose Coastal Wetland

R. K. Turner, I. J. Bateman, S. Georgiou, A. Jones, I. H. Langford,
N. G. N. Matias and L. Subramanian

Introduction

Wetland ecosystems account for about 6 per cent of the global land area and are among the most threatened of all environmental resources. The wetlands found in temperate climate zones in developed economies have long suffered significant losses and continue to face threats from industrial, agricultural and residential developments, as well as from hydrological perturbation, pollution and pollution-related effects (Turner, 1991).

Wetlands are complex ecological systems whose structure provides us with goods or products involving some direct utilization of one or more wetland characteristics (Maltby et al, 1996). Wetland ecosystem processes also provide us with ecologically related services, supporting or protecting human activities or human properties without being used directly. Wetland systems, as well as their distinctive landscapes, are also often significant socio-cultural assets. So, the stock of wetlands is a multifunctional resource generating substantial socio-economic values (Balmford et al, 2002; Turner et al, 2003). Sustainable management of these assets has therefore become a high priority. In this chapter, three interrelated management problems – (i) eutrophication of multiple use shallow lakes and connecting rivers; (ii) sea level rise and flooding risks; and (iii) tourism preferences and patterns – will be explored and analysed from an ecological-economic perspective in the context of the Norfolk and Suffolk Broads, UK. (see Figure 11.1). The overall management tasks in this area equivalent in size to a national park encompass the maintenance of public navigation rights and the area's biological diversity, sustainable utilization of the various functions the wetlands provide and the resolution of conflicts between stakeholder groups as a result of different usages of the area. The statutory duties of the management agency (the Broads Authority), however, constrain the range of options because no one interest (nature conservation, recreation and tourism promotion, or maintenance of navigation rights) can be given significant relative priority. The

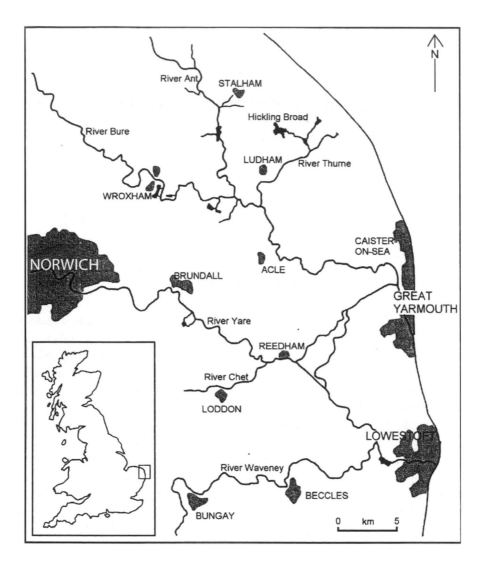

Figure 11.1 The Broads and its waterways

Authority has to operate by making often-pragmatic trade-offs, which can be subject to legislative constraints including EU Directives and the general guidance provided by the UK's sustainable development strategy.

Towards a framework for integrated wetland management assessment

The structure of and processes within wetland ecosystems generate a wide array of resources that directly or indirectly support the economic and social welfare of diverse groups of people. Sustainable development based on the maintenance of the functional diversity provided by wetland ecosystems will require careful management and evaluation of the different functions in terms of the welfare benefits they provide. In view of their complex, dynamic and co-evolving multi-functionality, a management approach is needed that addresses the pressures exerted on wetland ecosystems that threaten future flows of benefits. The Broads Authority has produced a strategic management and action plan (Broads Authority, 2004). The implicit aim is to achieve greater coordination between its three main functions – nature conservation, enhancement of recreation and quiet amenity, and the maintenance of rights of navigation – in order to fulfil sustainability goals. Integrated planning and management means combining assessments of the resources available to meet stated objectives; the formulation of a strategy or plan of action to use the resources in a wise way; and the implementation of the strategy in an orderly and efficient manner (Burbridge, 1994). Underpinning integrated management and planning is research that supports and informs such a management approach. A wetland research methodology somehow has to make compatible the very different perceptions of how a dynamic wetland ecosystem interacts with a co-evolving society (Clayton and Radcliffe, 1996; Brouwer and Crooks, 1998).

In this chapter, the driving–forces–pressure–state–impact–response (DPSIR) framework was used as a scoping device (Turner et al, 1998). This framework has been used to make explicit the means by which human activities in a given context and spatial area relate to the environmental pressures that impact wetland ecosystem states (see Figure 11.2) for an application to the Broads wetland (Broads Authority, 2004). These impacts cause environmental change, which, in turn, impact human beings, usually in some kind of societal response that feeds back into human activities. This feedback loop and any lags are important aspects of the human and natural systems interface.

The DPSIR framework provides a conceptual and organizational backdrop for the contributions of different disciplines to the description and analysis of environmental problems, given that the socio-economic aspects of environmental problems are an integral part of this co-evolutionary framework. It should be stressed that the DPSIR is a framework, not a model. Its main purpose is to make more manageable the complexity of environmental problems; for example in wetland ecosystems and related protection and sustainable management issues. It provides an important starting point on the road towards a common level of understanding and consensus between researchers, natural resource managers and policy makers as they debate the links between the various driving forces that pose a threat to the intrinsic functioning of a wetland ecosystem. In the case of the Broads, these pressures have included land conversion, agricultural development, hydrological perturbation and pollution, increasing flood risk perceptions, and their consequent impact on the various interests or tourism, stakeholder groups who utilize the goods and services provided by these ecosystems and/or contribute to the pressures on them. Moreover, there are likely to be differences in stakeholders' perceptions of pressures, impacts and environmental values (see Figure 11.2).

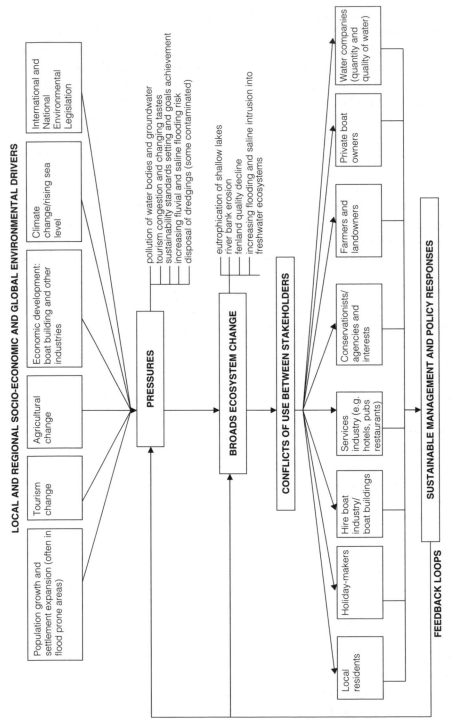

Figure 11.2 Pressures facing the Broads and consequent conflicts of use

Table 11.1 *Potential performance indicators*

Plan objectives and outcomes	Potential performance indicator
Living landscapes	
• Long-term vision for the Broads	Qualitative sustainability assessment degree of consensus among stakeholders
• Maintenance of Broads' landscape	Extent and percentage of flood plain maintained as open water, fen, grazing, marsh or open space
	Extent and voluntary uptake of agri-environmental schemes
• Sustainable land use plan	Percentage of appeals against planning decisions upheld by Planning Inspector
	Percentage of new homes built on previously developed land
• Flooding alleviation	Number of properties damaged by flooding
Water, habitats and wildlife	
• 'Good' status for all water bodies (Water Framework Directive)	Percentage of length of rivers and number of broads in 'good' status
• Biodiversity conservation enhancement	Percentage of sites of Special Scientific Interest in favourable condition
• Sustainable fen management	Total area of fen under appropriate management
Tourism and recreation	
• Risk reduction and boat safety enhancement	Number of incidents resulting in injury or death per annum
• Sustainable boating activity	Mean number of weeks per year that cruisers are hired
	Percentage of hire boats accredited under Quality Grading Schemes
	Percentage of boats meeting best available technology standards
	Percentage of boats violating speed restrictions
	Percentage of public rights of way easily accessible
• Enhanced access to land and water	Length of footpaths accessible to the disabled
• Tourism infrastructure quality enhancement	Number of catering establishments accredited under the Broads Quality Charter
Public understanding	
• Maximum awareness of national park principles and practice	Percentage of residents and visitors aware of national park status (survey monitoring)
• Maximum stakeholder inclusion	Number of organizations and community groups active in the plan implementation process

Source: Adapted from (Broads Authority, 2004).

In the context of complex decision making that aims to maintain functioning and ecological diversity in wetland ecosystems and satisfy multiple stakeholder groups, a range of protection and management options are likely to be available. Such options can be translated into management or development scenarios with each option likely to have different impacts on human and natural systems across different spatial and time scales. These impacts are often complex, but can, in principle, be measured with the help of indicators. Capturing the whole range of relevant impacts on natural and human systems within different protection or management scenarios, given the overall goal of sustainable development, will require a combination of environmental, social and economic indicators. Table 11.1 summarizes the indicators being developed by the Broads Authority alongside its 20-year plan.

Functions, uses, stakeholders, pressures and environmental changes

The Broads wetlands perform a variety of functions valued by a range of stakeholder groups living and working in the area or for those visiting the area. The main wetland functions are presented in Table 11.2. The table details the biophysical structure and processes maintaining the functions, their socio-economic uses and benefits, and threats to future availability of the functions. The Broads wetlands provide a buffer against extreme hydrological conditions; providing water storage in times of flood, and water release during a drought. Wetlands also have the capacity to change water quality through the removal of chemical pollutants such as nitrogen and phosphate. A third major function is the provision of a nationally and internationally important habitat for flora and fauna (including a number of rare species), which, in turn, along with the waterways themselves, attracts tourists to the area.

The Broads floodplain is at risk from two types of flooding: tidal flooding, caused by high sea levels, and fluvial flooding, caused by high river flows (Turner et al, 1995). Surge tides can cause saline flooding of land by breaching or overtopping flood banks. Saline intrusion also occurs in surge conditions as more salt water forces upstream between the banks. This can damage the ecology of normally freshwater reaches and cause extensive fish kills. Fluvial flooding, caused by heavy rainfall, is less damaging from an agricultural or conservation perspective, although flooding of any kind can damage property. If low river flow conditions occur in the autumn, normal high tides can cause the same saline intrusion effect (Turner and Brooke, 1988; Turner et al, 1995).

Besides the threat of increased salt water incursion and tidal salt water flooding, the Broads is threatened with another water problem: variable river flows and depleted groundwater. The Broads are part of a much wider catchment area. About 6 million people live in this area, which puts considerable demand on the region's water resources and poses a potential threat to the Broads. The region is furthermore the driest in Britain and droughts are a common feature of the area. Agriculture is another significant water user, in particular through spray irrigation of land in dry periods.

Table 11.2 *Wetland functions and associated socio-economic benefits in the Broads*

Function	Biophysical structure or process maintaining function	Socio-economic use and benefits	Threats
Hydrological functions			
Flood water retention	Short- and long-term storage of overbank flood water and retention of surface water runoff from surrounding slopes	Natural flood protection alternative, reduced damage to infrastructure (road network, etc.), property and crops	Conversion, drainage, filling and reduction of storage capacity, removal of vegetation
Groundwater recharge	Infiltration of flood water in wetland surface followed by percolation to aquifer	Water supply, habitat maintenance	Reduction of recharge rates, overpumping, pollution
Groundwater discharge	Upward seepage of groundwater through wetland surface	Effluent dilution	Drainage, filling
Sediment retention and deposition	Net storage of fine sediments carried in suspension by river water during overbank flooding or by surface runoff from other wetland units or contributory area	Improved water quality downstream, soil fertility	Channelization, excess reduction of sediment throughput
Biogeochemical functions			
Nutrient retention	Uptake of nutrients by plants (n and p), storage in soil organic matter, absorption of n as ammonium, absorption of p in soil	Improved water quality	Drainage, water abstraction, removal of vegetation, pollution, dredging
Nutrient export	Flushing through water system and gaseous export of n	Improved water quality, waste disposal	Drainage, water abstraction, removal of vegetation, pollution, flow barriers
Peat accumulation	In situ retention of carbon	Fuel, paleo-environmental data source	Overexploitation, drainage

Table 11.2 *Wetland functions and associated socio-economic benefits in the Broads* (Cont'd)

Function	Biophysical structure or process maintaining function	Socio-economic use and benefits	Threats
Ecological functions			
Habitat for (migratory) species (biodiversity)	Provision of microsites for macro-invertebrates, fish, reptiles, birds, mammals and landscape structural diversity	Fishing, wildfowl hunting, recreational amenities, tourism	Overexploitation, overcrowding and congestion, wildlife disturbance, pollution, interruption of migration routes, management neglect
Nursery for plants, animals, micro-organisms	Provision of microsites for macro-invertebrates, fish, reptiles, birds, mammals	Fishing, reed harvest	Overexploitation, overcrowding and wildlife disturbance, management neglect
Food web support	Biomass production, biomass import and export via physical and biological processes	Farming, fen biomass as alternative energy source	Conversion, extensive use of inputs (pollution), market failures

Source: Modified from Turner et al, 1997, and Burbridge, 1994.

Adequate groundwater levels and river flows are crucial for a number of reasons. First, sufficient water of good quality is vital for the wildlife diversity of the fens and marshes. The particular character of a fen is determined by its reliance on water supply: groundwater, river water, rainfall or a combination of the three. Also, the drained marshland depends upon an adequate freshwater supply to the dyke (field drains) systems. Many grazing marsh dykes rely on freshwater conditions to maintain the diversity of their aquatic flora. Dykes are also a source of drinking water for livestock on the marshes, especially during the summer.

Second, water abstraction decreases summer river flows, which in turn concentrates sewage discharges, reduces the flushing of algae from the Broads system and exacerbates the problem of saline intrusion. The increase in nutrient levels as a result of the introduction of river-based sewage works during the early part of the 20th century has, in particular, triggered an enormous change in the Broads water ecosystem, known as eutrophication. Eutrophication is essentially a fertilization of the water through nutrient enrichment. Two nutrients are involved: phosphates (P) and nitrates (N). Phosphates enter the system from sewage treatment works, while nitrates mainly come from the runoff from agricultural land within the Broads catchment, and to a lesser extent from sewage treatment works. Phosphorus comes from a limited number of sewage treatment works and can be removed before it is discharged into the water, and nitrogen comes from all over the catchment and is therefore difficult to control in the short term. Phosphorus levels have declined or are low in the main rivers, but nitrogen levels remain problematic. Only 12 of the 63 permanent water bodies are in good condition with stable aquatic plant populations and clear water (Broads Authority, 2004). We will return to the eutrophication problem in a later section.

Species conservation is a key management objective but the success of conservation or restoration generally, particularly in wetlands, depends upon restoration of wider ecosystem function (Moss, 1983; Scheffer et al, 1993; Moss et al, 1996; Holzer et al, 1997; Madgwick and Phillips, 1997; Pitt et al, 1997; Stansfield et al, 1997). One administrative issue arises from the difference between ecological and management authority boundaries that affects Broadland. The executive area of the Broads Authority of Norfolk and Suffolk follows the river valleys, but much of the Broads groundwater catchment, as well as the upper catchments of the main rivers that supply the Broads, are outside the direct influence of the Authority. The quantity and chemical quality of water received by the lakes and rivers of Broadland is thus, at least in part, outside the direct influence of the area's major management authority. Such administrative problems may prove a substantial impediment to the implementation of a holistic and integrated programme for Broadland management.

In succeeding sections, we highlight three policy challenges: (i) the multiple use management of the shallow lakes and rivers (Broads) given the threat posed by eutrophication; (ii) the provision of a selective flood alleviation scheme to protect nature conservation, recreation and other economic interests; and (iii) the need for better information on recreation/amenity users and their preferences, in order to promote sustainable tourism.

Sustainable tourism

Managing the water resources is also important for the public enjoyment of the area and navigation. Low freshwater flows can exacerbate problems of blue-green algae, botulism, salt water incursions and other water quality factors that severely affect people's enjoyment of the waterways, particularly those who participate in recreation or sports involving contact with the water. On the other hand, the visitors themselves, in aggregate, have put considerable strains on the area for a number of reasons with the risk of impairing those environmental features that people come to see and experience in the first place. Large numbers of visitors disturb local wildlife, especially during the breeding and nesting season. The expansion of boating activity in the past is believed to have confined wildfowl to less disturbed and non-navigable roads. The Broads provide an important habitat for a number of rare bird species such as the marsh harrier, bearded tit and the bittern.

The large numbers of visitors on boats, especially motorboats, result in considerable boat wash and, hence, river bank erosion and potential increased flood risk. Most hire boats are designed to meet comfort requirements, not to meet the specific environmental needs of the Broads. The river stretches are not particularly wide, while most of the broads cover less than 10ha. The size and shape of a craft significantly influences the amount of wash produced (May and Walters, 1986). Boat wash has an impact on the bankside vegetation and eventually the floodwall itself. A more sustainable approach to tourism is therefore an urgent requirement. It has been estimated that the overall value of tourism generated in the Broads area is approximately £47 million/annum. This financial flow supports 3107 full-time job equivalents. Some 4.4 million nights are spent in the area by visitors and around 1.3 million day visits are made to the Broads (Broads Authority, personal communication). However, the local hire boat industry has been negatively affected by changing consumer tasks and trends in recent years. The national leisure and tourism market is now characterized by trends such as the increase in holidays taken outside the UK, more frequent and shorter holidays and a much greater emphasis on high standards of service and value for one's money. These factors together with demographic changes have served to cause a significant fall in demand for the traditional Broads boating holidays, with subsequent negative economic multiplier impacts throughout the adjacent area. Recreation value can be estimated using an indirect travel cost (TC) method. Here, the relevant demand curve is assessed by comparing the number of trips taken by visitors with the cost of those trips in terms of direct expenditure upon travel and entrance fees and the indirect opportunity costs of travel time (Bateman, 1993; Bergin and Price, 1994). One aspect of TC analysis that has been a focus in recent research is the potential of the method for undertaking 'benefit transfer' analyses. Benefit transfer has been defined as 'the transfer of existing estimates of non-market values to a new study which is different from the study for which the values were originally estimated' (Boyle and Bergstrom, 1992). Within the Broads, the objective has been to construct models based upon data from a set of surveyed sites and use these to estimate the number of visitors to unsurveyed sites and their corresponding recreational values. This is an attractive procedure because it saves time and money on repeated studies, particularly as there are many forces that are likely to increase the demand for non-market benefit estimates over the next few years (McConnell, 1992).

Visitor arrivals functions can be estimated linking visits to a series of predictors, values for which can be collected for the target unsurveyed sites. An example of such a function is given as Equation (1) (see Table 11.3). This equation links the number of visits to a site to the time and distance cost of those visits (thereby allowing the estimation of visit values) and other predictors, including the type and quality of

Table 11.3 *Explanation of visitor arrival functions*

Visits	= f (	Price,	Socio-econ,	Quality,	Subs,	X)
No. of visits to undertake a given activity at a site. Expressed as either total visits of individuals or a visitor rate (e.g. per household pa)		Costs of a visit in terms of travel expenditure and the opportunity cost of travel time	Socio-economic factors (e.g. ownership, unemployment, etc.)	Type and quality of facilities provided at the site under consideration	Type, availability and quality of substitute sites	A matrix of other explanatory variables

facilities at the target site, the availability and quality of substitutes, socio-economic and possibly cultural factors and other explanatory variables.

$$\text{VISITS} = f(\text{PRICE}, \text{SOCIO} - \text{ECON}, \text{QUALITY}, \text{SUBS}, X) \qquad (1)$$

To date, relatively few benefit transfer analyses have been undertaken. This is largely because it is difficult to obtain accurate information on several important elements in the transfer function, such as travel times taken for visitors to reach the site, the availability of substitute sites and the definition of visitor zones of origin. However, recent advances in geographical information systems (GIS) technology have provided a superior foundation for implementing benefit transfer methods of placing economic values on recreational demand (Bateman et al, 1999; Brainard et al, 1999). In particular, GIS can help to resolve some of the spatial and data-handling problems associated with benefit transfer, while facilitating several methodological improvements.

The baseline data for our GIS-based transferable travel cost model is taken from a Broadland survey undertaken in 1996 and discussed in detail in a following section. This survey provides a total of 2098 visitor interviews conducted at 10 sites across the area. Trip origin information was collected from each survey respondent in the form of a full postcode of their home address (Bateman et al, 1996). The GIS was then used to interrogate the Bartholomew's 1:250,000 digital map database to extract data concerning the distribution and quality of the entire UK road network to permit computation of minimum travel time routes from all origin addresses to the survey site. Figure 11.3 illustrates some of the output from this analysis showing the diversity of outset origins and routes taken to reach Broadland.

The advanced spatial analytic capabilities afforded by a GIS permit the analyst to extract high-quality data on many of the other determinants of

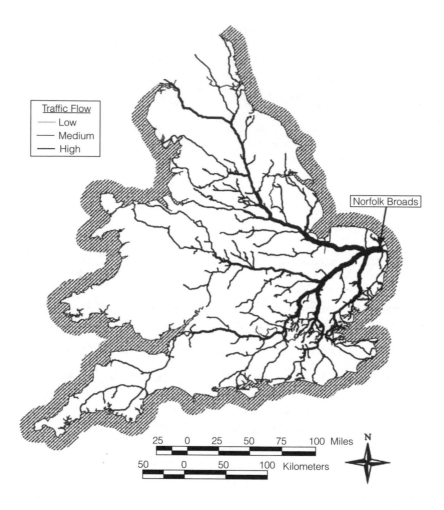

Figure 11.3 Holiday visitor traffic flows to the Norfolk Broads, simulated in a GIS

Equation (1), both for surveyed and unsurveyed sites. For example, interrogations of data sources such as the satellite-image based Institute of Terrestrial Ecology UK Land Cover Database, have, and are, being used to identify potential substitute destinations, and their accessibility is being estimated within in GIS (Brainard et al, 1999). Similarly, socio-economic data on both actual and potential visitors can be extracted from the UK Census of Population to examine the influence of deprivation indicators such as levels of unemployment and urbanization on visitor recreation demand in Broadland and to identify which groups do not visit sites (a factor that opens up previously unexplored avenues for distributional and equity analyses). A particular factor that merits attention is the possible existence of different sub-groups, with diverse priorities and recreational preferences within the catchment areas of the sites. The use of GIS allows a more sophisticated analysis of the nature of recreational interactions than is normally seen in conventional environmental value studies.

A range of interests have recently come together to set out a new strategy to combat the decline in tourism demand and to generate new economically and environmentally sustainable business growth. The ambitious vision is to foster a thriving boat hire industry and ancillary services via a quality experience based on customer needs. Over the medium term, the boat fleet will need to be made more environmentally efficient, with increased use of electric boats, solar boats and sail craft. A more niche-orientated marketing strategy is perceived to be required in preference to the old preoccupation with volume maximization, which will highlight environmental quality as the key Broads holiday characteristic (Strategic Leisure and TEP, 2001).

With this emerging context in mind, some recent research based on a combination of quantitative and qualitative social research approaches has focused on tourism overcrowding in the Broads. Face-to-face interviews of visitors who hire motorboats and group discussions with local residents who own motorboats were used to reveal stakeholder preferences and attitudes to perceived and actual problems (Brouwer, 1999; Brouwer et al, 2002). A majority of respondents felt that overcrowding was a real problem and that it was reducing the quality of the holiday/environmental experience, in terms of general amenity and peace and quiet. But there was also a sensitivity to increased hire prices as a mechanism to mitigate overcrowding. Water space zoning was another policy option that was met with significant opposition. The negative response to this instrument also served to uncover a deeper problem. Issues of trust, responsibility and blame seem to underlie opposition to change. The Broads Authority (BA) was seen as too remote and bureaucratic by the boaters and its motives were questioned. To the boaters, the hidden agenda appeared to be the eventual exclusion of boating from the Broads in favour of nature conservation. This group polarization has emerged despite the fact that the BA's stated and actual policy is one of balancing the main interests in a long-term management strategy. In recognition of this problem the BA has begun to institute a more overt stakeholder consultation process. This more inclusionary approach has been piloted in a localized problem case connected with one particular lake, Hickling Broad (Turner et al, 2003), and has been broadened out to discuss management issues across sub-catchment scales (known as the Upper Thurne River Catchment Group). It turned out that the 'local' problem was in fact symptomatic of causal mechanisms that were catchment-wide, including areas beyond the executive control of the BA. The new EU Water Framework Directive will also serve to emphasize the catchment-scale and management processes that are inclusionary. We now turn to examine these wider questions and the general problem of managing a rate of environmental change in a highly dynamic setting.

Managing dynamic ecosystem change: Combating eutrophication and feedback effects

It is expected that climate change, through, for example, alterations to the nutrient cycle, will exacerbate existing water quality problems such as eutrophication (Horne and Goldman, 1994). In addition, secondary effects upon water quality are expected through the role of climate change in increasing human demand for water services such as water provision, sewage treatment, etc. (Climate Change, 2001). The stresses put upon the integrity of freshwater sources are exacerbated by population growth. For example, in our study area of East Anglia, a region with higher than average population flows, there has been increasing pressure upon open-water resources such as rivers and lakes. A valuation study was undertaken whose main objective was to measure the benefits that individuals derive from preventing excess algae (eutrophication) impacts upon open water in rivers and lakes in East Anglia (see Bateman et al, 2004 for full details). A questionnaire based on the contingent valuation method (CVM) was used to estimate an individual's willingness to pay (WTP) for a scheme to prevent excess algae in the rivers and lakes in order to ensure continued access to the amenity and recreation facilities that each site provides. The scheme was based on a sewage treatment programme that would remove nutrients and reduce eutrophication.

The contingent valuation survey comprised a variety of sections including: assessments of present use of water bodies; reactions (including belief indicators) regarding the process by which water bodies and related activities may be affected by eutrophication; assessments of how such changes might impact upon usage of those water bodies; a valuation scenario section outlining the proposed scheme and a valuation task that examines households' WTP to avoid the specified eutrophication impacts. The valuation scenario included information on the rising population of East Anglia and increased pressure on sewage treatment works and the effects of changing weather patterns on water quality. Survey respondents were given a plausible solution to the potential problem of eutrophication in the form of, for example, a phosphate removal scheme at the sewage works. Respondents were told that such a treatment would increase their annual household water bill. After the presentation of the valuation scenario and payment mechanism, respondents were faced with the elicitation question, asking them how much they would be willing to pay for the good if given the opportunity to obtain it, under specified terms and conditions. The particular method of elicitation used was a relatively new approach, known as the one and one half-bound (OOHB) elicitation method (Cooper et al, 2002). Rather than facing a single yes/no response question about the cost of provision, the OOHB mechanism presents survey respondents with upper and lower bound cost estimates per household (or per individual) associated with the provision change under consideration. The precise values of these amounts (bids) are varied across the sample to permit estimation of survival functions and associated univariate

WTP measures such as the mean and median. Such an approach is considered to have greater statistical efficiency, plausibility and incentive compatibility than alternative mechanisms (Bateman et al, 2002). The contingent valuation survey approached 2321 households for face-to-face interviews; 1067 of these refused to take the survey, which contained one of the 13 bid (cost) treatments selected randomly so as to ensure equal sample size of each bid level. In order to obtain estimates of the WTP for the phosphorus removal scheme, it was assumed that a respondent's yes/no choice regarding the payment of a given bid amount to obtain a given improvement in environmental quality is made in the context of a utility maximizing choice by the respondent. In accordance with the random utility framework, the individual's WTP is a random variable with a cumulative distribution function whose parameters can be estimated on the basis of the responses to the contingent valuation survey (Bateman et al, 2002).

Table 11.4 presents the mean and median WTP values. Of the 1254 respondents sampled, only 1112 responses were used for the econometric analysis, since 142 responses had missing observations for significant explanatory variables. The mean household annual WTP for the total sample (n = 1112) was found to be £75.40. Protest bids were identified based on the answers to questions regarding the reasons for acceptance/refusal of a bid amount. The removal of the 232 protest bids produced no significant change to the WTP amount, which remained at £75.40/household/year. Aggregation of the sample WTP is crucial for benefit estimation to be used in a CBA. As the study was carried out in the East Anglia region, and had to do with the protection of lakes and rivers against eutrophication in this region, the aggregation was constrained to consider only the local population, and not to include the whole of the UK, although it is noted that non-use values would exist for individuals living elsewhere in the country. The sample mean WTP per household was thus multiplied by the number of households in East Anglia, which is 2.253 million, to give annual benefits of £169 million. Turning now to the cost of reducing eutrophication, compliance cost estimates from a previous study conducted by Pretty et al (2002) were obtained. The authors carried out a preliminary assessment of the environmental costs of eutrophication of freshwaters in England and Wales. The relevant compliance costs are those associated with sewage treatment. Sewage treatment companies incur costs to comply with

Table 11.4 *Mean and median WTP for avoiding eutrophication damages*

Mean WTP (£)	75.41
Median WTP (£)	69.07
95% confidence interval	69.41–84.36
Standard error	3.71

environmental legislation for the removal of phosphorus before it enters watercourses. Pretty et al (2002) predicted that nutrient removal at sewage treatment works, which come under the EC Urban Wastewater Treatment Directive, would cost water companies £50 million/year, with a further operating cost of £0.3 million/year for each year over the period 2000–2010. These costs are for the whole of England and Wales. As such, the comparison of aggregate benefits from the prevention of eutrophication just for the East Anglia region with the costs of a nutrient removal scheme for the entire English and Welsh region indicates that there are significant positive net benefits. Within the Broads (national park equivalent) area, however, complicated feedback effects have served to make practical management more difficult.

The Broads Authority's (BA) powers are similar to other UK National Park authorities, plus a navigation duty. But the BA is not subject to the Sandford principle, which mandates primary status for nature conservation in all the other UK National Park areas. The BA's statutory duties are focused around the requirement to balance navigation, nature conservation and recreation/amenity interests. This complex political, economic and environmental trade-off process is becoming even more difficult as the result of recent EU Directives (notably The Birds and Habitats Directive). This regulatory approach has at its core a rather 'static' interpretation of nature protection. Such an interpretation does not sit easily with the BA's remit of 'balancing' different interests in order to sustainably manage all the assets within its executive area. The navigation duty sometimes proves to be at odds with the provision of quiet public enjoyment and the conservation of the area's natural beauty.

The difficulties likely to be posed more generally by the Habitat Directive for management authorities such as the BA have been highlighted in the case of Hickling Broad (see Figure 11.1). This is a water body that over the last 30 years or so has become a focal point for private and other sail and power boaters. Rights of navigation are restricted to a specified channel, but boating has become possible over a large part of the surface of the water body. In more recent years, as water quality has been improved, aquatic plant growth has accelerated, and large sections of the water body have at times become virtually inaccessible to navigation.

Restoration policies promoted by the BA have reduced nutrient flow into the Norfolk Broads and greatly improved water quality. In Hickling Broad, these measures have proved to be especially successful insofar as they have encouraged the return of previously threatened aquatic plants. However, the thickness of plant growth sometimes slows boat traffic and adversely affects local sailing competitions. As part of its overall commitment to supporting the sustainable development of the Broads, the BA has a statutory duty to maintain the area for the purposes of navigation. It also tries to encourage environmentally friendly boating. However, the increasingly dense beds of aquatic plant (including a rare species of stonewort) growth can periodically destroy non-powered and electrically powered craft, and local boatyards may be tempted to revert back to using diesel-powered craft on Hickling Broad, thereby increasing noise and water pollution (Turner et al, 2003).

Clearly, management of a dynamic and multiple-use ecosystem is hindered if a 'static' interpretation of the EC Directives is adopted. A more flexible interpretation is essential to allow, in the Hickling case, experimental plant cutting and monitoring. Other management action to maintain navigation and recreation interests throughout the Broads executive area will also fall foul of a static interpretation of the provisions of the Habitats Directive. Some room for manoeuvre may be possible in terms of whether all management actions necessarily need to be interpreted as 'projects' and therefore as requiring impact assessments. For an authority like the BA, the cost implications alone would make such a ruling impracticable. From the UK government perspective, there is an element of 'wait and see' in its position, as it monitors how events play out in the Broads context. From the BA's perspective, there is a need to achieve a working compromise, or at least to engage stakeholders in an ongoing process of dialogue. Efforts are under way to promote such a deliberative and participatory process in order to achieve a reasonable compromise between navigation and conservation needs. It is also now clear that the management objective can only be the maintenance of relative stability in the Broad's conditions. The stakeholder dialogue process has been constantly widened and now has to encompass flooding risk management issues in the area.

Flood alleviation and sea level rise mitigation strategies for Broadland: Valuation analysis

In 1991 the National Rivers Authority (NRA), later named the Environment Agency (EA), initiated a wide ranging investigation to develop an: 'effective and cost-effective strategy to alleviate flooding in Broadland for the next 50 years' (Bateman et al, 1992).

The appraisal process consisted of five main components: hydraulic modelling, engineering, cost–benefit assessment, environmental assessment and consultation. The item of most relevance here is the cost–benefit assessment, which compared benefits of undertaking a scheme to provide a particular standard of flood protection to the costs of such an undertaking. Although market benefits from flood protection were considered in terms of agriculture, industry/residential and infrastructure (Turner and Brooke, 1988), the value of the non-market benefits from the area were uncertain.

As part of the cost–benefit assessment for the Flood Alleviation Study, a Broadland contingent valuation (CV) survey of recreational visitors was commissioned in 1991 to assess the WTP of individuals to preserve the existing

Broadland landscape, ecology and recreational possibilities (Bateman et al, 1992, 1994, 1995). Respondents were presented with two scenario:

1   'do nothing' in which due to saline intrusion virtually all the Broadland landscape and ecology would change in character;
2   implementation of an unspecified scheme for flood alleviation, which would preserve the current Broadland landscape and ecology.

The study consisted of two surveys: (i) a postal survey of households across the UK designed to capture the values that non-users might hold for preservation of the present state of Broadland; and (ii) an investigation of the values held by users for the same scenario as elicited through an on-site survey. Further theoretical and methodological investigations were undertaken via a second on-site survey conducted in 1996. Details of all three of these studies are presented below.

Non-user values were estimated by means of a mail survey questionnaire sent to addresses throughout Great Britain in order to capture both socio-economic and distance decay effects on stated WTP. Table 11.5 details the sampling strategy employed in this survey and the response rates achieved (Bateman and Langford, 1997).

The survey questionnaire was designed to best practice standards (Dillman, 1978). It was pre-tested through a focus group with pilot exercises, and included visual, map and textual information detailing the nature of Broadland, the flooding problems and flood defence options together with necessary details supporting a WTP question such as payment vehicle, payment time frame, etc. The survey achieved a typically modest response rate of some 31 per cent, however, initial analysis showed that this was heavily supported by past users of

Table 11.5 *Non-user survey response rate by sample group*

Sample group identification label	Distance zone[a]	Socio-economic class or area	No. of usable responses	Group response rate (%)[b]	Proportion of total usable responses (%)
1 M	1	Middle (2A)	58	34.7	18.7
2 M	2	Middle (2A)	66	39.5	21.3
3 M	3	Middle (2A)	59	35.3	19
4 M	4	Middle (2A)	47	28.1	15.2
3 U	3	Upper (1A)	54	31.1	16.8
3 K	3	Lower (4A)	28	16.8	9
Group mean			52	30.9	16.7
Total			310	—	100

Notes:
[a] Zone 1 = Central (Broadland) distance band (width approximately 40km); remaining zones are approximately 110km wide; 4 = most distant bank.
[b] 167 questionnaires mailed out to each sample group (total mailings = 1002).

Broadland who represented well over one-third of the responses in each distance category. Although experience of visiting the Broads declines significantly with distance from the area ($p < 0.0001$), this sample can best be characterized as a sample of dormant past users.

Analysis of the response rates detailed in Table 11.5 together with respondent characteristic data showed that response rates were negatively related to increasing distance from the Broads and positively related to respondent income. These relationships were further reflected within the replies of those who did return their questionnaires. When asked whether or not they agreed with the principle of incurring extra personal taxes to pay for flood defences in Broadland (the 'payment principle' question), 166 respondents (53.5 per cent) answered positively to the payment principle question. Determinants of these responses were investigated, yielding the model described in Equation (2):

$$\begin{aligned}
\text{LOGIT (YES)} = \ & 0.370 - 0.866 \text{ DISTANT} + 0.602 \text{ FISH} + 0.446 \text{ SOMEVIS} \\
& \ (0.61) \quad (2.59) \qquad\qquad (2.16) \qquad\quad (1.68) \\
& + 1.112 \text{ OFTVIS} + 1.458 \text{ INCMID} + 1.924 \text{ INCHI} \\
& \quad (2.23) \qquad\quad (2.81) \qquad\quad (3.45)
\end{aligned} \qquad (2)$$

where:

LOGIT (YES) = In $\{\pi_i/(1 - \pi_i)\}$ where π_i = the probability of the respondent saying 'yes' to the payment principle question.
DISTANT = 1 if respondent lives outside zone 1 (= 0 otherwise).
FISH = 1 if respondent participates in fishing at least occasionally (= 0 otherwise).
SOMEVIS = 1 if respondent sometimes but not often visits the countryside for relaxation/scenery (= 0 otherwise).
OFTVIS = 1 if respondent often visits the countryside for relaxation/scenery (= 0 otherwise).
INCMID = 1 if household income is £10–30k/annum (= 0 otherwise).
INCHI = 1 if household income exceeds £30k per annum (= 0 otherwise).
Scaled deviance = 378.89; df = 300; Figures in brackets are *t*-values.

Equation (2) also shows that even after controlling for proximity, participation in certain of the activities for which Broadland is synonymous (i.e. fishing, relaxing and enjoying scenery) is positively related to respondents agreeing to the payment principle.

Those respondents who accepted the payment principle were presented with an 'open-ended' format valuation question asking them to state the maximum amount of extra taxes they would pay WTP per annum to safeguard Broadland from the effects of increased flooding.

Including, as zero's, those respondents who refused the payment principle (i.e. those who stated they were not willing to pay to prevent flooding), this question elicited a whole-sample mean WTP of £23.29/annum (95 per cent confidence intervals: £17.53–32.45). It was also found that mean WTP decreases as the distance from Broadland increases, and previous Broadland visitors expressed a substantially higher WTP than those who have never visited the area. Aggregation of WTP estimates was conducted using three approaches, via the sample mean WTP, distance zone adjusted, and by bid functions (see Table 11.6 and Bateman et al, 2000). Analysis of the data that produced the results in Table 11.6 suggests that the simple 'Sample mean' and 'distance zone' approaches to aggregation yield substantial overestimates of total non-users benefits, which were very sensitive to the omission of any unusually high WTP responses. By contrast, the 'bid function' approach gave robust and stable estimates of aggregate value. In summary, the study of present non-users yields a consistent picture and provides the basis for some defensible estimates of aggregate benefits, which in turn yield an interesting commentary upon current practice. We now turn to consider the various on-site CV surveys of visitors to Broadland.

The 1991 user study generally conformed to the CV testing protocol subsequently laid down by the NOAA blue ribbon panel (Arrow et al, 1993). Survey design was extensively pre-tested with any changes to the questionnaire being retested over a total pilot sample of some 433 respondents. One of the many findings of this process was that a tax-based annual payment vehicle appeared optimal when assessed over a range of criteria (details in Bateman et al, 1993).

The final questionnaire was applied through on-site interviews with visitors at representative sites around Broadland, with 2897 questionnaires being completed. This sample was composed of 846 interviewees given the open-ended (OE) WTP questionnaire, and the remaining 2051 facing in turn the single-bound dichotomous choice (1DC) and interactive bidding (IB) questions. The 1DC elicitation method faces respondents with a single question such as 'are you willing to pay £x?' and then the bid level £x is varied across the sample. The IB method supplements the initial question with two further dichotomous choice questions reducing £x or increasing £x according to the answers given. The respondent is then finally given an OE question, the answer to which determines

Table 11.6 *The present non-user's benefits of preserving the present condition of Broadland aggregated across Great Britain using various procedures*

Aggregation approach	£ million/annum
(1) Aggregation using sample mean WTP	98.4–159.7
(2) Aggregation adjusting for distance zones	98.0–111.1
(3) Aggregation by bid functions:	
(i) using distance zone and national income	25.3–27.3
(ii) using country distance and regional income	24.0–25.4

the WTP value used by the analysts. Prior to any WTP question, respondents were presented with a 'payment principle' question. Negative responses to this question reduced sample sizes to 715 (OE) and 1811 (1DC/IB), respectively. Except where indicated, all those refusing the payment principle are treated as having zero WTP in calculating subsequent WTP measures.

The theoretical validity of responses to the various WTP questions was assessed through the estimation of a series of bid functions. The analysis indicated that a consistent set of predictors explain WTP responses, including measures of respondent income, experience of Broadland and participation in related activities, and interest in environmental issues.

As noted previously, the Norfolk Broads CV study was conducted in answer to a real-world question regarding the funding of flood defences in Broadland. The study fed into a wider cost–benefit analysis that also examined the agricultural, property and infrastructure damage-avoided benefits of such defences. The benefit–cost ratio of the latter items was calculated at 0.98 (National Rivers Authority, 1992). However, even if only a conservative measure of WTP for the recreational and environmental benefits of flood prevention is considered the benefit–cost ratio increases substantially to 1.94, indicating that the benefits of a flood alleviation strategy are almost twice the associated costs. The results, including findings from the CV study, were submitted to the relevant Ministry of Agriculture, Food and Fisheries as part of an application of central government funding support for the proposed flood alleviation strategy. Following lengthy consideration of this application, in 1997 the Environment Agency announced that it had received conditional approval for a programme for 'bank strengthening and erosion protection' (Environment Agency, 1997). The actual scheme has been taken forward since 2000 on the basis of a long-term private/public partnership scheme (between the EA and relevant government support ministries and a private engineering firm consortium).

Since the publication of Kahneman and Knetsch's (1992) 'embedding' critique of CV, there has been a wide-ranging debate over whether respondents give sufficient consideration of the specific characteristics of the goods valued when responding to CV questions. More specifically, the subsequent academic debate has focused on the sensitivity of WTP estimates to the scope of the good considered, where scope can be defined in terms of quantity and/or quality. A follow-up survey to the Broadland 1991 survey was therefore undertaken, which considered the circumstances under which sensitivity to scope occurs, where scope was defined in terms of the area protected by a flood alleviation scheme (FAS) for either the whole (W) of that area of Broadland that is under threat from saline flooding or a series of part (P) areas within that whole. As such, the P FASs are nested within the W FAS.

It was suggested by Carson and Mitchell (1995) that the most appropriate test of scope sensitivity is through the comparison of independent valuations from different levels of amenity. Such a test was undertaken in the Broadland

1996 survey by collecting two samples of users, the first of which faced questions concerning their WTP for the W scheme followed by their WTP for the P scheme (the 'top-down' W/P sequence sample); while the second sample faced the same questions but presented in reverse order 'bottom-up'; P/W sequence sample).

Full results of the Broadland 1996 survey are presented in Power (2000), however, they do not provide conclusive evidence for either CV supporters or their critics, and suggest instead that a mixture of economic and psychological influences are at work here. This points towards a complexity of preference motivations that is at the same time both unsurprising and challenging, and ought to be the future research agenda for CV research.

While the valuation work indicates that the public does put significant value on the environment that Broadland provides, the costs of flood protection provision are also very high. Over the 1990s, the Environment Agency has formulated a selective approach to flood alleviation and not a strategy that will provide an area-wide uniform level of protection. A number of communities and business sites are currently at high risk from flooding (so called 'undefended areas') as levels of protection vary across the area. The Broadland area is the subject of an experiment in terms of flooding alleviation scheme funding. A joint public and private funding initiative (PPP/PFI) has been launched that provides public funding over a 20-year period, which will be spent by a private consortium (Turner et al, 2003).

Conclusions and policy implications

The Broads wetland area is a multiple-use resource under heavy and sustained environmental pressure and subject to dynamic ecosystem change. The DPSIR organizing framework was successfully used to scope the magnitude and significance of the environmental change problems and consequent sustainable management policy response issues. The saline water inundation/flooding and its alleviation, tourism requirements and preferences and water quality-related conflict problems have been highlighted. Managing the rate of change in order to satisfy the many interest groups that live, work or visit in the Broads, or who merely appreciate from afar its unique characteristics, is the key challenge for the Broads Authority and its partners. The interdisciplinary research presented in this chapter seeks to improve our understanding of the Broads and thereto better inform the management process. The Authority's vision for the Broads, which is shared by many other interest groups, is an environment that is conserved but not fossilized in terms of natural systems, traditional activities and heritage landscape. Rather the aim is to allow for organic growth and changing human requirements and preferences, while ensuring that future generations receive the environmental, social and economic bequest that is their right. At the core of the vision is the acknowledgement that human activities, if they are to be sustainable, depend on the continued health and functioning of the Broads environment. Boating and other forms of recreation, for example, are intimately dependent on a good-quality environment, but equally the continued existence of such activities is a prime component of the local environs in terms of landscape, cultural heritage and amenity. An area largely devoid of humans and their activities is not the Broads, nor for that matter is it any of the other national parks in Britain.

Putting the vision into practice will require 'partnership' and 'consensus' in order to engage all interested parties in the implementation of a new (2004) Broads Plan (Broads Authority, 2004). Partnerships must be built on trust and accountability. The Authority has made, and is continuing to make, organizational changes to increase transparency and participation in order to enhance trust across all interests, while also ensuring best value (Turner et al, 2003). Increased scientific knowledge of wetland ecosystems and their benefits to society therefore has to be gained hand in hand with efforts to increase public awareness of these benefits. Such a communication is, however, only likely to be successful if due account is taken of the potential difference in worldviews between the scientists and the local people. Likewise, special attention should be paid to existing stakeholder structure, and potentially existing local ecological knowledge and local institutional arrangements for maintaining wetlands. Such institutions may constitute a basis for building wetland management processes that have already gained social acceptability at the local level, in contrast to governmental regulations imposed in a top-down fashion.

References

Arrow, K. J., Solow, R., Portney, P. R., Leamer, E. E., Radner, R., Schuman, E. H. (1993) 'Report of the NOAA panel on contingent valuation', *Federal Register*, vol 58, no 10, pp4602–4614

Balmford, A., Bruner, A., Cooper, P., Costanza, R., Farber, S., Green, R., Jenkins, M., Jefferises, P., Jessamy, V., Madden, J., Munro, K., Myers, N., Naeem, S, Paavola, J., Rayment, M., Roscendo, S., Roughgarden, J., Trumper, K., Turner, R. K. (2002) 'Economic reasons for conserving wild nature', *Science*, vol 297, pp950–953

Bateman, I. J. (1993) 'Valuation of the environment, methods and techniques: Revealed preference methods', in R. K. Turner (ed.), *Sustainable Environmental Economics and Management: Principles and Practice*, Belhaven Press, London, pp192–265

Bateman, I. J. and Langford, I. H. (1997) 'Non-users willingness to pay for a National Park: An application and critique of the contingent valuation method', *Regional Studies*, vol 31, no. 6, pp571–582

Bateman, I. J., Willis, K. G., Garrod, G. D., Doktor, P., Langford, I., Turner, R. K. (1992) 'Recreational and environmental preservation value of the Norfolk Broads: A contingent valuation study', unpublished report, Environmental Appraisal Group, University of East Anglia.

Bateman, I. J., Langford, I. H., Willis, K. G., Turner, R. K., Garrod, G. D. (1993) 'The impacts of changing willingness to pay question format in contingent valuation studies: An analysis of open-ended, iterative bidding and dichotomous choice format', Global Environmental Change Working Paper 93-05, Centre for Social and Economic Research on the Global Environment, University of East Anglia, Norwich and University College, London

Bateman, I. J., Willis, K. G., Garrod, G. D. (1994) 'Consistency between contingent valuation estimates: A comparison of two studies of UK national parks', *Regional Studies*, vol 28, no 5, pp457–474

Bateman, I. J., Langford, I. H., Turner, R. K., Willis, K. G., Garrod, G. D. (1995) 'Elicitation and truncation effects in contingent valuation studies', *Ecological Economics*, vol 12, pp161–179

Bateman, I. J., Garrod, G. D., Brainard, J. S., Lovett, A. A. (1996) 'Measurement, valuation and estimation issues in the travel cost method: A geographical information systems approach', *Journal of Agricultural Economics*, vol 47, no 2, pp191–205

Bateman, I. J., Lovett, A. A., Brainard, J. S. (1999) 'Developing a methodology for benefit transfers using geographical information systems: Modeling demand for woodland recreation', *Regional Studies*, vol 33, no 3, pp191–205

Bateman, I. J., Langford, I. H., Nishikawa, N., Lake, I. (2000) 'The Axford debate revisited: A case study illustrating different approaches to the aggregation of benefits data', *Journal of Environment Planning and Management*, vol 43, no 2, pp291–302

Bateman, I. J., Carson, R. T., Day, B., Hanemann, W. M., Hett, T., Jones-Lee, M., Loomes, G., Mourato, S., Ozdemiroglu, E., Pearce, D. W., Sudgen, R., Swanson, R. (2002) *Economic Valuation with Stated Preference Techniques: A Manual*, Edward Elgar, Cheltenham

Bateman, I. J., Day, B., Dupont, D., Georgiou, S., Matias, N. G. N., Morimoto, S., Subramanian, L. (2004) 'Does phosphate treatment for prevention of eutrophication pass the benefit cost test?', Mimeo, University of East Anglia

Bergin, J. and Price, C. (1994) 'The travel cost method and landscape quality', *Landscape Resources*, vol 19, pp21–22

Boyle, K. J. and Bergstrom, J. C. (1992) 'Benefit transfer studies: Myths, pragmatism, and idealism', *Water Resources Research*, vol 28, no 3, pp657–663

Brainard, J., Lovett, A., Bateman, I. (1999) 'Integrating geographical information systems into travel cost analysis and benefit transfer', *International Journal of Geographical Information Sciences*, vol 13, no 3, pp227–246

Broads Authority (2004) 'Broads plan: A strategic plan to manage the Norfolk and Suffolk Broads', Broads Authority, Colegate, Norwich

Brouwer, R. (1999) 'Public right of access, over crowding and the value of peace and quiet: The validity of contingent valuation as an information tool', GEC Working Paper 99-05, Centre for Social and Economic Research on the Global Environment (CSERGE), University of East Anglia, Norwich

Brouwer, R. and Crooks, S. (1998) 'Towards an integrated framework for wetland ecosystem indicators', GEC Working Paper 98-27, Centre for Social and Economic Research on the Global Environment (CSERGE), University of East Anglia, Norwich

Brouwer, R., Turner, R. K., Voisey, H. (2002) 'Public perception of overcrowding and management alternatives in a multi-purpose open access resource', *Journal of Sustainable Tourism*, vol 9, no 6, pp471–490

Burbridge, P. R. (1994) 'Integrated planning and management of freshwater habitats including wetlands', *Hydrobiologia*, vol 285, pp311–322

Carson, R. T. and Mitchell, R. M. (1995) 'Sequencing and nesting in contingent valuation surveys', *Journal of Environment Economics and Management*, vol 28, pp155–173

Clayton, A. M. H. and Radcliffe, N. J. (1996) *Sustainability: A Systems Approach*, Earthscan, London

Climate Change (2001) 'Impacts, adaptation and vulnerability', contribution of Working Group II to the *Third Assessment Report of Intergovernmental Panel on Climate Change*, J. McCarthy, O. F. Canziani, N. A. Leary, D. J. David, K. S. White (eds), Cambridge University Press, Cambridge, pp295–303.

Cooper, J. C., Hanemann, M., Signorello, G. (2002) 'One-and-one-half-bound dichotomous choice contingent valuation', *Review of Economic Statistics*, vol 84, no 4, pp742–750

Dillman, D. A. (1978) *Mail and Telephone Surveys – The Total Design Method*, Wiley, New York.

Environment Agency (1997) 'Broadland flood alleviation strategy: Banks strengthening and erosion protection', Environment Agency, Suffolk

Holzer, T. J, Perrow, M. R., Madgwick, F. J., Dunsford, D. S. (1997) 'Practical aspects of broads restoration', in F. J. Madgwick and G. L. Phillips (eds), *Restoration of the Norfolk Broads*, BARS 14e, Broads Authority and (P-91) Environment Agency, Norfolk

Horne, A. J. and Goldman, C. R. (1994) *Limnology*, 2nd edn, McGraw-Hill, New York, pp576

Kahneman, D. and Knetsch, J. L. (1992) 'Valuing public goods: The purchase of moral satisfaction', *Journal of Environmental Economics and Management*, vol 22, pp55–70

McConnell, K. E. (1992) 'Model building with judgement: Implications for benefit transfers with travel cost models', *Water Resources Research*, vol 28, no 3, pp695–700

Madgwick, F. J. and Phillips, G. L. (1997) *Restoration of the Norfolk Broads*, Final Report to E.C. Life Programme, BARS14, Broads Authority, Norfolk

Maltby, E., Hogan, D. V., McInnes, R. J. (eds) (1996) 'Functional analysis of European wetland ecosystems', Final Report Phase One, EC DG XII STEP Project CT90-0084, Wetland Ecosystems Research group, University of London

May, R. W. P. and Walters, C. B. (1996) 'Boat wash study', Broads Authority, Bars 12, Norwich

Moss, B. (1983) 'The Norfolk Broadland: Experiments in restoration of a complex wetland', *Biological Review*, vol 58, pp521–526

Moss, B., Stansfield, J., Irvine, K., Perrow, M., Phillips, G. (1996) 'Progressive restoration of a shallow lake: A 12-year experiment in isolation, sediment removal and biomanipulation', *Journal of Applied Ecology*, vol 33, no 1, pp71–86

National Rivers Authority (1992) 'A flood alleviation strategy for Broadland: Final Report Annex Four – cost benefit studies', NRA, Anglian Region, Peterborough

Pitt, J.-A., Kelly, A., Phillips, G. L. (1997) 'Control of nutrient release from sediments', in F. J. Madgwick and G. L. Phillips (eds), *Restoration of the Norfolk Broads*, BARS 14a, Broads Authority and Environment Agency, Norwich

Power, N. A. (2000) 'Contingent valuation and non-market wetland benefit assessment: The case of the Broadland flood alleviation scheme', PhD thesis, School of Environmental Sciences, University of East Anglia

Pretty, J. N., Mason, C. F., Nedwell, D. B., Hine, R. E. (2002) 'A preliminary assessment of the environmental costs of the eutrophication of fresh waters in England and Wales', University of Essex, Colchester

Scheffer, M., Hosper, S. H., Meijer, M.-L., Moss, B., Jeppesen, E. (1993) 'Alternative equilibria in shallow lakes', *Trends in Ecological Evolution*, vol 8, no 8, pp275–279

Stansfield, J., Caswell, S., Perrow, M. (1997) 'Biomanipulation as a restoration tool', in F. J. Madgwick and G. L. Phillips (eds), *Restoration of the Norfolk Broads*, BARS 14a, Broads Authority and Environment Agency, Norwich

Strategic Leisure and TEP (2001) 'Broads boat hire industry study: Draft strategy and action plan', c/o. Broads Authority, Colegate, Norwich

Turner, R. K. (1991) 'Economics and wetland management', *Ambio*, vol 20, no 2, pp59–63

Turner, R. K. and Brooke, J. (1988) 'Management and valuation of an environmentally sensitive area: Norfolk Broadland, England, case study', *Environmental Management*, vol 12, no 2, pp193–207

Turner, R. K., Adger, W. N., Doktor, P. (1995) 'Assessing the economic costs of sea level rise', *Environmental Planning A*, vol 27, pp1777–1796

Turner, R. K., van den Bergh, J. C. J. M., Barendregt, A., Maltby, E. (1997) 'Ecological–economic analysis of wetlands: Science and social science integration', in T. Soderquist (ed.), *Wetlands: Landscape and Institutional Perspectives*. Proceedings of the 4th Workshop of the Global Wetlands Economics Network (GWEN), Beijer International Institute of Ecological Economics, The Royal Swedish Academy of Sciences, Stockholm, Sweden, 16–17 November.

Turner, R. K., Lorenzoni, I., Beaumont, N., Bateman, I. J., Langford, I. H., Mcdonald, A. L. (1998) 'Coastal management for sustainable development: Analyzing environmental and socio-economic changes on the UK coast', *Geographical Journal*, vol 164, pp269–281

Turner, R. K., Geogious, S., Brouwer, R., Bateman, I. J., Langford, I. J. (2003) 'Towards an integrated environmental assessment for wetland and catchment management', *Geographical Journal*, vol 169, no 2, pp99–116

12

East African Cheetah Management via Interacting Political and Ecological Process Models

Timothy C. Haas

Introduction

Ultimately, the decision to implement ecosystem protection policies is a political one. Currently, the majority of ecosystem management research is concerned with ecological and/or physical processes. Management options that are suggested by examining the output of these models and/or data analyses may not be supported by the responsible Environmental Protection Agency (EPA) or affected human population unless the option addresses the goals of each involved social group (hereafter, *group*).

As a step towards meeting this need, an ecosystem management system (EMS) is described here that links political processes and goals to ecosystem processes and ecosystem health goals. This system is used to identify first the set of ecosystem management policies that have a realistic chance of being accepted by all involved groups, and then, within this set, those policies that are most beneficial to the ecosystem. Haas (2001) gives one way of defining the main components, workings and delivery of an EMS. The central component of this EMS is a quantitative, stochastic and causal model of the ecosystem being managed. The other components are links to data streams, freely available software for performing all ecosystem management computations and displays, and lastly, a web-based archive and delivery system for the first three of these components.

The 'new institutionalists' (see Gibson, 1999, pp9–14, 163, 169–171; Brewer and de Leon, 1983; Lindblom, 1980) draw on political economy theory to stress that (i) decision makers are pursuing their own personal goals, for example increasing their influence and protecting their job; and (ii) decision makers work to modify institutions to help them achieve these goals. This view of the policy-making process is particularly relevant for studying wildlife management in developing countries, as Gibson states:

> *New institutionalists provide tools useful to the study of African wildlife policy by placing individuals, their preferences, and institutions at the center of analysis. They begin with the assumption that individuals are rational, self-interested actors who attempt to secure the outcome they most prefer. Yet, as these actors search for gains in a highly uncertain world, their strategic interactions may generate suboptimal outcomes for society as a whole. Thus, rational individuals can take actions that lead to irrational social outcomes.* (Gibson 1999, pp9–10)

Another paradigm for political decision making is the *descriptive* model (see Vertzberger, 1990). This approach emphasizes that humans can only reach decisions based on their internal, perceived models of other actors in the decision-making situation. These internal models may in fact be inaccurate portrayals of the capabilities and intentions of these other actors.

Here, a rational actor decision-making paradigm is used that is similar to new institutionalism but modified to allow for perceptual distortions. See Haas (2004) and Appendix A for complete details of this approach. This group decision-making model is realized as an *influence diagram* (ID), see Nilsson and Lauritzen (2000). To incorporate the interaction between groups and the ecosystem, a set of IDs are constructed, one for each group, and then optimal decisions computed by each of these IDs through time are programmed to interact with decisions of other groups and with the solution history of the ecosystem ID. The model that emerges from the interactions of the set of group IDs and the ecosystem ID is called an *interacting influence diagrams* (IntIDs) model. In this model, each group makes decisions that they perceive will further their individual goals. Each of these groups, however, has a perceived, possibly inaccurate internal model of the ecosystem and the other groups. In other words, an IntIDs model has groups implementing decisions to maximize their own utility functions by using (possibly) distorted internal representations of other groups. A related group decision-making model is the beliefs, desires and intentions (BDI) model discussed in Kott and McEneaney (2006).

An IntIDs model is *actor oriented*. Such an architecture for modelling sociological phenomenon is seen by Hedstrom (2005, chs 1–3) as the approach most likely to break the current logjam in the development of sociological theory. Specific to the application presented in this chapter, Long and van der Ploeg (1994, pp64–65) argue for actor-oriented approaches to model the behaviour of agrarian groups. Jones (1999) applies a qualitative application of this approach to land degradation in Tanzania.

In the east African cheetah EMS described below, the IntIDs model represents (i) the president, EPA, non-pastoralist rural residents (hereafter, *rural residents*), and pastoralists of Kenya, Tanzania and Uganda; (ii) a single non-governmental organization (NGO) that seeks to protect biodiversity within these countries; and (iii) the ecosystem enclosed by these countries. By choosing from a predetermined repertoire of options, each group implements the option that maximizes their multiobjective (multiple goals) objective function. A schematic of the architecture of an IntIDs model is given in Figure 12.1.

Because this modelling effort draws on several disciplines, the goals that are driving the development of this EMS model need to be clearly stated. They are (in order of priority):

- *Usability*: develop a model that, because of its predictive and construct validity, contributes to the ecosystem management debate by delivering insight into how groups reach ecosystem management decisions, what strategies are effective in influencing these decisions, how ecosystems respond to management actions, and which management actions contribute to ecosystem health. In other words, by running different management scenarios through the model, stakeholders both within and outside the modelled countries can learn how political systems need to be changed to improve measures of ecosystem health, for example achieving the preservation of an endangered species.

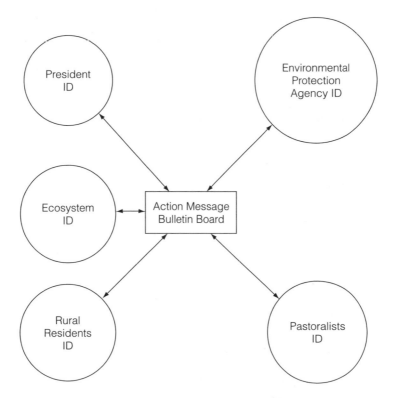

Figure 12.1 Schematic of the interacting IDs model of interacting political and ecological processes

- *Clarity and accessibility*: develop a model that can be understood by as wide an audience as possible.
- *Predictive validity*: in support of goal 1, develop a model that is not over-parameterized so that low prediction error rates can be achieved by the model after it has been fitted to data on group actions and ecosystem status. For the model to be useful, it needs to display prediction error rates that are lower than that of blind guessing.
- *Construct validity*: also in support of goal 1, develop a model that uses relationships, functions and mechanisms that operationalize the current state of understanding of how groups and ecosystems work.

Predictive validity will be assessed with the EMS model's one-step-ahead prediction error rate wherein at every step the model is refitted with all available data up to but not including that time step. Construct validity will be assessed by the degree to which the model's internal structure (variables and inter-variable relationships) agrees with current theories of group decision making and mathematical models of wildlife population dynamics.

There is a tension between predictive and construct validity in that the development of a model rich enough in structure to represent current theories of group decision making and ecosystem dynamics can easily become overparameterized which in turn can reduce its predictive performance. The approach taken throughout this work is to develop as simple a model as is faithful to group decision-making theory and ecosystem dynamics – followed by a fit of this model to data so as to maximize its predictive performance. These goals are seen as the most important for the development of a useful ecosystem management decision support system and are in agreement with Miles (2000).

This chapter proceeds as follows. The next section gives a brief overview of the architecture of a group ID and how model parameters are set to represent existing knowledge of group and ecosystem process behaviour. The subsequent section gives the EMS model of cheetah management across Kenya, Tanzania and Uganda. In the next section the model is statistically fitted to observations on several of the model's political and ecosystem variables. Prediction error rates of this fitted model are estimated in the following section, and the procedure for finding the most practical management strategy from the fitted model is given in the next. Conclusions are drawn in the final section. The software and data used in the cheetah management example are both freely available at www.uwm.edu/~haas/ems-cheetah/.

Overview of group and ecosystem IDs

Group IDs consist of variables that represent the group's assessment of input and output actions as they affect their economic, militaristic and political goals. Appendix A gives the details of these variables and how they relate to each other.

Based on input actions, groups select output actions and targets that they perceive will best serve their goals. Appendix A gives the details of this decision-making computation.

The ecosystem ID implements a cheetah population dynamics model in the form of a system of stochastic differential equations (SDE). Group IDs are influenced by outputs from this model and group ID output actions influence variables that in part determine the cheetah population's dynamics. Appendix B gives the mathematical form of the population dynamics model and how interactions between the group IDs and the ecosystem ID are implemented and computed.

Ecosystem management by these countries is simulated by having each country's EPA, rural residents and pastoralists select management actions that best satisfy their goals conditional on the actions of the other groups. Then, conditional on these implemented management options, the marginal distributions of all ecosystem status variables are updated. By simulating these between-group and group-to-ecosystem interactions many years into the future, long-term extinction probabilities of the wildlife populations represented in the ecosystem model can be computed.

The IntIDs model is fitted to data using a procedure called *Consistency Analysis*, described below. Consistency Analysis requires that each parameter in an ID be assigned an a priori value derived from expert opinion and/or subject matter theory. Let $\beta_H^{(j)}$ be such a value assigned to the ID's j^{th} parameter. Collect all of these *hypothesis parameter values* into the *hypothesis parameter vector*, β_H. See Haas (2005) for the subject matter heuristics used to assign values to β_H.

East African cheetah EMS

Background and region to be modelled

Cheetah preservation is a prominent example of the difficulties surrounding the preservation of a large land mammal whose range extends over several countries. The main threats to cheetah preservation are loss of habitat, cub predation by other carnivores and being shot to control their predation on livestock (Gros, 1998; Kelly and Durant, 2000).

Kelly and Durant (2000) note that juvenile survival is reduced by lion predation inside wildlife reserves because these reserves are not big enough for cheetah to find areas uninhabited by lions. Overcrowding of reserves in Africa is widespread (see O'Connell-Rodwell et al, 2000) and cheetah do not compete well for space with other carnivores (Kelly and Durant, 2000). Although many cheetah are currently existing on commercial land, this coexistence with man's economic activities may not be a secure long-term solution for cheetah.

One solution would be larger reserves that are free of poachers – possibly circled with an electric fence. Such a solution was found to be the most viable for keeping elephants from destroying crops in Namibia (see O'Connell-Rodwell et al, 2000). Pelkey et al (2000) also conclude that reserves with regular anti-poaching and anti-logging patrols are the most effective strategy for African wildlife and forest conservation.

A large portion of cheetah range is controlled by Kenya, Tanzania and Uganda (see Kingdon, 1977). Currently, the poverty rates in Kenya, Tanzania and Uganda are 52 per cent, 35.7 per cent and 44 per cent, respectively. The adult literacy rates are (90 per cent, 79 per cent) (males, females) for Kenya, (85 per cent, 69 per cent) for Tanzania and (79 per cent, 59 per cent) for Uganda (World Resources Institute, 2005). With close to half of the population living in poverty, many rural Africans in these countries feel that conservation programmes put wildlife ahead of their welfare and that large mammals are a threat to their small irrigated patches of ground and their livestock (Gibson, 1999, p123). For these reasons, many such individuals are not interested in biodiversity or wildlife conservation.

Gibson (1999, p122) finds that the three reasons for poaching are the need for meat, the need for cash from selling animal 'trophies', and the protection of livestock. Gibson's analysis suggests that to reduce poaching, policy packages need to be instituted that (i) deliver meat to specific families – not just to the tribal chief; (ii) increase the enforcement of laws against the taking of trophies; and (iii) improve livestock protection.

ID descriptions and hypothesis parameter values

Overview of IDs

According to Gros (1998) and Gibson (1999, p164), the groups that directly affect the cheetah population are EPAs, ranchers, rural residents and pastoralists. NGOs can be added to this list as they can engage in animal translocation. Each country's Presidential Office (hereafter *president*), legislature and courts indirectly affect the cheetah population through their influence on these primary groups. The EMS model represents (i) the presidents, EPAs, rural residents and pastoralists of Kenya, Tanzania and Uganda; (ii) a single, aggregate model of those NGOs that are working on wildlife conservation through operations in all three countries; and (iii) the shared cheetah-supporting ecosystem contained within the political boundaries of these three countries. This version of the model omits group IDs for legislatures, courts and large commercial ranches.

Table 12.1 lists the repertoire of output action–target combinations for a typical president ID. These actions are derived from observations on these countries taken over the period 1999 through 2006. The data sources and the collection protocol are given below. Table 12.2 collects all input action–actor combinations recognized by a typical president ID. This table also gives hypothesis values of resource change nodes under each action, and each action's hypothesis values for whether the action's effect will be immediate ($F^{(in)}$) and whether the action involves the use of force ($M^{(in)}$). Hypothesis parameter values for each ID in the EMS model are available at the aforementioned cheetah EMS website.

Table 12.1 *Output actions and viable targets for the President ID*

Output action	Viable targets
Request increased anti-poaching enforcement	EPA
Suppress riot	RR
Seize idle land for poor	RR
Declare tree planting day	RR
Open a wildlife reserve to settlement	RR, Pas
Create wildlife reserve	RR, Pas
Fund conservation project	RR
Sign inter-country customs pact	Presidents
Tighten wildlife agreement or laws	RR, Pas
Request ivory trade ban continuation	NGOs
Invest in tourism infrastructure	RR
Donate to establish wildlife trust fund	EPA
Host or attend conservation conference	NGOs
Punish or restrict domestic ministers	RR

Note: RR: rural residents, Pas: pastoralists

Table 12.2 *President DM-group input actions that change economic and/or militaristic resource nodes*

Actor	Input action	$CE_s^{(in)}$	$CM_s^{(in)}$	$M^{(in)}$	$F^{(in)}$
RR, Pas	Poach for food	−L	N	1	0
RR, Pas	Poach for cash	−S	N	1	0
RR, Pas	Poach for protection	−L	N	1	0
RR	Riot	N	−L	1	0
RR	Clear new land	−S	N	0	0
RR	Abandon settlement	−S	N	0	0
RR	Devastate a region	−L	N	0	0
RR	Murder game wardens	−S	−L	1	0
RR	Report: wildlife attack RRs	N	−S	0	0
Pas	Agree to create wildlife reserves	S	N	0	1
EPA	Decrease anti-poach	N	−S	1	1
EPA	Increase anti-poach	N	−S	0	1
EPA	Negative eco-report	−S	N	0	1
EPA	Positive eco-report	S	N	0	1
EPA	Suspend corrupt officers	N	−S	1	0
EPA	Plan water storage upgrade	−S	N	0	1
EPA	Seize elephant ivory	S	S	1	0
EPA	Encourage tourism	S	S	0	1
EPA	Detain RRs for encroachment	N	S	1	0
EPA	Translocate animals	−S	N	1	0
EPA	Use technology to locate habitat	−S	N	0	0
EPA	Host conservation conference	−S	N	0	0
EPA	Kill maurading wildlife	−S	N	1	0

Note: S: small, L: large, N: no change, +: increase, and −: decrease

The ecosystem ID is directly affected only by poaching activities, animal relocation, rural resident and/or pastoralist eviction and land clearing. Anti-poaching enforcement is directed towards rural residents and/or pastoralists – and may not be effective at reducing poaching activity. Likewise, the creation of a wildlife reserve or the opening of an existing wildlife reserve to settlement are actions directed towards rural residents and/or pastoralists. The following sections describe each group ID.

President IDs

Gibson (1999, pp155–156) argues in his case studies of Kenya, Zambia and Zimbabwe that the president in each of these countries has a different personal priority for protecting ecosystems. Further, presidents of politically unstable countries typically place a high priority on protecting their power and staying in office (Gibson, 1999, p7). These insights have motivated the following form of the president IDs (see Figure 12.2).

The president has direct knowledge of the actions of the country's rural residents and pastoralists. The president receives ecosystem status information exclusively from the EPA of that country. The president's audiences are campaign donors and the military. Aid-granting countries are not included as audiences in this version. The president's goals are to maintain political power and domestic order. Defending the country is not included as a goal in this version.

There is a tendency in African politics towards *neopaternalism* wherein the president is viewed as a strong man dispensing favours to loyal, children-like supporters. This is particularly true of President Yoweri Museveni of Uganda (see Kassimir, 1998).

Environmental Protection Agency IDs

EPA perceptions of the ecosystem's state are represented by cheetah prevalence and herbivore prevalence nodes. These nodes are influenced by the values of cheetah density, herbivore density and poaching rate in the ecosystem ID. The EPA's sole audience is the president. The EPA's goals are to protect the environment, and to increase the agency's staff and budget. The latter goal is motivated by an examination of the literature on bureaucracies. For example, Healy and Ascher (1995) note that during the 1970s and 1980s the USDA Forest Service, using FORPLAN output, consistently proposed forest management plans that required large increases in Forest Service budget and staff (see also Gibson, 1999, pp85, 115–116).

Rural resident IDs

The single ecosystem state node in these IDs is herbivore prevalence as influenced by the ecosystem ID's herbivore density node. A rural resident is pursuing the two goals of supporting his/her family and avoiding prosecution for poaching.

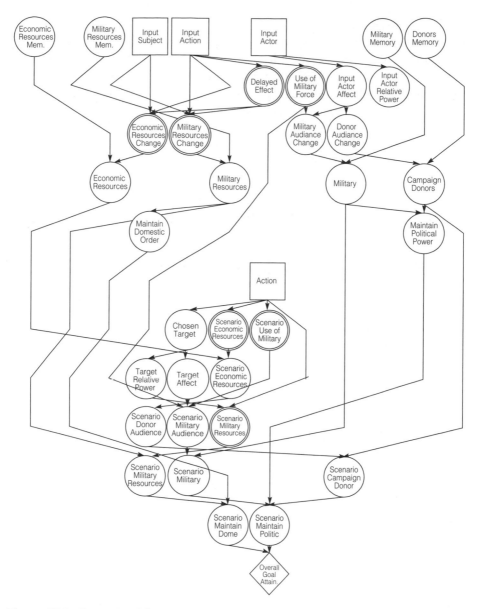

Figure 12.2 Kenya President Group ID

Note that here, in contrast to a political leader's ID, rural residents do have audience satisfaction as one of their goals.

Pastoralist IDs

Cheetah prevalence as influenced by the ecosystem ID's cheetah density node is the single ecosystem state node in these IDs. Pastoralists have the three goals of supporting their family, protecting their livestock and avoiding prosecution for poaching.

Wildlife conservation NGO ID

The NGO group's audiences are the governments of the three host countries as embodied in the presidential offices and the NGO group's financial backers, which are assumed to reside in other, developed countries. The NGO's three goals are to conserve wildlife, maintain productive relations with each host country's government and raise funds for its operations.

The NGO keeps track of changes in the poaching rate within each country. These changes affect the NGO's overall perceptions of cheetah and herbivore prevalence over the entire three-country area.

Because the NGO group's sole support is from external funds, only the contentment level of external donors and the previous time step's economic resources affects its budget status – input actions do not play a role.

Parameter estimation via consistency analysis

Overview

Consistency analysis is used to fit the EMS model to data. Let U be an IntIDs model's $r-$ dimensional vector of chance nodes. Partition U into $U^{(d)}$ and $U^{(ac)}$ – the vectors of discrete and absolutely continuous chance nodes, respectively. Let $g_S(\beta)$ be a *goodness-of-fit* statistic that measures the agreement of this distribution (referred to here as the $U|\beta$ distribution) and the (possibly) incomplete sample (or data set), S. Larger values of $g_S(\beta)$ indicate better agreement. Let $g_H(\beta)$ be the agreement between this distribution identified by the values of β_H (referred to here as the *hypothesis distribution*) and the $U|\beta$ distribution. Likewise, larger values of $g_H(\beta)$ indicate better agreement. Let *gsmax* be the unconstrained maximum value of $g_S(\beta)$ over all β. Similarly, let *ghmax* be the unconstrained maximum value of $g_H(\beta)$ over all β. Up to errors in the approximation of $g_H(\beta)$, this value is $g_H(\beta_H)$. The consistency analysis parameter estimator maximizes $g_{CA}(\beta) \equiv (1-c_H)g_S(\beta)/(|gsmax|+1) + c_H g_H(\beta)/(|ghmax|+1)$ where $c_H \in (0,1)$ is the analyst's priority of having the estimated distribution agree with the hypothesis distribution as opposed to agreeing with the empirical (data-derived) distribution. Let $\beta_C \equiv argmax_\beta \{g_{CA}(\beta)\}$ be the consistency analysis estimate of β. Hereafter, β_C will be referred to as the *consistent* parameter vector. See Haas (2001, Appendix) for suggestions on how to assign c_H, further details and a comparison with other parameter estimators.

Overall goal satisfaction priority weight coefficients (utility weights) are also adjusted until the actions history data set is matched by the model. This adjustment of a group's utility function to observations on the group's actions is similar to a utility function discovery algorithm reported by Chajewska et al (2001).

Agreement functions

Data (observations) agreement functions
For the entire IntIDs model, $g_S(\beta) = g_S^{Grp}(\beta) + g_S^{Eco}(\beta)$.

A sequence of computed group ID action–target combinations does not constitute a time series on a random process. This is because a decision from an ID is the action–target combination node values for which the conditional expected value of the Overall Goal Satisfaction node is maximized – making an ID's decision a function of expected values. Therefore, a computed action–target combination can be viewed as a hyper-parameter of the ID. Statistical methods that assume a data set consists of realizations on observable random variables are not appropriate for group action data. For this reason, alternate agreement measures have been developed as discussed next.

Agreement with actions history data
Call a time series of action–actor–target observations an *actions history* data set. To define a function that measures agreement between an actions history generated by an IntIDs model and an observed actions history data set, let $out_i^{(obs)}(t_j)$ be group i's observed output action–target combination at time t_j, $out_i^{(opt)}(t_j)$ be the action–target combination computed by the group's ID at that time and $M_{ij} = 1$ if $out_i^{(opt)}(t_j) = out_i^{(obs)}(t_j)$ and 0, otherwise. For m interacting group IDs, let $\beta = (\beta^{(1)\prime}, ..., \beta^{(m)\prime})'$, $EU_{i,j}^{(obs)}(\beta) = E\left[U_i^{(Sc)} \mid out_i^{(obs)}(t_j)\right]$, and $EU_{i,j}^{(opt)}(\beta) = E\left[U_i^{(Sc)} \mid out_i^{(opt)}(t_j)\right]$. Let $f_{acths}(\beta)$ be the agreement function at the point β (*acths* denotes 'actions history'). Define

$$f_{acths}(\beta) \equiv \sum_{i=1}^{m}\sum_{j=1}^{T} M_{i,j} + (1-M_{i,j})\left[EU_{i,j}^{(obs)}(\beta) - EU_{i,j}^{(opt)}(\beta) - 1/EU_{i,j}^{(obs)}(\beta)\right] \quad (1)$$

If no action–target combinations are matched and the model places low utility on the observed action–target combinations, f_{acths} is negative. If all observed action–target combinations are matched by the model, f_{acths} equals mT. Defining the objective function in this way discourages the search algorithm from driving both $EU^{(obs)}$ and $EU^{(opt)}$ to zero since a small value of $EU_{i,j}^{(obs)}$ will penalize the objective function more severely than a large value will improve it.

To summarize, for the collection of group IDs, the function that measures agreement between the actions history data set and the IntIDs distribution specified by β is $g_S^{Grp}(\beta) \equiv f_{acths}(\beta)$ and is a measure of agreement between an observed actions history data set and the actions history computed by the IntIDs model.

Agreement with ecosystem state data

Say that a multivariate time series of ecosystem node values has been observed. For example, here, cheetah and herbivore counts are observed over time. Denote with $u_{obs}(t)$ the vector of these values at time t. This vector constitutes a size-one sample on the observable ecosystem ID nodes at t. For such a sample, the negative Hellinger distance is $-\left|1 - \sqrt{\hat{pf}_{U|\beta}(u_{obs}(t))}\right|$ (see Appendix C and Lindsay, 1994, p1082). $g_S^{Eco}(\beta)$ is the sum of each of these negative Hellinger distances over each combination of region and time point. Say that there are R regions and T time points. If all m variables in the ecosystem model are discrete and each takes on N values, g_S^{Eco} *(uniform)* $= RT\left[\sqrt{1/N^m} - 1\right]$ and can be used to identify a lower bound. For example when $R = 5$, $T = 100$, $m = 10$ and $N = 100$, a lower bound for g_S^{Eco} is -500. When all variables in the ID are discrete, the upper bound is 0.

Hypothesis agreement function

The Hellinger distance between an ID's hypothesis distribution and its $U|\beta$ distribution can be approximated as follows. First, draw a size-m sample from a multivariate uniform distribution on the ID node vector: $u_1, \ldots, u_m$ and compute $\hat{pf}_{U|\beta}(u)$, a local, l nearest neighbour volumetric non-parametric density estimate (Thompson and Tapia, 1990, p179) at each of these points. The Hellinger distance approximation can then be computed as:

$$\hat{\Delta}(\beta, \beta_H) \equiv \left[\sum_{i=1}^{m}\left[\sqrt{\hat{pf}_{U|\beta_H}(u_i)} - \sqrt{\hat{pf}_{U|\beta}(u_i)}\right]^2\right]^{1/2} \tag{2}$$

The measure of agreement with the hypothesis parameter values is $g_H(\beta) = g_H^{Grp}(\beta) + g_H^{Eco}(\beta)$. For the collection of group IDs, $g_H^{Grp}(\beta) = \Sigma - \hat{\Delta}(\beta, \beta_H)$ where summation is over all combinations of time point, group and output node values considered by that group at that time point. For the ecosystem ID, $g_H^{Grp}(\beta) = \Sigma - \hat{\Delta}(\beta, \beta_H)$ where summation is over all combinations of region and time point.

Action taxonomy, data sources and coding protocol

Action taxonomies
To avoid creating a system that can only process a historical sequence of ecosystem management actions, a group output action classification system is needed that characterizes actions along dimensions that are not situation-specific. The idea is

to map a list of possible actions onto a set of dimensions that, taken together, describe an action. Several action taxonomies or classification systems have been developed in the political science literature, see Schrodt (1995). These taxonomies, however, lack a set of situation-independent dimensions for characterizing an action. The approach taken here is to base a set of action characteristics or *dimensions* on an existing action classification system. The Behavioural Correlates of War (BCOW) classification system is chosen for this extension for two reasons. First, BCOW is designed to support a variety of theoretical viewpoints (Leng, 1999) and hence can be used to code data that will be used to estimate a model of group decision making that synthesizes realist and cognitive processing paradigms of political decision making. Second, BCOW has coding slots for recording (i) a detailed description of an action; (ii) inter- and intra-country groups; and (iii) a short history of group interactions. This last coding category allows causal relationships to be identified and tracked through time.

The BCOW coding scheme consists of a nearly exhaustive list of actions grouped into Militaristic, Diplomatic, Economic, Unofficial (intra-country actor) and Verbal categories. The BCOW classification system exhaustively and uniquely characterizes a verbal action into either a comment on an action (Verbal: Action Comment), a statement that an action is intended (Verbal: Action Intent), or a request for an action (Verbal: Action Request). Here, the Unofficial Actions category of the BCOW coding system is not needed since groups internal to a country are modelled as having nearly the same range of output actions as a country-level group. Hence, all BCOW Unofficial Actions have been absorbed into one of the other action categories.

BCOW does not include many actions that are peculiar to ecosystem management. These actions are added to the BCOW taxonomy at the end of each Table in Haas (2005, Tables A1–A3). Further, many BCOW actions are very general such as 'Seizure'. The group IDs are sensitive to what particular form a general action takes on, for example seizure of elephant tusks is different than seizure of private land to be given to the rural poor. Therefore, several of the original BCOW actions have been given subcategories.

Only actions that physically affect the ecosystem are viewed as ecosystem management actions. Such actions include 'poach for cash', and 'translocate animals'.

Actions history data sources and coding protocol
An actions history data set is formed by coding stories posted on the websites of the following organizations: Earthwire, Africa Online, All Africa, Planet Ark, EnviroLink, UN Wire, Afrol, ENN, BBC News, World Bank DevNews, WildAfrica Environmental News, National Geographic News, LawAfrica, Kenya Government, Kenya Wildlife Service, Daily Nation, EastAfrican, IndexKenya, Tanzania News, Business Times, Business News, Sunday Observer, Family Mirror, The Guardian, The Express, Tanzania Lawyers' Environmental Action Team, Uganda Government, The Monitor, The New Vision, One World,

Uganda Ministry of Water, Lands and Environment and the Uganda Parliament. The data set currently contains stories from 1997 to 2007.

Currently, websites are scanned for stories every two months. If it can be assumed that a wide spread of random precipitating and response actions are observed under this two-month sampling protocol, then the temporal gaps in news story coverage may not have a large effect on the performance of the fitted model. This is because the model generates complete action–reaction pairs and action–reaction–re-reaction trios and is fitted to an observation record with temporal gaps. If the above assumption holds, the fitting procedure will encourage the model to produce either the observed precipitating or observed response action in a pair or trio. Under this assumption, actions are missing at random so that model disagreement with observed action pairs and action trios need not be systematically biased.

The following steps are followed to create an action-entry in the actions history data set.

- Go to one of the above websites and search for stories that concern one of the EMS countries and have as a subject either wildlife, wildlife habitat, national park, environmental policy, poaching, poachers or land management. Avoid opinion or 'study' stories.
- Read the article and create an entry in the group actions history database that consists of the fields: story date, story source, number of actors, actors, number of subjects, subjects, action, number of countries subjected to action, countries, number of regions, regions and date of action.
- Repeat for each country in the EMS.
- Add BCOW actions as necessary to the BCOW actions-and-codes file (see the 'Datasets' page at the Cheetah EMS website) to code-in raw actions that are not already represented by a BCOW code.

Cheetah and herbivore count data

Gros (1998, 1999, 2002) uses an interview technique to conduct cheetah count surveys in Kenya, Uganda and Tanzania, respectively. Herbivore count values for 1977–1985 in Kenya are found by summing over the numbers of impala *Aepyceros melampus* (40kg), Thomson's gazelle *Eudorcas thomsonii* (15kg), Grant's gazelle *Nanger granti* (40kg), lesser kudu *Tragelaphus imberbis* (40kg) and gerenuk *Litocranius walleri* (25kg) taken from Mbugua (1986) and Peden (1984). These herbivores are cited in Kingdon (1977) as being common prey for cheetah and are all under 60kg – an upper limit on the size of prey that can be brought down by a cheetah (Kingdon, 1977). The average mass of these cheetah-prey herbivores is 32kg. Call this collection of cheetah and herbivore observations the *true sample*.

Because the actions history data and the true sample do not overlap temporally, an artificial data set of wildlife counts is constructed here that has about the same mean and variance as the true sample but covers the time period 1999 through 2006 (see Table 12.3).

Table 12.3 *Artificial cheetah and herbivore count data*

Country	Region	Year	Herbivore D_t	Cheetah D_t
Kenya	Central	1999	0.3	0.04
Kenya	Central	2000	0.4	0.08
Kenya	Central	2001	0.3	0.08
Kenya	Central	2002	0.3	0.04
Kenya	Central	2004	0.2	0.04
Kenya	Central	2006	0.1	0.03
Kenya	Tsavo	2000	0.4	0.05
Kenya	Tsavo	2001	0.5	0.10
Kenya	Tsavo	2002	0.4	0.05
Kenya	Tsavo	2004	0.3	0.04
Kenya	Tsavo	2006	0.2	0.04
Tanzania	Morogoro	2000	0.3	0.04
Tanzania	Tanga	2005	0.2	0.03
Uganda	Yumbe	2001	0.4	0.07
Uganda	Kayunga	2006	0.2	0.04

Gros (1998) notes a distinction between reported and actual cheetah presence: the lack of a cheetah sighting within a district is not equivalent to zero cheetah count in that district. It is known that survey reports undercount cheetah numbers (Gros, 1998). Hence, use of interview-based survey count values will contribute to the fitted ecosystem model under-predicting true cheetah numbers.

The ecosystem ID represents this non-detection chance in the interview-based data with its 'Detection Fraction' variable (see Appendix B). This variable measures the fraction of a region over which cheetah (herbivores) are detected. Cheetah and herbivore counts are converted to Detection Fraction values before being used in the parameter estimation computation.

Combined data set

Consistency analysis is used to fit the IntIDs model to the data formed by combining the actions history data and the ecosystem state data. This combined data is referred to as *political-ecological* data and is exhibited in Figures 12.3–12.5. In these figures, an arrow's tail locates a group's action and the arrow's head indicates the reaction of the target group. Note that NGO actions and cheetah density averages are also displayed in all actions history figures.

Results

Optimization problem configuration

The time points at which the IDs read the bulletin board are aligned with those in the actions history data set. Doing so allows data-based causal chains of action and reaction to be learned by the model through the Consistency Analysis

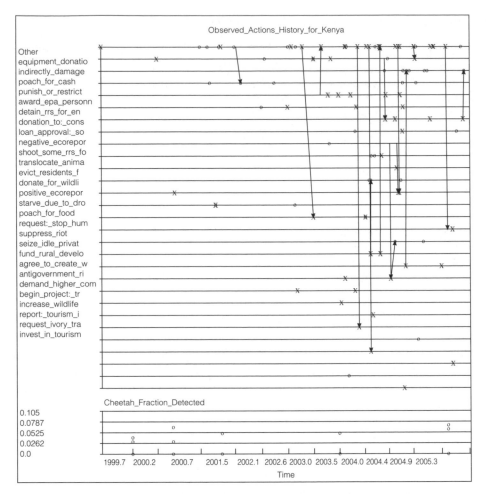

Figure 12.3 Observed output actions of Kenyan groups

parameter estimation procedure. The initializing actions are Tanzanian rural residents indirectly damaging wildlife habitat, and the Kenyan EPA increasing anti-poaching enforcement. To reflect the low reliability of the heuristics used to specify β_H, the Consistency Analysis was performed with $c_H = 0.01$.

Due to limited computing resources, optimization was performed sequentially by first fitting only parameters in Kenyan group IDs and those of the NGO ID, followed by a run to fit only parameters in Tanzanian group IDs plus the NGO ID, then only Ugandan group IDs plus those in the NGO ID. Finally, a run was made to fit the parameters of the ecosystem ID. This sequence of runs was repeated in a round-robin manner. Each of these optimization problems consisted of about 1200 parameters being adjusted in an effort to maximize the Consistency Analysis objective function. One evaluation of this objective function required the Monte Carlo simulation of 14 IDs per time step over about

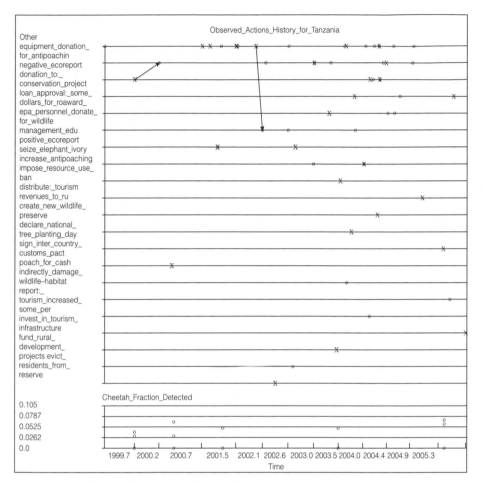

Figure 12.4 Observed output actions of Tanzanian groups

130 time steps. To perform such a large optimization analysis, a JavaSpaces cluster computing program was written and 28 PCs in a university student computer lab were employed to run a parallel version of the Hooke and Jeeves optimization algorithm.

Solution overview

Table 12.4 gives the final Consistency Analysis agreement functions and each function's bounds. Hypothesis agreement values are not reported because hypothesis distributions were assigned largely to give the optimization algorithm a starting point and were not themselves of interest to this present modelling effort.

For each group, Table 12.5 gives the fraction of model-generated action–target combinations that matched those observed. Out of 162 observed

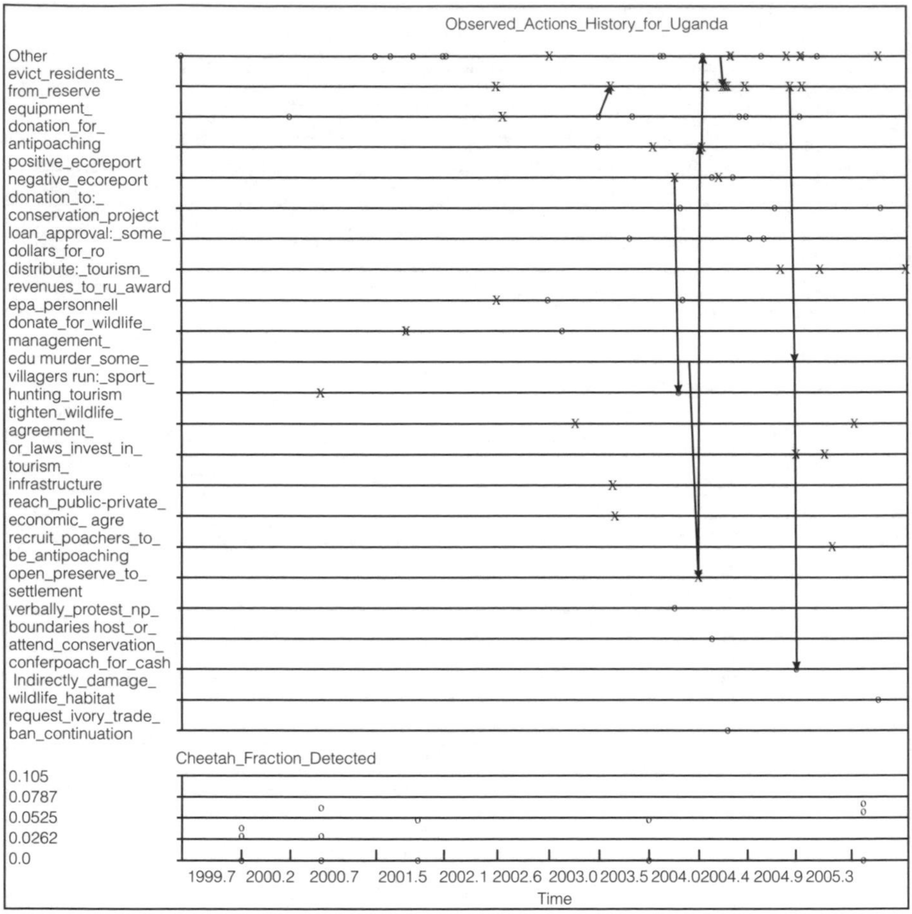

Figure 12.5 Observed output actions of Ugandan groups

Table 12.4 *Consistency analysis agreement function values and bounds*

Agreement measure	Lower bound	$\beta = \beta_c$	Upper bound
$g_s^{Grp}(\beta)$	$-\infty$	$-1.08E7$	142
$g_s^{Eco}(\beta)$	-500	-0.452	0
Match fraction	0	0.154	0.270

action–target observations, 32 (19.7 per cent) were matched by the model. The overall action match fraction was 0.197 and the overall target match fraction was 0.438. Also, the model produces cheetah and herbivore Detection Fractions that are similar to those in the artificial data set (see Table 12.3).

Figures 12.6–12.8 portray IntIDs model output over the same time period as the observations. Figures 12.9–12.11 plot only those observed action–reaction pairs that the Consistency Analysis-fitted IntIDs models replicated.

Table 12.5 *Action and target match fractions*

Group	Number of action–target combs.	Number matched	Match fraction	Number of matched actions	Match fraction	Number of matched targets	Match fraction
Kenpres	18	1	0.055	1	0.055	2	0.111
Kenepa	25	3	0.120	3	0.120	4	0.160
Kenrr	25	6	0.240	6	0.240	17	0.680
Kenpas	2	1	0.500	1	0.500	2	1.000
Tanpres	4	0	0.000	0	0.000	1	0.250
Tanepa	9	1	0.111	1	0.111	2	0.222
Tanrr	4	2	0.500	2	0.500	2	0.500
Tanpas	0	0	0.000	0	0.000	0	0.000
Ugapres	8	0	0.000	0	0.000	0	0.000
Ugaepa	23	6	0.260	6	0.260	15	0.652
Ugarr	6	2	0.333	2	0.333	2	0.333
Ugapas	1	0	0.000	0	0.000	0	0.000
NGO	37	3	0.081	7	0.189	7	0.189

Note: *combs.* = *combinations.*

One-step-ahead prediction error rates

As discussed in the Introduction, in order for an EMS model to be an effective management tool, its prediction error rate needs to be significantly lower than the prediction error rate of blindly guessing what actions will be taken by groups and what effect such actions will have on the ecosystem.

To this end, an estimate of the one-step-ahead error rate is needed. One approach is to refit the EMS model at each time point in the political-ecological data set using all data up to but not including that time point. Then, this refitted model is used to compute predictions of each group's output action–target combination and the ecosystem's state at that time point. These one-step-ahead predictions are compared to the observed values to produce an estimate of the one-step-ahead prediction error rate.

Specifically, starting back n_{pred} time points from the latest time point in the data set (T), an estimate of the one-step-ahead error rate for the group IDs, hereafter referred to as the predicted actions error rate (PAER), can be estimated as follows. First, refit the EMS model at time points $T - n_{pred} + i$, $i = 0, \dots, n_{pred} - 1$ using all observed action–target combinations up through time $T - n_{pred} + i$. Then, at each of these time points, use the refitted EMS model to predict all output action–target combinations at the time point $T - n_{pred} + i + 1$. The estimated PAER is

$$\hat{PAER} = \frac{1}{n_{pred}} \sum_{i=T-n_{pred}}^{T-1} 1 - \frac{n^{(i)}_{matched}}{n^{(i)}_{observed}} \tag{3}$$

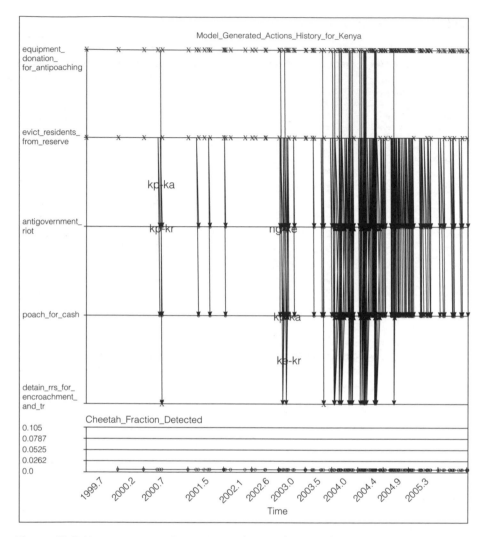

Figure 12.6 Kenyan group ID output action under β_c values

where $n^{(i)}_{matched}$ is the number of action–target combinations generated by the EMS model at time point i that match observed action–target combinations, and $n^{(i)}_{observed}$ is the number of observed action–target combinations at time point i.

To reduce the expense of computing $\hat{P}AER$, model refitting is performed only at every k^{th} time point. For example, if $k = 3$, the model would be refitted only at time points $T - n_{pred} + 3$, $T - n_{pred} + 6$, $T - n_{pred} + 9$, K, $T - n_{pred} + 3m$ where $m = floor\,(T/3)$.

Say that a group ID has m options. In the worst case, one of these options has a high probability of being chosen at each time point. Blind guessing, that is,

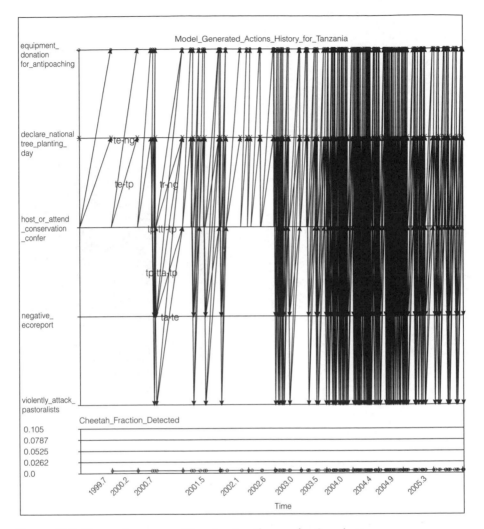

Figure 12.7 Tanzanian group ID output action under β_c values

assuming all options are equally likely, would predict this option with probability $1/m$ at each time point resulting in an error rate of about $1-1/m$. An ecosystem manager would prefer the EMS model's predictions over blind guessing whenever $\hat{P}AER < 1-1/m$.

For the ecosystem ID's continuously valued nodes, a commonly used measure of predictive accuracy is the root mean squared prediction error (RMSPE), which can be estimated with

$$\hat{RMSPE} = \left[\frac{1}{n_{pred}} \sum_{i=1}^{n_{pred}} \left(Y_{observed}^{(i)} - Y_{pred}^{(i)} \right)^2 \right]^{1/2} \tag{4}$$

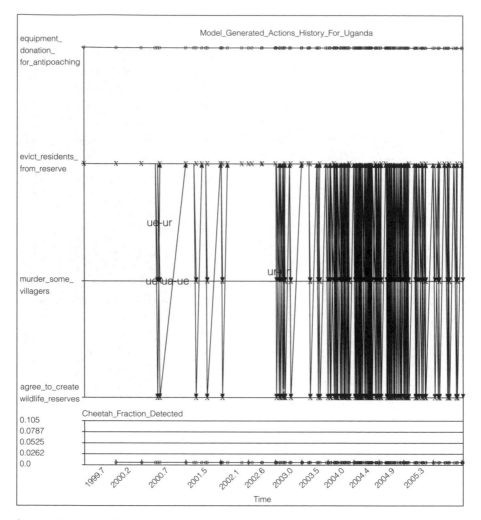

Figure 12.8 Ugandan group ID output action under β_c values

The cheetah management model's prediction error rates were estimated by fitting the model to political-ecological from 1999 to 2006. This fitted model was then used to compute predicted actions and ecosystem state values at each of the subsequent 36 observed action time points, which ended in the year 2006. These predictions produced a $\widehat{PAER}$ of 0.65 and a value of $\widehat{RMSPE}/\bar{D}_t$ of 0.076 where $\bar{D}_t$ is the average of the 36 observed cheetah fraction values. Since no refitting was performed over the 36 prediction time points, these error rate estimates are conservative. The actions prediction error rate is better than blind guessing and the relative size of a cheetah Detection Fraction prediction error is less than 8 per cent of the average observed cheetah Detection Fraction.

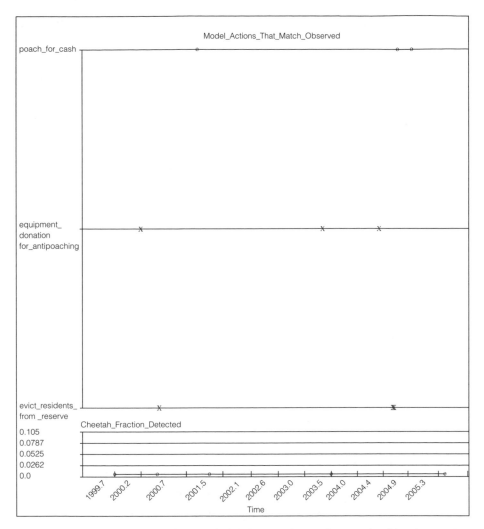

Figure 12.9 Kenyan group observed action–reaction pairs matched by the IntIDs model

EMS-derived practical management strategies

Once the EMS model has been fitted to a political-ecological data set, the model can be used to construct the most practical management strategy and to compare proposed management strategies to this most practical one. Here, a practical strategy is defined as one that demands the least change in group behaviour patterns for a desired improvement in ecosystem health as measured by the ecosystem output variables in the ecosystem ID.

One way to quantify this definition of practicality is to use the $g_H(\beta)$ value between the IntID model's parameters fitted to political-ecological data (β_C) – and

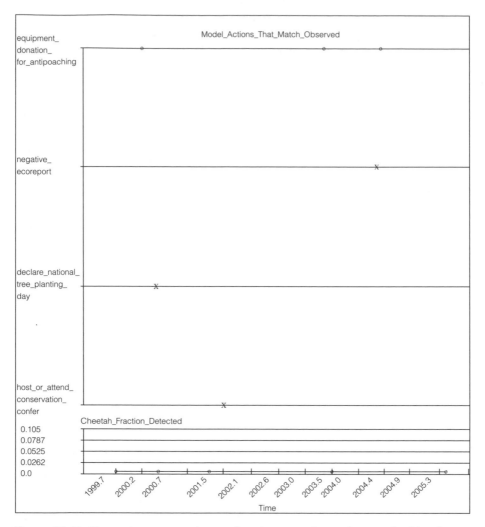

Figure 12.10 Tanzanian group observed action–reaction pairs matched by the IntIDs model

these same parameters modified so that a desired ecosystem state is achieved by a sequence of group ID actions over a future time period. The idea is to find the smallest changes in the beliefs of ecosystem-affecting groups that must occur before these groups change their behaviours enough to allow the ecosystem to respond in the desired manner. Hereafter, the management strategy that emerges by finding parameter values that result in a desired ecosystem state but that deviate minimally from β_C will be called the Most Practical Management Strategy (MPMS). The set of parameter values that achieves the MPMS will be designated by β_{MPMS}. Here, minimal deviation between two parameter vectors means that their $g_H(\beta)$ value is maximized.

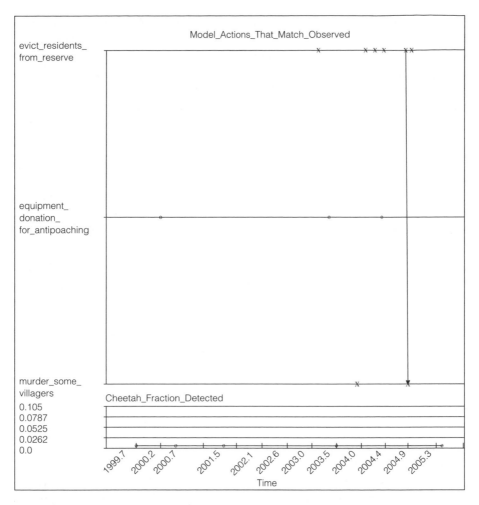

Figure 12.11 Ugandan group observed action–reaction pairs matched by the IntIDs model

One way to find the MPMS is to solve a constrained optimization problem as follows. First, set the Consistency Analysis hypothesis vector to the previously computed β_C. Let $H(\beta)$ be a vector of ecosystem state variables that is a function of β, the vector of group ID model parameters. For example, $H(.)$ could be cheetah count and herbivore count in the year 2057. Set $H(.)$ to a set of desired values, h, for example 2000 cheetah and 10,000 herbivores in 2057. Holding ecosystem parameters at their values contained in β_C, find a new set of group ID parameter values, β_{MPMS} for which $H(\beta_{MPMS}) = h$ and for which $g_H(\beta)$ is maximized.

$g_H(\beta)$ is an objective function that measures the agreement in belief systems of all managed groups from their data-based beliefs as represented by β_C – and those values needed to produce a sequence of action–target combinations that satisfy the above ecosystem state constraint.

In practice, the vector β_{MPMS} is found with Consistency Analysis wherein c_H is set to 1.0, β_C plays the role of the hypothesis parameter vector and h defines an equality constraint on the ecosystem ID's output vector. Because the smallest changes from β_C have been found, there are no other group-behaviour changes that are easier to achieve – hence these identified parameter value changes can be viewed as the most practical to attempt to implement in the real world.

Depending on the optimization algorithm used, a sequence of management actions may need to be used as a starting point for the algorithm so that the equality constraints for the desired ecosystem states are satisfied at the start of the search for β_{MPMS}.

To implement the MPMS in the real world, group belief systems would need to be changed. Methods currently used to change belief systems include educational programmes, workshops and advertising. If the needed degree of beliefs change appears to be beyond available resources, less practical strategies can be found by solving a constrained optimization problem wherein the parameters representing groups that will not have their beliefs modified are held at their consistent values. Such a strategy is referred to here as a Less Practical Management Strategy (LPMS).

It is possible that the desired ecosystem state values cannot be achieved within the EMS model by any pattern of group output actions. In this case, the desired ecosystem state is, according to the EMS model, impossible to achieve.

Example

Say that a cheetah conservation goal is to have an expected cheetah count of 200 individuals in the Tanzanian district of Tanga 50 years hence, that is in the year 2057. Say that only rural resident and pastoralist groups are to have their belief systems modified with all other groups having their parameters held at their β_C values.

One LPMS that meets this conservation goal is found by setting parameter values on the 'feed family' goal in these IDs so as to make it have no priority – and setting parameter values on the 'avoid prosecution' goal so as to make it have the highest priority. Under these new parameter values, poaching actions by these groups completely ceases over the next 50 years and the expected cheetah count for this district that begins with a population of 200 in 1999 has 188 individuals in 2057. When all parameters are left at their consistent values, the expected cheetah count for this district in 2057 is 0.

Conclusions

A general purpose EMS has been developed that can help decision makers manage an ecosystem that is being affected by human activities across several countries. Methods have also been developed for fitting the EMS model to political-ecological data, assessing the model's predictive validity and using the fitted model to identify the most practical and defensible management strategy to pursue. As an example, the system has been applied to cheetah conservation in East Africa.

The practical pay-off of this EMS is its step-by-step procedure for finding the most practical and defensible strategy for the management of an at-risk ecosystem through the computation of the MPMS. This strategy is practical because it requires the least change in the belief systems of the relevant social groups in order to reach desired conservation goals. This strategy is defensible for three reasons. First, an integrated model of both the decision making of groups that are impacting the ecosystem and that ecosystem's response to those impacts is derived from the most current theories of group decision making and ecosystem functioning. Second, this integrated model is fitted to data from both these social groups and the ecosystem. Third, questions and concerns about the model's ability to predict group behaviour and ecosystem response are answered through the predictive validity computations.

A future area of research is to extend the group IDs to allow learning to take place through time, that is developing a cognitively plausible learning algorithm in which a group, based on experience, learns to combine and/or modify their output action repertoire in an effort to further the group's goals.

Appendix A: Group ID architecture

Overview

In an EMS model, IDs are used to model the aggregate behaviour of homogeneous groups and homogeneous ecosystems. For the chapter's example of cheetah conservation in East Africa, the *types* of these homogeneous groups are (i) a country's president; (ii) a country's EPA; (iii) a country's rural residents; and (iv) a country's pastoralists. A modelled ecosystem consists of a population dynamics model for cheetah and the effects on this population from prey counts, habitat and physical management activities such as poaching and wildlife reserve creation.

A group's ID is partitioned into subsets of connected nodes called the *Situation* and *Scenario* subIDs. The Situation (*St*) subID is the group's internal representation of the state of the decision situation and contains *situation state* nodes. A node representing discrete time is in each ID's Situation subID. This node takes on the values $t_0, t_1, \ldots, t_T$ in steps of δt. Conditional on what decision option is chosen, the Scenario (*Sc*) subID is the group's internal representation of what the future situation, called the *scenario*, will be like after a proposed option is implemented. See Haas (1992) for the cognitive theory that supports this decision-making model architecture.

The following discussion focuses on the group ID of a political leader and his/her confidants. Modifications to the goal nodes of this model can yield models of bureaucratic agencies and family groups. Tables A12.1 and A12.2 collect all notation used to express this group ID while Figure A12.1 displays its architecture. To simplify this diagram, only one audience has been depicted. A circle denotes

Appendix Table 12.1 *Definition of symbols used to express the group ID's situation subID*

Symbol	Definition	Parents
$RE^{(St)}(t_i-1)$	Economic resources one time step back	root
$RM^{(St)}(t_i-1)$	Militaristic resources one time step back	root
$A_j^{(St)}(t_i-1)$	Audience j's contentment level one time step back	root
$InAc$	Input actor	root
$C^{(in)}$	Input action	root
InS	Input subject	root
AF_{InAc}	Input actor affect	$InAc$
AF_{InS}	Input subject affect	InS
RP_{InAc}	Input actor's relative power	$InAc$
RP_{InS}	Input subject's relative power	InS
$F^{(in)}$	Indicator that the input action's effect is delayed	$C^{(in)}$
$M^{(in)}$	Indicator that the input action uses military force	$C^{(in)}$
$CE_s^{(in)}$	Input subject's economic resources change	$C^{(in)}, F^{(in)}$
$CM_s^{(in)}$	Input subject's militaristic resources change	$C^{(in)}, F^{(in)}, RP_{InAc}$
$CA_j^{(St)}$	Situation change in audience j's contentment level	AF_{InAc}, AF_{InS}
$RE^{(St)}$	Situation economic resources level	$RE^{(St)}(t_i-1), InS, F^{(in)}, CE^{(in)}$
$RM^{(St)}$	Situation militaristic resources level	$RM^{(St)}(t_i-1), InS, F^{(in)}, CE^{(in)}$
$A_j^{(St)}$	Audience j's contentment level at the current time step	$A_j^{(St)}(t_i-1), CA_j^{(St)}$
$GE^{(St)}$	Situation economic resources goal	$RE^{(St)}$
$GM^{(St)}$	Situation militaristic resources goal	$RM^{(St)}$
$GMPP^{(St)}$	Situation goal of maintaining political power	$A_j^{(St)}$

Appendix Table 12.2 *Definition of symbols used to express the group ID's scenario subID*

Symbol	Definition	Parents
T	Output action's target	root
AF_T	Target affect	T
RP_T	Target's relative power	T
$C^{(out)}$	Output action	root
$M^{(out)}$	Indicator that the output action uses military force	$C^{(out)}$
$CE^{(out)}$	DM-group's economic resources changes in the scenario	$C^{(out)}$
$CM^{(out)}$	DM-group's militaristic resources changes in the scenario	$C^{(out)}, M^{(out)}, RP_T$
$RE^{(Sc)}$	Scenario economic resources	$RE^{(St)}, CE^{(out)}$
$RM^{(Sc)}$	Scenario militaristic resources	$RM^{(St)}, CE^{(out)}$
$CA_j^{(Sc)}$	Scenario change in audience j's contentment level	$CE^{(out)}, AF_T$
$A_j^{(Sc)}$	Audience j's scenario contentment level	$CA_j^{(Sc)}$
$GE^{(Sc)}$	Scenario economic resources goal	$RE^{(Sc)}, GE^{(St)}$
$GM^{(Sc)}$	Scenario militaristic resources goal	$RM^{(Sc)}, GM^{(St)}$
$GMPP^{(Sc)}$	Scenario goal of maintaining political power	$A_j^{(St)}, A_j^{(Sc)}$
U	Scenario overall goal satisfaction	$GE^{(Sc)}, GM^{(Sc)}, GMPP^{(Sc)}$

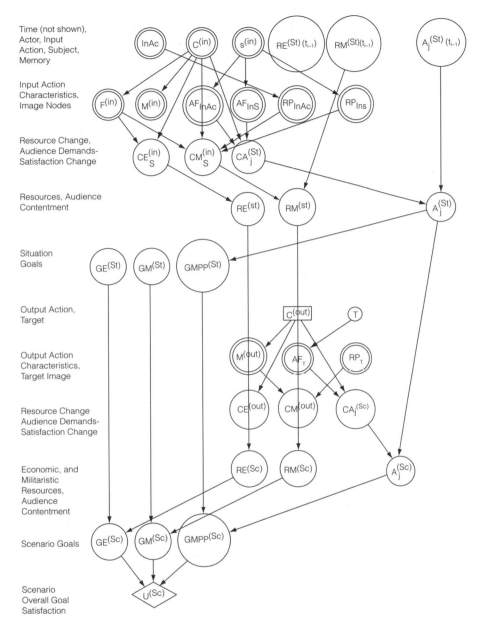

Appendix Figure 12.1 Group ID architecture

a chance (random) node; a double circle denotes a deterministic node; a square denotes a decision node; and a diamond denotes a utility or value node.

A decision option will hereafter be referred to as an *action*. Groups interact with each other and the ecosystem by executing actions. The decision-making group, referred to as the DM-group receives an *input action* that is executed by an *actor* referred to as the *input-action-actor* group or InAc-group. The *subject* of this action is the *input-action-subject* group or InS-group (which may or may not be the DM-group). The DM-group implements an output action whose subject is the *target* group or T-group. Let $C^{(action)}$ denote the input action when *action* equals *in* and denote the output action when *action* equals *out*. Let *InS* denote the input action's subject. Actions are either verbal (message) or physical events that include *all* inter- and intra-country interactions. Actions are represented by two fundamental characteristics: the actor's resource amount change as a result of the action and the subject's resource amount change as a result of the action. These characteristics are described below.

Conditional on an input action, the Situation subID is one way to represent a schema (see Rumelhart et al, 1986) or story that the decision maker invokes upon receipt of an input action.

Ecosystem state perceptions nodes

Quantities that measure the state of the ecosystem are input nodes to a group ID that is directly affected by the ecosystem. These nodes influence a node that represents how sensitive the group is to the value of the ecosystem state node. The idea is that a group is affected by the ecosystem but is only conscious of a certain 'filtered' or perceptual function of that ecosystem state variable.

A group ID is sensitive to the presence of a land animal such as the cheetah through the animal's density (number per hectare). This sensitivity is modelled by having the animal's density node influence a perceived animal prevalence node that takes on the values *none, few* and *many*.

Image nodes

The DM-group's set of dimensions that defines the DM-group's image of another group are Affect and Relative Power. Affect varies over the *enemy–neutral–ally–self* dimension (see Murray and Cowden, 1999; and Hudson, 1983, chs 2–4). Relative Power varies over the *weaker–parity–stronger* dimension. The Affect dimension's *self* category is needed because the subject of an InAc-group's action may be the DM-group itself.

Let AF_{InAc}, RP_{InAc} be the DM-group's Affect and Relative Power image nodes of the InAc-group, respectively. Define AF_{InS} and RP_{InS} similarly for the input action's subject.

Economic, militaristic and institutional goal nodes

It is assumed here that a group evaluates an input action directly on its perceived immediate and future impacts on economic, militaristic and institutional goals both in the present (Situation) and in the future (Scenario).

For economic and militaristic goals, this is a two-step process: first, the DM-group assesses how the input or output action changes their amount of economic or militaristic resources; then, an assessment is made of how this new resource level affects the associated economic or militaristic goal.

Only one institutional goal is modelled: Maintain Political Power. This goal is solely dependent on maintaining the contentment of several important *audiences*, discussed below. Denote Situation subID goal nodes with $GE^{(St)}$, $GM^{(St)}$ and $GMPP^{(St)}$. Define $GE^{(Sc)}$, $GM^{(Sc)}$ and $GMPP^{(Sc)}$ similarly for the Scenario subID. A goal node can take on the values *not-satisfied* and *satisfied*.

InAc-group image nodes, InS-group image nodes and the nodes representing the input action's immediate and future impact on the DM-group's resources affect goal status assessment. Scenario goals are influenced by Situation goals – if an output action does not cause a resource or audience node change, the mode of the Scenario goal's state equals the Situation goal state.

An example of how an input action affects goal node would be the president of Kenya creating a new wildlife reserve. For the rural resident DM-group, this action would cause $GE^{(St)} = GE^{(Sc)} = $ *not–satisfied* and $GM^{(St)} = GM^{(Sc)} = $ *satisfied*.

Audience effects

The influence of audiences on a decision maker is supported by research that suggests perceptions of present and future reactions of important audiences has an effect on decision making and bargaining, see Partell and Palmer (1999). The perceived impact of an input action on an audience is the believed effect of the action on audience demands. For example, an important audience for President Moi during his presidency of Kenya was his ethnic group, the Kalenjin (Throup and Hornsby, 1998, p8). President Moi knew that only actions that brought benefits to that tribe would be favourably received by them.

The effects of perceived audience reactions to input actions is modelled by having input action, actor and subject characteristics influence Audience Demands–Satisfaction Change nodes which in turn, influence Audience Contentment nodes.

Say that the DM-group ID has important audiences. Let the node $A_j^{(St)}$ denote the perceived contentment level of audience j. $A_j^{(St)}$ takes on the values *discontented* and *contented*. Let the node $CA_j^{(St)}$ denote the perceived change in audience j's demands–satisfaction level due to the input action and the DM-group's Affect perceptions of the Input Actor and Input Subject (perceptions that the DM-group assumes are shared by all audiences). $CA_j^{(St)}$ takes on the values *decreased, no change* and *increased*. Let $CA^{(St)} = (CA_1^{(St)}, \dots , CA_m^{(St)})$ and $A^{(St)} = (A_1^{(St)}, \dots , A_m^{(St)})$.

Likewise, in the Scenario subID, output action characteristics influence Audience Contentment nodes through the Audience Demands–Satisfaction Change nodes. Let $CA^{(Sc)} = (CA_1^{(Sc)}, \dots , CA_m^{(Sc)})$. These nodes are influenced by the output action and Target Affect nodes. This set of parents allows the modelling of perceived audience expectations for the DM-group to do something as a result of an input action. Audience Demands–Satisfaction nodes are not influenced by economic or militaristic change nodes.

Situation audience contentment level influences Scenario audience contentment: if there is no change to an audience's contentment level due to the output action, Scenario contentment level inherits the contentment level of the Situation audience node(s).

The Maintain Political Power goal, $GMPP^{(St)}$ is influenced by $A^{(St)}$ only – there is no goal to satisfy audiences because the decision maker has no concern for these audiences other than how they affect the decision maker's hold on political power.

Corruption

Audience effects on a decision maker can explain some aspects of governmental corruption. One of the many forms that corruption takes is the increased influence of a particular audience on the decision maker through payments of various kinds. Here, such corruption is modelled implicitly by having certain audiences exert a strong influence on the decision maker. The modelling of other forms of corruption is a topic for future research.

Overall goal satisfaction

Goal prioritization is modelled by a single node representing the DM-group's overall sense of well-being. This node, denoted by U, is a deterministic function of the goal nodes wherein the coefficients in this function are interpreted as goal-importance weights and hence can be assigned directly from knowledge of the group's goal priorities.

Group actions

Action characteristics and resource nodes

A *resource* is anything of economic or militaristic value to a group. Letting *subid* denote either *St* or *Sc*, define $RE^{(subid)}$ and $RM^{(subid)}$ to be the DM-group's absolute level of economic and militaristic resources, respectively. Resource nodes are modelled as random nodes because they represent a perceived amount of resources and hence are not typically known by the DM-group to an exact value. Typically, the decision maker has only a qualitative idea of their current levels of economic or militaristic resources. Here then, these nodes take on only the values *negligible, inadequate* and *adequate*. Militaristic resources is broadly defined to include military material, and territory won through military conquests.

Resource nodes specify the change in resources on separate economic and militaristic dimensions because an action can cause resource change on either or both dimensions. For example, a military blockade can have significant economic consequences for the subject. Define $M^{(action)}$ to be 1 if the action involves the use of military force and 0 otherwise.

Define $F^{(action)}$ if the action's resource changes will occur in the future ($F^{(.)} = 1$) or are immediate ($F^{(.)} = 0$). Define $CE_S^{(in)}$ to be the DM-group's perception of the subject's relative change in economic resources due to the input action. When this change is perceived to occur is defined by the action's value of $F^{(.)}$. Define $CE^{(out)}$ and $CM^{(out)}$ as the change in the DM-group's economic and militaristic resources, respectively due to the output action. These change nodes take on the ordinal values of *large_decrease*, *small_decrease*, *no_change*, *small_increase* and *large_increase*.

For each action, relative resource change node values are assigned subjectively. Except for certain extreme actions, the relative change caused by an action on the subject or DM-group is dependent on current levels of the group's resources and the specific nature of the action. Most BCOW actions are not specific enough to allow a change value to be assigned even if the action's actor and subject were specified. Therefore, change values are assigned locally, that is, a list of action–actor–subject triads is developed for the particular actions history being modelled. Then, change values for each action are assigned to be the maximum effect the action would have on the subject or DM-group.

Action and target nodes
Many actions in the BCOW classification system strongly imply only one or two possible target types, for example 'arrest poachers' would not be directed towards a president or an NGO. Hence, in the Scenario subID, the output action node influences the discrete chance node, 'Chosen_Target'.

Action–target combination perceived effectiveness
The DM-group's perception of the economic, or militaristic effectiveness of an output action is modelled by having the Target and Output Action nodes both influence Scenario Economic Resources Change, and Scenario Militaristic Resources Change nodes, respectively.

Output action messages and IntIDs model operation
A proposed action–target combination influences target image and action characteristic nodes. These nodes along with Situation goal nodes, influence Scenario goal nodes. Finally, Scenario goal nodes influence the Scenario Overall Goal Satisfaction node (see Figure A12.1). Each action–target combination is used to compute the expected value of the Overall Goal Satisfaction node. At time t, the action–target combination that maximizes this expected value is designated by $C_{optimal}(t)$. Computing the maximum utility output value is called *evaluating* the ID; see Nilsson and Lauritzen (2000).

After determining $C_{optimal}(t)$, the DM-group posts to a bulletin board an *action-message* consisting of (i) the time; (ii) the DM-group's name; (iii) the target's name; and (iv) the BCOW action code. At the next time point, all other groups read this message. Each group assigns the values on the action characteristics associated with the BCOW action code and assigns values to the InAc-group image and InS-group image nodes. Using these values, each group computes an optimal action–target combination and posts it to the bulletin board. When all groups have posted their output combination and the ecosystem ID has posted updated distributions on its state nodes, the time variable is incremented up to the next time point and the process is repeated.

Groups that are directly affected by the ecosystem, read an 'ecosystem state' action at every time step. All other group IDs react only to the actions of other groups. In this version of the IntIDs model, a group generates one action–target combination for each recognized input action–target combination on the bulletin board one time step back. These input action–subject combinations are read off the bulletin board in the same order as they are posted.

Group memory

A group's memory through time is modelled by having the nodes, $RE^{(St)}$, $RM^{(St)}$ and $A^{(St)}$ at the previous time step influence these same nodes at the current time step. See Haas et al (1994) for an example and the mathematical form of this approach to representing the passage of time with IDs.

This memory mechanism allows the modelling of changes in group perceptions through time. Examples include perceived resource depletion and accumulated resentment or desperation. Each of these nodes is given an initial distribution at time t_0 that represents the analyst's assessment of the group's perceived level of economic and militaristic resources and the group's perceptions of the contentment level of each audience ($A^{(St)}$).

Appendix B: Ecosystem ID

The ecosystem ID is a modified version of the cheetah population dynamics ID of Haas (2001) and consists of four subIDs: decisions, habitat, direct effects on population dynamics, and population dynamics (Figure A12.2). The decision nodes represent time (t), region (q) and management option (m) values at which ID outputs are desired. Cheetah habitat is characterized by chance nodes for the region's climate (CL), the proportion of a region's area that is protected ($R(t)$), and unprotected land use (U) – how land is used that is not designated as a national park or a wildlife reserve. A single direct effect chance node follows: within-region hunting pressure due to poaching or pest control (H_t). As more data become available, other direct effects such as disease could be added. See Haas (2001) for this model's Hypothesis parameter values.

Cheetah population dynamics is modelled with a system of stochastic differential equations consisting of the within-region nodes birth rate: (f_t), death

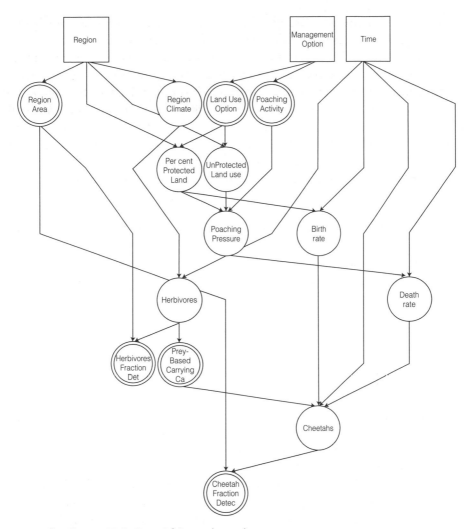

Appendix Figure 12.2 East African cheetah support

rate (r_t), number of herbivores (B_t), cheetah carrying capacity (K_t) and cheetah count (N_t). Note this ecosystem model is multivariate in that landscape nodes and prey nodes interact with the node of management interest: cheetah count.

The stochastic differential equation of herbivore count (B_t) is

$$\frac{dB_t}{dt} = \alpha_1 B_t (1 - B_t/\alpha_0) + \sigma dW_t \tag{5}$$

where $\alpha_0 = 10{,}000$ is the carrying capacity of the habitat, α_1 is the difference between the birth and death rates, $\sigma = 1.e-2$ is the diffusion parameter, and W_t is a Wiener process. The initial value is $B_0 = 0.6\alpha_0$. This model is a simplified version of the relationship given in Wells et al (1998) derived by assuming that the probability of a litter upon the meeting of a male and female is 1.0.

The ecosystem ID has two root nodes: Time and Poaching Pressure. These two nodes jointly influence Herbivore Count. If $B_t < 2000$, the rural resident Herbivores Prevalence node is set to *none*, if $2000 < B_t < 10,000$ this node is set to *few*, and if $10,000 < B_t$ this node is set to *many*. Poaching affects the value of α_1: under *moderate poaching*, or *suppress riot*, $\alpha_1 = 0.3$. The reasoning is that police forces normally assigned to poaching control must be reassigned to riot suppression with a consequent increase in poaching pressure.

As described in Haas (2001), the distribution of f_t at t is the solution to the SDE

$$df_t = -.5(\alpha_f + \beta_f^2(2f_t - 1))(1 - (2f_t - 1)^2)dt + .5\beta_f(1 - (2f_t - 1)^2)dW_t^{(f)} \quad (6)$$

This SDE was chosen because its solution is bounded between 0 and 1 making f_t a dimensionless, fractional birth rate. A similar development for the death rate leads to the stochastic differential equation

$$dr_t = -.5(\alpha_r + \beta_r^2(2r_t - 1))(1 - (2r_t - 1)^2)dt + .5\beta_r(1 - (2r_t - 1)^2)dW_t^{(r)} \quad (7)$$

Note that the birth rate decreases as α_f becomes increasingly positive and the death rate decreases as α_r becomes increasingly positive.

The tendency of more females to have litters within protected areas (see Gros, 1998) is represented by having the parameter α_f be conditional on the region's status. Similarly, to represent the effect of poaching and pest hunting on r_t, α_r is conditional on poaching pressure. The variability of the sample paths of f_t and r_t are controlled by the parameters β_f and β_r, respectively. Although the SDE's for f_t and r_t are not derived from biological theory, their use allows birth and death rates to be modelled as bounded, temporal stochastic processes with parameters that can represent different temporal trends (with α) and different amounts of variability (with β).

All other unmodelled effects (such as migration and/or parameter values that are age-dependent) that could influence the within-region cheetah count differential (dN_t) are represented by the derivative of a Wiener process in the cheetah count SDE:

$$dN_t = \left[f_t(1 - P^{cN_t}) - r_t - (f_t - r_t)\frac{N_t}{K_t} \right] N_t dt + \beta_N dW_t^{(N)} \quad (8)$$

where P, c, N_0, and β_N are fixed parameters and K_t is a deterministic function of the B_t temporal stochastic process. The parameter P is the probability that a meeting does not result in a litter, c is the proportion of animals that meet over a short time period, N_0 is the initial population size, and β_N is the noise coefficient.

To give some interpretation to this model, recall that the Malthusian growth model is $dN = (f - r)Ndt$, and the Pearl–Verhulst density-dependent growth model (logistic equation) is $dN = [(f-r) - (f-r)N/K]Ndt$. The first term in the cheetah count SDE is a simple birth rate effect adjusted for missed or barren unions, and the second term is a simple death rate effect. These first two terms make up the standard Malthusian growth model that has been modified to account for the chance of missed or barren unions. The third term is the Pearl–Verhulst addition to the Malthusian growth model to incorporate density-dependent population growth and has a negative effect when the birth rate exceeds the death rate – or a positive effect when the birth rate is smaller than the death rate. This effect, either way, is in proportion to the population size relative to the Carrying Capacity. For example, if the birth rate exceeds the death rate and the population size exceeds the Carrying Capacity, this density-dependent effect will be negative – one specific mechanism might be high infant mortality due to scarce food resources.

The cheetah population is said to be *viable* if $E[N_{t_F}]>0$ at a distant, future time, t_F.

As presented in Haas (2001), the final output variable, 'Detection Fraction' (D_t) measures the fraction of a region's area over which cheetah have been detected. Let a_r be a region's surface area and $d = N_t/a_r$, i.e. the density of cheetah in the region. An observation on D_t can be computed from maps of cheetah presence/absence by district. This is done by dividing the sum of all areas of districts in the region on which cheetah have been detected by a_r. The influence diagram models D_t as a deterministic function of N_t and a_r as follows. Let ξ be the minimum cheetah density that results in a cheetah detection report. Let ρ be a cheetah density above which cheetah are certain to be reported. Then $D_t = 0$ if $d < \xi$, $= (d-\xi)/(\rho - \xi)$ if $d \in (\xi, \rho)$, and $= 1$ if $d > \rho$. Note that it is possible for N_t to be positive but D_t to be zero, that is ξ can be interpreted as the minimum density detection limit.

Ecosystem state output nodes are herbivore and cheetah detection fractions. Because the ecosystem ID is conditional on region, computed herbivore and cheetah detection fractions are region-specific. Since the group IDs are not regionally indexed, these region-specific ecosystem ID outputs need to be aggregated across regions. Here, this aggregation is accomplished by computing, at each time step, a weighted average of the expected values of ecosystem output nodes with region area as the weighting variable. These weighted averages are written to the bulletin board.

Outputs are averaged over districts in Kenya (11 districts), Tanzania (19 districts) and Uganda (55 districts). Averaged output from this model is read by a group ID as if it is the averaged ecosystem response to inputs from any of the three countries being modelled.

Of course, ecosystem health is incompletely characterized by herbivore and cheetah detection fractions. Future model versions will have nodes representing other species and the spatial distribution of vegetation.

Appendix C: Hellinger distance

The Hellinger distance is defined in terms of a hybrid probability function that is given as follows. The joint cumulative distribution function of U can be decomposed as $F_U(u) = F_U^{(d)}(u) + F_U^{(ac)}(u)$ where $F_U^{(d)}(u)$ is the pure discrete component – completely determined by the probability mass function (PMF), $P(U = u)$, and $F_U^{(ac)}(u)$, the pure absolutely continuous component – completely determined by the probability density function (PDF), $F_U(u) = \partial F_U^{(ac)}(u)/\partial U$ (Koopmans, 1969). Koopmans gives a hybrid of the PMF and PDF called the *probability density–probability function* (PDPF) that is convenient for computing joint probabilities of U. The PDPF is defined as:

$$pf_U(u) \equiv \frac{\partial}{\partial U^{(ac)}} P(U^{(d)} = u^{(d)}, U^{(ac)} \le u^{(ac)}) \qquad (9)$$

Several agreement functions used in Consistency Analysis are based on the Hellinger distance between two probability distributions. This distance is:

$$\Delta(\beta_1, \beta_2) \equiv \left[\int \left(\sqrt{pf_{U|\beta_1}(u)} - \sqrt{pf_{U|\beta_2}(u)} \right)^2 du \right]^{1/2} \qquad (10)$$

(see Tamura and Boos, 1986). It can be shown that $0 \le \Delta(\beta_1, \beta_2) < \sqrt{2}$.

References

Brewer, G. and de Leon, P. (1983) *Foundations of Policy Analysis*, Dorsey Press, Homewood, IL

Chajewska, U., Koller, D., Ormoneit, D. (2001) 'Learning an agent's utility function by observing behavior', in *18th International Conference on Machine Learning (ICML '01)*, www.robotics.stanford.edu/Çlurszula/, pp35–42

Gibson, C. C. (1999) *Politicians and Poachers*, Cambridge University Press, Cambridge

Gros, P. M. (1998) 'Status of the cheetah *Acinonyx jubatus* in Kenya: A field-interview assessment', *Biological Conservation*, vol 85, pp137–149

Gros, P. M. (1999) 'Status and habitat preferences of Uganda cheetahs: An attempt to predict carnivore occurrence based on vegetation structure', *Biodiversity and Conservation*, vol 8, pp1561–1583

Gros, P. M. (2002) 'The status and conservation of the cheetah *Acinonyx jubatus* in Tanzania', *Biological Conservation*, vol 106, pp177–185

Haas, T. C. (1992) 'A Bayes network model of district ranger decision making', *Artificial Intelligence Applications*, vol 6, no 3, pp72–88

Haas, T. C. (2001) 'A web-based system for public–private sector collaborative ecosystem management', *Stochastic Environmental Research and Risk Assessment*, vol 15, no 2, pp101–131

Haas, T. C. (2004) 'Ecosystem management via interacting models of political and ecological processes', *Animal Biodiversity and Conservation*, vol 27, no 1, www.bcn.es/museuciencies, pp231–245

Haas, T. C. (2005) *Ecosystem Management via Interacting Models of Political and Ecological Processes*, Technical Report, School of Business Administration, University of Wisconsin-Milwaukee, Milwaukee, WI, www.uwm.edu/~haas/ems-cheetah/poleco.pdf

Haas, T. C., Mowrer, H. T., Shepperd, W. D. (1994) 'Modeling aspen stand growth with a temporal Bayes network', *Artificial Intelligence Applications*, vol 8, no 1, pp15–28

Healy, R. G. and Ascher, W. (1995) 'Knowledge in the policy process: Incorporating new environmental information in natural resources policy making', *Policy Sciences*, vol 28, pp1–19

Hedstrom, P. (2005) *Dissecting the Social: On the Principles of Analytical Sociology*, Cambridge University Press, Cambridge, chs 1–3

Hudson, V. M. (1983) *The External Predisposition Component of a Model of Foreign Policy Behavior*, PhD Dissertation, Ohio State University

Jones, S. (1999) 'From meta-narratives to flexible frameworks: An actor level analysis of land degradation in highland Tanzania', *Global Environmental Change*, vol 9, pp211–219

Kassimir, R. (1998) 'Uganda: The catholic church and state reconstruction', in L. A. Villalón and P. A. Huxtable (eds), *The African State at a Critical Juncture*, Lynne Rienner Publishers, Boulder, CO, pp233–254

Kelly, M. J. and Durant, S. M. (2000) 'Viability of the Serengeti cheetah population', *Conservation Biology*, vol 14, no 3, pp786–797

Kingdon, J. (1977) *East African Mammals: An Atlas of Evolution in Africa*, Academic Press, London

Koopmans, L. H. (1969) 'Some simple singular and mixed probability distributions', *The American Mathematical Monthly*, vol 76, no 3, pp297–299

Kott, A. and McEneaney, W. M. (2006) *Adversarial Reasoning*, Chapman and Hall, London

Leng, R. J. (1999) *Behavioral Correlates of War, 1816–1979* (Computer File), 3rd Release, Middlebury College, Middlebury, VT, 1993, available for download as Study Number 8606 from the Inter-University Consortium for Political and Social Research (ICPSR), Ann Arbor, MI, www.icpsr.umich.edu

Lindblom, C. (1980) *The Policymaking Process*, Prentice-Hall, New York

Lindsay, B. (1994) 'Efficiency versus robustness: The case for minimum Hellinger distance and related methods', *Annals of Statistics*, vol 22, pp1081–1114

Long, N. and van der Ploeg, J. D. (1994) 'Heterogeneity, actor and structure: Towards a reconstitution of the concept of structure', in D. Booth (ed.), *Rethinking Social Development: Theory, Research and Practice*, Longman Scientific and Technical, Essex, ch. 3

Mbugua, S. W. (1986) 'Monitoring livestock and wildlife in Kenya', in *Range Development and Research in Kenya*, Winrock International Institute for Agricultural Development, Morrilton, AR

Miles, S. B. (2000) 'Towards policy relevant environmental modeling: Contextual validity and pragmatic models', United States Geological Survey Open-File Report 00-401

Murray, S. K. and Cowden, J. A. (1999) 'The role of "enemy images" and ideology in elite belief systems', *International Studies Quarterly*, vol 43, pp 455–481

Nilsson, D. and Lauritzen, S. L. (2000) 'Evaluating influence diagrams using LIMIDs', in C. Boutilier and M. Goldszmidt (eds), *Proceedings of the Sixteenth Conference on Uncertainty in Artificial Intelligence*, Morgan Kaufmann Publishers, San Francisco, pp436–445

O'Connell-Rodwell, C. E., Rodwell, T., Matthew, R., Hart, L. A. (2000) 'Living with the modern conservation paradigm: Can agricultural communities co-exist with elephants? A five-year case study in east Caprivi, Namibia', *Biological Conservation*, vol 93, pp381–391

Partell, P. J. and Palmer, G. (1999) 'Audience costs and interstate crises: An empirical assessment of Fearon's model of dispute outcomes', *International Studies Quarterly*, vol. 43, pp389–405

Peden, D. G. (1984) *Livestock and Wildlife Population Inventories by District in Kenya 1977–1983*, Technical Report 102, Kenya Rangeland Ecological Monitoring Unit, Nairobi

Pelkey, N. W., Stoner, C. J., Caro, T. M. (2000) 'Vegetation in Tanzania: Assessing long term trends and effects of protection using satellite imagery', *Biological Conservation*, vol 94, pp297–309

Rumelhart, D. E., Smolensky, P., McClelland, J. L., Hinton, G. E. (1986) 'Schemata and sequential thought processes in parallel distributed processing models', in D. E. Rumelhart, J. L. McClelland and the PDP Research Group, *Parallel Distributed Processing: Exploration in the Microstructure of Cognition, Volume 2*, The MIT Press, Cambridge, MA, pp7–57

Schrodt, P. A. (1995) 'Event data in foreign policy analysis', in L. Neack, J. A. K. Hey and P. J. Haney (eds), *Foreign Policy Analysis*, Prentice-Hall, Englewood Cliffs, NJ, pp145–166

Tamura, R. N. and Boos, D. D. (1986) 'Minimum Hellinger distance estimation for multivariate location and covariance', *Journal of the American Statistical Association*, vol 81, no 393, pp223–229

Thompson, J. R. and Tapia, R. A. (1990) *Nonparametric Function Estimation, Modeling and Simulation*, Society for Industrial and Applied Mathematics, Philadelphia, PA

Throup, D. and Hornsby, C. (1998) *Multi-Party Politics in Kenya*, Ohio University Press, Athens, OH

Vertzberger, Y. Y. I. (1990) *The World in Their Minds*, Stanford University Press, Stanford, CA

Wells, H., Strauss, E. G., Rutter, M. A., Wells, P. H. (1998) 'Mate location, population growth and species extinction', *Biological Conservation*, vol 86, pp317–324

World Resources Institute (2005) *Population, Health and Human Well-Being Country Profiles*, http://earthtrends.wri.org

13
Co-management of Protected Areas: A Case Study from Central Sulawesi, Indonesia

Regina Birner and Marhawati Mappatoba

Introduction

Negotiated agreements between local communities and state agencies concerning the management of natural resources have gained increasing importance in recent years. Examples include negotiations on water rights (Bruns and Meinzen-Dick, 2000) and biodiversity conservation (Venema and Breemer, 1999). Negotiation approaches have been identified as a promising strategy to overcome shortcomings of conventional participatory approaches, such as the neglect of power relations and conflicts of interests (Leeuwis, 2000; Agrawal, 2001; Cook and Kothari, 2001; Hildyard and Pandurang, 2001). Protected areas in developing countries are one of the fields where negotiation approaches are particularly promising, because conflicts of interests are frequently observed and conventional strategies of state management have often failed. Negotiation approaches can be used to establish systems of collaborative management (co-management), which involve a sharing of rights and responsibilities between state agencies and the local population. Moreover, negotiated co-management agreements promise to overcome the problems of managing protected areas by state agencies alone, because they are voluntary and have better prospects of taking into account the development aspirations and the indigenous knowledge of the local people living within the surroundings of a protected area (Borrini-Feyerabend et al, 2000; Meinzen-Dick et al, 2001).

While the potential of negotiated co-management agreements is increasingly acknowledged in the literature, published empirical analyses of such agreements are still limited. Wilshusen et al (2002) reviewed the debate that has emerged on the topic, following the criticism of conservation biologists that involving local communities has largely failed to promote better conservation outcomes. This debate still continues, as the contribution by Locke and Dearden (2005) shows; these authors call for a rethinking of protected area categories that aim at linking conservation and development. Mburu and Birner (2002) analysed the efficiency of collaborative wildlife management in Kenya, taking transaction costs into account. Carlsson and Berkes (2005) reviewed concepts and methodological implications of co-management, emphasizing that co-management should be considered as a problem-solving process. More recently, Keough and Blahna (2006) identified factors for the successful involvement of local communities and other stakeholders in collaborative ecosystem management.

The present chapter uses the case of the Lore Lindu National Park in Central Sulawesi, Indonesia, as an empirical example to study the potentials and the challenges of the co-management approach. In cooperation with several non-governmental organizations (NGOs), the administration of the Lore Lindu National Park has played a pioneering role in promoting negotiated community agreements on conservation (Kesepakatan Konservasi Masyarakat, KKM). The agreements aim to overcome the major threats to the National Park, which consist in the conversion of the forest inside the park for agricultural land (encroachment), the extraction of rattan, logging, hunting of protected endemic animals, such as anoa (*Bubalus spp*) or babyrussa (*Babyrousa babyrussa*), and the collection of the eggs of the protected maleo bird (*Macrocephalus maleo*) (ANZDEC, 1997). At the time of this research (2000–2002), efforts to establish community agreements on conservation have been started in approximately 40 of the 60 villages located close to the National Park, and more than 10 villages have already signed an agreement. The agreements are promoted by three NGOs that differ with regard to their approaches and goals. Therefore, the case of the Lore Lindu National Park provides an excellent opportunity for an explorative study of negotiated co-management agreements.

The chapter is organized as follows: the next section presents some theoretical considerations on negotiated agreements from the perspectives of resource economics and policy analysis. The subsequent section gives an overview of the research area and outlines the methods used for the study. The following section introduces the approaches to establish community agreements pursued by three different NGOs in the area that differ in their value orientation and objectives. The empirical results of a household survey conducted in three villages are presented in the next section while the following one discusses the empirical results on the basis of the theoretical framework. In a final section some conclusions are drawn.

Conceptual framework

Negotiated agreements as a Coase solution to externalities?

From the perspective of environmental economics, problems of nature conservation arise due to negative external effects that are associated with the use of natural resources. External effects are defined as actions of economic agents that affect the production or consumption possibilities of others in a way that is not captured by the market mechanism. The conversion of tropical rainforests for agricultural production, for example, causes negative external effects because it reduces biological diversity. The costs arising to the society and future generations caused by reducing biological diversity are not considered in the farmers' decision to convert tropical rainforest. The environmental economics literature proposes three classical solutions to the problem of externalities: (i) state regulations that restrict the actions leading to external effects; (ii) Pigou taxes that internalize the costs caused by the external effects; and (iii) bargaining between the party causing the external effect and those affected by it (Coase, 1960).

Protected areas – so far the globally most important approach in nature conservation – are a prime example of the first solution: state regulations. From the perspective of environmental economics, regulations are generally considered as less efficient than taxes or the bargaining solution, because they create no incentive to reduce the externality further than the limit stated by the regulation and they do not usually achieve the required reduction of the negative environmental effects with the lowest possible costs. However, as Horbach (1992) showed, they are characterized by a higher political feasibility than taxes, which may explain the wide use of regulatory instruments in environmental policy. State regulations are also associated with considerable enforcement problems, especially if the number of producers causing external effects is high and the capacity of state agencies is limited. This is typically the case in protected area management in developing countries, where comparatively few park guards have to deal with thousands of land users. Taxes, the second solution to the external effects mentioned above, are hardly applied in nature conservation. The enforcement problems of this solution would probably be similar or even higher than those arising in the case of state regulations. Collecting taxes from a high number of partly or even largely subsistence-oriented farmers is obviously difficult.

Negotiated agreements on nature conservation represent the third solution to the externalities mentioned above: the bargaining solution proposed by Ronald Coase in 1960 in his paper on 'The problem of social cost'. As a starting point of his analysis, Coase emphasized the reciprocal nature of externality problems:

> *To avoid the harm to B would inflict harm on A. The real question that has to be decided is: should A be allowed to harm B or should B be allowed to harm A? The problem is to avoid the more serious harm.*
> (Coase, 1960, p2)

With regard to nature conservation, this aspect is crucial. Taking the example of rainforest conversion, one has to acknowledge that 'to avoid the harm to B', which is in this case the society suffering from reduced biological diversity, 'would inflict harm to A'. In this case, A stands for the farmers, who suffer an income loss, if they are not allowed to use the land for agricultural production.

Coase showed that if property rights are fully specified, transaction costs are zero and distributional aspects do not matter, voluntary bargaining between agents will lead to an efficient outcome, regardless of how property rights are initially assigned. Even though this insight later became known as the Coase Theorem, the major focus of Coase in his 1960 paper was to show that transaction costs are rather important in most real life situations. Therefore, the initial distribution of property rights is relevant for the design of efficient solutions to externality problems. One can add that the initial distribution of property rights is also important with regard to distributional questions. A number of other assumptions of the Coase Theorem are discussed in the literature, as well, such as perfect knowledge of one another's production and profit or utility functions, profit-maximizing producers and expected-utility maximizing consumers, and the assumption that agents strike mutually advantageous bargains (Hoffman and Spitzer, 1982, p73).

With regard to negotiated agreements on nature conservation, one can conclude that this instrument has, according to the Coase Theorem, a considerable potential for leading to an efficient internalization of the external effects underlying nature conservation problems. At the same time, the assumptions of the Coase Theorem point to the questions that have to be studied empirically in order to assess this policy instrument:

1   How are the property rights considered to be originally assigned? To what extent do state agencies acknowledge the customary property rights of the local population?
2   To what extent are the negotiated agreements based on cost–benefit considerations and self-interested negotiation?
3   What role do transaction costs play in the process of establishing and negotiating co-management agreements?

Negotiating agreements as a case of empowered deliberative democracy?

While environmental economics focus on a normative evaluation of the economic efficiency of negotiated co-management agreements, one can also consider the negotiation of such agreements as a political process, which can be studied from a political science perspective. Thomas (2001) considered negotiated agreements on habitat conservation in the US as a case of 'Empowered Deliberative Democracy' (EDD). The EDD model was developed by Fung and Wright to analyse cases that 'have the potential to be radically democratic in their reliance on the participation and capacities of ordinary people, deliberative because they institute reason-based decision making, and empowered since they attempt to tie action to discussion' (Fung and Wright, 2001, p7). This framework appears to be suitable for analysing the agreements in the Indonesian case. As

Indonesia is in a process of democratic transition, the question of whether such agreements constitute innovative models of democratic decision making is not only of academic interest, it also has significant practical relevance. The main elements of the EDD model developed by Fung and Wright (2001) are presented in Box 13.1. As can be seen from this box, the EDD model offers a different interpretation for the negotiated community agreements than does the Coase Theorem. As a mode of social choice, Coase assumes strategic bargaining of self-interested parties with fixed preferences and given cost and benefit functions. The EDD model suggests deliberation as an alternative mode of social choice. Deliberative decision making describes a process in which participants listen to each other's position, offer reasons that others can accept and generate group choices after appropriate consideration. Deliberation assumes that a process of social learning will take place, leading to the change of preferences. However, as Fung and Wright explain:

> *The ideal does not require participants to be altruistic or to converge upon a consensus of value and strategy, or perspective. Real-world deliberations are often characterized by heated conflict, winners, and losers. The important feature of genuine deliberation is that participants find reasons that they can accept in collective actions, not necessarily that they completely endorse the action or find it maximally advantageous.* (Fung and Wright, 2001, p19)

Forero Pineda (2001) considers deliberation as the key criterion to define participatory democracy, which he distinguishes from direct democracy (decision making by referendum, without citizen deliberation and without intermediaries) and from representative democracy (decision making by intermediaries, without citizen deliberation). Forero Pineda draws attention to the fact that participatory democracy may or may not involve intermediaries, and there may be an interaction with some authority elected through the channels of representative democracy (Forero Pineda, 2001). For the case under consideration, one also has to consider that traditional authorities may play a role as intermediaries. They derive their legitimacy from indigenous systems of law and traditional systems of authority (compare Weber's (1922) types of legitimate rule), which do not necessarily involve elections held according to western principles of representative democracy. It will be a question for the empirical analysis to assess the impact of different types of intermediaries on the negotiated agreements.

As other modes of social choice besides deliberation, Fung and Wright (2001, p20) discuss strategic negotiation, command and control by experts, and aggregate voting. The conventional approach of declaring protected areas is an example of the command and control strategy, which the negotiated agreements on conservation attempt to overcome. Strategic negotiation is the mode of social choice that is implicitly assumed by the Coase Theorem. Aggregate voting, the decision mode characterizing direct democracy according to the above classification, was not observed as a method to deal with nature conservation problems in the Indonesian case study. From a theoretical perspective, this mode is characterized by the problem that Arrow's Impossibility Theorem (1950) describes: there is no social choice rule that would allow for passing from individual preferences to social preferences, if some very reasonable and basic conditions are to be met.

Box 13.1 The model of Empowered Deliberative Democracy

Design principles

1 Practical orientation
   Development of governance structures geared to concrete concerns.
2 Bottom-up participation
   Those most directly affected by targeted problems – typically ordinary citizens and officials in the field – apply their knowledge, intelligence and interest to the formulation of solutions.
3 Deliberative solution generation
   Participants listen to each other's position and, after due consideration, generate group choices. This distinguishes deliberation from three other familiar modes of social choice: command and control by experts, aggregative voting and strategic negotiation.

Design properties

1 Devolution
   Administrative and political power is devolved to local units, which are not merely advisory and voluntaristic, but rather creatures of a transformed state endowed with substantial public authority.
2 Centralized supervision and coordination
   Linkages of accountability and communication connect local units to superordinate bodies, which reinforce the quality of local democratic deliberation, for example by coordinating and distributing resources, diffusing innovation and learning, and rectifying incompetent decision-making.

Enabling conditions

1 Balance of power between actors
2 Others, for example, literacy

Criteria for evaluation of empirical cases

1   Genuine deliberation
2   Role of intermediaries in the deliberation process
3   Effective translation of decision into action
4   Effective monitoring of the implementation of the decisions
5   Achievement of alleged benefits of centralized coordination
6   Function of deliberative processes as schools of democracy
7   Outcomes superior to those of alternative arrangements

Potential problems of the model

1   Problems of power and domination inside deliberative arenas may jeopardize the democratic character of the process. More powerful, or especially well-informed or interested parties may capture deliberative institutions for rent-seeking.
2   Powerful actors may use deliberative arenas only when it suits them ('forum shopping').
3   Empowered deliberation may demand unrealistically high levels of popular participation. Therefore, deliberative experiments may initially enjoy successes but may be difficult to sustain in the long run.

Source: Adapted from Fung and Wright, 2001 and Forero Pineola, 2001.

Value orientation as a factor influencing community agreements

The agreements in the Lore Lindu area are promoted by NGOs that have different objectives and value orientations. As these differences may well have an impact on the type of agreements they promote, we include the consideration of value orientations in our analysis. Among organizations dealing with issues of nature conservation and rural development, one can typically distinguish three different value orientations, or ideologies (compare Dauvergne, 1994; Wittmer and Birner, 2005):

1   the 'conservationist' orientation;
2   the 'developmentalist' orientation;
3   the 'eco-populist' or 'indigenous rights advocacy' orientation.

These value orientations underlie the objectives and the factual and evaluative beliefs of different actors. In the public discourse, they are typically expressed in a flexible and strategic way (compare van Dijk, 1998). The conservationist discourse focuses on nature conservation as a goal in its own right. Organizations with a conservationist orientation are typically concerned with the protection of certain wildlife species and their habitats, or, more generally with the protection of biological diversity.

Conservationist organizations have increasingly included rural development activities in their agenda. Their experience has shown that development activities, for example in the buffer zones of protected areas, help to reach conservation objectives more effectively. However, such activities may also indicate that conservationist organizations have broadened their set of objectives. In the 'developmentalist discourse', poverty, population increase, and lack of appropriate technology are considered to be the major driving forces of the destruction of natural resources. In rural areas, organizations with a developmentalist orientation typically concentrate on activities such as agricultural extension, transfer of technology and infrastructural development. Techniques of ecologically sustainable resource management and issues of nature conservation have increasingly become parts of the programmes of developmentalist organizations, both due to the need to conserve the production basis in the long run, and as an indication of a broadened value orientation of such organizations. In the 'eco-populist' discourse, ecological issues are placed in the context of advocacy for the rights of local and indigenous communities. Organizations with an eco-populist agenda typically consider local communities as the true stewards of natural resources and place more trust in traditional institutions of resource management than in the capacity of state agencies.

With regard to the different modes of social choice discussed above, 'command and control by experts' has traditionally played a larger role in organizations with a developmentalist or a conservationist background, while empowerment and deliberative solution generation is more prominent in eco-populist organizations. However, the intensive debate on participation in rural development during the last decades has had a profound impact on the strategies of all three types of organizations. Even though the term deliberation is hardly used in the literature on participation in rural development, this literature is motivated by similar ideas of empowerment, social learning and consensus building. However, in the more recent literature on participation one can observe an increasing criticism of participatory approaches (Cook and Kothari, 2001). The issues criticized resemble the problems of the deliberative model mentioned in Box 13.1. The dissatisfaction with participatory approaches refers to the neglect of power structures and the limited capacity of conventional participatory methods to deal with conflicts of interests. Some authors suggested strategic negotiation, a further mode of social choice mentioned above, as a means to overcome these problems (Leeuwis, 2000; Agrawal, 2001). Against this background, it is a question for the empirical analysis to study how the value orientation of an organization influences the negotiation approach they promote.

Figure 13.1 summarizes the framework for the analysis of negotiated agreements on nature conservation based on the above theoretical considerations. As the agreements selected for the empirical case study of this chapter were completed comparatively recently, a final analysis of the outcome based on ecological or socio-economic impact indicators is not yet possible. While this is planned for later stages of this research, the focus of this chapter is placed on the process of establishing the agreements.

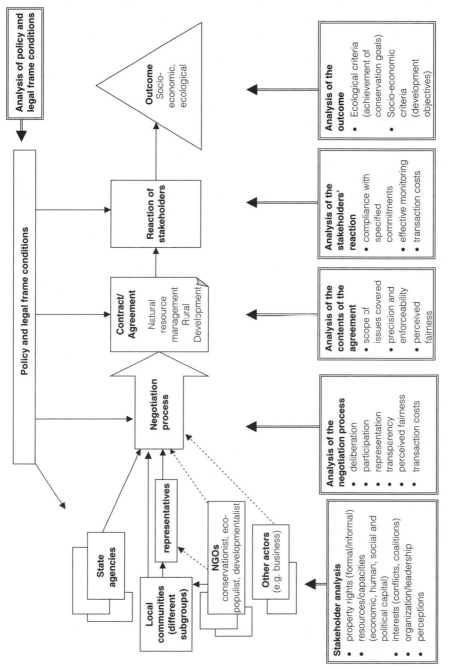

Figure 13.1 *Analytical framework of negotiated agreement on nature conservation*

Research area and methods

The Lore Lindu National Park is located in Central Sulawesi, Indonesia, and covers an area of 229,000ha. The region in which the Park is located is characterized by a high ecological and socio-cultural diversity. Due to its rich biodiversity and its high endemism, the park was declared as a World Heritage Site by UNESCO. The park is managed by the Balai Taman Nasional Lore Lindu (BTNLL), an administrative office that reports directly to the Ministry of Forestry at the national level. There are approximately 120 villages in the five sub-districts in which the park is located. Half of these villages are located close to the park, some in enclaves inside the park. As mentioned in the introduction, efforts to establish 'community agreements on conservation' (Kepasakapatan Konservasi Masyarakat, KKM) are already ongoing in approximately 40 of these 60 villages. At present, there are three NGOs promoting these agreements: (i) a local NGO (receiving international funds) with an 'eco-populist' orientation according to the classification outlined above, which specializes on advocacy for indigenous rights; (ii) a large international NGO with a 'developmentalist' orientation, which focuses on the provision of rural development services; and (iii) a large international NGO with a 'conservationist' orientation, engaged in nature conservation and protected area management. Hereafter, these NGOs will be referred to as the 'Advocacy NGO', the 'Rural Development NGO' and the 'Conservation NGO', respectively. The Conservation NGO had a local sister organization that focused on community activities, which was later integrated into the Conservation NGO. After this merger, the Conservation NGO continued the work of its earlier local sister organization on community agreements. To avoid confusion, we deal with both organizations together here under the label 'Conservation NGO'. Altogether, there were around 30 NGOs and one large integrated development and conservation project funded by the Asian Development Bank (ADB) operating in the area of the Lore Lindu National Park at the time of this research. Twenty-six of the NGOs, which worked on issues related to the Park, have formed the Lore Lindu Communication Forum.

Three research methods were combined for the empirical study on the community agreements:

1 interviews with state agencies, NGOs and development projects at the provincial level;
2 stakeholder interviews in ten selected villages to study different processes of establishing a village agreement;
3 a survey of a random sample of households in three selected villages, where the process of establishing an agreement was already completed.

The research was carried out between 2000 and 2002. The selection of villages covered all three NGOs facilitating the agreement, and all sub-districts where the agreement approach is being implemented. Only villages where the process of establishing an agreement was already advanced or completed were chosen. Between seven and ten stakeholders were interviewed in each village, starting with the village headman. Other interview partners were identified using the snowball system, for example by following the recommendations of former interview partners.

The household survey was conducted in three villages in which an agreement had already been established. Hereafter, these villages will be referred to as Villages A, B and C. Village A was selected as an example of the approach adopted by the Rural Development NGO. Staff members of this organization recommended this village as the one where they considered the agreement approach to be most successful. The other two villages were selected as examples of the approach promoted by the Advocacy NGO. Three villages had signed an agreement promoted by this NGO, but the third village was not included in the household survey because of some special circumstances applying to this village. Agreements promoted by the Conservation NGO were not included in the household survey, because none of the villages had signed an agreement at the time of conducting the survey.

To select the households, a simple random sample of 10 per cent of the households (at least 20 households) was drawn in Villages A and C. In Village B, which is twice the size of the other two villages, 5 per cent of the households were interviewed. The sampling frame included only households that do not have official functions in the village such as village headman, member of the traditional village council, etc., because the purpose of the household survey was to collect information on the knowledge, participation and perceptions of the 'common villager'. The interviews were conducted in a semi-structured form, using interview guidelines.

Approaches to establish community agreements

Overview

The approaches to establishing community agreements on conservation differed considerably between the organizations promoting this approach. Table 13.1 gives an overview of the strategies applied by the three NGOs under consideration.

The approach of the Advocacy NGO

The organization referred to as 'Advocacy NGO' in this chapter (see previous section) has a strong focus on advocacy for indigenous people's rights. The conservation of natural resources is a major goal of this NGO, too. The

Table 13.1 *Overview of the agreement strategies of different NGOs*

Type of organization	Local advocacy NGO with international funding	International development NGO, with international and local staff	International conservation NGO (with a local sister organization focusing on community activities)
Focus of activities in general	Advocacy for indigenous rights, 'watchdog' of government and international activities	Rural/community development (agricultural extension, infrastructure provision, etc.), sustainable management of natural resources	Community development activities as complementary measure for nature conservation activities (such as improved park management)
'Logic' behind community agreement	Commitment to keep rules on conservation, enforced and sanctioned by traditional village institutions, as part of a strategy to regain traditional resource use rights in the park	Rules on conservation as part of a general set of rules of conduct within the village; prerequisite required for providing development services, including infrastructure development	Commitment to keep clearly specified rules on conservation in exchange for provision of development services and infrastructure by government organizations and projects
Selection of villages	Villages that request assistance for agreement; at present: only indigenous villages	All villages where the NGO conducted activities in Phase 1 of its programme in the Lore Lindu region	Villages where conflicts concerning the protection of the National Park appear severe
Role of the NGO concerning the agreement	Facilitator of agreement, provider of support for social mobilization and capacity building in the village, promoter of policy dialogue with various organizations	Facilitator of agreement and provider of development services and infrastructure	Facilitator of agreement, broker between conservation organization and organizations/projects providing development services and infrastructure
Representation of the villagers concerning the agreement	Traditional village institutions (Lembaga Adat)	Formal village government (Kepala Desa)	Representatives of the village chosen especially for the purpose of the village agreement
Mapping of resource use	Community-based mapping of traditional resource use rights (using global positioning system (GPS), but not GIS)	So far not applied	Community-based mapping of actual resource use (with GPS and GIS)

Source: Compiled by the authors.

interviews with the NGO's representatives showed that they regard the indigenous population as the best steward of the natural resources because of their traditional rules and institutions for sustainable resource management. The NGO considers the activities of state agencies and internationally funded projects with a critical distance and expresses doubts concerning their capacity to protect the natural resources of the region. The NGO had successfully launched a campaign to avoid the construction of a large hydropower dam in the area of the Lore Lindu National Park. With regard to the considerations on discourses in natural resource management outlined earlier, the position of this NGO can be characterized as 'eco-populist'.

The NGO promoted the first community agreement on conservation in a village located inside the park that was supposed to be resettled under the ADB project mentioned above. The NGO received support from international organizations that had already acquired experience with community-based mapping and the negotiation of such agreements. In that first village, the process of establishing the agreement lasted approximately two years and involved several steps, including awareness creation and mobilization within the village, community-based mapping, policy dialogue with various state agencies and other external stakeholders, and finally the negotiation of the community agreement on conservation with the management of the National Park on the one hand, and the traditional village council, Lembaga Adat, as the representative of the village, on the other hand. The agreement includes restrictions concerning the use of land for agricultural production and restrictions on the extraction of forest resources, such as rattan. The advocacy NGO invested approximately Rs15 million (approx. US$1580) and the salary of three staff members for this process, which lasted two years. The villagers had a strong incentive to reach such an agreement, because it was essential for avoiding the resettlement of the village.

In the case of the two villages included in the household survey (named Village B and Village C) where the Advocacy NGO also facilitated an agreement, the incentives of the villagers to make such an agreement were not equally obvious. The villages were not under a threat of resettlement. In contrast to the approaches applied by the Conservation NGO and the Rural Development NGO (see below), there was no explicit or implicit provision for development services, infrastructure or other benefits, in exchange for the conservation commitment. However, in both cases, the village leaders themselves approached the Advocacy NGO and asked for assistance in establishing such a community agreement on conservation, after they had heard about the case of the first village. According to the interviewed village leaders, the most important reason to promote an agreement was to stop public allegations that the villagers were destroying resources inside the park. According to the village leaders, external actors with commercial interests such as logging companies or sawmill operators were in fact responsible for this destruction. The interviews suggest that the village leaders also promoted the agreements:

- as a strategy to avoid the degradation of natural resources with negative impacts on the village (water shortages, flooding, etc. as a consequence of deforestation);
- as part of a strategy to regain traditional resource use rights inside the park;
- as a means to strengthen the traditional village institutions (Lembaga Adat), which (re-)gain functions concerning the control of resource use that were formerly taken up by the Park officials, including the issue of sanctions.

The research in Villages B and C where the Advocacy NGO facilitated the agreement indicated that the process of establishing an agreement there involved a lower level of consultation with government agencies and other external stakeholders than in the case of the Village A. In Village C, for example, the text of the village agreement was decided upon within a community meeting and signed by the Lembaga Adat. Only afterwards did the director of the National Park write an official letter to back up the community agreement. Although the park director had been consulted during the process in the village, the agreement cannot exactly be considered as the outcome of a negotiation process between the community and the park administration. This type of procedure may be due to the fact that the first village served as a pioneer case, which can now be followed more easily by other villages. So far, the Advocacy NGO promotes agreements only in indigenous villages, for which they consider the approach they developed to be most suitable. The NGO does not exclude the possibility of working later in villages with a higher percentage of immigrants, but the interviewed NGO leaders mentioned that it might be necessary to develop a different methodology for these villages.

The Administration of the National Park (BTNLL) has expressed its full support for the community agreements on conservation supported by the Advocacy NGO. According to his own statement, the leadership of the BTNLL that was in place at the time of this research followed an 'eco-populist approach', which places a high level of trust in the capacity of the indigenous communities to manage the natural resources inside and outside the park in a way that is sustainable in the long-term. Moreover, as a BTNLL representative explained, the new Forest Law of 1999 increased the scope for such community agreements, because it could be interpreted in a way that allows villagers to use certain natural resources inside the park for home consumption. This opportunity, which was not possible under the prior law, could now be specified in the community agreements.

The approach of the Rural Development NGO

The organization referred to as 'Rural Development NGO' here has several decades of international experience in promoting community-based development in rural areas. In recent years, it has increasingly included the protection of natural resources into its development activities. Within the programme implemented by this NGO in the Lore Lindu area, the community agreements on conservation were, however, only one component of a broader community development programme that included, among others, the following activities: (i) provision of physical infrastructure, for example for drinking water; (ii) promotion of an increase in agricultural productivity, for example by agricultural extension and the provision of inputs such as seedlings; (iii) the introduction of soil conservation techniques, such as the establishment of contour bounds cropped with legumes; (iv) improvement of marketing facilities; and (iv) promotion of non-traditional income-generating activities, such as fish ponds. The NGO selected 22 target villages among the 60 villages located close to the Lore Lindu National Park. Their location close to the park and their poverty level were the major selection criteria. Within the target villages, the NGO organized the poorer households in groups, which then participated in the programme activities.

The establishment of a community agreement was an integral component of the NGO's programme in each of its target villages. It was mainly the task of the NGO staff member in charge of the respective village to promote such an agreement. The agreement did not only concern National Park regulations, but also general rules of conduct within the village. This agreement was described by one respondent as a prerequisite to the success of the NGO's development activities. One could also interpret the agreement as an implicit contract, according to which the community commits itself – in exchange for receiving development assistance – to follow certain rules of conduct, including observation of the official regulations concerning the National Park. In practice, however, the agreements were not handled as a prerequisite to the implementation of the NGO's development activities, because in many of the target villages an agreement was only signed shortly before the programme was terminated.

In contrast to the approach followed by the Advocacy NGO, the interaction with the Administration of the National Park in the establishment of the agreements appeared rather low. In the village included in the household survey (Village A), the local Park Guard, who has his office in the village, was involved, but the NGO did not solicit an official approval of the agreement from the BTNLL head office. This may be due to the fact that the agreement was not specific to the National Park, as mentioned above. Moreover, the agreement did not refer to any indigenous rights to resources in the park, which were to be acknowledged. It rather demanded that the villagers obey the official regulations of the National Park.

The Rural Development NGO and the Advocacy NGO also differed in their strategy for dealing with traditional leadership. The Advocacy NGO dealt with the traditional village council, the Lembaga Adat, as the responsible representative of the villagers with regard to the agreement, while the Rural

Development NGO mainly addressed the official village headman, the Kepala Desa. This strategy may be influenced by the fact that the Rural Development NGO also worked in villages with a large proportion of immigrants, where the Lembaga Adat does not have the same authority and recognition as in the indigenous villages.

The approach of the Conservation NGO

Through its local sister organization, the 'Conservation NGO' started to promote the establishment of community agreements on conservation in 12 villages located close to the National Park. This NGO described the approach of establishing community agreements explicitly as a 'co-management' (collaborative management) strategy and placed it in the context of developing a management and zoning strategy for the National Park. Biological surveys, conducted by the Conservation NGO, were used to suggest the boundaries for different zones from a nature conservation point of view. Community mapping, conducted by the local sister organization, was seen as an instrument to determine the resource use demands of the local communities. In case of conflicting interests between nature conservation and resource use by the communities, negotiating an agreement was envisaged as a tool to solve such problems and agree on a zoning plan. Similar to the approach of the Rural Development NGO, the local sister organization of the Conservation NGO had the plan that development services should be offered to the villagers in exchange for a commitment to keep certain conservation rules. However, unlike the Rural Development NGO, the Conservation NGO and its local sister organization did not have the capacity to offer substantial development services themselves. Their activities focused on small-scale activities such as butterfly farming and bee-keeping. Their major focus of activities was environmental education, for example in schools. Therefore, they considered themselves as a 'broker' and aimed to channel development assistance and infrastructure development supplied by government organizations and development projects such as the ADB project to communities that were willing to engage in a community agreement. It was envisaged that the provision of development assistance would be specified in the agreements.

The Conservation NGO also had the idea that the villagers should elect a number of representatives especially for the purpose of negotiating the agreement. In addition, the NGO tried to involve both the official village government (Kepala Desa) and the traditional village council (Lembaga Adat). Like the Advocacy NGO, this NGO intended to introduce traditional sanctions, such as paying a fine in the form of livestock, for violations of nature conservation rules established under the agreement. Due to limitations of funding and the re-integration of the local sister organization into the Conservation NGO, the activities had not yet led to the final signing of an agreement in any of the villages at the time of this research. The Conservation NGO, however, planned to continue the establishment of community agreements according to concepts similar to its former sister organization.

Interestingly, there are villages in which community agreements on conservation were promoted by two or even all three different NGOs. The stakeholder interviews left the impression that the coordination among the NGOs concerning these activities was not very intensive. It rather appeared that each NGO promoted 'its own' agreement, even if they were working in the same village.

Participation and perceptions of the villagers

This section is based on the household surveys conducted in the three sample villages.

Socio-economic background of the villages and the sample households

Table 13.2 summarizes some general characteristics of the three case study villages. The population in Village A comprises both indigenous people and immigrants who came from areas other than Central Sulawesi and who belong to different ethnic groups. Villages B and C can be characterized as indigenous villages. Table 13.3, which refers to the sample households, also reflects this village composition. As shown in Tables 13.2 and 13.3, no paddy land is available in Village A. Village B has the highest population density and the lowest average size of land holdings. The low population density in Village C, in combination with very limited access to markets due to unfavourable road conditions, leads to a comparatively high proportion of unused land in Village C (see Table 13.3). In Village B, the availability of land is restricted due to the close vicinity of the National Park, which surrounds the entire village area. Village A, in contrast, still has forest resources located in its village territory, which can be converted into agricultural land, according to their official classification. One also has to take into account the inequality of land distribution. In Village B, 16 of the 25 sample households had less than 0.5ha of paddy land, and another three households had no paddy land at all. In Village C, six of the 20 sample households had less than 0.5ha paddy land. A comparison between Tables 13.2 and 13.3 shows that the sample households own less land than the village average. This indicates that the households included in the sampling frame (those without official functions in the village) own, on average, less land than those with functions.

As a measure of poverty, a housing score ranging from 1 (good) to 3 (poor) was applied. As shown in Table 13.3, Village A had the highest proportion of poor households according to this criterion, while Village C had a more equitable distribution of housing quality.

Table 13.2 *Characteristics of the case study villages*

	Village A	Village B	Village C
Organization promoting the agreement	International Rural Development NGO	Local Advocacy NGO	
No. of households[a]	240	530	180
No. of households in household survey	25	25	20
Population density (persons per km²)[a]	20	35	5
Ethnic composition	mixed	indigenous	indigenous
Access to markets/quality of roads	good	medium	low
Av. size of paddy land per household (ha)	no paddy land	0.9	3.1
Av. size of upland per household (ha)	3.0	0.9	1.1
Av. area of forest per household (ha)[b]	13	41	87

Notes: [a] Figures are rounded; [b] average calculated as forest area that belongs to the administrative village area divided by the number of households; includes forest area located inside the National Park.

Source: Authors' interviews and data derived from a village survey conducted by Miet Maertens and Marhawati Mappatoba in 2001.

Table 13.3 *Characteristics of the sample households*

	Village A	Village B	Village C
Percentage of household heads born in the village (per cent)	20	56	70
Percentage of immigrants that came from other provinces than Central Sulawesi (per cent)	25	0	33
Average size of cultivated paddy land (ha)	no paddy	0.5	1.1
Average size of cultivated upland (ha)	1.1	0.9	0.9
Average size of unused land (ha)	0.4	0.2	1.5
Households with high housing score (per cent)[a]	4	4	26
Households with low housing score (per cent)[a]	52	40	21

Note: [a] Quality of housing, as an indicator of poverty, was ranked on a scale from 1 (high) to 3 (low).

Source: Authors' household survey (2001).

Knowledge of sample households about the agreement

Table 13.4 shows that there are considerable differences between the three villages concerning the knowledge of the respondents about the agreement.

In Village A, only one-third of the respondents immediately knew what the interviewer's question concerning the community agreement on conservation referred to. In Village B, the percentage of respondents in this category was almost 50 per cent and in Village C it was as high as 80 per cent. In Village A,

Table 13.4 *Knowledge of respondents on community agreements (percentage of respondents)*

	Village A	Village B	Village C
Respondent knows agreement without further explanation	32	48	80
Respondent recognizes agreement after explanation	36	44	15
Respondent never heard about agreement	32	8	5

Source: Authors' household survey (2001).

one-third of the respondents only recognized what the question the interviewers were referring to after the type of agreement was explained to them. Another third of the respondents answered that they had never heard about such an agreement. In Village B and Village C, the percentage of respondents in this last category was very low, as indicated in Table 13.4.

When interpreting these figures, one has to keep in mind that the agreement in Village A had been established four years ago, while in Villages B and C it was only established within the year before the interview. Moreover, knowledge concerning the agreement is related to the involvement of the households in the meetings held in relation to the agreement, which is discussed further below. Table 13.5 indicates the depth of the respondents' knowledge concerning the contents of the agreements. With regard to this question the respondents were divided into three groups: (i) respondents who only know that the agreement exists, but were not able to mention to which activities it refers; (ii) respondents who mentioned in general to which activities the agreement refers (e.g. restrictions on collection of rattan and harvesting of timber inside the park); and (iii) respondents who knew details of the agreement, for example concerning sanctions. As Table 13.5 shows, the percentage of respondents with knowledge of the details of the agreement was highest in Village C and lowest in Village A. In Village B, the percentage of persons who knew only that the agreement exists was higher than in the other two villages. These figures have to be interpreted

Table 13.5 *Depth of knowledge about agreement (percentage of respondents)*

	Village A	Village B	Village C
Specific knowledge on details	29	39	65
General knowledge on contents	47	26	15
Only knows that agreement exists	24	35	20

Source: Authors' household survey (2001).

with care, since categorizing the answers necessarily involves a qualitative judgement.

Involvement of sample households in the process of establishing the agreement

As Table 13.6 shows, there were considerable differences concerning the participation of the sample households in the meetings dealing with the agreement. These differences correspond to the findings concerning the knowledge of the respondents about the agreement, as presented in the last section. The percentage of villagers participating in at least one meeting related to the agreement was highest in Village C and lowest in Village A. As Table 13.6 also indicates, the respondents who participated in the meetings in Village B attended on the average more meetings than the respondents in Villages A and C.

A comparison of the households that were participating in meetings concerning the agreement (participants) with those that were not participating (non-participants) indicated a tendency for the participants to be better off with regard to the welfare indicators of landholding and housing, but the differences were not large (see Table 13.7). The household survey also included a question on village organizations, such as religious groups, labour sharing groups, sports groups, etc., in which the household members participate. The number of groups

Table 13.6 *Participation in meetings related to the agreement*

	Village A	Village B	Village C
Respondents who remembered that they participated at least in one meeting (per cent)	16	24	60
Average number of meetings attended by the participants	4.0	5.6	3.8

Source: Authors' household survey (2001).

Table 13.7 *Characteristics of participants and non-participants*

	Participants	Non-participants
Welfare indicators		
Average area of cultivated land (ha)	2.0	1.6
Percentage of households with housing score 1 (good)	10.6	9.1
Percentage of households with housing score 3 (poor)	36.4	40.4
Social capital indicator		
Average number of organizations in which household members participate	5.1	3.6

Source: Authors' household survey (2001).

in which the household members participate is considered here as a measure of the household's social capital.

As Table 13.7 shows, the participants had, on average, a higher level of social capital than the non-participants. The results also show that the participants were, on average, older than the non-participants. Two reasons may account for this difference: first, it may conform to customary rules that decisions concerning the village are made by elder members of the village community. Second, younger persons may have higher opportunity costs of participating in the meetings.

Interpreting the figures on the involvement of the households in meetings concerning the agreement, one has to consider that different 'models of participation' that were implemented in the different villages. In Village A, the meetings concerning the agreement were linked to the general development activities of the Rural Development NGO, which targeted the poorer section of households. The participants in these activities were more involved in the meetings concerning the agreement, even though, in principle, the agreement concerned all villagers. In Village B, the model of participation was such that the village leaders selected the persons who should participate in the meetings concerning the agreement, even though all villagers were allowed to participate. It appears that, mostly, persons who have functions in the village were among those selected to participate, which explains the comparatively low percentage of participants among the sample households (which were sampled only among households without functions in the village). Asked why they did not participate, most of the interviewed non-participants in Village B indicated that they were not invited or that they would not feel entitled to participate and even speak in such meetings, if they were not explicitly invited (see Table 13.8). The village leaders in Village B also explained that they had to speed up the process of negotiating the agreement, because they wanted to have it signed before the end of 2000. In the beginning of 2001, a far-reaching new legislation concerning regional autonomy entered into force, and the village leaders were not sure whether it would still be possible to make the agreement as planned under this new legislation. According to the village leaders, this time constraint limited the possibilities to communicate the village agreement among the population. Nevertheless, 36 meetings were held in connection with the agreement, which is the highest number in the three sample villages.

After signing the agreement, the village leaders in Village B placed a high emphasis on making the agreement known to the villagers. They relied heavily on the assistance of the religious leaders and other multiplicators in the village, such as the midwives. As Table 13.9 shows, the church and the mosque were the most important sources of knowledge among the sample households in Village B. The process of making the agreement known to the villagers can be considered as very successful, since 92 per cent of the sample households were aware of the existence of the agreement (see Table 13.4).

Table 13.8 *Reasons for non-participation (number of respondents)*

	Village A	Village B	Village C
Not in the village, when agreement was made	3	1	3
Never received an invitation/no knowledge about meetings	6	15	3
Thought that meetings were only for those who participate in the other activities of the NGO	3	—	—
Did not feel entitled to participate in such meetings	—	2	—
Not enough time/money to participate in the NGO's activities	2	1	—
Very new in the village	2		—
Other reasons (age, family reasons, lack of interest, etc.)	3	2	—
Total	19	21	6

Source: Authors' household survey (2001).

Table 13.9 *Source of knowledge about the agreement (number of respondents)*

	Village A	Village B	Village C
Participation in agreement meetings	5	4	12
Heard from neighbours/friends/relatives	13	4	6
Heard from announcement in church/mosque	—	12	1
From neighbours and announcement	—	4	—
Total	18	24	19

Source: Authors' household survey (2001).

In Village C, the goal of the village leaders was to reach a high participation of all groups of villagers. This is reflected in the comparatively high proportion of sample households who participated in at least one meeting (see Table 13.6). The differences in the participation models between Village B and Village C occurred in spite of the fact that the agreements were promoted by the same NGO. This indicates the strong influence of the village leadership on the structure of the process of establishing the agreement.

When assessing the participation of the villagers in meetings related to the agreement, one also has to keep in mind the problem of opportunity costs. Table 13.8 does not indicate that this was a major constraint to the participation of villagers in the meetings. However, 23 per cent of the respondents who participated in at least one meeting mentioned that they stopped going there, because they needed to spend this time working. An indication that opportunity costs are an obstacle to participation can also be seen in the fact that even in Village B, where the number of meetings attended was the highest (see Table 13.6), this number was still considerably lower than the total number of meetings held in this village (less than 6 of 36 meetings).

Knowledge on sanctions and violations of the agreement

As outlined above, monitoring is an important aspect of assessing a community agreement on conservation. In Villages B and C, the agreement stipulates that the traditional village council, the Lembaga Adat, will be in charge of deciding upon the sanctions to be imposed, if villagers or outsiders are found to have violated the regulations of the agreement. This function is in line with the traditional role of the Lembaga Adat as a village court. Usually, the Lembaga Adat imposes traditional fines, such as sacrificing an animal, the value of which depends on the severity of the violation. The strongest sanction is to evict a person from the village. For instance, in Village B, it was reported that up to colonial times, villagers who were not able to pay the sanctions imposed by the Lembaga Adat became slaves of those community members who paid the fine for them. To assist the Lembaga Adat in enforcing the agreement, two committees, each consisting of six persons, were appointed as guards. In Village C, no violation of the agreement had occurred since the community agreement was established. In this village, no special persons were appointed for controlling the agreement. Rather, every villager was expected to report violations of the agreement to the village authorities.

In Village B, three violations of the agreement, all concerning illegal logging, were reported – so far. In all three cases, the Lembaga Adat imposed traditional fines that were paid by the culprits. Ninety per cent of the respondents were aware of at least one of these violations and the imposed sanction. On average, the respondents were aware of 1.8 violations of the agreement. Violations of the agreement concerning rattan collection, encroachment or poaching were not reported. The interviews in Village B, however, left the impression that the prohibition of rattan collection under the agreement was a problem for poor households, especially for those with limited access to land, who had depended on this activity as an important income source before the agreement was made. In Village C, the collection of rattan appeared to have been less important due to limited possibilities for marketing rattan. No violation of the agreement was reported – so far.

In Village A, the interviewed stakeholders mentioned only one sanction, which had been suggested by the village headman in relation to the agreement. This sanction was that rattan collected inside the National Park was to be confiscated by the village headman and sold for the benefit of the village. However, this sanction was never implemented as it contradicts the regulation of the National Park, according to which the Park Guard has to cut the rattan into pieces, if he finds someone collecting rattan inside the park. The interviewed stakeholders in Village A reported that after the agreement, a group of villagers was assigned the task of watching whether the agreement was violated. However, this control group stopped its activities after some months. One of the reasons reported for this was the unclear situation of what should happen in case of detecting rattan collection. Moreover, the problem of rattan collection inside the Park appears to be less important than in Village B due to the fact that the

Table 13.10 *Knowledge on sanctions (percentage of respondents)*

	Village A	Village B	Village C
Only national regulations known	76	20	50
Specific knowledge on sanctions of agreement	0	24	25
General knowledge on sanctions of agreement	0	44	20
No knowledge on sanctions	4	4	5
No answer	20	8	0

Source: Authors' household survey (2001).

villagers in Village A also have access to forest resources outside the National Park where rattan can be collected.

Table 13.10 displays the knowledge of the respondents concerning sanctions for illegal activities inside the National Park. In Village A, the majority of the respondents were only aware of the sanctions applied by the Park Guard according to the national regulations, that is confiscation of the rattan in case of illegal rattan collection. In the case where a person is found collecting rattan again after having been warned, he will be handed over to the police. Fifty per cent of the respondents remembered at least one case in which the national regulations were applied. On average, the number of cases remembered by the respondents was 1.6. Only 10 per cent of the respondents had some general knowledge that the community agreement was also associated with sanctions, and 5 per cent said that they had no knowledge about sanctions. In Village B, more than half of the respondents had a general knowledge on the sanctions associated with the agreement, and a quarter were able to mention details. In Village C, a higher percentage of the respondents were only aware of the national sanctions, probably due to the fact that no case of violation of the community agreement had yet occurred. Table 13.10 also indicates the percentage of respondents who did not answer the question concerning the sanctions, indicating that they felt uncomfortable with this topic or were afraid. This points to one constraint of the interview method with regard to such sensitive topics as sanctions. Interestingly, in Village C this problem did not occur.

Villagers' views on advantages and problems concerning the National Park

The household survey also included questions on the perceptions of the villagers concerning advantages and problems related to the National Park. Only 10 per cent of the respondents did not mention any positive aspects that the protection of the forest through the National Park may have for their community. As Table 13.11 shows, more than two-thirds of the respondents mentioned the prevention of erosion and ensuring the water supply as advantages of the protection of the forest. Other advantages mentioned by the

Table 13.11 *Advantages of forest protection mentioned by respondents (per cent)*

Advantage	Per cent of respondents
Erosion prevention	69
Water supply	67
Prevention of floods	61
Prevention of landslides	46
Protection of animals	31
Timber for future generations	24
Better air quality	16
Medicinal plants	7

Source: Authors' household survey (2001).

participants included the prevention of floods and landslides, the protection of animals, the availability of timber for future generations, better air quality and the protection of medicinal plants. Asked about the source of their knowledge concerning these advantages, the respondents mentioned mostly officials such as Park Guards, representatives of the Forestry Department and the village headman, as well as the radio. The number of respondents who indicated that this was their traditional knowledge or had been passed on by traditional village leaders was higher in the indigenous Villages B and C than in Village A, where the percentage of immigrants was high.

Even though some of the respondents may have given the answers they felt expected to give, one can certainly consider it as an advantage with respect to the enforcement of the agreement that more than two-thirds of respondents were able to link forest protection with advantages for their community.

During the interviews, 80 per cent of the respondents mentioned at least one problem, which the National Park caused for them or their community. This does not mean that the other respondents do not feel that the park leads to problems, they may also have felt unsure of whether or not they could talk freely about such problems. About half of the respondents mentioned that they were afraid that, due to the National Park, there will not be enough land available for their children. Even in Village C, where land scarcity is not yet a problem, 55 per cent of the respondents expressed this concern. Table 13.12 distinguishes between participants and non-participants and lists the problems mentioned by the respondents. The second most important problem identified was that lands on which they held traditional property rights were located inside the park. While the agreement allowed them to collect certain non timber forest products inside the National Park, it did not allow them to use their traditional land for agricultural purposes. The loss of the income provided by rattan collection was mentioned as the third most important problem. Some respondents in Village B mentioned that the villagers depending on this income had no other possibility than going to other villages to collect rattan after the implementation of the agreement. The village leaders in this village are well aware of

Table 13.12 *Problems with National Park mentioned by respondents (percentage)*

Type of problem[a]	Participants	Non-participants
Land scarcity for children may occur	67	45
Traditional land use rights inside the park	67	30
Rattan collection needed for income	38	24
Lacking possibility to catch birds	10	9
Timber would be needed (in general)	19	19
Timber needed for house construction	10	9
Timber needed for village development	14	7
Lack of fire wood	10	7

Note: [a] Open question, multiple answer possible, table lists percentage of respondents who mentioned the respective problem.

Source: Authors' household survey (2001).

this problem. There are plans to distribute land of a former concession area to villagers who have only little or no land. The leaders have also discussed the possibilities of sustainable rattan harvesting techniques, such as rotational harvesting. Other problems indicated by the respondents refer to restrictions on timber and fuelwood collection and on the hunting of birds. As Table 13.12 shows, the villagers participating in the meetings felt more affected by the problems with the park. This may indicate a motivation for their participation; it may, however, also indicate that the participation led to a higher sensibility concerning these issues.

Assessment of the conservation agreements

Are the agreements a 'Coase solution' to an externality problem?

From the perspective of environmental economics, the agreements on conservation can be considered as the 'Coase solution' to an externality problem. This solution assumes a strategic negotiation between the actors causing the externality and the actors affected by it. According to Coase, the interpretation of who causes the externality depends on the question of how the property rights are initially assigned. If property rights are held by the state, the local farmers converting forest or extracting forest resources would have to be considered as the party causing the externality. The state, as representative of the society, would then be considered as the party affected by the external effect. If the local farmers hold the property rights in land and forest resources, the state is to be considered as the party causing the externality, when restricting these property rights by declaring a protected area. As outlined above, this leads to the question of whether or not the state acknowledges customary property rights that already existed before the area was declared a National Park. Empirically, this question was very relevant: as shown in Table 13.12, two-thirds of the participants in the meetings and one third of the non-participants considered it as a major problem that, in their village, customary property rights were located inside the National Park.

As the empirical evidence shows, the state had not acknowledged the customary property rights located inside the National Park at the beginning of the negotiation process in any of the cases under consideration. In the agreements promoted by the Advocacy NGO, the recognition of customary rights to control the use of resources inside the Park was a subject, not an initial condition, of the negotiation. The 'deal' between the state agency and the local community can be interpreted as follows: the traditional village council receives a formal recognition of their traditional rights to regulate the management and use of the natural resources located inside the park. In exchange, the village council commits itself to making sure that the resources are used in a sustainable way. Although the formal recognition of customary rights by the Park Management was a considerable advantage for the community, a more far-reaching legal backing of this acknowledgement would have been desirable as a guarantee in the long term. The approaches promoted by the Rural Development NGO and the Conservation NGO envisaged compensation in the form of development services of the income forgone by the villagers due to the restrictions posed by the National Park and the commitment to obey them in the agreement. Even though this can be interpreted as an acknowledgement of the fact that state protection causes costs to the farmers – in the sense of causing an external effect according to the Coase Theorem, a formal recognition of the farmers' customary property rights is not foreseen in the agreements promoted by these NGOs.

The empirical investigation also shows that not all community agreements can be considered as a strategic negotiation between two parties, one representing the party causing the externality and the other representing the party affected by it. In the case of the agreements promoted by the Rural Development NGO (see the household survey in Village A), a negotiation with state agencies did not take place at all. It was rather a negotiation between the villagers and the NGO. In the other cases, an interaction with the BTNLL, the state agency in charge of the National Park, did take place. However, in the case of Village C, this interaction was limited to consultation and an ex-post approval of the agreement by the state agency.

As outlined earlier in the chapter, the Coase Theorem also assumes that bargaining is based on a consideration of marginal costs and benefits, which determine the willingness to pay and to accept. The costs of conservation mainly consist of opportunity costs due to income losses from restrictions on resource use. Based on data of a household survey conducted by a research group under the STORMA (Stability of Rainforest Margins) research group (Schwarze et al, 2002), the gross margins for major crops grown on upland fields (the land type most strongly competing with protection), such as coffee, cocoa and maize, were in the range from Rs.690,000 to Rs.7,700,000 (US$73–810) per ha per year. As family labour and fixed costs are not considered in the gross margin calculation, these figures indicate an upper limit of the order of magnitude of the opportunity costs of protection per hectare of land. The gross margin, and therewith the opportunity costs, depend essentially on the output prices, which fluctuate considerably between seasons as well as between years. The calculation of the benefits of conservation in monetary terms would require methods such as contingent valuation, which have not yet been applied in the area of the Lore Lindu National Park. During the research, no evidence could be found that the stakeholders involved tried to value the costs and benefits of nature conservation in the Lore Lindu area in monetary terms in order to use the figures in the negotiation process. Next to valuation problems, it is doubtful to what extent the stakeholders would share the view that all the costs and benefits of nature conservation could be evaluated in monetary terms. However, even though monetary figures on cost and benefits were not used in the negotiation, one can assume that the bargaining partners followed their perception, or their implicit subjective valuation, of the costs and benefits involved. The benefits may also include intangible 'political' benefits such as increased authority for the community. These considerations show that more empirical research on the valuation of costs and benefits and more long-term observation would be necessary to judge the third question raised at the outset, whether the bargaining led, in an economic sense, to mutually advantageous outcomes.

The empirical investigation also shed light on the third question raised in the theoretical framework, which concerns the role of transaction costs in the process of establishing and negotiating co-management agreements. Even though a monetary calculation of all transaction costs involved in the agreements was beyond the scope of this research, one can derive some preliminary conclusions from the figures available. As mentioned above, the Advocacy NGO spent, apart from the salary of local staff, around Rs.15,000,000 (US$1600) for the village with the most intensive negotiation process they facilitated so far. One possibility for assessing the magnitude of such a figure is to compare it with other important costs that are incurred for nature conservation. The highest costs usually arise in the form of the opportunity costs of land that is set aside for conservation. A common method of estimating these opportunity costs is to calculate the income forgone from agricultural production (Hampicke, 1991). Making a conservative assumption on the basis of the above figures that the opportunity costs of land are in the range of Rs.600,000 (US$63), the transaction costs of Rs.15,000,000 (US$1580) quoted above correspond to the opportunity costs arising for the protection of 25ha of land. One has to take into account that the opportunity costs of land arise every year, whereas the establishment of the agreement is an investment that can be depreciated over a longer period. This hypothetical calculation should help to relate the transaction costs arising for NGOs promoting an agreement to other costs arising for nature conservation. A transaction cost calculation also has to take into account the opportunity costs of the farmers for attending the meetings. Even though these costs can be an obstacle to the participation for farmers with a high time depreciation, they would also lose their relative importance, if the series of meetings needed to establish an agreement is considered as an investment for a longer period of time. Even though further research into this issue is necessary, it appears reasonable to conclude that – as compared to the opportunity costs of protection in the form of income forgone from agricultural production – the transaction costs of negotiation are not a major factor affecting the efficiency of nature conservation. Nevertheless, considering the other aspects discussed above, one can conclude that the Coase Theorem, with its focus on the strategic bargaining of two parties over an externality, is not sufficient to capture all relevant aspects of the community agreements on conservation observed in this case study.

Are the agreements a case of 'Empowered Deliberative Democracy'?

The empirical results indicate that one can distinguish stakeholders at two levels: NGOs, development projects and state agencies at the regional level, and groups of households, which differ in socio-economic status and in their dependence on natural resources at the village level. At the regional level, the NGOs pursued their interests in promoting different kinds of agreements with comparatively little coordination and cooperation among each other. The limited coordination can, at least partly, be attributed to the different value orientations of the NGOs concerned. These differences seem to have led to communication problems and strategic barriers to interaction. The case study also indicated that there were different interest groups within the villages. The households with little access to land are more seriously affected by restrictions on rattan collection than better-off villagers, who do not depend on this income source. However, the households were not organized along these lines. According to the field observations, none of the NGOs promoting the agreements took these differences in interests explicitly into account in the organization of the negotiation process. However, the negotiation meetings provided a forum for the discussion of different interests. Therefore the essential question is who participated in this forum and how the decision making there took place.

Applying the model of Empowered Deliberative Democracy (EDD) outlined in Box 13.1, the analysis shows that the negotiated agreements fulfil important aspects of the design principles of the model. They focus on a concrete concern, in this case the improvement of nature conservation in the area of the Lore Lindu National Park. Depending on the NGO promoting the agreement, they also focus on rural development as another concrete concern (see Table 13.1). The series of meetings held in connection with the agreements indicate that bottom-up participation and a process of deliberation were clearly envisaged by the organizations promoting the agreements. The interviews with the participants indicated that the process had deliberative qualities as described above: after intensive discussion of different viewpoints, the aim was to reach a consensus that was acceptable to all participants. The research method of participant observation, however, would have been necessary to reach a final assessment on this point. Using the number of meetings held as an indicator, the deliberation process was most intense in Village B and least intense in Village A.

The research also showed that the models of participation differed between villages. In Villages A and C, the direct participation of, as far as possible, all villagers was envisaged. While this goal was achieved to a considerable degree in Village C, in Village A, the participation was mostly limited to official village leaders and some of the beneficiaries of the Development NGO promoting the agreement.

In Village B, participation was limited to the customary and formal village leaders and the persons appointed by them to join the meetings. With regard to the considerations outlined above, this model can be considered as deliberative democracy involving intermediaries. While formal village leaders are intermediaries who are elected through the usual mechanism of representative democracy, the traditional village leaders involved in the deliberation process derive their legitimacy from customs and tradition. The question in these cases is the extent to which the intermediaries represent and accommodate the interests of all groups in the village, especially of those who are likely to be disadvantaged by the regulations of the agreement. During the household survey, direct criticism concerning the terms of the agreement was limited. This may, however, be attributed to the interview situation. Nevertheless, as Table 13.12 indicates, a considerable proportion expressed their concerns with regard to the loss of income from rattan. Some villagers directly mentioned that they see no other possibility than going to other villages for rattan collection. This can be seen as an indication that the interests of the villagers depending on rattan as an income source were not fully taken into account by their intermediaries. Phrased differently, the possibility that more powerful actors impose their version of the agreement on less powerful groups did exist. The village leaders did, however, search for potential solutions to compensate for income losses from rattan collection, such as providing increased access to land. This potential solution was outside the scope of the agreement. Agreements that directly link conservation goals with development services, such as those promoted by the Development NGO and the Conservation NGO, also provide the possibility of overcoming such conflicts of interest.

The research showed that the agreements also fulfil some of the design properties of the EDD model (see Box 13.1). The approval of the conservation agreements by the Administration of the Lore Lindu National Park can be considered as an act of devolution because it indeed shifted management authority to governance bodies at the community level that are not merely advisory. As the case of Village B shows, the local bodies in charge of exercising authority over natural resource management (Lembaga Adat, village headman, guard groups), can be very effective in implementing and monitoring the agreement, and in applying sanctions in case the rules are violated. Nevertheless, the devolution criterion of the EDD model (see Box 13.1) was not fully met, because this act of devolution was a voluntary decision in the discretion of the Park administration. Therefore, the local units that were in charge of resource management according to the agreement could hardly be considered as 'creatures of a transformed state endowed with substantial public authority', as the EDD model demands.

In principle, the park administration can also play the role of a central authority to supervise and coordinate the agreement processes around the park, a function that is another design property of the EDD model. As the case study showed, the involvement of the park administration in the negotiation process differed considerably between the villages, depending on the strategy of the NGOs promoting the agreements. In general, the National Park administration strongly supported the agreement approach, especially in its eco-populist version. In the absence of specific legislation on such agreements, the willingness of the Park Manager to acknowledge indigenous resource rights and to trust in the capacity of indigenous communities was certainly an essential in promoting the agreements. This earned the Park Manager the appreciation of advocacy-oriented groups at national and even international level, while conservationist groups remained sceptical of this approach.

Box 13.1 also lists some potential problems of the EDD approach. As indicated above, the research was conducted at a stage when it was too early to assess the agreements on the basis of their outcome in terms of ecological and socio-economic indicators. One problem, however, could already be seen in the fact that the contents of the agreements were not very specific. In the cases under consideration, the agreements were not accompanied by a management plan that specified, for example, the quantities of the resources that can be extracted for home consumption. Likewise, the draft of an agreement by the Conservation NGO that intended to offer development services in exchange for a conservation commitment, did not specify these services in terms of time frame and responsibility. This lack of specification can be considered as a hindrance to effective implementation and monitoring. One possible way to overcome such problems is to create a mechanism that allows the parties concerned to adapt and to renegotiate the agreements in the course of time. Other potential problems listed in Box 13.1, such as an unequal power structure among the participants, also existed, as has been discussed above.

Conclusions

Even though a final assessment of the effectiveness of community agreements on conservation in the Lore Lindu area was not possible in the time frame of this research, the case study shows that such agreements have a considerable potential for improving nature conservation and rural development in the region. The agreements constitute an interesting and instructive example of the devolution of authority in natural resource management, which can serve as a model for other regions of Indonesia. As the agreements are negotiated at the local level, they can take the specific ecological, socio-economic and cultural conditions at the local level into account. Due to their voluntary character, they can reduce conflicts and the problems of state regulations, which represent the 'command-and-control approach' to protected area management. The case study showed that the effort to establish such agreements can lead to intensive processes of deliberation on self-governance at the village level, which can be considered as 'schools of democracy' that are important for the process of democratization Indonesia is undergoing. As the differences between the three study villages showed, the achievement of this goal depends on the implementation of the agreement approach, which is influenced by the visions and value orientations both of the organizations facilitating the agreements and of the village leaders responsible for the implementation at the local level.

The case study also revealed some areas that deserve further consideration by the organizations, agencies and policy makers promoting such negotiated agreements. The problem of unequal power relations and conflicts of interest within the villages may well jeopardize the deliberation process. The role of intermediaries, or representatives, should, therefore, be considered carefully. Acting as representatives of the villagers in the negotiation process, both formal and customary village leaders may well take the interests of all villagers into account. However, this should not be taken for granted, as the question of rattan harvesting in the case study indicates. One could also consider the option of letting the villagers vote on the outcome of the deliberation process. This combination of the deliberative with the direct democracy model could be an instrument to increase the legitimacy of the agreement, especially in cases where the broad participation of the villagers in the deliberation process is difficult to achieve. This shows that it would be useful for the actors promoting community agreements to discuss the question of participation and legitimacy more explicitly and consider the advantages and disadvantages of different models.

The results of this case study also have implications for other countries. As indicated in the introduction, co-management of protected areas is widely considered to be a promising approach to overcoming conflicts between nature conservation and economic development. In particular, negotiated agreements between communities and the management of protected areas, often facilitated by NGOs, are a major approach to co-management (Borrini-Feyerabend et al, 2000). The case study indicates that a variety of approaches to establishing such agreements are possible, and that the type of approach used is likely to depend on the value orientation of the NGO facilitating the agreement. One can derive from this case study that environmental NGOs that do not have major expertise in rural development may face difficulties in offering attractive development options in return for a self-commitment of local communities to restrict the use of natural resources. They may, however, play the role of a 'broker', but a careful assessment is needed to find out whether they actually have enough leverage over other organizations that have the resources to promote development. In contrast, NGOs that focus on rural development may lack the specific knowledge in conservation biology that would be useful to draft conservation agreements.

The case study also points to coordination challenges between NGOs, a challenge that may also be relevant in other countries. In the areas surrounding protected areas, the density of NGO activity is particularly high. Different value orientations may prevent NGOs from working together. As the experience of other countries shows, the value orientation described here as 'eco-populism' often clashes with the value orientations characterized as 'conservationism' and 'developmentalism', which can pose problems for coordination (Wittmer and Birner, 2005). Still, the case study shows that by coordinating their activities, NGOs could combine their strengths in the different fields that are important for co-management, including nature conservation, advocacy for indigenous rights and rural development.

The case study indicates that a lack of coordination may not only be a problem between different NGOs, but also between NGOs and park management. In some types of conservation agreements, the involvement of the park management was rather marginal, which may jeopardize the long-term viability of the agreements. Another lesson to be derived from the case study is the need for a legal framework, which provides a basis for co-management agreements. In the case under consideration, the absence of a clear legal framework can be considered as a potential problem for the long-term viability of the agreements as well, since they largely depended on the discretion of the Park Manager.

Finally, the case study shows that both the Coase model of bargaining over externalities and the model of Empowered Deliberative Democracy are useful for analysing different aspects of negotiated agreements. A further development of the theory, which combines aspects of environmental economics with the analysis of policy processes, is promising for better understanding and implementation of the agreement approach. The Coase model draws attention to the need to clarify the allocation of property rights, and to take the benefits and the costs, including the transaction costs, into account in order to reach efficient solutions. However, depending on the value orientation and objectives of the organization involved, the agreements do not necessarily correspond to the model of self-interested strategic bargaining underlying the Coase Theorem. The case study showed that valuable insights can be gained by studying the agreements as a potential instance of EDD, which considers citizen deliberation, rather than strategic bargaining or command and control by experts, as the preferred mode of social choice.

Acknowledgements

The authors would like to thank all stakeholder representatives and all villagers that were interviewed in the course of this research. Special thanks are due to

Heidi Wittmer for valuable comments. The grants from TOEB-GTZ (Tropical Ecology Support Program of the German Agency for Technical Co-operation) and from DFG (German Research Council) for the project SFB 522 STORMA (Stability of Rainforest Margins) are gratefully acknowledged.

References

Agrawal, B. (2001) 'Participatory exclusions, community forestry, and gender: An analysis for South Asia and a conceptual framework', *World Development*, vol 29, no 10, pp1623–1648

ANZDEC (1997) *Central Sulawesi Integrated Area Development and Conservation Project*, TA NO 2518 – INO, Indonesia

Arrow, K. J. (1950) 'A difficulty in the concept of social welfare', *Journal of Political Economy*, vol 58, pp328–346, reprinted in Kenneth J. Arrow (1984) *Social Choice and Justice*, Basil Backwell, Oxford, pp1–29

Borrini-Feyerabend, G., Taghi Farvar, M., Nguinguiri, J. C., Ndangang, V. (2000) *Environmental Management, Co-management of Natural Resources, Organising, Negotiating and Learning-by-doing*, Eschborn, IUCN, GTZ

Bruns, R. B. and Meinzen-Dick, R. (eds) (2000) *Negotiating Water Rights*, IFPRI, ITDG Publishing, London

Carlsson, L. and Berkes, F. (2005) 'Co-management: Concepts and methodological implications', *Journal of Environmental Management*, vol 75, pp65–76

Coase, R. H. (1960) 'The problem of social cost', *Journal of Law and Economics*, vol 3, pp144

Cook, B. and Kothari, U. (eds) (2001) *Participation – The New Tyranny?* Zed Books, London, New York

Dauvergne, P. (1994) 'The politics of deforestation in Indonesia', *Pacific Affairs*, vol 66, no 4, pp497–518

Forero Pineda, C. (2001) 'Participatory democracy in Latin America – A comparative analysis', paper presented at the Annual Conference of the International Society for New Institutional Economics

Fung, A. and Wright, E. O. (2001) 'Deepening democracy: Innovations in empowered participatory governance', *Politics and Society*, vol 29, no 1, pp5–41

Hampicke, U. (1991) *Naturschutz-Ökonomie* (Natural Economics), Verlag Eugen Ulmer, Stuttgart

Hildyard, N. and Pandurang, H. (2001) 'Pluralism, participation and power: Joint forest management in India', in B. Cook and U. Kothari (eds), *Participation – The New Tyranny?* Zed Books, London, New York, pp56–71

Hoffman, E. and Spitzer, M. L. (1982) 'The Coase Theorem: Some experimental tests', *Journal of Law and Economics*, vol 25, pp73–98

Horbach, J. (1992) *Neue politische Ökonomie und Umweltpolitik*, Campus Verlag, Frankfurt (Main)

Keough, H. L. and Blahna, D. J. (2006) 'Achieving integrative, collaborative ecosystem management', *Conservation Biology*, vol 20, no 5, pp1373–1382

Leeuwis, C. (2000) 'Reconceptualizing participation for sustainable rural development: Towards a negotiation approach', *Development and Change*, vol 31, pp931–959

Locke, H. and Dearden, P. (2005) 'Rethinking protected area categories and the new paradigm', *Environmental Conservation*, vol 32, no 1, pp1–10

Mburu, J. and Birner, R. (2002) 'Analyzing the efficiency of collaborative wildlife management: The case of two community wildlife sanctuaries in Kenya', *Journal of Organizational Theory and Behaviour*, vols 3&4, pp359–397

Meinzen-Dick, R., Knox, A., Di Gregorio, M. (2001) *Collective Action, Property Rights and Devolution of Natural Resource Management – Exchange of Knowledge and Implications for Policy*, CAPRi, ICLARM, ZEL/DSE, Eurasburg.

Schwarze, S., Nuryartono, N., van Rheenen, T., Ebel, C. (2002) 'Gross margin calculations of major crops grown in the area of the Lore Lindu National Park, Results from a Household Survey', STORMA A4 research group, unpublished figures

Thomas, C. W. (2001) 'Habitat conservation planning: Certainly empowered, somewhat deliberative, questionably democratic', *Politics and Society*, vol 29, no 1, pp105–130

Van Dijk, T. (1998) *Ideology. A Multidisciplinary Approach*, Sage Publications, London

Venema, B. and v. d. Breemer, H. (eds) (1999) *Towards Negotiated Co-management of Natural Resources in Africa*, Lit Verlag, Münster

Weber, M. [1922] (1990) *Wirtschaft und Gesellschaft – Grundriss der verstehenden Soziologie* [*Economy and Society – Foundations of Sociology*] 5th rev edn, J.C.B. Mohr (Paul Siebeck), Tübingen

Wilshusen, P. R., Brechin, S. R., Fortwangler, C. L., West, P. C. (2002) 'Reinventing a square wheel: Critique of a resurgent "protection paradigm"', *International Biodiversity Conservation. Society and Natural Resources*, vol 15, pp17–40

Wittmer, H. and Birner, R. (2005) 'Between conservationism, eco-populism and developmentalism – discourses in biodiversity policy in Thailand and Indonesia', CAPRi Working Paper, IFPRI, Washington, DC

4

IPRs AND PROTECTION OF INDIGENOUS KNOWLEDGE

14

Intellectual Property Rights and Problems in the Protection of Indigenous Knowledge: A Case Study of the Philippines Legal Reforms

Timothy Swanson, Ray Purdy and Ana Lea Uy

Introduction

This chapter sets out some recent attempts by the government of the Philippines to reform and revise its intellectual property rights (IPR) laws, in order to take into account all of the various forms of knowledge that contribute to the conduct of research and development (R&D) in the biological sector. There are certain industries (the life sciences) in which R&D may be a more complex sector than usual, involving contributions from natural capital and traditional capital as well as more modern forms of capital. For this reason there has been significant pressure for the development of IPR systems that recognize these forms of contributions, and which allocate the rents from innovation accordingly.

It is extremely complicated to generate these reforms, both for reasons of pre-existing IPRs and on account of the complexity of the problem in isolation. Pre-existing IPR laws have emphasized one particular path to the generation of R&D and one particular point for IPR implementation. That model has assumed that useful innovations have flowed exclusively from investments of modern forms of capital (formal education, investments in technology) and that property rights should be made to inhere at the level where the final product is marketed. It is difficult to see how new forms of IPRs, based on very different assumptions, might be made compatible with this pre-existing model.

In any event, the idea of implementing property rights at earlier stages of the R&D industry is complex, as the nature of the information is relatively intangible and non-segregable at this juncture. It is far more difficult to claim property rights in information before it is embodied within a specific good (intermediate or final). It is also far more difficult to segregate between different pieces of information, and hence to separate between contributions, before that information is embodied. These problems must be dealt with successfully under any set of reforms to address this problem.

To illustrate these difficulties, we wish to use a case study of the recent attempts at intellectual property right reform in the Philippines. One important reason for choosing the Philippines as a case study is that it has been a leader in the development and implementation of legislation concerning the protection of biological resources. Much of this legislation was occasioned by the state's international obligations as a signatory to the Convention on Biological Diversity (CBD). The Philippines was one of the first developing countries to pass national legislation regulating access to genetic and biological resources in accordance with the CBD, and this legislation is now being used as a model throughout much of Asia (see below).

The CBD established for the first time under international law the doctrine of national sovereignty over the natural resource of genetic resource (or biological) diversity, and refuted the previously existing doctrine of common heritage (see Swanson, 2002). In the Philippines this created a national interest in the protection and management of genetic resource diversity. This then resulted in Executive Order 247 (EO247) in 1995 in the Philippines, establishing a system for managing the use of national biological and genetic resources. EO247 and its implementing regulations represented the first attempt by the Philippines to create a comprehensive system for a new right within this system.

The second movement for IPR reform in the Philippines derives from the country's obligations as a signatory to the World Trade Organization's Agreement on Trade Related Aspects of Intellectual Property Rights (TRIPs). Under TRIPs the Philippines must adopt a system for the protection of innovations in plant genetic resources, either the already existing plant breeders' rights (PBR) or some other equivalent (or 'sui generis') system. The recently adopted Plant Variety Protection Act of 2000 (PVPA) establishes a system of PBR in the Philippines but exempts pre-existing varieties and provides for a farmers' 'own use' exemption. The adoption of a PBR system demonstrates that the Philippines continues to standardize its existing IPR system, while simultaneously developing a significant alternative. The tensions and conflicts between the two systems are apparent in the very different forms of legislation being adopted in this one country (see below).

The main reason for selecting the Philippines as a case study is on account of its large indigenous population, and recent movements to protect indigenous peoples' rights. It is estimated that the Philippines has a population of 12 million indigenous peoples, which amounts to about 20 per cent of the total population. There are also approximately 110 indigenous groups, made up of tribes such as the Kaigorotan, Lumad, Aeta, Tagbanuas, Mangyans and Badjos. These indigenous groups have collected a large amount of varied traditional knowledge that still influences their lives today. Filipino traditional knowledge includes health care, agriculture, forestry systems, mining, arts and crafts, music, dancing and literature. The Philippines Constitution of 1987 has recognized the value of these communities; section 17 of Article XIV provides that 'the State shall recognize, respect and protect the rights of indigenous cultural communities to preserve and develop their cultures, traditions and institutions. It shall consider these rights in the formulation of national plans and policies.'

We will consider in particular detail the legislation that has been implemented and/or proposed for the protection of the rights of indigenous communities in relation to their traditional knowledge and resources. The primary piece of legislation concerned is the Indigenous Peoples Rights Act of 1997 (IPRA), which contains the explicit recognition of indigenous peoples' rights to utilize and to develop the natural resources on their ancestral lands, as well as the state's recognition of their right to ownership and control over their indigenous knowledge and systems. IPRA is in the very early days of its formulation and definition, but it represents an important basis for believing that the IPR regime within the Philippines will have to develop down an alternative route. IPRA represents a commitment to ensure that the IPR regime in the Philippines recognizes alternative as well as more standardized forms of R&D processes. This commitment is also present in a newly adopted system of laws developed to protect and to promote the use of traditional health practices, the Traditional and Alternative Medicine Act of 1997 (TAMA), discussed below.

Although the substance of the rights established under IPRA is relatively undefined, there has long been a bill before the Philippines' legislature (SB101) to provide for the creation of a formal system of 'Community Intellectual Rights Protection'. This proposed system of protection for indigenous peoples' 'community knowledge' is discussed in detail below. This discussion raises the many problems and complexities involved in developing an alternative model for IPR protection. The movement in the Philippines demonstrates how complicated the task must be.

In short, the Philippines sits at a crossroads (along with the rest of the world) where the pre-existing system of IPRs is being globalized under TRIPs at the same time that a newly developing system of IPRs is being initiated. There are clear conflicts between the systems, and yet to be solved complications in instituting the latter. In this chapter, which is part of a larger study on 'Traditional Knowledge and its Management', we attempt to illustrate both phenomena by reference to the current state of the Philippines' debate on the subject.

The implementation of the CBD and EO247

The Convention on Biological Diversity (CBD) laid down the basic principles for the use of biological and genetic resources. It established the doctrine of national sovereignty toward any given country's biological and genetic resources.[1] Although the Convention laid down this principle, it was up to contracting parties to put into place a national legal structure implementing its provisions. As a signatory to this Convention, the Philippines has now introduced legislation to comply with the CBD, which attempted to regulate access to genetic resources for the equitable sharing of benefits arising from their sustainable utilization.

Executive Order 247

The Philippines Executive Order No. 247 ('Prescribing Guidelines and Establishing a Regulatory Framework for the Prospecting of Biological and Genetic Resources, their By-Products and Derivatives, for Scientific and Commercial Purposes, and for Other Purposes') (EO247) represents the Philippines' attempt to implement Article 15 of the CBD. EO247 was signed into law by President Ramos in May 1995 and became effective in June 1996.[2] Under the constitution of the Philippines, an Executive Order is only legally binding during the term of the President that signs it and is only normally chosen as a means to set up legal rules quickly in cases of emergencies. In principle, it continues to be legally binding during the next Presidential term, unless repealed, amended or revoked by the President's successor.[3]

Executive Order 247 covers the prospecting of all biological resources in the public and private domains.[4] The Executive Order also extends to cover the by-products and derivatives of biological and genetic resources.[5] As the scope of the legislation is limited to genetic resources (i.e. physical materials), it does not extend to the associated traditional knowledge. The Philippines legal controls uses the basic mechanisms of any access system concerning biological and genetic resources, including: the prior informed consent of the state, the prior informed consent of local communities, provision for benefit sharing, an implementing agency and sanctions for non-compliance.

Executive Order 247 requires that anyone, whether a national or a foreign entity, wishing to access biological resources to enter into a formal research agreement with the government. Executive Order 247 distinguishes between two types of research agreements, depending on whether the bioprospecting is intended for academic purposes (academic research agreement (ARA)) or for commercial purposes (commercial research agreement (CRA)). The requirements of an ARA are less stringent, but both have minimum requirements and there are no exemptions for the need for some form of permit.

Any form of access to biodiversity, either through an ARA or a CRA, is strictly illegal without the prior informed consent (PIC) of the appropriate local authority: the Protected Area Management Board; the indigenous and local communities; or the private landowner.[6] The burden lies with the applicant to commence the PIC procedure and to inform the affected community of their intentions through public notice, consultation and outline of benefits. A PIC certificate will not be issued by the government without the consent of the head of an affected indigenous community, as confirmed by a signature from the relevant local authority.[7]

Although the PIC procedures brought about a great deal more involvement of indigenous people in the decision-making process in principle, the actual practice has been heavily criticized (Zamora, 1997). It is argued that the requirements are more procedural than substantive in nature, in that access requires no more than the notification of the local community and the signature of the head of an indigenous community to confirm the mere fact of notification.[8] In part this might be attributed to the absence of a procedure defining the indigenous peoples' rights regarding the refusal of access or rights to benefits, but it is more likely to be the case that the rights are readily waived or acquired.

Although EO247 is intended to implement an equitable benefit sharing system based on the CBD, it does not elaborate precisely how the indigenous peoples and local communities stand to benefit. In order to ensure that some benefit sharing results from bioprospecting, a set of minimum conditions is established in order for the government to authorize the issuance of either an ARA or a CRA. These general conditions provide for the following: duplicates of samples should be deposited with local agencies; citizens should retain right of access to the materials and any products developed from them; technology should be transferred; and nationals should participate and be trained in the prospecting process. In addition to these minimum requirements for the issuance of a research agreement, Executive Order 247 further stipulates that any prospecting activities must not directly or indirectly harm the biological diversity, ecological balance or the inhabitants of the area where the collection is undertaken. In order to assess the state of compliance with these requirements, a status report on the ecological state of the area and/or species concerned is to be undertaken by the bioprospector at regular intervals.

Finally, the conditions for the issuance of a prospecting permit provide that the rights to the underlying genetic resources cannot be transferred. That is, the ownership of the biological resources should always remain with the state, and a separate agreement should issue on the sharing of royalties. This implicitly confers some sort of 'genetic resource right' status upon the subject resources, although its universal validity and ultimate value would remain the subject of some debate.

How does EO247 generate benefits in practice? An example of the benefit sharing developed under Executive Order 247 can be seen in a CRA issued to a partnership consisting of the University of the Philippines and the University of Utah in the US. This provides for a fixed bioprospecting fee of 10,000 Philippine Pesos (US$200 at 2002 exchange rates) per year for three years paid directly to the government. Further the collector agrees to pay 5 per cent of the net revenue derived from any royalties based on the development and commercialization of any material; this payment would be made to the Department of Agriculture, the local community or private person concerned, depending on the source of the materials. Ancillary benefits from the agreement include: the establishment of an education module programme and information campaigns on resource conservation and environmental protection for communities, the training of one government representative; the establishment of scholarship programmes; a guarantee that Filipino scientists are to be involved in the research and collection process; the involvement of Philippine universities and research institutions and the transfer of equipment to them; and the agreement that the biological or genetic resources must be made available to a designated Philippine institution for commercial and local use without royalty payments to the collector (Barber and La Vina, 1998).

In sum, access legislation has generated a large set of procedural hurdles that must be satisfied prior to making legal access to biological resources, but much less in the way of substantive rights. It extends these largely procedural rights only to the biological/natural resources important to the R&D sector, but not to the human resources involved in the traditional sector.

The ASEAN Declaration on access to biological resources: Impending conflicts

The legislation that has been introduced in the Philippines has also been used as the basis for a model law on access and benefit sharing for other national systems in Asia, by the Association of South East Asian Nations (ASEAN).[9] The member states of the ASEAN group (which includes the Philippines) produced a draft framework agreement document in 2000,[10] which will eventually lead to the adoption of legislation at the regional level.[11]

This ASEAN framework agreement sets the minimum requirements for the national implementation of legislation promoting the conservation and sustainable use of biological and genetic resources. This agreement seeks to protect ASEAN biological and genetic resources by implementing the provisions contained in the CBD. It encourages states to claim sovereignty over their resources; set up a system where PIC is required from them and local indigenous peoples before access can take place; and ensure fair and equitable sharing of benefits arising from the utilization of biological and genetic resources (and lays down the minimum set of benefits that should be received).[12]

Interestingly the framework agreement also provides that ASEAN member states shall not allow the patenting of plants, animals, microorganisms or any parts thereof, or the associated traditional and indigenous knowledge.[13] This is inconsistent with these states' obligations under the WTO Agreement on TRIPS, in which these states are required to implement a patent system for microorganisms (and at least a sui generis system for plants). This is one example of the inconsistencies that are beginning to appear between the laws developing within the two sectors.[14] In general, this is representative of some of the inherent conflicts between the expanding genetic resource right system and the globalizing IPR system for biotechnology.

Conclusion: The movement for creation of rights in biological resources

The creation of the CBD and the enunciation of EO247 represent one movement that has occurred within the Philippines over the past decade. This is the movement to assert national sovereignty over the biological and genetic resources occurring within national boundaries. For many decades the legal status of these natural resources was unclear, but these movements toward asserting rights is making clear that national governments do not intend for these resources to be common property. The manner in which countries protect these rights, and appropriate benefits from them, remains unclear. The approach based on written agreements for access and benefit sharing has yet to evolve into a meaningful assertion of substantive rights. Too often this approach takes the ultimate form of a procedural checklist for access, and a general commitment to collaboration and cooperation.

Nevertheless the attempt to assert property rights in these natural resources represents a substantial departure from prior experience in the R&D sector of these industries. It remains to be seen whether these rights are incorporated in a meaningful way into the approach taken to R&D and rent distribution. But it represents a substantial movement to require that the role of natural resources in biological R&D be appreciated.

The implementation of TRIPs and the PVPA

At about the same time that the CBD was developing the framework for managing access and rights to genetic resources, the TRIPs agreement was finalizing the standards for biotechnologies and plant varieties. The potential for conflict between the two is clear, although their subject matters are very different. The CBD is advocating the assertion of rights in the underlying genetic and biological resources (the natural capital that contributes to the production of information), while the TRIPs agreement is standardizing the systems of already existing IPR (the rights in the final and intermediate goods embodying innovations). In this section, we will recount the recent developments in the Philippines in relation to its TRIPs obligations, and indicate where it might intersect with the developments in other areas.

TRIPs and PBRs

The Philippines passed the Intellectual Property Code of the Philippines into law on the 1 January 1998, as Republic Act No. 8293. This code consolidated the existing laws of the Philippines on intellectual property rights (IPRs) and supplemented these with the minimum standards required by TRIPs.[15]

Under s.27(3) of the TRIPs agreement, member states are required to provide a patent system for microorganisms as well as a system for plant genetic resources. The Intellectual Property Code of the Philippines therefore established patent protection for microorganisms under section 22.4 (see Annex IV in Swanson, 2002b). An interesting observation regarding this section of the Code is that it appears to run counter to the Philippines Constitution. Under Article XII,

Section 2, of the 1987 Constitution, the State is the owner of all 'flora and fauna' and 'with the exception of agricultural lands, all other natural resources shall not be alienated'. This would arguably render the patenting of microorganisms unconstitutional. As mentioned above, section 22.4 of the Code also appears to be in conflict with the ASEAN Framework Agreement on Access to Biological and Genetic Resources, to which the Philippines is a signatory.

The TRIPs agreement also requires member states to introduce either patent or sui generis protection for plant varieties. The latter option resulted from the fact that many developing countries argued against the patenting of plant varieties during the TRIPs negotiations, as it was believed that patent based restrictions were too inflexible to handle the complications arising in this context: the 'own use' exemption, the problem of food security, the sharing of benefits. Instead, the developing countries argued for a novel, or 'sui generis' system of property rights in plant varieties, in order to suit the particular needs of the agricultural context. Section 22.4 of the Intellectual Property Code of the Philippines therefore excludes plant varieties from patent protection, and leaves this to be developed by an effective sui generis system. This system is currently being adopted in that country as the Plant Variety Protection Act of 2002.

The Plant Variety Protection Act 2002

At the time of writing, the Plant Variety Protection Act 2002 (PVPA 2002) was going through its final stages of passage in the Philippines Senate.[16] The PVPA 2002 will be implemented in order for the Philippines to comply with the WTO TRIPs agreement. As mentioned above, Article 27.3(b) of TRIPs allows countries to exclude plants from patentability, so long as there is some form of effective form of sui generis system in operation. The PVPA 2002 therefore proposes a sui generis system of protection and exclusive rights with respect to innovations in plant varieties. There is no further guidance in TRIPs concerning what is an 'effective sui generis system', so many developing countries have adopted the model prevalent throughout the developed world, one that is based on the International Convention for the Protection of New Varieties of Plants (UPOV) 1961.[17]

Once adopted, the PVPA 2002 will implement UPOV as the sui generis system. The PVPA 2002 approximates reasonably closely to the International Convention for the Protection of New Varieties of Plants (UPOV) 1961, as amended. The Philippines has consulted UPOV on the conformity of this Act with the UPOV Convention, although it has not yet formally initiated the accession procedure that requires the signature of the President.

Under the provisions in the PVPA 2002, intellectual property rights are given to plant breeders who develop new varieties through conventional means, genetic engineering or biotechnology. A certificate of plant variety protection will be granted to the breeder[18] if they can show that they have met the internationally recognized criteria of 'distinctness, uniformity, stability and novelty' in developing the new plant variety.[19] The certificate protects the plant breeder's commercial rights over their variety for 25 years for trees and 20 years for plants.[20] The breeder can then use a trademark, trade name or other similar indication on the protected plant variety when it is sold or marketed.[21] A yearly fee has to be paid by the plant breeder to the Philippines Plant Variety Protection Board during the period covered by the certificate to maintain their intellectual property rights.[22]

Interestingly the first bill of the Plant Variety Protection Act (Senate Bill 1912), which was subsequently replaced, appears to have offered greater protection to the rights of indigenous peoples and farmers. Section 5 in the original bill states that a publicly known plant variety shall not be considered new, if at the date of filing of the application for a certificate the variety is publicly known or is used by others. Although this principle is true under generally held principles of intellectual property law, this is an important exception to the general allowance of plant breeding rights. The exemption for prior use or knowledge is useful in protecting indigenous communities' knowledge and biological resources because so many genetic resources are in use by groups who do not know that they could apply for a certificate protecting their intellectual property rights.

Another important exemption regarding plant genetic resources is the 'own use exemption', which had been available to farmers to enable their own reuse of purchased seeds. One of the principles of the PVPA 2002 is that the 'use of intellectual property bears a socio-economic function. To this end, the State shall promote the diffusion of technology and information for the promotion of national development and progress for the common good.'[23] The legislation seeks to promote farmers' rights by allowing small farmers on their own landholdings to be exempted from plant variety protection in order to ensure that small farmers have continued access to seeds and planting materials.[24] This provision is, however, extremely unclear as drafted, and is subject to conditions that will be defined at a later stage by the Plant Variety Protection Board.[25] This represents another conflict within the Philippines IPR regime that remains to be finally decided.

The protection of traditional folklore, music and dances, etc.

The Philippines Intellectual Property Code also allows for the protection of what is called derivative works. Section 173 allows for the copyrighting of dramatizations, translations, adaptations, abridgments, arrangements and other alterations of literary or artistic works; and collections of literary, scholarly or artistic works, and compilations of data and other materials that are original by reason of the selection or coordination or arrangement of their contents (see Annex IV in Swanson, 2002). Although this could in theory be used to protect indigenous peoples' cultural resources, it seems unlikely that copyright could be granted unless an identifiable author could be found. In general the Philippines IPR code makes no other special provision for folklore or traditional knowledge.

Conclusion: The movement for the standardization of IPRs in the Philippines

At the same time that the Philippines has been extending property rights in novel directions (in accordance with its obligations under the CBD), the Philippines is also making significant progress in reforming its IPR code in order to bring it into uniformity with the requirements of TRIPs. One of the major components of the TRIPs negotiations involved the discussions concerning the biological sector (plant breeding and biotechnology generally) and so specific revisions were agreed and reforms required under s.27(3). The Philippines is now in the final stages of the passage of the bills required to implement these reforms, in regard to both the plant breeding sector and the biotechnology sector.

Therefore, at the same time that the Philippines is advocating substantial change to the IPR system in one bill, it is engaged in the adoption of the agreed standardized forms in another. These two movements are proceeding in tandem, and are indicative of the fact that the next round of negotiations regarding IPR are likely to be very complicated.

This complexity is going to arise out of the demands of countries (such as the Philippines) for the reciprocal recognition of their rights to their capital inputs into the R&D process. The preceding TRIPs negotiations focused on the modern forms of capital contributing to R&D, while leaving other international negotiations (e.g. CBD) to negotiate the terms for the recognition of the natural forms of capital. The next stage of negotiations is likely to see the need to merge the two discussions.

There is one final movement to consider within the Philippines, and this concerns its attempt to incorporate traditional forms of capital inputs that are not natural in origin but human. Unlike the movement for rights in natural resources, this is a movement that has been occurring on the domestic stage rather than the international. Nevertheless, this movement is equally important to countries such as the Philippines, and it will equally appear on the agenda for the next stage of the global IPR discussions.

The Philippines' movement to protect indigenous peoples' rights

The Philippines is a nation comprised of many indigenous peoples and a long history of successive regimes (indigenous, Spanish, American, Philippine National). This has resulted in a nation that has several systems of rights and laws, which overlay one another. While some indigenous peoples and the rules governing their communities have continued in existence from time immemorial, the national laws were first established by the Spanish a few hundred years ago and then their American successors about one hundred years ago. Each regime was dramatically different from its predecessor, and so there were some laws and systems that continued in existence from the predecessors, while new layers were added. In general the national system has predominated while some local and regional aspects of the predecessor systems (where not in conflict) were tolerated. For this reason, there are some aspects of local tribal systems that have continued for hundreds of years, while the national governments have come and gone.

The 1987 Constitution represented the point at which the national government determined that it was important to reconcile these various pre-existing rights and regimes. In particular the new constitution recognized 'the rights of indigenous communities to their cultures, traditions and institutions'. The constitution required the government to enact plans and policies to give effect to these rights. Out of this new constitution flowed a new system for the recognition of indigenous peoples' rights to their own cultures and traditions. From this point onwards, the problem concerns how to reconcile all of the institutions that emanate from the various cultures that coexist within the Philippines.

To a great extent, this same phenomenon that is happening in the Philippines is also occurring on a global basis. The problems faced by the Philippines will be faced by the global community as it attempts to reconcile and make coherent the various approaches and methods for conducting R&D. In this case the Philippines may be seen as a laboratory for considering solutions to the problems concerning property rights that are affecting the R&D sector globally.

The Indigenous Peoples Rights Act

The protection of indigenous peoples' resources and their knowledge base was established under Philippines law when Republic Act 8371, known as the Indigenous Peoples Rights Act[26] (IPRA) was approved in October 1997. The IPRA gave the indigenous peoples rights over their ancestral lands and rights to utilize and develop natural resources found in their ancestral domains.[27] This allowed them the right to either prohibit access to the resources on their lands or to enter into access agreements for their use, so long as this was done in accordance with national and customary laws. The IPRA created a National Council for Indigenous Peoples (NCIP) as the agency responsible for overseeing the issuance of permits for access to indigenous peoples' lands. (IPRA is contained in Annex VII of Swanson, 2002b.)

Similar to the provisions of EO247 the doctrine of PIC was adopted as the basis for access to indigenous peoples' resources. However, IPRA extends the regime beyond natural resources to include new rights extending to the intellectual creations of indigenous communities. IPRA confers onto indigenous peoples the right to full ownership and control over their indigenous knowledge and systems. Indigenous knowledge systems and practices are defined as 'systems, institutions, mechanisms, technologies comprising a unique body of knowledge evolved through time embodying patterns of relationships between and among peoples, their lands and resource environment, including spheres of relationships which may include social, political, cultural, economic, religious and which are the direct outcome of the indigenous peoples responses to certain needs consisting of adaptive mechanisms which have allowed indigenous peoples to survive and thrive within their socio-cultural and biophysical conditions.'[28]

The indigenous peoples were given the right to introduce 'special measures to control, develop and protect their sciences, technologies and cultural manifestations, including human and other genetic resources, seeds, including derivatives of these resources, traditional medicines and health practices, vital medicinal plants, animals and minerals, indigenous knowledge systems and practices, knowledge of the properties of fauna and flora, oral traditions, literature, designs, and visual and performing arts.'[29] Access to these resources is again subject to the PIC of the indigenous peoples.[30] Other operational requirements also provide for the necessity of a written agreement between the parties seeking access and the indigenous peoples; the acknowledgement of all data provided by the indigenous peoples in any publications; and a percentage of royalties from any commercial product or publications that result from access.

Thus, the IPRA extended the system of controlled access far beyond the scope of biological and genetic resources. It is now arguable that any of the traditional forms of assets held by indigenous peoples are subject to strict control and regulated access. The primary form of regulation is the PIC system utilized in the context of genetic resources, but the IPRA also enables any 'special measures to control, develop and protect indigenous peoples' sciences, technologies and cultural manifestations'. Clearly, the intention of IPRA is to extend the rights of indigenous peoples far beyond the realm of biological resources and to provide more substance than was available under the PIC system of access.

The Indigenous Peoples Rights Act (IPRA) legislation demonstrates this intent by the recognition of the concept of 'community intellectual property rights' over indigenous peoples' rituals, customs, practices and customary laws that relate to rights over resources. This includes the protection of archaeological and historical sites, artefacts, designs, ceremonies, technologies and visual and performing literature, religious and spiritual properties, human and other genetic resources, seeds, medicines, health practices vital medicinal plants, animals, minerals, indigenous knowledge systems and practices, resource management systems, agricultural technologies, knowledge of properties of flora and fauna, language, music, dances, script, histories, oral traditions, conflict resolution mechanisms, peace building processes, life philosophy and perspectives,; and teaching and learning systems.[31] Therefore, the creation of the concept of community intellectual property rights represents the first step beyond the formalistic concept of 'access agreements' and toward the creation of a substantive right of ownership. We will return to it again below.

Although the IPRA remains in its infancy, it appears that it will provide impetus for substantial amounts of change to the IPR law of the Philippines. The hurdles that remain concern the development of the implementing rules and regulations that will give fruition to these goals and objectives. In particular, the challenge lies in giving both form and substance to the concept of 'community intellectual property rights' enunciated within IPRA.

The protection of traditional and alternative health care

One of the primary functions of traditional knowledge is as a contributor to health care, as an input into R&D systems and in other ways. In 1992, a traditional medicine programme was established in the Philippines under Administrative Order No.12. The purpose of this programme was to promote and advocate traditional medicine worldwide. The perceived success of the programme led to the creation of legislation covering the development of traditional and alternative health care in the Philippines. The Traditional and Alternative Medicine Act 1997 (TAMA 1997) was approved by the Senate on 9 December 1997.[32] TAMA 1997 can be seen in Annex VI of Swanson (2002b).

The main purpose of the legislation is for the state to improve the quality and delivery of health care services through the development of traditional and alternative health and its integration into the national health care system.[33] The main objectives of TAMA 1997 are to encourage scientific research on and to develop the traditional and alternative health care systems that have direct impact on public health care; to promote and advocate the use of traditional, alternative, preventive and curative health care; and to formulate policies for the protection of indigenous and natural health resources and technology from unwarranted exploitation, for approval and adoption by the appropriate government agencies.[34]

The last of these objectives is significant because it seeks to protect traditional medicines and other health care resources that are in the possession of indigenous peoples. The definitions of 'traditional and alternative health care',[35] 'traditional medicine'[36] and 'alternative health care modalities'[37] in TAMA 1997 also seem to extend this protection not only to a natural resource used by indigenous peoples, but also to their traditional knowledge in using and developing this natural resource. In some of the Philippines' indigenous communities, traditional knowledge in the medical field has accumulated over many generations and it has its basis as much in human as in natural resources. It has significance for general medicine in its prior identification of useful medicinal treatments. Some of the commercially available traditional medicines that have originated from the Philippines include Ascof (lagundi or *Vitex negundo* L.) for coughs and asthma and Re-Leaf (sambong or *Blumea balsamifera*) for the dissolution of kidney stones. It has great significance for the protection of the health of indigenous peoples because many would not be aware of medical alternatives, or could not afford expensive western treatments.

The TAMA 1997 legislation recognizes the value of traditional medicine and traditional health knowledge and attempts to secure the rights of indigenous peoples in its use and exportation. The legislation confirms this by stating that 'it shall also be the policy of the state to seek a legally workable basis by which indigenous societies would own their own knowledge of traditional medicine. When such knowledge is used by outsiders, the indigenous societies can require the permitted users to acknowledge its source and can demand a market share of any financial return that may come from its authorized commercial use.'[38] Section 4(i) of TAMA 1997 says that IPRs '[are] the legal basis by which the indigenous communities exercise their rights to have access to, protect, control over their cultural knowledge and product, including but not limited to, traditional medicines, and includes the right to receive compensation for it'. Although section 4(i) says that indigenous people can use IPRs, this provision is contained in the definitional section of the legislation that merely defines 'intellectual property rights'. Intellectual property rights are not mentioned in any other part of the legislation, and thus none are operationalized in this act. TAMA 1997 is supposed to be supplemented by a set of implementing rules and regulations.[39] It seems that TAMA is a form of framework legislation and these implementing regulations will have greater significance concerning how the legislation operates in practice.

The agency directly responsible for the organizational and management side of the legislation is the Philippine Institute for Traditional and Alternative Health Care (PITAHC), which was created under the legislation.[40] The purposes of the PITAHC is to promote traditional and alternative health care through international conventions, etc.;[41] to conduct research and development into the areas of traditional and alternative health care;[42] to verify, package and transfer economically viable technologies in the field of traditional and alternative health care;[43] sustain production, marketing and consumption of traditional and alternative health care products;[44] to acquire charters, franchises, licenses, rights, privileges, assistance, financial or otherwise, and concessions as are conductive to and necessary or proper for attainment of its purpose and objectives;[45] to receive and acquire from any person and/or government and private entities, whether foreign or domestic, grants, donations and contributions consisting of such properties, real or personal, including funds and valuable effects or things, as may be useful, necessary or proper to carry out its purpose and objectives and administer the same in accordance with the terms of such grants, donations and contributions, consistent with its purpose and objectives;[46] to enter into, make and execute contracts and agreements of any kind or nature; and to formulate and implement a research programme on the indigenous Philippine traditional health care practices performed by 'traditional healers' using scientific research methodologies.

It is noticeable that the functions of this organization appear to be primarily to promote, negotiate and organize the selling of traditional knowledge and medicines for export; it does not provide the organization with the express obligation to do so on the behalf of the indigenous communities. While the legislation legally entitles the PITAHC to examine the traditional health care practices of indigenous peoples and to control their export, it offers no substantive basis for how indigenous peoples can object to this knowledge being sold or how they can set up contracts with commercial interests. It is worth noting that the PITAHC is overseen by a Board of Trustees, which was also established under the legislation.[47] An interesting observation is that there are no representatives of indigenous groups on this Board of Trustees; in contrast, the Inter Agency on Biological and Genetic Resources (IACBGR), which was established under Executive Order 247, allows for representation from an indigenous organization in its composition.[48] There is no further provision anywhere in TAMA 1997 for even the consultation of indigenous peoples, for such things as monitoring their health care practices.

Therefore, TAMA 1997 is a fascinating example of a piece of legislation that attempts to halt the unauthorized appropriation of traditional knowledge regarding medicines in the Philippines; however, it does not provide any rights-based foundation for stemming this tide. It creates an agency (PITAHC) to promote and to appropriate these benefits, but it does little to channel them to the communities from which they emanate. TAMA is important as the first piece of law recognizing rights to traditional knowledge (as opposed to natural resources) within the Philippines, but it gives little or no substantive basis for those rights. The Philippines continues to await its first law that will give real substance to the concept of traditional knowledge rights.

Community intellectual property rights

A bill has been introduced by Senator Flavier in the Congress of the Philippines to provide for a formal system of community intellectual rights protection. Senate Bill 101 (otherwise known as 'An Act Providing for the Establishment of a System of Community Intellectual Rights Protection') allows for the registration of traditional knowledge as a form of intellectual property protection, with ownership and the benefits that derive from it flowing to the community. This bill has not yet received assent and the proposals for implementation will be discussed further below. It is reviewed here only to indicate a possible direction for the development of rights in traditional knowledge, and the problems and hurdles that remain.

The concept of community IPR protection was adopted because the Philippine government thought that the traditional system of intellectual property protection could not protect the indigenous knowledge systems. This is because traditional IPR protection rests on the notion of an individual author or an inventor who came up with the invention, innovation or idea. The explanatory note to the legislation confirms this by saying that 'the existing legal framework for intellectual property rights (IPR) in the country today recognizes only the dominant industrial mode of innovation. It has failed to recognize the more informal, communal system of innovation through which the farmers and indigenous communities produce, select, improve, and breed a diversity of crop and livestock varieties – a process which takes place over a long period of time. The existing IPR framework effectively sidesteps the traditional knowledge of indigenous communities'.

SB101 would rectify this problem by instituting a system for the registration and recognition of traditional knowledge by the community concerned. This registered knowledge would then become the exclusive property of the community. Since the specific provisions of SB101 are not yet approved and so may change significantly in coming months, they are not surveyed further here. Most of the bill's substance is apparent when the problems with implementing Community Property Rights are assessed below.

Conclusion: The movement for the protection of indigenous rights

The third great upheaval within the system of IPR in the Philippines has been generated by that country's attempt to reconcile the various important cultures and traditions that coexist within that country's borders: traditional Philippines, Spanish, American and modern Philippines. This movement for change has been sourced in the constitutional admonition to recognize and support the rights of indigenous communities, but it represents a broad-based movement for reconciling the various traditions and cultures that make up the people of this country.

This is the movement that represents the potential for greatest change in the IPR law of the country. The different peoples of the Philippines have very different cultures that must somehow be made to coexist within a single combined legal system (rather than a single imposed one). Some of these peoples participate within a traditional model of biological R&D (biological resources and traditional human capital) and many exist entirely within a traditional 'life sciences' sector altogether. There are others in the Philippines whose engagement is principally or entirely with modern life sciences. The creation of a legal system that is capable of combining this wide range of approaches is an important implication of the Philippines' recognition of indigenous rights.

Similarly the globe itself consists of many different forms of capital inputs contributing to the R&D industry in the life sciences. The Philippines' attempt to aggregate these various approaches within a single system is important as a learning experience for the undertaking of the same task at this higher level. For this reason the Philippines' experiment with the creation of community intellectual property rights is interesting to observe and to examine. We turn now to an analysis of the questions raised in the attempt to generate these novel forms of property rights.

Implementation of the Community Intellectual Rights Protection Act: Problems in the creation of new property rights and reconciliation with the old

This section lists the various issues that must be covered in any law purporting to establish a system of rights to traditional knowledge, and lists some of the problems that are generated in addressing them. Here we use the 'community property rights' structure set out in the Philippines bill as a case study in the problems of resolving these issues, in order to give concrete examples of the issues involved. We also make reference to official comments and reports from the Patent Office of the Philippines, which voice the concerns of the other branches of the government about the workings of this sort of proposed legislation.[49]

In addition to addressing the current terms of SB101, in the course of the preparation of this report a Roundtable discussion was held with several Philippine organizations concerned with the implementation of the concept of community property rights. These organizations were asked to voice their concerns about the current draft, and to give their opinions on the direction in which this legislation should be taken.[50]

All of these comments and discussions generate a significant amount of detail regarding the nature of the problems associated with the creation of a novel regime of property rights in traditional knowledge. These problems primarily emanate from the disembodied nature of the knowledge concerned, and from the conflicts and inconsistencies between this proposed legislation and already-existing IPR laws. In any event, it is difficult to conceive of an approach to these new forms of property rights that would not be afflicted with the same sorts of problems.

In the following section we discuss the terms of the Community Intellectual Property Rights Act (CIPRA), and ask questions about how (and whether) it can be implemented in a meaningful and effective manner. In each subsection we set out the substance of the CIPRA provision and the comments from the Philippines' government on its implementation, but also ask questions about the capacity to solve these problems more generally. The intent is to use the CIPRA bill as a case study for the understanding of the complexities involved in completing the task that the Philippines has undertaken.

What is the traditional knowledge that is to be protected?

The Explanatory Note to the CIPRA bill states that its objective is to provide for a system of community IPR protection that acknowledges the innovative contribution of local and indigenous cultural communities with respect to the development of genetic resources and the conservation of the country's biological diversity. Section 4 of CIPRA expands on this and lists the things that are declared to be the intellectual property of the communities of the Philippines. This includes an extremely long list of items and practices[51] and concludes with the inclusive 'all other products or processes not made by a single person or juridical personality, which was discovered through a community process, or when the individual making the innovation does not claim the knowledge as his own, provided that any individual or juridical personality making such a claim should present proof of innovation or a history leading to the discovery that would justify his claim.'

Thus, the key to the understanding of the scope of protected subject matter is the term 'community process'. The legislation is not intended to extend to any innovation that is generated by means of individual processes of innovation, but only to those that are generated by a group. Clearly, this is intended to stave off the greatest amount of conflict with the existing IPR laws, which are of course focused on the concept of individual innovation; however, it does not solve the problem since it begs the question concerning the meaning of 'community process'.

What is community generated knowledge?

Community (as opposed to individually generated) traditional knowledge is defined in CIPRA section 3(d) as: '…knowledge from a community process are those whose discovery or development could not be ascribed to a single individual or juridical person, and/or which resulted from the contributions of different groups or generations'. However, section 4(f) says that community intellectual property rights can be recognized in relation 'to all other products or processes not made by a single person or juridical personality, which was discovered through a community process, or when the individual making the innovation does not claim the knowledge as his own, provided that any individual or juridical personality making such a claim should present proof of innovation or a history leading to the discovery that would justify his claim'.

It seems that further clarification is required in the bill as to how the community intellectual property will be affected by claims of individuals against the community. The Intellectual Property Office (IPO) of the Philippines has commented that the bill should clarify the effect of the proposed definition of community intellectual property with regard to the innovations of an individual, who is a member of the community or who has lived in the community and who claims that such innovation is his knowledge notwithstanding the claim of his community. It certainly seems that the bill as it stands is a little unclear as to what happens where a community has used or expanded on an individual's innovation or vice versa. Presumably an individual can register for normal intellectual property rights if he can prove he is the owner or inventor. In cases where an agreement cannot be reached between an individual and a community over the contributions made to the knowledge process, the IPO have suggested that there should be provision in the bill for the establishment of some form of alternative dispute resolution mechanism that is not limited to arbitration and mediation. In any event, it seems clear that the creation of legal systems providing rights only to groups (while other systems provide rights to individuals) is likely to generate significant conflicts within the groups. In short, the attempt to avoid the conflict with the existing individual-based IPR system is likely to merely shift the conflict rather than resolve it.

The language of the bill also indicates that it may be possible for an individual to sign over its invention or process to the community (by agreeing not to raise any claim). This raises the issue of transferability of traditional knowledge rights generally. Are they transferable? Can a group establish rights and then make them available to others, even if those others are not a designated group (or potentially not even a group at all)? Presumably it is the case that these rights are not transferable (except in very limited manners as discussed below) and this would imply significant reductions in the value of any rights that are conferred.

Who qualifies for protection?

Section 2(a) of CIPRA says that the state recognizes the original rights of indigenous peoples and local communities over plant and genetic resources, traditional medicines, agricultural methods and local technologies that they have discovered and developed. While 'indigenous peoples' is a term defined in section 3(i), 'local communities' has been left undefined in the definitional section. However, the nature of what is a community has been elaborated in section 5, providing that it is 'any group of people living in a geographically defined area with common history and definitive patterns of relationship'.

This is indicative of the problem concerning any attempts to restrict the availability of these rights to certain groups. If the rights are recognized when held by certain groups, then what is the value of these virtually non-transferable rights? Could an indigenous group enter into a joint venture with other groups, or a partnership, or would this represent an unlawful transfer of rights? If it is not unlawful to enter into joint ventures, then what is to prevent unscrupulous groups or individuals from entering into broad and unclear agreements that enable them to make use of any and all of the groups' potential rights (in a sort of undefined partnership)? In the absence of fully recognized transferability, it is difficult to see how such rights will rise to any substance greater than the already existing access and benefit sharing agreements.

Even if the rights are restricted to indigenous groups, problems arise as to whether CIPRA will cover the protection of traditional knowledge practices of lowlanders and other communities who may not necessarily be classified as indigenous peoples (e.g. the medical and healing traditions of the people in Siquijor). In practice it seems that the use of the words and 'other communities' throughout the act would cover the Siquijor and other groups. However, the Philippine Council for Agriculture (PCA), Forestry and Natural Resources Research and Development (PCAARD) and the Department of Science and Technology (DOST) have commented that further evaluation is needed over the effectiveness of having a largely geographical-based definition of the community. Although the impetus is arising from recognizing the contributions of indigenous peoples in the Philippines, it seems arbitrary to restrict the availability of rights to specific groups over others who are contributing to the R&D sector today.

How will indigenous knowledge be registered?

Under the first paragraph of section 5 of CIPRA, a local community should be registered with the appropriate government agency in order to exercise their rights over their product or traditional knowledge. The second sentence of this same paragraph, also says that 'their failure to do so shall not prejudice its status as custodians or stewards of its traditional knowledge'. The second paragraph says that 'a community shall automatically become the general owners of any product or traditional knowledge', once this is entered into the registers. It seems that to exercise their rights the indigenous peoples or community must therefore jump two hurdles: registering as a community and registering the traditional knowledge.

Section 6 of CIPRA provides for the registration of community intellectual property in indigenous knowledge registers. All identified and documented community intellectual property shall be entered by government agencies into one of three registers. A national inventory of plant varieties will be maintained by the National Commission on Plant Genetic Resources to register plants and seeds; a national register of indigenous cultural heritage will record cultural products and heritage at the National Museum; and the Bureau of Patents, Trademarks, and Technology Transfer Inventions will have responsibility for everything else. This will include industrial designs, utility models, agricultural practices, devices developed from indigenous materials, customs and knowledge, medicinal products and medicinal herbs.

There could be a number of problems in the establishment of these registers. Section 6 provides that 'in consultation with the concerned local communities, academic experts, and non-government organizations, the State shall take the initiative in providing technical and other related forms of assistance in the documentation, identification and characterization of community intellectual property. The State shall also promote rules whereby non-government organizations can extend similar assistance to local communities.' It seems that the state have taken on a substantial commitment in taking the initiative in identifying traditional knowledge, when considering there are approximately 7000 islands that comprise the Philippines. The process of registration will entail significant government expenditure because of the geographical isolation of many of these communities and it remains to be seen whether the government will be able to implement this in practice.

As a result of the significant amount of human and other forms of resources that should be required in the documentation, identification and characterization of community IPRs, the Intellectual Property Office (IPO) have called for further clarification in the bill as to the identity of the government agencies that will be involved. The IPO also thought clear mandates should be provided in the bill as to the responsibilities of these government agencies that will provide technical and other related forms of assistance. The IPO suggested model would be the establishment of an inter-agency body that could act as a national focal point assisted by regional agencies.

The South East Asia Regional Initiatives for Community Development (SEARICE) have also made a number of suggestions about how to make the identification and registration process operate more effectively in practice. They have pointed out that a number of other bodies that are already mandated by legislation to the protection of indigenous peoples' rights could also play a role. They have suggested that the Philippine Institute for Traditional and Alternative Health Care (PITAHC), which was established under Republic Act 842, could assist in the CIPRA implementation process in relation to national and local registries of medicinal and herbal medicines and associated knowledge. SEARICE have also noted that the scientific and academic communities have established through an Administrative Order issued by the Department of Science and Technology (DOST) in 2000 a National Commission on Genetic Resources (NCGR), which serves as a policy advisory body on issues involving genetic resources conservation and development within the formal system. They consider that the possibility of utilizing this inter-agency body in some way in the implementation of the CIPRA should be reviewed.

It is plausible that if the state does not take the initiative in registering community rights, it would be unlikely that many indigenous peoples will either find out about their community intellectual protection rights or be able to travel to register such rights. There could be difficulties in registering rights at the local level for the reason that not many people understand what it is about and do not care to know what good it can do the community. It is a common observation that some communities are suspicious and adverse to the institutionalization of intellectually property protection over their traditional knowledge. There is a need in the bill to provide a more solid provision concerning the education of communities about the value of their indigenous knowledge and the modes of protection that can be instituted.

The South East Asia Regional Initiatives for Community Development (SEARICE) have also suggested that there should be some provision for setting up an information and education campaign to raise the awareness and capacities of communities of the CIPRA and the registration system. Whether provisions for this should be contained in the CIPRA bill is questionable. SEARICE has also suggested that to complement the national registration scheme, local registration schemes initiated by communities (registered or not) and civil society organizations should also be encouraged under the proposed CIPRA legislation. They consider this beneficial as they consider local registration schemes will stimulate direct community participation in the implementation of the law and will minimize the problems arising from the bureaucratic processes involved in the national registration system. This seems like a particularly good suggestion, although it could become a bureaucratic nightmare if there is an not an adequate focal government agency coordinating this. The structure of the organization of the registration scheme will therefore be significant in the implementation and effectiveness of the legislation, if adopted, in practice.

How will the registers operate?

It is important that the information on the register be made public so as to establish a claim of prior possession; however, the placement of traditional knowledge within the public domain creates several problems. It raises the question of how the register will intersect and interact with other systems of property rights and rights registration.

First, placing any specific traditional knowledge on the register would place it within the public domain and give it the status of prior art, thereby barring future registration under the patent system. The Intellectual Property Office has suggested that until this problem is resolved they recommend that caution must be taken in documenting traditional knowledge that is not in the public domain, as it could prejudice its protection. There should therefore be a provision in the bill that clarifies this and sets out what constitutes indigenous knowledge in the public domain.

Second, the same concern applies with regard to the protection of traditional knowledge under other systems such as trade secret or confidentiality laws. It must be recognized that the use of the register implies a trade-off with other forms of protection, and that some protection will be lost in exchange for the protection afforded by the register.

A further concern with the establishment of these registers is that there is no method in place to regulate access to them. A provision should be put in place that in some way regulates or allocates access on a licensed basis. The cost of deterring any unauthorized or improper use of registered information would otherwise be excessive.

Who owns specific community knowledge?

Another potential problem with the effectiveness of the CIPRA legislation in practice is the difficulty of proving authorship or ownership of a specific piece of information/knowledge. This will always be a problem with any attempt to register disembodied information (i.e. information in any form other than a marketable good) but the following discussion illustrates the range of complexities that would arise in this context.

It will be extremely difficult to determine ownership if traditional knowledge was built from previous knowledge of other communities. The definition of 'innovation' in section 3 of CIPRA says that it 'refers to the processes or products derived from such processes, whether documented in written, recorded or oral form, which constitute an introduction of new changes, including alteration, modifications or improvements'. There could be disputes amongst different indigenous peoples as to the significance of the changes that have taken place.

There could be a great deal of difficulty in determining ownership of some materials, knowledge, practices and processes that are claimed by one indigenous community, if another indigenous community also claims it as theirs. It is very difficult to establish in which community or area the specific indigenous knowledge originated. This is compounded by the fact that certain indigenous groups or individuals could have moved around a country, or even have originated from another country, and passed on this knowledge. As most indigenous knowledge has been passed down through oral traditions it will be extremely difficult to establish who is the actual owner, and to disentangle the various contributors to the development of any specific practice or method.

A long-standing problem in this area has been the practice of claiming rights based on minor modifications; for example, one party used some form of indigenous knowledge and then produced a new product slightly different to the original (e.g. a plant variety could be used to make a synthetic counterpart like a pill). There are obvious parallels concerning whether one indigenous tribe could take some form of indigenous knowledge and modify it to form something new. Would such a minor modification truncate the scope of the pre-existing claim?

Section 5 of CIPRA says that a community shall automatically become the general owners of any form of traditional knowledge, once this is entered in any of the registers. There is very little in the CIPRA Bill that gives any indication as to how the validation process would work. Would the registration office make any effort to confirm that they are the rightful 'owners' or custodians of this knowledge? It is feasible to require some form of audit trail to qualify for normal forms of intellectual property protection, but this is unlikely to work in relation to indigenous knowledge that is passed down through oral traditions. There are also questions concerning who would bear the burden of proof and expense in investigating the cultural and historic background in disputes over community rights protection. The party with the burden of proof (and thus the expense of a serious anthropological project) is the likely loser. It therefore seems that the bill could be improved by clarifying the validation procedure and establishment of some form of dispute resolution committee that specializes in indigenous knowledge. The Philippine Council for Agriculture, Forestry and Natural Resources Research and Development (PCAARD) and Department of Science and Technology (DOST) have raised this as a potential problem with the CIPRA Bill as it stands and have requested further clarification.

A further potential problem with multiple claims over the use of the same knowledge base is that, if one group receives community IPR protection and the other does not, then in theory they would have to compensate the group who received the protection, even if the community practice is one that they have exercised for millennia. Under section 5 of CIPRA owners of community IPRs are entitled to collect a justifiable percentage from all profits derived from the commercial use of their knowledge for a period of 10 years. This means that if one indigenous group sold, for example, craftworks to tourists, that have protected rights belonging to another group, they will have to pay them a percentage of all their profits received. This could cause resentment if the group without the protected right had relied on that knowledge base for hundreds of years and relied upon it for its income.

How are the benefits from ownership to be exercised?

The CIPRA Bill builds on earlier Philippine legislation by introducing provisions concerning access agreements and benefit sharing for community IPRs. Section 2(c) of the CIPRA Bill says that 'all benefits arising from the knowledge and innovations by indigenous and local communities should accrue to their development and welfare and should therefore be equitably shared'.

Interestingly, the third paragraph in section 5 states that 'all benefits shall be given directly to the organization that effectively represents the community's interests. In the absence of such an organization, the benefits will be held in trust by the State and will be released only by legislation enacted in favour of the community.' The IPO have expressed their reservation regarding this clause and are seeking clarification as to whether an indigenous community or an organization of indigenous peoples in a particular community, which is not duly registered with the appropriate agency, would still be entitled to the benefits envisioned by the Senate Bill. The IPO believes that the absence of registration should not prevent the indigenous peoples from the equitable sharing of benefits from the use of traditional knowledge and genetic resources. They have likened this situation to that which took place after the introduction of the coconut levy, which created an undesirable conflict among stakeholders and the government. This provision relies on the local communities registering, which in theory relies on the government's successful promotion of the registration scheme in the first place. The fact that funds flow to the government in the absence of registration creates a clear disincentive for the registration process to be undertaken efficiently in the first place.

Section 5 of CIPRA also states that royalties are required to be paid to the community owners for a period of 10 years starting from the date of registration. There is no provision concerning the percentage of these payments, or the period of time that other benefits such as technology transfer might take place. Presumably this is left for communities to negotiate during access agreements. This means that academic researchers or scientists who wish to have access to these resources would have to deal with the Council of Elders and comply with their requirements, in the absence of any stated percentage. The South East Asia Regional Initiatives for Community Development (SEARICE) have suggested that there should be clear provisions in CIPRA concerning information and education campaigns to raise the awareness and capacities of communities of not only their rights to register but to negotiate for a fair and equitable share in benefits arising from the commercialization of their interests.

Are there conflicts with other laws?

A potential problem with the CIPRA Bill is its interaction and overlap with other instruments. Section 11 of CIPRA states that 'all laws, executive orders, presidential decrees, rules and regulations or parts thereof which are inconsistent with the provisions of this Act are hereby repealed, amended or modified accordingly'. The following laws are those that are expressly impacted.

(1) Plant Variety Protection Act 2002

The Plant Variety Protection Act 2002 (PVPA 2002) is being adopted in order for the Philippines to achieve compliance with the WTO TRIPs agreement. The PVPA 2002 did this by introducing a sui generis system of protection, which approximates very closely to the International Convention for the Protection of New Varieties of Plants (UPOV) 1961, as amended. Under the provisions of the PVPA 2002, IPRs are given to plant breeders who develop new varieties and a certificate of plant variety protection will be granted if the breeder can show that they have met the internationally recognized criteria of 'distinctness, uniformity, stability and novelty' in developing the new plant variety.

There is concern that the end-of-pipeline rights generated by the PVPA Bill might be in conflict with the fundamental principles of the CIPRA Bill, which provide for community IPRs in the parent strains and genetic material discovered or selected and conserved by local communities, which are used in the development of new plant varieties.[52] SEARICE have commented that the PVPA does not give due recognition and reward to community innovations in plant genetic resource conservation and development. PCAARD and DOST have also recommended that close attention is paid to the implications of the primary and residuary title provision in the issuance of a Plant Variety Protection (PVP) certificate.

Section 77 of the PVPA Bill says that 'all laws, decrees, executive orders, and rules and regulations, or parts thereof which are inconsistent with this Act are hereby repealed or modified accordingly'. There is also an identical provision in Section 11 of the CIPRA Bill. It is clear that some provision should be added into one or both of these bills to indicate how they are intended to interact.

(2) The Civil Code of the Philippines: Community Ownership

Another potential conflict could in principle occur between the CIPRA Bill and the Civil Code of the Philippines concerning the legal status of 'ownership'. Under the Civil Code ownership is recognized where an individual has title or property to the exclusion of all others. Under section 4 of the CIPRA Bill the communities are considered 'at all times and in all perpetuity the holders of primary and residuary titles to community property'. There is a clear conflict between the concept of ownership in the general code and the concept of community ownership in the CIPRA.

(3) Conflicts with International Legal Regimes: TRIPs

Interestingly, the explanatory note to the CIPRA Bill states that 'its central thesis aims to overthrow the long-standing paradigms embodied in such international institutions as the World Trade Organisation (WTO) – formerly the GATT – and the Food and Agricultural Organisation (FAO) which recognize genetic resources as a "universal heritage" in order to guarantee free access for the "first world commercial interests to the raw materials of the south"'. It seems that the Philippines government could be headed for a collision with the TRIPs agreement over its community intellectual rights protection for plant varieties under the CIPRA legislation.

The adoption of the sui generis system under the PVPA 2002 meets the requirements of the TRIPs agreement, but the adoption of a bill something like CIPRA would create a second system of rights running in parallel to that under UPOV. It is possible that the combination of the two systems will be seen to be an unacceptable sui generis regime, but this remains to be seen in the next round of negotiations.

Conclusion: Problems in implementing systems of novel property rights

This discussion of the system of property rights being considered for implementation in the Philippines indicates the scale of the task that is being faced. The adoption of a system that recognizes property rights in traditional knowledge faces substantial obstacles on three counts: (i) the community rather individual nature of ownership; (ii) the disembodied nature of the subject innovation; and (iii) the conflicts with the already-existing regime.

The communal nature of the proposed property rights system raises many difficult questions. First, what is a community that is able to take the right? And, to what extent does the limitation on owners imply restrictions on transferability? Second, how are the apparent conflicts between innovative individuals and their resident community to be resolved? How do conflicts between the individual-based systems and the community-based systems get resolved? All of these questions arise on account of the attempt to sidestep the existing IPR laws, and they generate more problems than solutions. It indicates that there is very little value to be had out of moving toward community-based notions of IPR, rather than individual-based notions that might be claimed by a community as well.

The potentially disembodied nature of the innovation also represents very serious problems for defining property rights. How is it possible to segregate between various claims to the same knowledge? Does a minor modification/ improvement truncate a pre-existing claim? Does prior registration make another community's use of the same knowledge invalid? How should registration and the burden of proof regarding ownership be handled? If it is not based on first registration alone, who bears the expense and burden of the anthropological task of disentangling traditional knowledge? All of these problems indicate that the proposed system must come to terms with the need to develop a clear method for embodying traditional knowledge in some tangible form, as a means of demarcating the various rights and halting the disputes that might rage over any single claim.

Finally, it is clear that it is the intention to develop such systems as an alternative to the already-existing systems of IPR, and this implies that there are going to be conflicts. How is the PVPA supposed to interact with the community property rights legislation? Is ownership going to be expanded to include communities as well as individuals? The conflicts between pre-existing and newly developing regimes are symptomatic of the differences between countries in their IPR systems. These differences need to be worked out in a common framework, rather than in competing ones.

Conclusion

This chapter has set forth the three movements that constitute the dramatic change that has occurred within the Philippines IPR system over the past decade. These three movements represent: (i) the movement to create rights in biological and genetic resources (as set out in the CBD); (ii) the movement to standardize and formulate TRIPs-compatible IPR systems; and (iii) the movement to recognize rights of indigenous peoples to their own resources and institutions.

The movement to create rights in biological resources was initiated by the CBD as an alternative to the pre-existing system of universal access and common heritage. States with significant amounts of biological resources (useful in the R&D sector) no longer wished to make these available on this basis, and national sovereignty was claimed over domestic genetic resources. The doctrine of PIC was adopted to implement this claim, and contractual agreements for access and benefit sharing have been the norm. Although this system has not yet developed any new individual-based property rights in genetic resources, it has established the fact that other, more traditional forms of capital are important contributors within the R&D process. And, although the claimed rights are more procedural than substantive in nature, the recognition of these claims constitutes the first step towards agreeing to the overhaul of existing IPR regimes.

The second step is being taken at present in the form of the advocacy of property rights to useful traditional knowledge. Traditional human capital is the other form of input that has been useful in R&D within the biological sector; the recognition of claims of rights to traditional knowledge would be an even more important step toward the overhaul of the existing IPR system.

This is because, unlike natural resources, there is no confusion concerning the status of human resources; these have always been resources attributable to a specific state. The creation of rights in traditional knowledge would therefore represent more of a recognition of the need to alter the existing system of rent creation and rent sharing, rather than the alteration of the system of national sovereignty. It implies more in terms of change for the IPR system than did the debate over natural resources, as human resource inputs can only be compensated through that sort of system.

Thus, the third movement requires the consideration of the manner in which the two preceding movements may be combined and made consistent with the third: the movement for the globalization of a standardized regime for IPR protection. The need to recognize the wide range of capital that supplies inputs to the R&D process in the biological sector indicates that significant changes remain to be made. The progress of the Philippines in their attempts to create such change indicates that the nature of those changes require a lot more thought and discussion.

Notes

1. Article 15, Convention Biological Diversity.
2. EO 247 provides the basic legal framework for access and benefit sharing. (see EO 247 in Annex II). This was then supplemented by a set of implementing rules and regulations in 1996 under Administrative Order 96-20: Implementing Rules and Regulations on the Prospecting of Biological and Genetic Resources (Implementing Regulations). This Administrative Order can be seen in Annex III.
3. The Executive Order established an Inter-Agency Committee (IAC), which is responsible for the implementation and review of the Order. The IAC is composed of individuals from the Department of Environment and Natural Resources, Department of Science and Technology, the Department of Agriculture, Department of Health, the Department of Foreign Affairs, as well as representatives from the Philippines scientific community, the National Museum, non-governmental organizations and significantly a representative from indigenous communities. In practice a Technical Secretariat conducts the initial review and evaluation of the application and supporting documentation, and, within 30 days of receiving all the required documentation from the collector, submits its results, including, where appropriate, a draft research agreement, to the Inter-Agency Committee for final evaluations.
4. Biological resources includes genetic resources, organisms or parts thereof, populations or any other biotic component of ecosystems with actual or potential value for humanity such as plants, seeds, tissues and other propagation materials, animals, microorganisms, live or preserved, whether whole or in part thereof. Section 2g. Administrative Order 96-20: Implementing Rules and Regulations on the Prospecting of Biological and Genetic Resources.

5. Section 2j and 2m, Administrative Order 96-20: Implementing Rules and Regulations on the Prospecting of Biological and Genetic Resources.

6. This obligation is consistent with Article 15(5) of the B.

7. Section 4 of EO247 states that the proposal must be submitted to the recognized head of the indigenous community and s.2 states that prospecting can only occur with the prior informed consent of the communities.

8. Prior informed consent is defined circularly as the consent obtained from the local community. Section 2(w), Administrative Order 96-20: Implementing Rules and Regulations on the Prospecting of Biological and Genetic Resources (Implementing Regulations).

9. ASEAN is made up of the following members: Brunei Darussalam, Cambodia, Indonesia, Malaysia, the Philippines, Singapore, Thailand and Vietnam.

10. The ASEAN Framework Agreement on Access to Biological and Genetic Resources, Draft Text, 24 February 2000.

11. The ASEAN Framework Agreement is attached in Annex I.

12. Article 2, The ASEAN Framework Agreement on Access to Biological and Genetic Resources.

13. Article 4, The ASEAN Framework Agreement on Access to Biological and Genetic Resources.

14. However, in practice and as will be discussed below, the Philippines has recently implemented a patent system for microorganisms (Republic Act 8293. Intellectual Property Code of the Philippines) and a system of PBR protection.

15. These were introduced under a bilateral US–Philippine agreement to strengthen protection of intellectual property rights in the Philippines.

16. Senate Bill 1865.

17. The UPOV Convention was established to encourage innovation in plant breeding by giving breeders exclusive rights to a plant variety that they have developed, so long as basic criteria are met.

18. Section 4, Plant Variety Protection Act 2002.

19. Sections 6, 7 and 8, Plant Variety Protection Act 2002.

20. Section 33, Plant Variety Protection Act 2002.

21. Section 16, Plant Variety Protection Act 2002.

22. Section 34, Plant Variety Protection Act 2002.

23. Section 2, Plant Variety Protection Act 2002.

24. Section 43(d), Plant Variety Protection Act 2002.

25. Ibid.

26. IPRA. An Act to Recognize, Protect and Promote the Rights of Indigenous Cultural Communities, Creating a National Commission for Indigenous Peoples, Establishing Implementing Mechanisms, Appropriating Funds Therefore, and For Other Purposes.

27. Section 7(b), IPRA.

28. Section 14, IPRA Implementing Rules and Regulations.

29. Section 34, IPRA.

30. Section 15, IPRA Implementing Rules and Regulations.

31. Section 10, IPRA Implementing Rules and Regulations.

32. Republic Act No. 8423

33. Section 2, Traditional and Alternative Medicine Act 1997.

34. Section 3, Traditional and Alternative Medicine Act 1997.
35. Section 4(a), 'Traditional and alternative health care' – the sum total of knowledge, skills and practices on health care, other than those embodied in biomedicine.
36. Section 4(b), 'Traditional medicine' – the sum total of knowledge, skills and practice on health care, not necessarily explicable in the context of modern, scientific philosophical framework, but recognized by the people to help maintain and improve their health towards the wholeness of their being the community and society, and their interrelations based on culture, history, heritage, and consciousness.
37. Section 4(d), 'Alternative health care modalities' – other forms of nonallopathic, occasionally non-indigenous or imported healing methods.
38. Section 3(e), Traditional and Alternative Medicine Act 1997.
39. Section 4(i), Traditional and Alternative Medicine Act 1997.
40. Section 5, Traditional and Alternative Medicine Act 1997.
41. Section 3(g), Traditional and Alternative Medicine Act 1997.
42. Section 6(a), Traditional and Alternative Medicine Act 1997.
43. Section 6(b), Traditional and Alternative Medicine Act 1997.
44. Section 6(c), Traditional and Alternative Medicine Act 1997.
45. Section 6(f), Traditional and Alternative Medicine Act 1997.
46. Section 6(g), Traditional and Alternative Medicine Act 1997.
47. Section 7, Traditional and Alternative Medicine Act 1997.
48. Section 10.1(i), Implementing Rules and Regulations on the Subject of Bioprospecting of Biological and Genetic Resources – Department Administrative Order No. 96-20.
49. Patent Office, Report on SB101, December 2001.
50. See Uy, 'Memorandum on the Status of SB101', memorandum, March 2002.
51. These include: parent strains and genetic material discovered or selected and conserved by local communities, which were used in the development of new plant varieties, and which can be harnessed for other potential uses; seeds and other reproductive materials selected, cultivated, domesticated and developed by local communities *in situ*; agricultural practices and devices developed from indigenous materials, customs and knowledge; medicinal products and processes developed from the identification, selection, cultivation, preparation, storage and application of medicinal herbs by local communities and indigenous peoples; cultural products from local communities, such as weaving patterns, pottery, painting, poetry, folklore, music, and the like.
52. Section 4 CIPRA Senate Bill No. 101.

References

Barber, C. V. and La Vina, A. G. M. (1998) *Implementing Benefit-sharing: The Philippine Experience on Executive Order 247*, World Resources Institute, Washington, DC

Convention on Biological Diversity (2000) *An Information Package for Pacific Island Countries; 2000*, South Pacific Regional Environment Programme

La Vina, A. G. M. and Calida, B. Baylon, R. (1997) *Regulating Access to Biological and Genetic Resources in the Philippines*, A Manual on the Implementation of Executive Order No. 247, Foundation for the Philippine Environment (FPE) and World Resources Institute (WRI)

Leonen, M. and La Vina, A. G. M. (1994) 'Obstacles to harnessing creativity: Philippine efforts to conserve biodiversity and to use biological resources sustainably', in A. F. Krattiger, J. A. McNeely, W. H. Lesser, K. R. Miller, Y. St. Hill, R. Senanayake (eds), *Widening Perspectives on Biodiversity*, International Academy of the Environment and IUCN, Geneva

Patent Office of the Philippines (2001) Comments on CIPRA, Memorandum, 2001

Swanson, T. (2002) *Problems in the Protection of Indigenous Knowledge in the Philippines: A Study on Traditional Knowledge and its Management*, World Bank, Washington, DC

Uy, A. L. H. (2001) 'The right of indigenous people over natural resources in their ancestral domain: Analysis of Philippine experience', Masters of Law (LLM) Dissertation, University of London

Uy, A. L. H. (2002) Roundtable Discussion on the CIPRA. Memorandum for the World Bank Project on Traditional Knowledge, February

Zamora, O. B. (1997) 'The Philippines: A bridle on bioprospecting?' *The Quarterly Newsletter of Genetic Resources Action International*, June, http://www.grain.org/seedling/?id=13, accessed 6 November 2008

15

Protecting Traditional Knowledge: A Holistic Approach based on Customary Laws and Bio-cultural Heritage

Krystyna Swiderska

The privatization of community knowledge

Indigenous communities have accumulated a wealth of traditional knowledge (TK) through centuries of close dependence on nature – including knowledge about medicinal plants, wild foods and agricultural practices, and knowledge embodied in the native seed varieties and livestock breeds that they have improved and conserved. In recent years, indigenous organizations have become increasingly concerned about the privatization of their knowledge and bio-resources, alienation of their rights and unfair exploitation of these resources, without permission or respect of customary laws. IPR regimes – such as patents and plant variety protection (PVP) – are becoming increasingly strong and ubiquitous as a result of trade agreements of the WTO and the proliferation of bilateral Free Trade Agreements. This is accelerating the commercial use and privatization of indigenous knowledge and resources (Swiderska, 2006).

A number of international and national policy initiatives are seeking to respond to the challenge of ensuring that the rights of indigenous and local communities over their traditional knowledge are respected and protected. Many people agree that existing intellectual property rights – such as patents and PVP – are not suitable for protecting traditional knowledge and that alternative 'sui generis'[1] systems are needed. Intellectual property rights (IPRs) are designed to protect commercial inventions and mostly grant individual and exclusive rights; whereas traditional knowledge of communities is first and foremost for subsistence and is largely held collectively, as ancestral heritage.

However, some people (e.g. industrialized country patent offices at World Intellectual Property Organisation (WIPO) meetings) argue that sui generis systems should be consistent with existing IPR standards. Parties to the Convention on Biological Diversity (CBD) see sui generis systems largely as mechanisms for sharing benefits with communities from the commercial use of TK, including the use of IPRs. Many indigenous organizations, on the other hand, feel that a completely different approach is needed, which responds to the distinct customary laws and worldviews of traditional knowledge holders, rather than western commercial norms. For them, the spread of IPRs is a significant concern because they clash with the indigenous values of ancestral heritage and free sharing/open access that sustain livelihoods and biodiversity; and can undermine local control over resources and development pathways. There is a fear that IPRs will eventually replace these 'commons' values with private property values (Swiderska, 2006). If the less industrialized countries and communities are forced to accept IPRs from which they can derive little benefit, it seems only fair that industrialized countries should accept mechanisms to protect traditional knowledge based on customary laws.

Despite these divergent perspectives, there is some acceptance in international policy fora of the need to recognize customary laws and practices as one part of measures to protect traditional knowledge. There is, however, little understanding of what this means in practice.

An action-research approach using an indigenous conceptual framework

The International Institute for Environment and Development (IIED) is working with research and indigenous partners in India, China, Kenya, Peru and Panama (see Box 15.1) to develop mechanisms to protect TK that are based on

---

Box 15.1 Collaborative research on TK protection and customary law

This chapter draws on the work of a number of organizations engaged in the project 'Protecting community rights over traditional knowledge: Implications of customary laws and practices': Asociación ANDES (Peru), Fundación Dobbo Yala (Panama), Ecoserve (India), Centre for Indigenous Farming Systems (India), Herbal and Folklore Research Centre (India), Centre for Chinese Agricultural Policy (China), Southern Environmental & Agricultural Policy Research Institute (Kenya) and Kenya Forestry Research Institute. These organizations are working with indigenous and local communities in areas of important biodiversity (medicinal plants/forests and centres of origin of rice, potatoes and maize): Quechua farmers in Peru; indigenous Adhivasis in Chattisgarh; Lepchas in the Eastern Himalayas; Yanadi tribals in Andhra Pradesh; Mijikenda in Kenya; Kuna and Embera-Wounaan in Panama; and indigenous farmers in Guangxi, SW China.

The studies are applying the Code of Ethics of the International Society of Ethnobiology. The project is supported by IDRC, DGIS and The Christensen Fund.

For more information, see www.iied.org/NR/agbioliv/bio_liv_projects/protecting.html.

the customary laws and practices of indigenous and local communities rather than being modelled on western norms. Through participatory action-research with indigenous communities, the project is developing local tools for TK protection, including community knowledge registers, community access protocols and an inter-community agreement for equitable benefit sharing.

Policies on TK protection and access to genetic resources (GRs) and benefit sharing (ABS) tend to recognize rights to TK only and not to associated genetic resources, which are assumed to be owned by the state as per the CBD's principle of 'state sovereignty' (IIED et al, 2006). They focus on protecting only the intangible aspect of TK systems, abstracted from the web of elements which sustain them – bio-genetic resources, traditional territories, cultural and spiritual values and customary laws. Yet, in the holistic indigenous worldview, tangible and intangible heritage are inextricably linked and cannot be separated.

For indigenous communities, TK and genetic resources need to be sustained primarily for customary use by communities, and external users should also comply with customary norms relating to their use. As our research has found, customary laws promote ecological sustainability and social equity (Swiderska et al, 2006a). They also provide the basis for development that is endogenous, rather than externally driven, and are fundamental for indigenous self-determination. Yet, they are rarely recognized by governments or the judiciary, and need to be strengthened in order to address the growing threats to culture, biodiversity and traditional economies.

The project is using the holistic concept of 'Collective Bio-Cultural Heritage' as the common conceptual framework for action-research, which encompasses not only traditional knowledge, but knowledge systems as a whole. At a workshop in Cusco in May 2005, the project partners defined 'Collective Bio-Cultural Heritage' as:

> *Knowledge, innovations and practices of indigenous and local communities which are collectively held and are inextricably linked to: traditional resources and territories, local economies, the diversity of genes, varieties, species and ecosystems, cultural and spiritual values, and customary laws shaped within the socio-ecological context of communities.*[2]

As a mixed group of indigenous and non-indigenous researchers (including natural scientists and lawyers), using an indigenous vision to guide the research brings important 'internal' capacity building within the group.

The above definition of Collective Bio-Cultural Heritage builds on a whole body of work by communities such as Quechua farmers in the Andean Potato Park; anthropologists such as Darrell Posey's work on Traditional Resource Rights; and various indigenous fora, for example the guidelines for the protection of indigenous heritage developed by Erica Daes of the UN-Working Group on

Indigenous Populations. Thus, it is not a new concept, but represents a renewed effort to promote holistic approaches for the protection of indigenous peoples' heritage, by the project partners and other indigenous organizations such as Call of the Earth/Llamado de la Tierra.[3] The UN Permanent Forum on Indigenous Issues (UNPFII) held a Technical Workshop on Indigenous Knowledge in Panama, September 2005, which recommended that 'the UNPFII should encourage further elaboration of the concept of "Collective Bio-cultural Heritage" as the framework for standard setting activities on indigenous traditional knowledge'.

While the term is increasingly appearing in international fora, there is still limited work on its application in practice. At a recent workshop in Panama, November 2007,[4] the project partners noted that the concept of bio-cultural heritage (BCH) has provided a very useful conceptual framework for action-research, on a number of levels:

- for understanding complex TK systems and the interconnections between their different components and how external factors affect them;
- for developing local tools for TK protection (e.g. community registers, access protocols, benefit-sharing agreements) that reflect and strengthen BCH linkages, the community vision and indigenous values;
- for communicating and collaborating with communities and their institutions;
- for communicating the community view of TK systems and genetic resources with policy makers and others;
- for developing the overall framework for action-research and organizing ideas so that they reflect indigenous perspectives – as the Peru study found, BCH is more useful than using pure ecology/biology or western concepts as it better reflects reality.

TK systems are complex as they are influenced by different interacting elements and by external conditions and changes (e.g. economic development) that affect their 'internal' dynamics. Thus, complexity theory may provide a useful tool for better understanding TK systems and the linkages between the different components of BCH. This requires an interdisciplinary approach (involving both TK and science). For example, as ANDES (Peru) has found, applying complexity theory to BCH registers also means including associated scientific knowledge, policy context and all the elements that can help prevent the loss of the TK/resource. The community view can provide the starting point and then science/other disciplines can be used to further understand the linkages between the different elements (knowledge, resources, landscapes, customary laws, etc).

A number of the project partners are working with communities to develop registers of TK and bio-resources that include sub-fields on the associated elements of BCH – cultural values, customary laws and landscapes – in order to strengthen the linkages. As the Kenya/Mijikenda case noted, the management of BCH, traditions and customary laws used to be more intimately connected – the BCH contributes to healing the divide brought about by modernization, religion, western education and marginalization of traditional institutions. In this and other cases, the registers are being developed using computerized databases. Planning software could also be applied to database registers for computer modelling to help analyse/understand TK systems, and provide a tool for landscape management as well as the protection and promotion of TK.[5]

Comparing ABS, IPR and customary law models

Over 11 UN agencies are carrying out activities on the protection, preservation and promotion of traditional knowledge, within their particular mandates and spheres of competency. While many valuable activities are underway, it is evident that there are also gaps in their alignment with indigenous peoples' perspectives, needs and aspirations. Most of the UN processes – with the exception of indigenous and human rights fora – address traditional knowledge separately from traditional resources and territories and customary laws, deal with TK issues within a paradigm of property, and marginalize the ancestral rights-holders from decision making (IIED et al, 2006).

The CBD's ABS framework recognizes the sovereign rights of states over natural resources and the authority of states to decide over the use of genetic resources. Although the principle of 'state sovereignty' is important in promoting equitable benefit sharing between countries, it is generally interpreted as government *ownership* of genetic resources, with the rights of other actors, notably indigenous and local communities, often unclear or unrecognized. The CBD only requires the prior informed consent (PIC) of state parties for access to genetic resources, and not of indigenous and local communities. Thus, it separates rights over natural and genetic resources, which are 'owned' by the state, and rights to traditional knowledge, which are 'owned' by indigenous and local communities. Yet many genetic resources originate from indigenous territories, even if they are now held *ex situ* (in botanic gardens, Consultative Group on International Agricultural Research (CGIAR) centres, etc.) and some, such as traditional crop varieties, are themselves the innovations of indigenous farmers.

Given the obligation on states to facilitate access to genetic resources, the ABS framework effectively facilitates access by outsiders (e.g. companies and researchers) to community resources, whether held *in situ* or *ex situ*. Addressing customary laws and traditional resource rights in this framework would imply a requirement for PIC of indigenous communities for the use of bio-genetic resources from their territories, a reciprocal or two-way access framework that also facilitates access to genetic resources by communities, and an emphasis on ensuring continued access to resources for customary use by communities.

The FAO Treaty on Plant Genetic Resources for Food and Agriculture has also adopted the CBD's ABS framework. As with the CBD, it separates genetic resources from the customary laws of indigenous communities that govern their access and use, and ensure continued access to these resources for food security, health, poverty reduction and cultural and spiritual life.

The World Intellectual Property Organisation's (WIPO) Inter-Governmental Committee on Genetic Resources, Traditional Knowledge and Folklore has developed useful guiding principles for policies for the Protection of Traditional Knowledge.[6] However, being situated within an IPR body and composed mainly of representatives from national patent offices, its work has a distinct leaning towards existing IPR models. Even though the recognition of customary laws is amongst the issues being discussed, a number of parties continue to emphasize the need for protection of traditional knowledge to be consistent with IPR standards, which largely separate traditional knowledge from the cultural and spiritual values that establish its collective ownership.

While ABS and IPR regimes are essentially commercially oriented, customary laws relating to the protection of TK and bio-resources often have a strong spiritual character. Most customary rules and principles have their roots in the long and continuous use of natural resources in a locality. The environment shapes livelihoods and cultural and spiritual identity. Unlike the western concept of law, 'customary laws' include values and practices that are upheld/practised by society but are not bound by law, as well as some which take on the force of law over time (IIED and Fundacion Dobbo Yala, 2007). They are often based on fundamental values of respect for nature or Mother Earth, social equity and harmony, and serving the common good. Traditional knowledge and resources are seen as collective ancestral heritage that no individual can own as they are believed to come from God (Swiderska et al, 2006a).

Three key Andean customary principles or values were identified, which were found to be very similar for all the other studies:

1   *reciprocity*: what is received has to be given back in equal measure; it encompasses the principle of equity, and provides the basis for exchanges between humans, and with Mother Earth;
2   *duality*: everything has an opposite that complements it; behaviour cannot be individualistic;[7]
3   *equilibrium*: refers to balance and harmony, in both nature and society – for example respect for nature and resolving conflicts. Equilibrium needs to be observed in applying customary laws, all of which are essentially derived from this principle (Swiderska, et al, 2006a).

The core idea of customary law is *sharing*, even where cultural values are less strong (e.g. China). This supports protection of TK from loss, but might appear to go against protection from misappropriation. However, the customary practice of sharing helps to protect TK rights by strengthening community commons (Swiderska, 2006; IIED and Fundacion Dobbo Yala, 2007).

Customary laws are usually orally held rather than written down or codified, which is important for maintaining flexibility. The best use of customary laws is to develop local tools and practical mechanisms to protect TK – that strengthen customary laws in practice – because customary laws are associated with practices and are dynamic. But in order to be recognized externally, some elements of customary law may have to be written down. A key challenge is how to move from an oral to a written paradigm without losing adaptability and meaning – writing down customary law is 'like putting it in the freezer' (A. Argumedo, personal communication). Furthermore, customary laws and practices may not exist for a particular purpose, for example regulating external access to bio-resources, which means that derivatives may need to be identified to apply to a new situation, based on underlying customary values/principles, and established community practices for access to resources, distribution of wealth/benefits, etc.

'Collective bio-cultural heritage' as the basis for TK protection

Having emerged from a community context, the concept of collective bio-cultural heritage reflects the holistic worldview of indigenous peoples. It addresses biodiversity and culture together, rather than separating them; recognizes collective as opposed to individual rights; and places them in the framework of 'heritage' as opposed to 'property'. It explicitly recognizes that the heritage of indigenous peoples includes biological resources and traditional territories, and not only TK and culture (IIED et al, 2006).

The concept emphasizes the need to protect rights not only to traditional knowledge, but to all the interlinked components of knowledge systems – including bio-genetic resources, landscapes, cultural and spiritual values, and customary laws and institutions. It therefore sets out a framework to develop mechanisms to protect traditional knowledge that are holistic and based on human rights, including rights to land and natural resources, and the right to self-determination. The concept also emphasizes the need for the restitution of rights over indigenous heritage that has been taken away.

Collective bio-cultural heritage offers much potential for addressing the gaps in existing initiatives on TK protection at international, national and local levels. It identifies core elements, which could provide the basis for a common international policy, while allowing flexibility for approaches to be adapted to diverse local needs and contexts (IIED et al, 2006).

At the local level, the establishment of indigenous-controlled Community Conserved Area – or 'Indigenous Bio-Cultural Heritage Areas' – offers a means to protect indigenous knowledge *in situ*, as part of indigenous culture and territories. Using this model, the protection of indigenous knowledge is achieved through: the recognition of collective land rights; the strengthening of community-based management of natural resources, biodiversity and knowledge; strengthening of cultural and spiritual values; strengthening of customary laws and institutions; and strengthening local economies and poverty reduction. Thus, protection of BCH provides a means of preventing the loss of TK as well as protecting indigenous rights, under a system of community stewardship. For many rural communities, protecting TK from loss is the main priority, hence mechanisms to protect TK from misappropriation must address this also. The concept establishes not only rights, but also the *responsibility* of indigenous peoples to conserve their heritage and transmit it to future generations. Furthermore, it emphasizes development processes that are based on local knowledge and leadership, and are endogenous as opposed to externally driven.

Andes (Peru) together with Quechua farmers are using this concept as a guiding framework to shape a range of responses for TK protection. These include the establishment of an Andean Potato Park as an Indigenous Bio-Cultural Heritage Area; development of a web-based multimedia community bio-cultural register (using open-source software); application of collective trade marks to bio-cultural products; an agreement for repatriation of, and reciprocal access to, potato varieties with a CGIAR centre (the International Potato Centre (CIP)); and an inter-community agreement for equitable benefit sharing based on customary laws.[8] These two agreements are legal contracts and therefore provide a mechanism for the recognition of customary law in formal law. Furthermore, the return of lost varieties will restore associated TK, practices and beliefs (e.g. traditional recipes and rituals). Over 500 traditional varieties have been returned to the communities of the Potato Park, which will be shared widely amongst the 5000 residents of the park based on reciprocity and open access, to improve community nutrition and health; as well as helping to generate revenue (e.g. through the traditional restaurant). The CIP has also agreed to prevent any patents from being taken on the potato varieties obtained from the park (hence 'repatriating' them).

By engaging the six communities of the park to develop responses for the park as a whole, the research process is helping to strengthen collective organization and control of bio-cultural heritage as community commons in the face of multiple external threats. Customary laws and the search for legal pluralism are at the heart of this endeavour. They are being used to guide all the activities in the park so that the communities can defend their resource rights and take advantage of development opportunities without losing their cultural values that sustain biodiversity and livelihoods. Similarly, the other studies have also found that linking TK/BCH and economy, through value addition, marketing, etc. is critical to generating incentives for their conservation. Using the BCH concept to guide such market-based responses helps to maintain the indigenous value framework.

Conclusions and recommendations for the protection of indigenous knowledge

1   There is a need for an entirely new approach. Sui generis systems for protecting the knowledge, innovations and practices of indigenous and local communities should not be consistent with existing IP models that protect individual rights and whose objectives are exclusively commercial.[9] Instead, they should be tailored to the distinct characteristics of traditional knowledge and innovation processes. Even if new elements are incorporated into IP systems, the continuation, dynamic and adequate protection of TK cannot be guaranteed, since structurally many traditional societies do not respond to the western system, but have their own methods of economic, political, social and cultural articulation. Systems of free sharing and exchange of resources, collective custodianship and spiritual beliefs, which underpin traditional livelihoods and customary laws, are at odds with systems that protect commercial interests and thereby commodify TK. However, 'soft' IPRs that recognize collective rights (e.g. collective trade marks, copyright and geographical indications) may be useful to provide additional protection.

2   Sui generis systems should recognize the holistic character of traditional knowledge – that is its close linkages with biodiversity, traditional territories, cultural values and customary law, all of which are vital for sustaining TK systems. They should therefore protect the rights of indigenous and local communities *to all these components* of TK systems – or 'collective bio-cultural heritage'.

3   While the CBD recognizes national sovereignty over natural resources and the authority of states to decide over genetic resources, indigenous and human rights instruments recognize the rights of indigenous and local communities to own and decide over these resources. International human rights law recognizes the right of all peoples to freely dispose of their natural resources. ILO Convention 169 recognizes the rights of indigenous and tribal peoples to their natural resources and territories. The recently adopted UN Declaration on the Rights of Indigenous Peoples also recognizes indigenous rights to TK, GRs, territories and cultural heritage. Sui generis systems should therefore be consistent with indigenous and human rights instruments, and not only with the CBD and ABS regimes, so that the rights of indigenous and local communities over their bio-genetic resources are also recognized.

4   Active participation and leadership of indigenous and local communities is crucial. Sui generis systems, ABS regimes and other tools (e.g. biodiversity registers) at local, national and international levels should be developed and administered by and with indigenous and local communities.

5   The best way for communities to protect their rights over their knowledge and resources is at the local level – where they can directly control and safeguard their resources. Community-based natural resource management, together with secure land tenure, provides a means to strengthen governance

and control of natural resources, maintain traditional knowledge, conserve biodiversity and improve livelihoods. For example, through the establishment of community-controlled 'Indigenous Bio-Cultural Heritage Areas'.

6   Protecting TK requires the use of markets, databases, strengthening natural resource management systems/commons – not just policy and law. Linking TK/BCH and economy (e.g. through value addition) is critical to generating incentives for conserving it. Using BCH to guide such activities can help to ensure that an indigenous value framework is maintained. Benefit sharing needs to be promoted from all external use of community GRs and TK (not just use by foreign companies). National institutions in different sectors should also recognize and reward the contribution of community TK and genetic resources – for example the role of traditional healers in health care, and of farmers in plant breeding and participatory plant breeding.

7   ABS systems should not only focus on facilitating access to community resources, but also on facilitating access by communities to resources in *ex situ* collections. Vast collections of traditional varieties were made in the 1950s and 1960s, and are now held by universities, companies, etc., yet communities are rarely allowed access. With genetic erosion caused by modern agriculture, development, etc., many communities need to restore diversity to cope with climate change. Strengthening TK and BCH as a whole is important for adaptation to climate change. Adaptation depends not only on local genetic diversity, but on traditional knowledge and practices that enhance diversity and enable communities to cope with environmental stress.

8   The customary laws and authorities of indigenous and local communities should be recognized in policies for ABS and TK protection, including in determining rights over resources, procedures for PIC and equitable benefit sharing. While customary laws vary considerably between different communities, there are strong commonalities in underlying customary principles or values – such as equilibrium, duality and reciprocity. Such principles should form the basis for sui generis systems at all levels. Given that TK and GRs are often shared freely between communities, even across borders, the need for collective rights, collective decision making and benefit sharing amongst neighbouring communities should be recognized.

9   The international regime on ABS should fully recognize and protect the rights of indigenous and local communities to their knowledge, genetic resources and territories, and be developed and administered in close collaboration with them, rather than being a government-centric framework where the local custodians of genetic resources loose out. The current process needs to be broadened to enable representatives of indigenous and local communities to participate fully in the decision-making process.

10 More supportive policy frameworks are also needed across a range of 'sectors' – conservation, agriculture, health, education, economic sectors, trade and IPRs. Currently these sectors largely undermine TK and bio-culturally diverse production systems.

The UNPFII is uniquely placed to take a leading role in developing a global system for the protection of collective bio-cultural heritage. Unlike most other UN organizations addressing TK protection, the forum aims to promote the well-being of indigenous peoples, with the active participation of indigenous peoples as well as governments. First and foremost, the stewardship role of indigenous people and provides an opportunity for putting forward proposals to initiate such a process. Such a process could entail regional consultations with indigenous peoples on the concept of bio-cultural heritage and mechanisms for its protection, under the leadership of indigenous organizations.

Notes

1. Meaning unique or 'of its own kind'.
2. Protecting Community Rights over Traditional Knowledge: Implications of Customary Laws and Practices. Research Planning Workshop, Cusco, Peru, 20–25 May 2005, IIED and Andes, available at www.iied.org/NR/agbioliv/bio_liv_projects/protecting.html
3. See Aroha Te Pareake Mead, paper for UNPFII Workshop in Panama, September 2005: 'Emerging issues in Maori traditional knowledge: Can these be addressed by United Nations Agencies?'
4. Research Partners' Workshop in Panama, 19–23 November 2007, organized by IIED and Fundacion Dobbo Yala.
5. See note 4.
6. Revised Draft Provisions for the Protection of Traditional Knowledge: Policy Objectives and Core Principles, WIPO/GRTKF/IC/9/5, available at www.wipo.int/tk/en/consultations/draft_provisions/draft_provisions.html.
7. This Andean understanding of duality views two parts (e.g. male and female, mind and matter) as part of a unified whole; whereas in western science, duality means two separate parts.
8. For more information, see Graham Dutfield forthcoming: 'The Potato Park as a sui generis system for the protection of traditional knowledge'. See also reports from the project 'Protecting Community Rights over Traditional Knowledge', available at www.iied.org/NR/agbioliv/index.html.
9. Alejandro Argumedo, ANDES, unpublished report of the Peru case study, 2006.

References

IIED, Andes and Call of the Earth (2006) Towards a holistic approach to indigenous knowledge protection: UN activities, collective bio-cultural heritage and the UNPFII, Joint Statement at the Fifth Session of the UN Permanent Forum on Indigenous Issues, 15–26 May, New York, available at www.iied.org/NR/agbioliv

IIED and Funducion Dobbo Yala (2007) *Report of Research Partners Workshop* held in Panama, 19–23 November, International Institute for Environment and Development and Fundacion Dobbo Yala Panama

Swiderska, K. (2006) *Banishing the Biopirates: A New Approach to Protecting Traditional Knowledge*, IIED Gatekeeper Series 129, International Institute for Environment and Development (IIED), London

Swiderska, K., Argumedo, A., Pant, R., Vedavathy, S., Nellithanam, J., Munyi, P., Mutta, D., Song, Y., Heraclio, H., Barrios, H. (2006a) *Protecting Community Rights over Traditional Knowledge: Implications of Customary Laws and Practices*, interim report (2005–2006), International Institute for Environment and Development (IIED), London, available at www.iied.org/NR/agbioliv/documents/TK%20Interim%20report-23%20Nov.pdf

Swiderska, K., Argumedo, A., Pant, R., Vedavathy, S., Nellithanam, J., Munyi, P., Mutta, D., Song, Y., Heraclio, H., Barrios, H. (2006b) *Protecting Community Rights over Traditional Knowledge*, folder on emerging findings, International Institute for Environment and Development (IIED), London

5

CLIMATE CHANGE,
BIODIVERSITY AND ECOSYSTEM
SERVICES

16

Adaptation to Climate Change and Livestock Biodiversity: Evidence from Kenya

Jane Kabubo-Mariara

Introduction

Livestock constitutes 47 per cent of the agricultural gross domestic product (GDP) and contributes over 12 per cent to total GDP in Kenya. Most of the production is, however, sustained by the arid to semi-arid lands (ASALs), which are estimated to support about 25 per cent of the nation's human population and slightly over 50 per cent of its livestock. The ASALs cover more than 80 per cent of the land in Kenya and are characterized by low, unreliable and poorly distributed rainfall, and are thus mainly used for extensive livestock production and wildlife. The country can be divided into seven agro-climate zones using a moisture index based on annual rainfall expressed as a percentage of potential evaporation (Sombroek et al, 1982). Areas with an index greater than 50 per cent have high potential for cropping and are designated zones I, II and III. These zones account for about 18 per cent of Kenya's land area. The semi-humid to arid regions (zones IV, V, VI and VII, referred to as ASALs) have indexes of less than 50 per cent and a mean annual rainfall of less than 1100mm. Ninety per cent of the arid and semi-arid areas lie below 1260m and mean annual temperatures range from 22°C to 40°C (Kabubo-Mariara and Karanja, 2006).

With the increased fragility of the ASALs, it has become increasingly difficult for the livestock sector to sustain production. It is estimated that the annual growth rate of livestock production in Kenya declined from 3.5 per cent in 1980–1990 to –1.3 per cent in 1990–2000. The largest decline was in cattle (from 3.3 per cent to –1.6 per cent), while the growth rate of sheep and goat production declined from 4.0 per cent to –0.7 per cent. It is estimated that production of other species (chicken, pigs, camels, etc.) recorded increased growth rates. Trends in annual production of some animal products also recorded increased growth rates while others remained constant. Production of all meat products stagnated at 2.2 per cent in the two periods, springing from a rise in the growth rate of beef and pig and a decline in mutton, goat and poultry production. Milk and egg production also recorded declining growth rates (FAO, 2005).

Although the above changes are not due to climate change, more adverse effects are expected from climate change. There is increased evidence that it is getting hotter and there is also enough scientific evidence to show that any significant change in climate on a global scale will affect local agriculture and therefore the world's food supply (Houghton et al, 2001). The highest damages from climate change are predicted to be in the agricultural sector in sub-Saharan Africa because the region already endures high heat and low precipitation and also because of the semi-arid nature of a large portion of the continent, frequency of droughts and scarcity of water. In Kenya, global circulation models predict that global warming will lead to increased temperatures of up to 8.7°C and cause variability of rainfall by up to 34 per cent by the year 2100 (Strzepek and McCluskey, 2006). From these predictions, the two extreme climate events that may adversely affect the agricultural sector are drought (crop water stress leading to declining yields) and flooding (resulting in water logging) in both the arid and semi-arid lands and the high potential areas. The ASALs will, however, bear the largest impact of global warming (Galvin et al, 2001). Water resources in the country are most vulnerable in the ASALs where severity of drought and floods is expected to increase, while the already strained ground water resources in the coastal regions will be most vulnerable in the future (Kabubo-Mariara and Karanja, 2007). In addition to the predicted climate change scenarios, unpredicted climate events such as high frequency of flooding may still occur.

Climate can affect livestock both directly and indirectly and climate shocks can have devastating effects among the poor (Luseno et al, 2003; McPeak, 2006). Direct effects from air, temperature, humidity, wind speed and other climate factors influence animal performance: growth, milk production, wool production and reproduction (Houghton et al, 2001). Indirect effects include climatic influences on the quantity and quality of feedstuffs such as pasture, forage, grain and the severity and distribution of livestock diseases and parasites (Seo and Mendelsohn, 2006a). Adaptation options and other strategies for farmers to reduce the adverse impact of global warming are therefore crucial, more so in the ASALs. In Kenya, however, climatic uncertainty and drought as well as environmental changes driven by shifts in land use patterns have seriously diminished the ability of livestock-dependent communities to cope using traditional strategies (Kabubo-Mariara, 2005). Both risk minimization and loss management strategies are therefore quite crucial to counter the expected damage from global warming. Mixed crop livestock enterprises, holding diverse portfolios of livestock species and the introduction of more drought resistant livestock species are some of the most important forms of adaptation of livestock management to counter the risks and losses occasioned by climate change (Kabubo-Mariara, 2008a, 2008b).

Against the above background, this chapter contributes to the limited empirical evidence on the impact of and adaptation to climate change by examining the impact of climate change on livestock production and choice of livestock biodiversity in Kenya. The chapter further simulates the expected effect of various long-term climate change scenarios on livestock production and management based on different atmosphere-ocean global circulation Models (AOGCMs).

The rest of the chapter is organized as follows. The next section presents climate change predictions based on AOGCMs and Special Report on Emissions (SRES) scenarios and is adapted from Kabubo-Mariara (2008c). The next section presents the methods of analysis, while the following section briefly presents the data types and sources; and the next presents the results; these three sections draw heavily from Kabubo-Mariara, (2008a, 2008b). The final section presents the conclusions.

AOGCMs and climate change scenarios

The IPCC predicts emission scenarios on the basis of complex climate models. A range of scenarios of future greenhouse gases and aerosols emissions have been developed based on certain assumptions of population and economic growth, land use, technological change and energy availability (Houghton et al, 2001). Although there are a wide range of Special Report on Emissions Scenarios (SRES), only A2 and B2 have been integrated by many AOGCMs because of the assumptions on which each is based.[1] These scenarios represent a range of equally plausible future climates (expressed as anomalies of the baseline 1961–1990 climate) with differences attributable to the different climate models used and to different emission scenarios that the world may follow. For Kenya, 10 scenarios are derived by using five different models Commonwealth Scientific and Industrial Research Organisation model (CSIRO2), Hadley Centre coupled model (HADCM3), coupled general circulation model (CGCM2), European Centre Hamburg model (ECHAM) and parallel climate model (PCM)[2] in conjunction with two different emission scenarios (A2 and B2) (Strzepek and McCluskey, 2006). Strzepek and McCluskey obtained climate change estimates for Kenya between 2000 and 2100 by using the two scenarios to modify real-time climate information. In each scenario, climate values at the Global Resources Information Database (GRID) cell level were summed to predict climate change.

The predicted temperature and precipitation for the period 2000–2100 are presented in Table 16.1. Table 16.2 shows the predicted decadal average changes in annual climate variables for 2050 and 2100, relative to the year 2000. In reality, the predictions for precipitation can be positive or negative because some regions are expected to gain in terms of rainfall but others are expected to lose (Kabubo-Mariara and Karanja, 2006). For instance, the CGCM2-A2 scenario predicts that precipitation could increase in some regions by 6 per cent but fall in others by 6 per cent. The figures for temperatures are predicted increases in degrees Celsius. The highest predicted global warming impacts are from the HADCM3 and

Table 16.1 *Climate predictions of AOGCMs and SRES for 2000–2100*

			2000	2020	2050	2080	2100
SRES	Model	Temp.(°C)					
A2	CSIRO		21.81	23.59	25.24	27.93	29.92
	CGCM2		21.81	23.41	24.94	27.43	29.23
	ECHAM		21.81	23.27	24.78	27.26	29.07
	HADCM		21.81	23.69	25.52	28.50	30.66
	PCM		21.81	22.98	24.10	25.91	27.19
B2	CSIRO		21.81	23.77	25.41	27.03	28.09
	CGCM2		21.81	23.31	24.56	25.76	26.55
	ECHAM		21.81	23.32	24.63	25.91	26.75
	HADCM		21.81	23.80	25.48	27.08	28.13
	PCM		1.81	23.07	24.07	25.01	25.60
		Precip.(mm)					
A2	CSIRO		82.92	87.68	91.23	97.20	101.63
	CGCM2		82.92	84.70	85.76	87.66	89.16
	ECHAM		82.92	88.01	92.44	99.74	105.04
	HADCM		82.92	87.73	90.85	95.93	99.61
	PCM		82.92	86.03	88.23	91.77	94.27
B2	CSIRO		82.92	86.06	87.78	89.48	90.61
	CGCM2		82.92	85.41	86.70	88.03	88.93
	ECHAM		82.92	89.51	94.71	99.76	103.08
	HADCM		82.92	86.78	89.05	91.25	92.68

Source: Computed from raw data provided by Strzepek and McCluskey, 2006.

Table 16.2 *Predicted decadal average changes in annual climate variables: 2050–2100*

	Precipitation (change, base = 100)									
	CGCM2		CSIRO2		ECHAM		HADCM3		PCM	
Year	2050	2100	2050	2100	2050	2100	2050	2100	2050	2100
A2-Scenarios	106	116	109	123	113	134	110	124	106	115
B2-Scenarios	104	109	105	109	116	129	108	115	106	110
	Temperature (increases °C)									
	CGCM2		CSIRO2		ECHAM		HADCM3		PCM	
Year	2050	2100	2050	2100	2050	2100	2050	2100	2050	2100
A2-Scenarios	3.0	7.4	3.4	8.2	2.8	7.2	3.6	8.7	2.2	5.4
B2-Scenarios	2.7	4.7	3.6	6.3	2.8	4.9	3.6	6.3	2.3	3.8

Source: Strzepek and McCluskey, 2006.

CSIRO scenarios, but the lowest are from the PCM. For precipitation, the highest predicted changes are from the ECHAM but the lowest are from the CGCM2 and the PCM. From the predicted scenarios, one can observe that temperatures are predicted to rise by between 2.2°C and 8.7°C, while precipitation is expected to vary by between 4 per cent and 34 per cent by the year 2100.

Methods of analysis

Impact of climate change on livestock values

We evaluate the impact of climate change on livestock incomes using the Ricardian approach (Mendelsohn et al, 1994). The Ricardian approach is a cross-sectional model that takes into account how variations in climate change affect net revenue or land value. The model has also been utilized to study the response of livestock values to climate change (Seo and Mendelsohn, 2006a; Kabubo-Mariara, 2008b) inspite of certain criticisms.[3] Following Seo and Mendelsohn (2006a), we start by assuming that the farmer maximizes net income by choosing which livestock to purchase and which inputs to apply:

$$Max \; \pi = P_{qj}Q_j(L_G,F,L,K,C,W,S) - P_G L_G - P_F F - P_L L - P_K K \quad (1)$$

where: π is net income, P_{qj} is the market price of animal j, (though optional, q is included to denote that this is the price of animals and thus to distinguish this price from other prices), Q_j is a production function for animal j, L_G is grazing land, F is a vector of feed, L is a vector of labour inputs, K is a vector of capital inputs, C is a vector of climate variables, W is available water, S is a vector of soil characteristics, P_G is price of grazing land, P_F is a vector of prices of each type of feeds, P_L is a vector of prices for each type of labour, P_K is the rental price of capital.

The farmer chooses the species j and the number of animals that maximize profits. The resulting net income can be defined as:

$$\pi^* = f(P_q,C,W,S,P_X,P_L,P_K) \quad (2)$$

The Ricardian function is derived from the profit maximizing level of Equation (2) and explains how profits change across all the exogenous variables facing a farmer. The change in welfare (ΔU) resulting from climate change from C_0 to C_1 can be measured using the Ricardian function as follows:

$$\Delta U = \pi^*(C_1) - \pi^*(C_0) \quad (3)$$

The Ricardian model treats a farmer as though he is an income generating entity. Seo and Mendelsohn (2006a) have shown that although this assumption fits large farms, it can be applied to small farms by addressing issues of valuation of household labour and own consumption.

The estimated model is specified as:

$$\pi = \alpha_0 + \alpha_1 T + \alpha_2 T^2 + \alpha_3 R + \alpha_4 R^2 + \alpha_5 Z + \varepsilon \quad (4)$$

where T and T^2 capture levels and quadratic terms for temperature, R and R^2 capture levels and quadratic terms for precipitation, Z is a vector of socio-economic variables and ε is a random disturbance term. The quadratic terms for temperature and precipitation are expected to capture the non-linear shape of the climate response function. With a negative linear term, when the quadratic term is positive, the net revenue function is U-shaped and the reverse yields a hill-shaped function.

Determinants of decision to manage livestock and choice of livestock biodiversity

To model the decision to hold livestock, we start by assuming that a livestock farmer chooses the outputs and inputs that maximize net revenue subject to the prices, climate and other external factors that he or she faces (Seo and Mendelsohn, 2006a; Kabubo-Mariara, 2008a). The farmer must first determine whether or not it is profitable to engage in livestock management and also choose the livestock biodiversity to manage.

Suppose the profit from managing livestock for farmer i is given by $\pi_i^* = X\beta - \varepsilon$ where X is a vector of regressors composed of climate and the socio-economic characteristics of the farmer. The disturbance, ε, is unknown to the econometrician but may be known to the farmer (the farmer is more likely to choose an animal that is most profitable (Seo and Mendelsohn, 2006b), but the cumulative distribution function (CDF) is a function $f(\varepsilon)$ that is known up to a finite parameter vector.

The profit maximizing farmer will then choose to keep livestock if $\pi_i^* > 0$ or $\varepsilon < X\beta$. The probability that this occurs, given X, is $P(\varepsilon < X\beta) = F(X\beta)$. The likelihood function can be defined as:

$$L = \prod_{\pi_i^* < 0} F(-\beta X) \prod_{\pi_i^* > 0} \left[1 - F(-\beta X)\right] \tag{5}$$

If $F(\varepsilon)$ is a standard logistic CDF, then the probability can be defined as

$$P_i = \frac{\exp(X\beta)}{1 + \exp(X\beta)} \tag{6}$$

If instead we assume that ε is $IN(0,\delta^2)$, the decision to hold livestock can be estimated using a probit model (Maddala, 1995). If we define y_i as a binary response variable, the probit model can be defined as:

$$P_i(y_i \neq 0 \,|X) = F(X\beta) \tag{7}$$

The farmer compares the profits from different livestock species in order to choose which one to adopt. The farmer has to determine whether a species is profitable. The more profitable the species, the more likely it is that the farmer will adopt it.

The data

The primary data on which this chapter is based was drawn from a sample of 722 households. The data were collected from 38 districts drawn from six out of eight provinces in Kenya between June and August 2004. The districts chosen captured variability in a wide range of agro-climatic conditions (rainfall, temperatures and soils), market characteristics (market accessibility, infrastructure, etc.) and agricultural diversity, among other factors. Each district was divided into agro-ecological zones and samples of three different farm types/sizes, large, medium and small, purposely chosen from each ecological zone. The data were collected using a common questionnaire designed jointly by the School of Forestry and Environmental Studies of Yale University and the Centre for Environmental Economics and Policy in Africa (CEEPA), University of Pretoria for 11 countries participating in the regional Global Environmental Facility/World Bank project.[4]

In addition to the household data, the study also makes use of satellite and ARTES (Africa rainfall and temperature evaluation system) climate data. The temperature data came from satellites that measure temperatures twice daily via a Special Sensor Microwave Imager mounted on US Defense Department satellites (Basist et al, 1998). The ARTES dataset was interpolated from weather stations by the National Oceanic and Atmospheric Administration based on ground station measurements of precipitation and minimum and maximum temperature (World Bank, 2003). The data were constructed from a base with data for each month of the survey year and for morning and evening. The monthly mean temperatures were estimated from approximately 14 years of data (1988–2003) and the mean monthly precipitation was estimated for 1960–1990 to reflect long-term climate change.

Empirical results

Descriptive statistics

In this subsection, we examine the sample characteristics of the key variables of interest: namely household level and climate variables.[5] The primary data suggests that only 8 per cent of all households in the sample specialized in livestock production, while 12 per cent of the households specialized in crop production. Mixed crop livestock farmers constituted 80 per cent of the sample (722 households). The key household variables of interest for this chapter include diversified livestock species held by farmers, costs associated with livestock inputs (including labour) and household characteristics. The data show that households hold a diversified portfolio of animal species, with cattle, chicken, goats and sheep forming the main livestock types. The major livestock types by average endowments and agro-ecological zone are presented in Table 16.3. The table shows that dairy cattle and chicken were reared by the largest percentage of households. Consequently, the main livestock products were milk and eggs. The data further revealed that although households located in low potential zones rely more on livestock than those in high-potential zones, there is significant livestock production in high potential zones as well, with dairy cattle, goats and chicken as the main species. Dairy cattle are much more important for households in high potential than those in low-potential zones, who keep relatively more beef cattle. Although sheep are reared by a relatively small number of households in high potential zones, these households keep much more sheep than their counterparts in low potential zones. Some farmers owned additional animals and species such as camels, donkeys, rabbits, ducks, turkeys, bees and fish. Large standard deviations across all livestock species reflect large disparities in livestock holding among farming households in Kenya.

In Table 16.4, we present the average sales of livestock products and prices. Imperfections in livestock markets make it difficult to obtain accurate prices of animals and products. For this reason, although the survey collected data on livestock prices from households, we used the median prices for each animal and livestock products in each district in order to make our prices as robust as possible. The results show that although relatively fewer households kept sheep compared to other livestock species, the highest sales of livestock products was from sheep.

In this study, net revenue is defined as gross revenue less total variable costs associated with livestock production (the cost of feed, hired labour, transportation, packaging, storage, veterinary). It is, however, important to caution that the estimated net values are rough estimates of the actual net worth because of several difficulties of measuring net livestock revenue: first, though farmers gave actual estimates of all costs, it is difficult to account accurately for the cost of livestock production because most inputs are not always traded in the market. Second, it is very difficult to measure the actual amount of land devoted to livestock production, more so in mixed cropping areas. Some households may also use common property resources for grazing, while others may rely on zero grazing especially for dairy cows. For this reason, we defined net revenue as revenue per total farmland in hectares due to the lack of a better measure. Third, there is a large non-marketed output of livestock products, which is valued at the prevailing market prices because the data suggest that households consume a large fraction of their output (Seo and Mendelsohn, 2006a).

The sample statistics for climate data are presented in Table 16.5. The long and short rains refer to the extended wet and dry conditions respectively. In Kenya, long rains fall between March and May and short rains between October and December. The extended rains seasons are, however, longer to cover the whole cropping season. Long rain crops planted in early March are harvested in August. Farms are then prepared and planted in September and the crops

Table 16.3 *Average livestock holdings by agro-ecological zone*

Livestock type	High potential zones			Medium and low potential zones			Full sample		
	% of Households	Mean	Std. Dev.	% of Households	Mean	Std. Dev.	% of Households	Mean	Std. Dev.
Beef cattle	9	337	965	14	926	4833	23	695	3822
Dairy cattle	29	399	2961	37	127	1224	66	247	2170
Bulls	6	23	93	9	40	217	15	34	180
Goats	23	491	2454	19	466	2412	42	479	2431
Sheep	13	626	3995	22	227	1137	35	375	2597
Pigs	3	10	45	3	4	14	6	7	32
Oxen	6	4	12	9	4	7	15	4	9
Chicken	30	66	260	36	27	90	66	45	188
Other	4	87	159	3	160	405	7	121	298

Table 16.4 *Annual livestock product sales and prices (US$)*

Variable	No. of households	Sales		Price (US$)	
		Mean	Std dev.	Mean	Std dev.
Milk (kg)	505	426.77	5593.00	0.26	0.04
Beef (kg)	15	29.52	45.46	1.62	0.15
Sheep (kg)	27	1180.56	6095.66	2.06	0.17
Goats (kg)	13	7.33	13.72	2.16	0.19
Chicken (kg)	24	961.83	2183.07	2.06	0.20
Eggs (number)	185	4.59	14.99	0.06	0.01
Wool (piece)	14	1.07	1.54	0.52	0.10
Leather (piece)	21	3.29	13.39	0.89	0.38
Other	37	290.47	601.12		

Table 16.5 *Sample statistics for temperatures and precipitation by season*

Season	Temperatures (°C)		Precipitation (mm/mo)	
	Mean	Std dev.	Mean	Std dev.
Fall (December–February)	19.29	2.67	88.80	41.45
Summer (March–May)	19.07	2.74	103.71	31.57
Winter (June–August)	18.50	2.36	62.40	40.82
Spring (September–November)	19.09	2.66	71.89	26.95
Annual average	18.99	2.58	84.53	18.60
Long rains (March–August)	19.33	2.73	90.90	34.97
Short rains (September–February)	18.65	2.46	81.27	23.71

harvested in February. In this chapter, the long rains season is therefore defined as March to August and the short rains season as September to February.

Impact of climate change on livestock production

Ricardian model regression results

In this section, we present the results for the impact of climate change on the net value of stock (all animals valued at mean prices) and also from the sale of livestock products. In addition to seasonal climate variables, we test for the impact of household size, age of household head and average education level. The Chow test results show that the overall models are stable at the 1 per cent level of significance, but the R^2 shows that the models explain only about 22 per cent of the total variation in net value of livestock (Table 16.6). Although this is quite low, it is consistent with most findings in cross-sectional studies.

The results show that climate variables have a large and significant impact on stocking in Kenya. The results indicate that high summer temperatures discourage livestock keeping while high winter temperatures are beneficial. Specifically, the response of net value of livestock to summer temperatures is U-shaped, but the response to winter temperatures is hill-shaped. The results support the usual situation in Kenya. Although the average summer temperatures in Kenya are quite modest at 19°C, the temperature can soar to more than 35°C in the arid and semi-arid zones, which are the main stocking areas. In years of extreme temperatures and droughts, farmers will be forced to reduce their stock levels or risk losing them altogether. Field observations indicated that high winter temperatures encourage growth of fodder and grass, holding precipitation constant and will therefore encourage farmers to increase their stocks. The hill-shaped relationship suggests that excess winter temperatures are, however, harmful to stocking levels. The results further show that climate exhibits a non-linear relationship with livestock production.

Table 16.6 *Ricardian regression estimates of the net value of livestock: seasonal model*

Variables	Climate only variable model	All variables model
Summer temperature	−478.2471	−483.0355
	[1.87]*	[1.95]*
Summer temperature squared	11.8038	11.3584
	[1.73]*	[1.73]*
Winter temperature	714.3908	711.6473
	[2.25]**	[2.33]**
Winter temperature squared	−17.8406	−17.0378
	[2.04]**	[2.05]**
Winter precipitation	41.036	35.3146
	[2.01]**	[1.70]*
Winter precipitation squared	−0.2193	−0.1904
	[2.02]**	[1.72]*
Spring precipitation	−82.2547	−71.1886
	[2.18]**	[1.90]*
Spring precipitation squared	0.4412	0.39
	[2.27]**	[2.03]**
Log of household size		−40.9314
		[0.53]
Age of household head		−4.6685
		[2.19]**
Average years of education of household members		5.6595
		[1.08]
Observations	722	722
R-squared	0.22	0.23
F(*,*)	38.81	30.59
Robust *t*-statistics in brackets		

Note: * Significant at 10%; ** significant at 5%; *** significant at 1%.

Winter precipitation exhibits a hill-shaped relationship with the net value of stock, implying that increased rainfall in winter is beneficial. The quadratic term, though negative, has a relatively small impact and suggests that excess winter precipitation will be harmful. Spring rainfall exhibits a U-shaped relationship with the net value of stock. The negative impact of the linear term implies that excess rainfall in spring would result in damage to the stocking rate function. This is consistent with findings by Seo and Mendelsohn (2006a), which show that livestock production in Africa is quite sensitive to changes in precipitation. This is also consistent with what has been observed in Kenya following excessively heavy rains. For instance, flash floods have caused the loss of livestock in Kenya in the past, while excess short rains towards late 2006 led to an outbreak of Rift Valley fever that caused livestock and human deaths in late 2006 and early 2007. The linear and quadratic terms show that, like temperature, precipitation exhibits a non-linear relationship with the net value of livestock.

The introduction of household characteristics affects the magnitudes and significance of the climate variables but the results are robust with the climate variable only model. We uncover no significant impact of household size and education on the net value of stocks. The age of the household head is, however, negatively and significantly correlated with net value of stocks, implying that controlling for climate change, older heads are likely to keep less livestock than their younger counterparts.

The regression results for net revenue from livestock sales are presented in Table 16.7. The results show that the models perform much poorer in terms of overall goodness of fit compared to the net value of livestock models. The models explain only about 5 per cent of the total variation in net revenue, but fit the data better than an intercept only model. The results are, however, robust with the model for net value of stocks. Summer temperatures exhibit a U-shaped relationship with net revenue, implying that excess summer temperatures will result in a negative response and thus a damage on livestock production. The response of net revenue to winter temperature is hill-shaped. The same intuition used to explain the impact of winter temperatures on the net value of animals can also be used here. High temperatures in winter encourage the growth of fodder and grass, which increases milk production, while stocks and prices of livestock and livestock products remain the same. The results also show that the impact of precipitation is consistent with the net value of livestock model. Specifically, winter precipitation exhibits a hill-shaped relationship, while spring rainfall exhibits a U-shaped relationship with net revenue. The results further show that climate exhibits a non-linear relationship with the net revenue from livestock flows. This supports the results of studies on the impact of climate change on animal husbandry in Africa (see Seo and Mendelsohn, 2006a, 2006b).

Table 16.7 *Ricardian regression estimates of the net sales of livestock products*

Variables	Climate only variable model	All variables model
Summer temperature	−13,833.68	−13,286.70
	[1.72]*	[1.67]*
Summer temperature squared	359.4537	352.9907
	[1.69]*	[1.66]*
Winter temperature	14,357.87	12,905.32
	[1.78]*	[1.66]*
Winter temperature squared	−356.7878	−329.8338
	[1.72]*	[1.63]
Winter precipitation	235.4268	168.1665
	[2.02]**	[2.02]**
Winter precipitation squared	−1.4331	−1.0497
	[1.98]**	[1.99]**
Spring precipitation	−501.4938	−391.7901
	[2.00]**	[2.01]**
Spring precipitation squared	3.1656	2.5068
	[2.03]**	[2.06]**
Log of household size		3.927.13
		[1.74]*
Age of household head		−7.8623
		[0.39]
Average years of education of household members		64.5347
		[0.68]
Observations	722	722
R-squared	0.06	0.06
F(*,*)	4.13***	7.69***
Robust *t*-statistics in brackets		

Note: * Significant at 10%; ** significant at 5%; *** significant at 1%.

Predicting impact of global warming on livestock values

We use the Ricardian model coefficients and respective variable means to project the impact of global warming on livestock incomes. The results for different AOGCM predictions are presented in Table 16.8. All models predict that global warming will have adverse effects on the net value of livestock. The largest losses are predicted from the HADCM and CSIRO models for both sets of SRES. The lowest losses are predicted from the PCM and CGCM models. The results are consistent with findings obtained by Seo and Mendelsohn (2006a, p31), for large farms, although the authors predicted much more modest losses and potential gains for small farms except from the PCM model (see Kabubo-Mariara, 2008b).

The simulated climate scenarios for net revenue (Table 16.9) suggest that global warming will result in gains in net revenue from livestock production. The results support findings by Seo and Mendelsohn (2006a, pp30, 32) who found

Table 16.8 *Predicted damage in net livestock value from different AOGCM scenarios*

Scenario				A2			B2	
Model	Year	Predicted net value	Loss (US$)	% Damage	Predicted net value	Loss (US$)	% Damage
CSIRO	2020	256	37	−13	262	31	−11
	2060	158	135	−46	181	112	−38
	2100	−132	425	−145	47	246	−84
CGCM	2020	275	18	−6	272	21	−7
	2060	203	90	−31	225	68	−23
	2100	−34	327	−112	149	144	−49
ECHAM	2020	259	34	−12	149	144	−14
	2060	174	119	−40	186	107	−37
	2100	−61	354	−121	99	194	−66
HADCM	2020	254	39	−13	257	36	−12
	2060	138	155	−53	169	124	−42
	2100	−201	494	−169	36	257	−88
PCM	2020	272	21	−7	269	24	−8
	2060	224	69	−23	233	60	−21
	2100	92	201	−69	182	111	−38

Note: *Base net value = US$292.90.

that, except for the PCM model, all other models predict increased livestock income from small farms but losses from large farms. The largest and lowest gains are predicted to spring from the CGCM and the PCM models respectively in the A2 scenarios, but from the CSIRO and ECHAM models respectively in the B2 scenarios. Increased net revenue in the face of the falling value of livestock may be due to livestock adaptation and a change in the species managed by households (Kabubo-Mariara, 2008a). Seo and Mendelsohn (2006b), for instance, predict that farmers in Africa may reduce the amount of beef cattle and chicken but increase the number of dairy cattle, goats and sheep per farm (Seo and Mendelsohn, 2006b, p37). The overall effect for all farm types is, however, a fall in the expected livestock income, although small farms were predicted to reduce the number of all other animals except beef cattle (Seo and Mendelsohn, 2006b, p37). A fall in net income per animal is also predicted (Seo and Mendelsohn, 2006b, p38).

The AOGCM simulations presented above only take into account increased precipitation combined with global warming. A sensitivity analysis that allows precipitation to fall shows that, initially, livestock farmers may gain in terms of the value of stock from increased temperatures combined with reduced precipitation (CSIRO model only) but, thereafter, losses set in. Similar simulations suggest that net revenues are predicted to fall with a fall in precipitation in the CSIRO model but increase for all other models.

Table 16.9 *Predicted damage in net livestock revenue from different climate scenarios (US$)*

Scenario		A2			B2		
Model	Year	Predicted net value	Loss (US$)	% Damage	Predicted net value	Loss (US$)	% Damage
CSIRO	2020	2236	607	37	2468	52	839
	2060	3202	1573	97	3526	116	1897
	2100	4815	3186	196	4589	182	2960
CGCM	2020	2376	747	46	2262	39	633
	2060	3536	1907	117	3056	88	1427
	2100	5378	3749	230	3826	135	2197
ECHAM	2020	2029	400	25	1932	19	303
	2060	2777	1148	70	2378	46	749
	2100	4052	2423	149	2839	74	1210
HADCM	2020	2288	659	40	2427	49	798
	2060	3393	1764	108	3474	113	1845
	2100	5412	3783	232	4449	173	2820
PCM	2020	2027	398	24	2043	25	414
	2060	2706	1077	66	2575	58	946
	2100	3774	2145	132	3075	89	1446

Note: *Base net value = US$1628.94.

Livestock management and biodiversity adaptation to climate change

Decision to engage in livestock management

In the previous section we have shown that livestock production is responsive to seasonal climate variations. Evidence also shows that, in addition, production is responsive to wet/dry conditions and annual climate variations (Kabubo-Mariara, 2008b). In this section, we model the impact of annual rather than seasonal climate variables on the decision to hold livestock because households need time to adapt their portfolio of livestock biodiversity as climate changes. For instance, a decision to switch from cattle to small ruminants resulting from climate change is a long-term decision that is likely to be affected more by annual rather than seasonal temperature variations. The results in Table 16.10 present the marginal effects of each variable on the likelihood of engaging in livestock production. The results indicate that climate change significantly affects livestock holding decisions. The Chow tests (Wald chi²) show that although the overall fit of the model is quite poor, the model fits the data better than the intercept only model. The individual results can be interpreted as follows: a 1°C change in the linear annual temperature will increase the probability of holding livestock by 0.38, but a similar change in the quadratic value will lead to a 0.009 decline in the probability of holding livestock. Further computations would be needed to derive the total marginal impact of temperature on the decision to hold livestock. All other probit results can be interpreted in the same manner. The results show that all climate variables have significant impacts on the decision to hold livestock. Further, the results also show that the livestock response to annual temperature is U-shaped but the response to precipitation is hill-shaped. Although the coefficients of the climate variables are significant in both models, the marginal effects are almost zero for the quadratic term. The results suggest that the probability of engaging in livestock production decreases up to some threshold with an increase in annual temperatures, then increases, but the reverse effect is observed for precipitation. The non-linear relationship between global warming and the decision to engage in livestock production suggests that farmers make adjustments to climate change as global warming rises. The marginal impacts of temperature are much higher than for precipitation.

The last column shows that the introduction of household characteristics increases the overall fit of the model by 4 per cent. The results suggest that larger households are more likely to engage in livestock production than smaller households. Although livestock production may not be labour intensive in pastoral regions, it is quite labour intensive in small holder farming where households have to spend time looking for fodder and other animal feed, due to the scarcity of pasture. Larger households will therefore be less labour constrained than their smaller counterparts. The age of the household head is positively

Table 16.10 *Probit model results (marginal effects) of whether or not to hold livestock*

Variables	Climate variable model	All variable model
Annual temperature	−0.3832	−0.3384
	[4.52]***	[4.17]***
Annual temperature squared	0.0093	0.0081
	[4.49]***	[4.11]***
Annual rainfall	0.0601	0.061
	[5.32]***	[5.60]***
Annual rainfall squared	−0.0003	−0.0004
	[5.40]***	[5.67]***
Log household size		0.1206
		[3.97]***
Age of household head		0.0021
		[2.66]***
Average years of education of household members		−0.0027
		[0.89]
Observations	722	722
Wald chi²(*)	34.26***	59.22***
Pseudo R-squared	0.0620	0.1056
Robust z statistics in brackets		

Note: * Significant at 10%; ** significant at 5%; *** significant at 1%.

correlated with the probability of engaging in livestock production. This could be explained by the fact that most rural dwellers who own land are the more elderly members of society and therefore have more resources to keep livestock than their off-springs (younger adults). These results are not uncommon in the literature (Dercon, 1998; Imai, 2003; Kabubo-Mariara, 2005).

Choice of livestock species

We further investigate the choice of livestock biodiversity to hold upon making the decision to engage in livestock production. The results focus on the decision to hold dairy and beef cattle, goats and sheep, chicken and all other livestock biodiversity combined (bulls, oxen, camel, pigs, etc.). The results (Table 16.11) suggest that the models fit the data quite well, and the Wald chi² tests show significant results for all individual probits. The overall fit of the models is, however, poor, which is not uncommon in cross-sectional data. The coefficients for the climate variables are all significant for the choice of cattle and chicken, but not consistent for the other livestock biodiversity.

The results suggest that global warming affects the choice of livestock biodiversity kept by households. The results are, however, complex and differ from species to species. The probability of holding dairy cattle exhibits

Table 16.11 *Probit model results for choice of livestock species*

Variables	Dairy cattle	Beef Cattle	Goats	Sheep	Chicken	Others
Annual temperature	-0.7956	0.2845	0.0456	0.157	-0.4905	-0.1286
	[6.01]***	[2.63]***	[0.31]	[1.21]	[3.74]***	[1.17]
Annual temperature squared	0.0181	-0.0063	0.0005	-0.0043	0.0116	0.0034
	[5.73]***	[2.45]**	[0.13]	[1.37]	[3.69]***	[1.28]
Annual rainfall	0.11	-0.057	0.0389	-0.0251	0.1172	0.0257
	[6.15]***	[3.59]***	[2.02]**	[1.36]	[6.37]***	[1.70]*
Annual rainfall squared	-0.0007	0.0003	-0.0002	0.0001	-0.0007	-0.0001
	[6.43]***	[3.68]***	[1.87]*	[1.11]	[6.31]***	[1.57]
Log household size	0.0971	0.1494	0.161	0.0678	0.0862	0.0962
	[1.78]*	[3.05]***	[2.53]**	[1.24]	[1.55]	[2.04]**
Age of household head	0.0006	0.003	0.0045	0.004	-0.001	0.0033
	[0.41]	[2.45]**	[2.89]***	[2.76]***	[0.72]	[2.67]***
Household's average years of education	0.0074	-0.0031	-0.0125	-0.0103	0.0117	-0.0124
	[1.50]	[0.65]	[2.20]**	[2.02]**	[2.31]**	[2.94]***
Number of observations	722	722	722	722	722	722
Wald chi² (7)	58.15	46.25	96.77	37.52	37.40	24.06
Pseudo R-squared	0.07	0.06	0.11	0.04	0.05	0.03

Notes: Robust z statistics in brackets.

* Significant at 10%; ** significant at 5%; *** significant at 1%.

a U-shaped relationship with annual temperature, but a hill-shaped relationship with precipitation. The marginal effects of individual variables suggest that temperature changes are the key drivers of the decision to hold dairy cattle. The results are consistent with Seo and Mendelsohn (2006a) who find an inverted U-shaped response of dairy cattle to summer temperature. Household size has a positive impact on the probability of holding dairy cattle but we uncover no significant impact of the age and education variables. The impact of climate variables on the probability of holding beef cattle is the reverse of the impact on dairy cattle. The probability of keeping beef cattle exhibits a hill-shaped relationship with annual temperatures, while annual precipitation exhibits a U-shaped relationship. The largest marginal effect is from the linear term of annual temperature but this is quite modest compared to the impact on the decision to hold dairy cattle. The impact of the linear precipitation variable for beef cattle supports previous studies on drought and livestock in Africa (Swinton, 1988; Seo and Mendelsohn, 2006a, 2006c). A unit increase in annual rainfall would increase the probability of selecting beef cattle by 0.11.

The different effects of global warming on the probability of engaging in dairy and beef cattle management supports findings on droughts and consumption smoothing, which have shown that households may or may not adjust herd size to droughts depending on prevailing factors (Fafchamps et al, 1998; Kazianga and Udry, 2004). Fafchamps et al (1998) has also shown that two distinct forces are capable of inducing producers to hold onto livestock even when they anticipate losing many of their animals to global warming: (i) the desire to smooth consumption when livestock make an essential contribution to household income and other assets are not available; and (ii) the desire to maximize profits when demand for livestock products is inelastic. Kazianga and Udry (2004), however, find that households in Burkina Faso rely almost exclusively on self-insurance in the form of livestock sales to smooth out consumption.

Goats and sheep are less responsive to climate change than cattle. Although the probability of holding goats and sheep shows a hill-shaped relationship with temperature, we uncover no significant impact and the marginal effects are quite modest. Annual precipitation exhibits a hill-shaped relationship with the probability of engaging in goat rearing. Both the linear and quadratic terms are significant but the marginal probabilities are very low. None of the climate variables are significant for the sheep model. Although this result does not support findings on the impact of climate change and livestock adaptation in a group of African countries (Seo and Mendelsohn, 2006a, 2006c), it seems to support literature that argues that small ruminants are more adaptable to harsh agro-climatic conditions than cattle (Kabubo-Mariara, 2008a). Only the age of the household head and the household's average level of education significantly affect the probability of holding sheep. Age is particularly significant, although the marginal effect is quite low. The elderly without labour support may turn to sheep (and goat) rearing because these activities are less labour demanding.

Education is negatively correlated with the probabilities of rearing both sheep and goats. This supports studies that suggest that more educated farmers are likely to keep less livestock than their less educated counterparts because education broadens alternative income earning opportunities (Kabubo-Mariara, 2008a). The probability of rearing chicken is significantly affected by all climate variables and the marginal effects are quite high compared to the impact on other livestock biodiversity. Annual temperatures exhibit a U-shaped relationship with this decision choice, but rainfall exhibits a hill-shaped relationship. Education is positively correlated with the decision to hold chicken, implying that although education may give the household alternative income earning opportunities outside livestock, some basic skills are required. The decision to hold other livestock types does not seem to be sensitive to climate change, except for rainfall, whose linear term is significant. The results imply a hill-shaped relationship between rainfall and the probability of holding other livestock types.

Predicting the impact of global warming on choice of livestock biodiversity

We use the probit regression coefficients for choice of livestock biodiversity and variable means to predict the impact of global warming on livestock choice. We examine a set of climate change scenarios predicted by atmosphere-ocean general circulation models (AOGCMs). These climate scenarios reflect the A1 scenarios in the IPCC's Special Report on Emissions Scenarios (SRES) (IPCC, 2001) from the following models: Canadian Climate Center (CCC), Center for Climate System Research (CCSR) and parallel climate model (PCM) (Kurukulasuriya et al, 2006, Seo and Mendelsohn, 2006a). In 2100, PCM predicts a 2°C increase, CCSR a 4°C increase and CCC a 6°C increase in temperature in Africa. For precipitation, PCM predicts an average 10 per cent increase, CCC a 10 per cent decrease and CCSR a 30 per cent average decrease in rainfall in Africa. Although the scenarios may not have a uniform impact across all Africa, and differ from the scenarios presented earlier in Table 16.2, they cover the range of all the general circulation models that have been found to give reasonable climate forecasts for Kenya (Kabubo-Mariara and Karanja, 2006; Kabubo-Mariara, 2008a, 2008b).

To get the new climate for each district, we added the predicted change in temperature from each AOGCM to the benchmark values, and then evaluated the impact on the probability of choosing different livestock species. We also adjusted benchmark precipitation by the predicted percentage to get the new precipitation levels. The results (Table 16.12) suggest that global warming will reduce the probability of keeping dairy cattle. The highest fall will be from warming predicted by the CCSR model (43 per cent and 23 per cent from rainfall and temperature changes respectively). The CCSR also predicts the highest combined decline in the probability of holding dairy cattle. At low levels of temperature, the choice of

Table 16.12 *Change in probabilities of selecting livestock biodiversity from different climate scenarios*

Climate change scenario	Dairy cattle	Beef cattle	Goats	Sheep	Chicken	Other livestock
PCM: +2°C temperature	−20.51	26.50	30.44	−5.92	−8.88	12.68
CCSR: +4°C temperature	−23.05	33.88	62.31	−17.68	−6.54	43.19
CSIRO2: +6°C temperature	−12.34	21.91	91.80	−33.74	4.17	90.80
PCM: +10% rainfall	−12.78	21.99	2.52	−8.68	−6.48	3.01
CCC: −10% rainfall	−3.00	12.10	−7.32	14.33	−10.57	−8.07
CCSR: −30% rainfall	−43.26	110.27	−35.57	59.15	−53.25	−36.84
PCM: +2°C tempt & +10% rainfall	−24.81	51.79	31.93	−14.06	−12.81	16.50
CCSR: +4°C tempt & −30% rainfall	−51.05	132.95	87.47	38.61	−54.52	−3.20
CCC: +6°C tempt & −10% rainfall	−10.27	21.92	26.79	−22.39	2.08	80.72
Base probabilities	0.66	0.22	0.41	0.35	0.65	0.22

livestock biodiversity seems to be more sensitive to temperature than to precipitation changes. The predicted changes in probabilities of holding beef cattle are exactly opposite those of dairy cattle. The probability of holding beef cattle increases as global warming rises. This implies that with warming, households substitute dairy for beef cattle. Consistent with the results for dairy cattle, the highest predicted changes are from the CCSR model. Unlike the predictions for cattle, goat, sheep, chicken and other livestock show mixed results. Increased temperatures and precipitation increase the probability of holding goats and other livestock, but decrease the probability of holding sheep and chicken. However, higher temperatures increase the probability of keeping chicken. The predictions imply interesting scenarios in the response of different animal biodiversity to climate change. Dairy cattle and beef portray a reversed non-linear response to changes in temperature and precipitation. Goats, chicken and other livestock portray a rising response to changes in temperature but sheep have a falling response. The response to changes in precipitation is falling for goats, chicken and other livestock but rising for sheep. The combined impacts suggest a difference in the response of livestock biodiversity to changes in temperature and precipitation. For instance, it seems that dairy cattle are much more responsive to changes in temperature than to precipitation, but the reverse is the case for beef cattle.

Conclusion

Global warming is a matter of grave concern, especially in low income countries that depend on the natural resource base, more so rain-fed agriculture. In Kenya, global circulation models predict that global warming will lead to increased temperatures of about 4°C and cause a variability of rainfall by up to 20 per cent by the year 2100. It is also predicted that, although drought and flooding are two extreme climate events that may adversely affect the agricultural and livestock sectors countrywide, the ASALs will bear the largest impact of global warming, which will thus lead to devastating impacts for the livestock sector.

This chapter examines the impact of climate change on livestock production and choice of livestock biodiversity in Kenya. The analysis is based on primary data collected from a sample of 722 households from 38 districts in 2004. The primary data are enriched with secondary climate data, which reflect long-term climate change in Kenya. The impact of climate change on livestock production is analysed using the Ricardian approach. The probability of engaging in livestock management is analysed using the probit model and is based on the entire sample. For households engaged in livestock management, the choice of species from feasible livestock biodiversity is analysed using the probit model. The chapter further examines the impact of different climate change scenarios predicted by AOGCMs on livestock production and also on the choice of livestock species.

The Ricardian model results show that livestock production in Kenya is highly sensitive to climate change and that there is a non-linear relationship between climate change and net livestock incomes. The results further show that the response of net value of livestock to summer temperatures is U-shaped, but the response to winter temperatures is hill-shaped. We also find a hill-shaped response of net value of livestock to winter precipitation but a U-shaped response to spring precipitation. The response of net revenue to summer temperatures is U-shaped, suggesting that excess summer temperatures will result in a negative response and thus cause damage to livestock production. The response to winter temperature change is hill-shaped. The predicted impacts of climate change from AOGCMs suggest that a combined impact of increased temperature and precipitation will result in a reduced net value of livestock, reflecting livestock biodiversity adaptations. Warming makes it less profitable to keep dairy and beef cattle (high-value animals), but favours small ruminants. Predictions for changes in net revenue, however, suggest gains in the value of livestock flows resulting from a combined effect of rising temperatures and increased precipitation. This is attributable to an intensified rearing of diversified livestock species by small farmers (Kabubo-Mariara, 2008a).

The probit model results for the decision to engage in livestock management show that the response of the probability of engaging in livestock management to variations in annual temperature is U-shaped but the response to changes in precipitation is hill-shaped. The difference in the curvature of the response functions reflects the expected relative magnitudes of seasonal climate variations (Kabubo-Mariara, 2008a). The non-linear relationship between climate variables and the decision to engage in livestock production suggests that farmers adapt their livestock management decisions (by varying the likelihood of keeping livestock) to climate change.

The results for choice among livestock biodiversity suggest that global warming affects livestock adaptation in Kenya. The marginal impacts of temperature are much higher than the impacts of precipitation. The response of the choices of dairy cattle, chicken and other livestock exhibit a U-shaped relationship with temperature, but a hill-shaped relationship with precipitation. The reverse is observed for beef cattle, goats and sheep. The results strongly suggest that with increased warming, farmers will move from dairy to beef cattle farming. Goats are less responsive to climate variations than all other livestock species irrespective of the estimation approach. Goats and sheep are less responsive to temperature change than cattle, implying that they can withstand harsher climate conditions than cattle. The predicted probabilities of adopting different livestock species suggest that increased temperatures lead to adjustments in the decision to keep dairy cattle. When it becomes extremely hot, farmers may opt to move towards beef cattle and reduce the demand for dairy cattle. The probability of choosing goats and other livestock (oxen, bulls, camels, bees, pigs and rabbits) also increases with global warming while the demand for sheep rearing declines. The corresponding impact of warming through reduced rainfall also leads to substitution between dairy and beef cattle, and also goats and other livestock instead of sheep. Dairy cattle are much more sensitive to rising temperatures than to falling precipitation.

Notes

1. The A1 scenario assumes very rapid economic growth and the rapid introduction of new and more efficient technologies among other assumptions. The A2 and B2 scenarios assume that per capita economic growth and technological change are more fragmented and slower than in the A1 scenario (IPCC, 2001). A2 and B2 are therefore more realistic than the A1 for Kenya and are likely to give more accurate results than the A1 scenario.

2. CGCM2 is a Canadian model, CSIRO2 is an Australian model, ECHAM is a German model, HADCM3 is a British model, PCM is a parallel climate model.

3. See Mendelsohn et al, 1994; Seo and Mendelsohn, 2006a and Kabubo-Mariara, 2008b for the advantages and limitations of the Ricardian model.

4. The other countries are South Africa, Zambia, Zimbabwe, Ethiopia, Egypt, Ghana, Niger, Cameroon, Burkina Faso and Senegal (Dinar et al, 2006).

5. The choice of variables used in this paper was limited by the available data and I acknowledge that there are a number of other factors that could be important for livestock choice and productivity. Specifically, soil and hydrological data were available but these factors did not seem to matter, unlike in crop farming (Kabubo-Mariara and Karanja, 2007). Geographical factors were considered in choice of sample but no variables were generated to capture actual agro-ecological zones. Regional dummies were dropped from the analysis because they were found to be correlated with climate variables, which are measured at district level. The survey did not collect any data on cultural factors.

References

Basist, A., Grody, N. C., Peterson, T. C., Williams, C. N. (1998) 'Using the special sensor microwave imager to monitor land surface temperatures, wetness, and snow cover', *Journal of Applied Meteorology,* vol 37, no 8, pp888–911

Dercon, S. (1998) 'Wealth, risk and activity choice: Cattle in Western Tanzania', *Journal of Development Economics,* vol 55, pp1–42

Dinar, A., Hassan, R., Kurukulasuriya, P., Benhin, J., Mendelsohn, R. (2006) 'The policy nexus between agriculture and climate change in Africa. A synthesis of the investigation under the GEF/WB Project, Regional Climate, Water and Agriculture: Impacts on and adaptation of agro-ecological systems in Africa', CEEPA Discussion Paper No. 39, Centre for Environmental Economics and Policy in Africa, University of Pretoria

Fafchamps, M., Udry, C., Czukas, K. (1998) 'Drought and saving in West Africa: Are livestock a buffer stock?' *Journal of Development Economics,* vol 55, pp273–305

Food and Agriculture Organization (FAO) (2005) Kenya: Livestock Sector Brief: FAO and Livestock Information, Sector Analysis and Policy Branch (AGAL), www.fao.org/ag/againfo/resources/en/publications/sector_briefs/lsb_KEN.pdf, last accessed July 2007

Galvin, K. A., Boone, R. B., Smith, N. M., Lynn, S. J. (2001) 'Impacts of climate variability on East African pastoralists: Linking social science and remote sensing', *Climate Research,* vol 19, no 1, pp161–172

Houghton, J. T., Ding, Y., Griggs, D. J., Noguer, M., van der Linden, P. J., Dai, X., Maskell, K., Johnson, C. A. (2001) *Climate Change: The Scientific Basis. Contribution of Working Group I to the Third Assessment Report of the Intergovernmental Panel on Climate Change,* Cambridge University Press, New York

Imai, K. (2003) 'Is livestock important for risk behaviour and activity choice in rural households? Evidence from Kenya', *Journal of African Economies,* vol 12, pp271–295

Intergovernmental Panel on Climate Change (IPCC) (2001) *Climate Change: The Scientific Basis,* Cambridge University Press, New York

Kabubo-Mariara, J. (2005) 'Herders response to acute land pressure under changing property rights: Some insights from Kenya', *Environment and Development Economics,* vol 10, no 1, pp67–85

Kabubo-Mariara, J. (2008a) 'Climate change adaptation and livestock activity choices in Kenya: An economic analysis' *Natural Resources Forum,* vol 32, pp131–141

Kabubo-Mariara, J. (2008b) *A Ricardian Analysis of the Economic Impact of Climate Change on Livestock Husbandry in Kenya,* Mimeo, University of Nairobi, Nairobi

Kabubo-Mariara J. (2008c) 'Crop selection and adaptation to climate change in Kenya', *Environmental Research Journal,* vol 2, no 2/3, pp177–196

Kabubo-Mariara, J. and Karanja, F. (2006) 'The economic impact of climate on Kenyan crop agriculture: A Ricardian approach', CEEPA Discussion Paper No. 12, Centre for Environmental Economics and Policy in Africa, University of Pretoria

Kabubo-Mariara, J. and Karanja, F. (2007) 'The economic impact of climate change on Kenyan crop agriculture: A Ricardian approach', *Global and Planetary Change,* vol 57, pp319–330

Kazianga, H. and Udry C. (2004) 'Consumption smoothing and livestock in rural Burkina Faso', Economic Growth Center, Working Paper 898

Kurukulasuriya, P., Mendelsohn, R., Hassan, R., Benhin, J., Deressa, T., Diop, M., Eid, H. M., Fosu, K. Y., Gbetibouo, G., Jain, S., Mahamadou, A', Mano, R., Kabubo-Mariara, J., El-Marsafawy, S., Molua, E., Ouda, S., Ouedraogo, M., Séne, I., Maddison, D., Seo, N. S., Dinar, A. (2006) 'Will Africa survive climate change?' *The World Bank Economic Review*, vol 20, no 3, pp67–388

Luseno, W. K., McPeak, J. G., Barrett, C. B., Little, D., Gebru, G. (2003) 'Assessing the value of climate forecast information for pastoralists: Evidence from Southern Ethiopia and Northern Kenya', *World Development*, vol 31, no 9, pp1477–1494

McPeak, J. (2006) 'Confronting the risk of asset loss: What role does livestock transfers in northern Kenya play?' *Journal of Development Studies*, vol 81, pp415–437

Maddala, G. S. (1995) *Limited Dependent and Qualitative Variables in Econometrics*, Cambridge University Press, New York

Mendelsohn, R., Nordhaus, W., Shaw, D. (1994) 'The impact of global warming on agriculture: A Ricardian analysis', *American Economic Review*, vol 84, pp 753–771

Seo, S. N. and Mendelsohn, R. (2006a) 'The impact of climate change on livestock management in Africa: A structural Ricardian analysis', CEEPA Discussion Paper No. 23, Centre for Environmental Economics and Policy in Africa, University of Pretoria

Seo, S. N. and Mendelsohn, R. (2006b) 'Climate change impacts on animal husbandry in Africa: A Ricardian analysis', CEEPA Discussion Paper No. 9, Centre for Environmental Economics and Policy in Africa, University of Pretoria

Seo, S. N. and Mendelsohn, R. (2006c) 'Climate change adaptation in Africa: A microeconomic analysis of livestock choice', CEEPA Discussion Paper No. 19, Centre for Environmental Economics and Policy in Africa, University of Pretoria

Sombroek, W. G., Brown, H. M. H., Van Der Pouw, B. J. A. (1982) 'The exploratory soil map and agro-climate zone map of Kenya (1980) scale 1:1,000,000', *Exploratory Soil Survey Report E1*, Kenya Soil Survey, Nairobi

Strzepek, K. and McCluskey, A. (2006) 'District level hydroclimatic time series and scenario analysis to assess the impacts of climate change on regional water resources and agriculture in Africa', CEEPA Discussion Paper No. 13, Centre for Environmental Economics and Policy in Africa, University of Pretoria

Swinton, S. (1988) 'Drought survival tactics of subsistence farmers in Niger', *Human Ecology*, vol 16, pp123–144

World Bank (2003) *Africa Rainfall and Temperature Evaluation System (ARTES)*, World Bank, Washington, DC

17

Socio-economic Impacts of Climate Change on Coastal Ecosystems and Livelihoods: A Case Study of Southwestern Cameroon

Ernest L. Molua

Introduction

Cameroon has a long coastline drained by rivers with diverse regimes of lakes and springs. The most interesting sectors are the tidal mangrove reaches, creeks and islands with huge amphibious colonies found in the estuaries of huge rivers, such as the Wouri, Sanaga and Nyong. Cameroon opens into the Atlantic Ocean through the Littoral and Southwest provinces, respectively. The estuary of Wouri and the sea around the port city of Limbe, formerly Victoria, contains a diversity of plants and fish unmatched in Africa, and continues to provide food, shelter and income to about 5 million people in Cameroon. The importance of the biodiversity of freshwater and marine ecosystems provides a rationale for economic exploitation and need for conservation (Pearce et al, 1990; McAllister et al, 1997; Myers, 1997; Shumway, 1999). However, the biological productivity of marine resources along the coast has over the years been challenged by climatic factors (Sackey et al, 1993; Jones, 1994). Future climate change stemming from global warming poses an immense challenge to stakeholders in the region.[1]

Evidence of global warming abounds and data on satellite-measured sea level change indicate a sustained rise in levels and increased precipitation intensities, resulting in increased flood risk. The fourth report of the Intergovernmental Panel on Climate Change (IPCC) has shown that the rapid rise in mean global temperature seen in the last century was exceptional in the context of the last millennium. This warming is predicted to lead to thermal expansion of sea water, along with partial melting of land-based glaciers and sea ice resulting in a rise in sea level that may range from 0.1 to 0.5 metres by the middle of the 21st century (IPCC, 2007). Mean global temperatures of both land and sea surfaces increased by 0.6°C ± 0.2°C in the 20th century and the heat content of oceans, integrated to 3km depth, has increased since 1950. There is now a scientific consensus that these increases are attributable to an even greater rate of increase seen in greenhouse gases. According to the IPCC (2007), surface temperatures are expected to increase by a further 1.4–5.8°C by 2100. It is likely that changes in temperature at this scale and rate will have a pronounced effect on coastal assets and marine ecology. The risks of changing climate conditions in relation to higher temperatures, changes in precipitation, increased climate variability and extreme weather events can result in strong significant impacts on marine biodiversity and coastal livelihoods.[2]

Cameroon is located at the centre of Africa, near the Equator (Figure 17.1). This location endows the country with great biodiversity potential. With a total land area of about 475,440km[2] and a coastline of 402km, Cameroon is an ecologically diverse country in the central Africa sub-region.[3] The country extends for 800km between longitudes 9° and 16°E and 1300km between latitudes 2° and 13°N. The four major ecological zones in the country include a tropical forest zone; a coastal and maritime zone; a savanna zone; and a sudano-sahelian zone. From south to north, there are various types of tropical mountain rain forests, humid savannah, forest galleries and dry forests. Where the climate is drier, dry savannah, steppes and the *yaeres* prevail.[4] Apart from these natural ecosystems, there are also man-made agro-systems consisting of large rubber (*Hevea brasiliensis*), banana (*Musa* spp.), palm tree (*Elaeis guineesis*), cocoa (*Theobroma cacao*) and coffee (*Coffea robusta*) plantations. Both the Rio del Rey basin and the Cameroon estuary attract small and large businesses exploiting renewable and non-renewable natural resources. While Cameroon's wealth of crude petroleum is embedded in the underbelly of the Rio del Rey Basin, its fishery production for both domestic and foreign market is harvested exclusively from its Atlantic coast and the rivers that empty into Cameroon estuary.

Cameroon's rich fauna and flora makes it a versatile location for studies on environmental change (Ngantou and Braund, 1999). The fauna component consists of about 540 fish species of which 90 are endemic, over 15,000 butterfly species, more than 270 species of mammals, 160 reptile species and 3 crocodile species. There are also about 850 bird species, and more than 8000 plant species of which roughly 150 are endemic. For timber production, approximately 630 species of actual or potential commercial value have been identified (Gartlan, 1989; Benhin and Barbier, 1999).

For Cameroon the risk of climate change or even prolonged extreme climatic events could therefore have dramatic impacts on its economy and natural systems, with the potential in some cases for irreversible damages to ecosystems. With a population of about 18 million, Cameroon's human development indicators are those of a middle income developing country (UNDP, 2006). Income per capita is estimated at US$800 (US$2350, in purchasing power parity terms) and life expectancy at birth is 56 years (UNDP, 2006). Adult literacy is estimated at 63 per cent (75 per cent for males and 53 per cent for females), 82 per cent of the population have access to safe water and 92 per cent to sanitation (UNICEF, 2006). Recently, Cameroon has been ranked 125th out of 173 in the

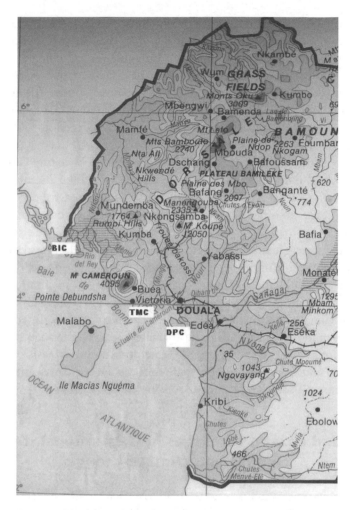

Figure 17.1 Geographical location of Southwestern region of Cameroon

Human Development Index of the United Nations Development Programme (UNDP, 2006). Compared with other countries in sub-Saharan Africa, Cameroon has one of the most diversified production and resource bases, as it produces and exports a broad range of non-oil commodities.[5] Cameroon is a net petroleum product exporter, with oil exports amounting annually to 37 million metric tons representing about 10 per cent of gross domestic product (GDP). However, agriculture and exploitation of natural resources still remain the mainstay of the economy. Agriculture, including livestock production, water and forest resources, as well as biodiversity, are among the most vulnerable systems. Cameroon is an agricultural country where half of the population is living in rural areas. A significant proportion of Cameroon's population inhabit the coastal areas and eke out a living from fishery and the exploitation of mangroves.

This chapter explores the links between climate change, biodiversity and the economic activities that are dependent on that biodiversity. Specifically, the potential environmental and economic consequences of climate change for Cameroon's coastal zones are examined through the perception of communities residing and utilizing mangroves and fishery resources under the influence of extreme climatic events. This is done because it is well known that weather events and sea level rise will impact on the ecological characteristics of key coastal habitats in the region, for example sandy beaches, coral reefs and mangrove forests. Fishing is one of the largest employment sectors in coastal Cameroon, as there is a lack of industrial development, and tourism is in its infancy. About 40 per cent of the total workforce is full-time unregistered fishers. Subsistence fishers are already amongst the poorest members of the community, and the situation looks set to worsen if fisheries continue to decline. A critical step in improving the management of Cameroon's biodiversity and ecosystems is to take stock of their economic importance and establish the perceptions of the exploiters on the resilience and capacity of the coastal ecosystem to maintain the flow of goods and services in the years to come. To put these into context, we review the interplay of climate and coastal resources in the next section. In the following section we examine the socio-economic characteristics and the adaptation choices of coastal communities in Southwestern Cameroon. Empirical tests of perception on adaptation and livelihood are performed in the subsequent section, followed by conclusions and some recommendations in the last section.

Marine and coastal resources in Cameroon: Interplay of climate and climate change

Cameroon's marine systems are particularly rich, with different types of organisms than are found on- and offshore. The Wouri estuary is one of the global marine biodiversity hotspots, and the Idenau–Limbe coastline has an amazing wealth of marine species and habitats. Economically active locations along the West coast of Cameroon include the regions of Bamusso–Isangele, Tiko–Mungo Creeks and Douala–Pongo. While these zones account for significant population levels and economic activity, climatic variation and incidences of extreme weather conditions have been noted. Marine biodiversity in the region is important, for the growing human population and economic agents, for a number of reasons. First, people rely on life in the seas for food, medicines, employment and income. Second, the rich marine ecosystems attract tourists. Third, the marine ecosystems provide services such as protection from environmental extremes; for example, mangroves that act as a buffer zone in the coastal areas, protecting against the worst effects of storms (Appolinaire, 1993; Adegbehin, 1993). Finally, the diverse and interesting environment adds to the quality of life.

However, current climate fluctuations are already causing extensive shifts in species distribution and local biodiversity. The challenges of exploiting terrestrial biodiversity to meet rising food needs and the attendant environmental consequences (Adams, 1990), are extending into aquatic biodiversity, especially in the Southern region of Cameroon. Future climate change and fishing pressures may further interact to exacerbate the risk of collapse of fish populations to below the level at which the biodiversity can support fisheries. This is because climate change can impact on biodiversity in several ways, including species extinction, stock extinction, loss of alleles or genotypes and adverse changes in genotypic frequency (Moyle and Leidy, 1992; Edwards et al, 2001). In addition, this may induce change in distribution and abundance. Climate change and sea level rise effects are probably severe for some sensitive systems, such as coral reefs and mangroves, and these also affect fish populations. *El Niño* has a strong effect on phytoplankton, zooplankton and fish dynamics. It is therefore evident that natural resources, productivity and biodiversity are at risk. The resultant changes in ecosystems will not only affect the distribution and productivity of plant and animal species, water supply and other services, and possibly accelerate losses in biodiversity,[6] but also highlight the need for intensive effort in the management of coastal zones (Agyepong et al, 1990).

Studies highlight the fact that climate change is already impacting on natural ecosystems (Parmesan and Yohe, 2003; IPCC, 2007) and research indicates that many ecosystems and species could be adversely affected by increases in global mean temperatures of 1–2°C not just in terms of their range or existence, but also their ability to deliver various services to humans (Leemans and Eickhout, 2004). Gitay et al (2002) and Reid et al (2005) suggest that a rise beyond 2°C is unacceptable for ecosystems and biodiversity. In addition to increasing temperatures, scientific evidence indicates that the current rate of sea level rise is three times the historical rate and sea levels have already risen by 10–20cm in the last century. The IPCC (2001) predicts that global sea levels will rise between 0.09 and 0.88m by 2100. An increased sea level rise will lead to sea water intrusion into freshwater bodies and aquifers.[7]

Mangroves are directly exposed to climate change. Cameroon's huge mangrove forests and tropical intertidal habitats in the Southwestern and Littoral regions are extensively developed on its accretionary shorelines. The mangroves provide important services for adjacent ecosystems (Ajao, 1993; Postel and Carpenter, 1997), and also supply many useful products to more than 103 villages and communities along Cameroon's Atlantic coastline. The mangroves shown in Figure 17.2 provide (i) nursery habitats for many species of fish and invertebrates that spend their adult lives on coral reefs; (ii) sediment trapping to sustain offshore water quality for coral reefs; (iii) protection for inland sites from storm surges and flooding; (iv) building materials; (v) traditional medicines; (vi) firewood; and (vii) food. As the coastal populations have expanded, the shortage of productive land has led to the clearance of large areas of mangrove for

Figure 17.2 Mangroves in muddy ground in the coastal zone

agriculture and aquaculture production. Demands for timber for charcoal and building, and coastal development space have equally been highly damaging. In some portions of the Rio del Rey basin, mangrove forests have been reduced to mere relics of their former ranges as a result of human exploitation.

In addition to these pressures, mangroves are threatened by sea level rise. A sea level rise of between 0.09 and 0.88m/year, poses a major threat to these mangrove ecosystems through sediment erosion, inundation stress and increased salinity at the landward zones. These problems may be exacerbated for mangrove stands that are subjected to 'coastal squeeze', that is, where landward migration is restricted by topography or human developments (World Bank, 1992; Appolinaire, 1993). Increased air temperatures and atmospheric carbon dioxide concentrations from the nearby metropolis of Douala and Limbe are likely to affect the productivity and range of mangrove forests, as well as change the phenological patterns.[8] These changes have serious implications for water resources, food security, the spread of disease, the productivity of natural resources and sea level rise.

Climate change, coastal biodiversity and socio-economic consequences

Primary survey of marine locations

Cameroonian households' interconnection with natural resources means they are vulnerable to climate hazards, which will become even more frequent as climate change accelerates. Subsistence production being characterized by low levels of input use reinforces the vulnerability of human settlements whose well-being revolves entirely around ecosystem supplies (Isebor and Awosika, 1993; Makaya, 1993). This study uses longitudinal data gathered in three areas along the Atlantic Coast of Cameroon, from Rio del Rey to the Estuary of Cameroon (Figure 17.3). Settlements and communities in the (i) Bamusso–Isangele Creeks (BIC) on the Rio del Rey basin; (ii) Tiko–Mungo Creeks (TMC); and the (iii) Douala–Pongo Creeks (DPC) on the Cameroon estuary are studied.

These locations provide rich marine and coastal biodiversity for study, providing nursery and feeding areas for marine fishes. The climate is primarily humid and tropical. Annual rainfall varies from a mean of 2000mm at the DPC to 5000mm around the BIC. Some villages in the three study locations provide an intersection of marine and freshwater ecosystems, exhibiting features of both, as they not only supply and maintain good quality water for domestic, agriculture and industrial use, but they also provide fish for food, assimilate and dilute wastes, undertake nutrient cycling, provide recreational opportunities, aesthetic values and facilitate transportation for both people and goods. A significant threat to livelihoods in the region is the impact on future water supply (Gliessman, 1990; Avakyan and Iakovleva, 1998; Alcamo et al, 2000).

Varied species of mangroves in three families are found primarily in the Creeks and all along this region, including the red mangroves, *Rhizophora racemosa*, *R. mangle* and *R. harrisonii*; in the white mangroves *Avicennia*

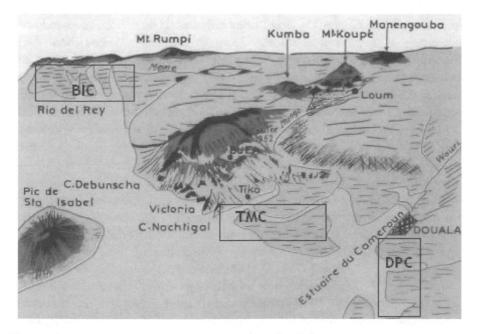

Figure 17.3 Cameroon's southwestern coast and relief

germinans and *Laguncularia racemosa*. *Rhizophora racemosa* is the primary colonist in the open lagoon systems, whereas *Avicennia africana* is the primary colonist in closed systems. Vegetation varies depending on whether the soils consist of sandy troughs or muddy hollows. These mangroves contain no endemic species, they are known for their diverse pelagic fish communities, including some narrowly distributed species, abundant avifauna and the presence of some rare mammals and turtles. While the ecoregion provides spawning and nursery areas for the fisheries in the Gulf of Guinea, Hippopotamus (*Hippopotamus amphibius*), Nile crocodiles (*Crocodylus niloticus*) and a variety of amphibians are also found in the rivers and floodplains surrounding the ecoregion. However, in recent times habitat degradation, physical alteration canals, overharvesting and pollution have all taken a heavy toll on biodiversity in the region, and this highlights the value of water (Chambers et al, 1989; Barbier and Thompson, 1998). Rising national demand for water and food will increase the already considerable pressures on the region's ecosystems, putting more of the species and ecosystem processes at risk (Falkenmark and Widstrand, 1992).

Data collection

The data from the locations studied were obtained using surveys and unobtrusive observation. Both households and focus groups were surveyed and interviewed. Within the selected study sites of Bamusso–Isangele Creeks (BIC), Tiko–Mungo Creeks (TMC) and Douala–Pongo Creeks (DPC), villages were identified and grouped into clusters of four villages. Each of the three sites had three clusters. Two clusters were then randomly selected from each site. Hence, a total of six clusters comprising 24 villages were studied. From each village, 25 households were randomly selected for interviews. Thus 100 households per cluster (or 200 households per site of BIC, TMC and DPC, respectively) were sampled and interviewed. In total 600 households were studied.[9] In addition to households, nine focus groups, three from each of the locations, were selected and discussions held.

The enumerators conducted face-to-face interviews with household heads, eliciting information on their demographic profiles and economic activities. Discussions with the focus groups sought to establish their perceptions on changing climate and corresponding impact on livelihood. The questionnaire administered to the households was retrospective in nature, recording information for four time periods per year for each of the years 2001, 2004 and 2007. Within a year, the four time periods correspond to the bimodal rainfall pattern of the area: the long rains, the dry season following these rains, the short rains and the dry season following these rains. Each period is roughly three months in length. Respondents were asked to report the following variables for each time period: age of household members; household size; household member's occupation; average fish production from the household per day; other aquatic products; total sales per period; and other sources of household income.

Socio-economic characteristics and livelihood of households

Close to 80 per cent of households make their living from exploiting the surrounding water and associated marine resources (Figure 17.4). The fishery subsector employs the majority of the residents, with about 23 per cent engaging in non-fishery activities such as processing, arts and crafts, trading and marketing. Approximately 65 per cent of households in the subregion have household sizes ranging from three to seven persons living under the same roof, engaged in the harvesting of aquatic resources (fish, crabs, etc.), which is practised by several generations of the villagers. Mean annual per capita household incomes vary from US$450 in BIC to US$675 in TMC, and US$824 in DMC. The gendered division of labour ensures that 92 per cent of women are engaged in fish, crabs and crayfish processing as major income earning activities, supplemented with fuelwood drying and a home-based cottage industry. Roughly 84 per cent of males are employed in fishery exploitation. Their income is supplemented by other activities such as electronic repairs, wood splitting for fuel, fishing-net weaving and wooden boat construction. With the unavailability of commercial credit opportunities, 74 per cent of economic operators in the region rely on financing from family sources, friends and rotating-savings. The existing social relationships and family support provide insurance for health, education and homecare.

Communities in the three zones attach religious reverence to the mangroves that protect the coast from erosion and surge storms, especially during tornadoes. In addition to open water fishery, the inhabitants exploit the mangroves and associated resources. The mangroves host a wide variety of commercially important species of fish and crustaceans and a range of economic

Figure 17.4 Fishing on the Cameroon Estuary

organisms, including oysters, shrimps, crabs, mud lobsters, sponges, algae, barnacles and bryozoans. Although 43 per cent of men and 40 per cent of women report some schooling, 85 per cent of household heads appreciate the economic and ecological importance of the marine environment. They acknowledge that their livelihood depends on the continued productivity of the creeks and mangrove-swamps and that certain practices by some members of their community interfere with the productivity of the environment. Control is undertaken both through peer pressure and sanctions in village councils. Fines are levied on community members found guilty of employing either fish or woodfuel harvesting methods that the village council has identified as detrimental to the community. This environmental awareness and ability to control has been attained through regular contact with non-governmental organizations (NGOs) working in the region. Six of the focus groups report at least one visit in the last five years by agriculture and fishery extension service agents and officials of NGOs, apart from holding seminars or workshops on production techniques and the environment.

Climate change and coastal biodiversity: Perception, adaptation and mitigation

Perception of coastal communities on climate change

Local knowledge systems contribute to information on climate and climate change. Table 17.1 indicates that more than 90 per cent of locals used natural indicators such as wind direction, storm intensity and flood frequency, and biological indicators such as the flowering of plants, behaviour of fish and other animals. Historical knowledge of a changing climate is obtained from elders. Only 16 per cent have used the mass media to follow debates and accrue knowledge on climate change, with more than 20 per cent relying on neighbours. Information received from technical personnel from governmental and non-governmental organizations created awareness of climate change for about 35 per cent of the inhabitants. While the residents in the marine zones relied on local and traditional knowledge to understand climate, more than 90 per cent reported with certainty that weather patterns in the region have changed over their lifetime. These observations by the residents are corroborated by climate information and trends from weather stations in the region. Although there are concerns on the amount of mangrove area lost to urbanization, industrialization and agriculture, as well as impacts from timber and petroleum exploitation in the region,[10] there is clear evidence that climatic derivatives of storms, floods, increased salinization and steady warming influence the performance of marine ecology and the harvests from the study zones. Increasing temperature and precipitation trends are reported at the Douala weather observatory (Molua, 2006).

Table 17.1 *Sources of information on changing climate*

Factors that contribute to knowledge about climate	Respondents Yes (%)
Technical personnel from organizations or institutions	35
Information from radio, TV or newspapers	16
Natural indicators (winds, storms, floods)	90
Biological indicators (flowering of plants, fish, birds, other animals)	95
Knowledge from grandparents	63
Neighbours in community	28
Neighbours in other communities	21
Other: Dreams, God's disposition	23

Higher temperatures impact on marine ecosystem well-being through coral bleaching, reduction in species diversity and greater susceptibility to pathogens and diseases. Coral bleaching affects cultural services, and the increased coral mortality and eutrophication in lagoons and estuaries cause a reduction in fish yields. Changes in patterns of phytoplankton growth affect productivity and ecosystem balance (Clark and Edwards, 1994). This affects food security and livelihoods. About 68 per cent of fishery operators report an increasing need for deep-water fishery. Approximately 85 per cent of respondents interviewed and eight focus groups examined report increasing rainfall within their community. Increased precipitation retards growth, productivity and seedling survival in mangroves. The attendant increase in the flooding of sand dunes, lagoons and estuaries reduces the regulatory services of the mangroves. Six of the focus groups contend that the changes in species composition affect goods provided by mangroves, for example food, firewood and other non timber forest products. This in turn affects the security of resource access and livelihoods of the coastal communities.

With 58 per cent of coastal community residents over the age of 55 reporting having observed increased storms over the last 30 years, they attribute the mass mortality of mangroves species as a consequence of the increased frequencies of hurricanes. This further aggravates the erosion of dunes and beaches and exacerbates flooding in lagoons and estuaries. About 62 per cent of those interviewed, and four of the focus groups opine that climate extremes affect their economic activity through loss of man-days of labour, destruction of fishing equipment and damage to homesteads with its associated economic costs. These impacts on communities may be reinforced further through reductions in the protective and regulatory functions of coral reefs, mangroves, sand dunes, lagoons and estuaries, leaving the coastal communities more vulnerable to natural disasters.

The reported increase in wave activity, floods and rise in sea levels affects not only coral growth but also reduces the reef's abilities to protect shorelines. Land occupied by mangroves is lost, affecting not only the provisioning services but also the protective services provided by mangroves. Salinity in lagoons and estuaries increases and affects species composition and, in turn, affects the provisioning services of mangrove ecosystems. Inundated lagoon banks and coastal wetlands leads to changes in species composition, which in turn affects goods provided by mangroves (Hughes and Hughes, 1992). The attendant declines in food, firewood and other non timber forest products impact on household income and livelihoods. About 64 per cent of women primarily employed in woodfuel trading report a reduction in their activities as a result of a decline in wood supplies over the last eight years. This decline is largely due to the growth in population and increased demand for charcoal. However, the decline in woodfuel supplies is also due to the loss of the protective covering of mangroves, which tends to leave the coastal communities more vulnerable to natural disasters (EC, 1992; Diop, 1993).

Mitigation and adaptation to climate change

Adaptation is vital to avoid the unwanted impacts of climate change, especially in sectors and ecosystems vulnerable to even moderate levels of warming (Clark and Edwards, 1994). Different communities within the three locations studied have developed a variety of different ways to use marine resources. Each form carries with it a particular suite of ecological benefits. The rationale for this is that changes in biosphere, biodiversity and natural resources unfavourably affect quality of human life and further exacerbates the problem of poverty. Figure 17.5 shows the percentage of respondents engaging in different adaptations, with more than 70 per cent of residents employing more than one method to cushion the impacts of environmental change. The planned adaptation options adopted include the reinforcement of homesteads against storms, deep-water fishing, increased night time fishing, increased visits to soothsayers to predict weather events and prayers for Divine intervention.[11] The extent of adaptation is shaped by the ability of households and individuals to access resources and the investment decisions they make with observed and expected climate change, economic events, policies and institutional change. In areas of greater risk, such as the BIC, household strategies are more diversified as a mechanism to minimize the effects of possible shocks from negative climatic events. Households with portfolios of economic activities that are diversified and have less covariant activities are observed to be better able to cope with climate risk.

Figure 17.6 reveals a correlation of perception of climate change and adaptive responses. Those who agree that they have over the years seen changes in climate and are certain that climate change has occurred and are no conducting longer business as usual have employed more adaptation. A stronger response to adapt and

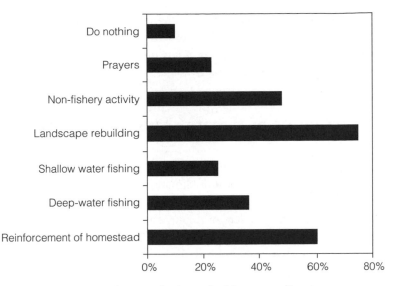

Figure 17.5 Management changes by households responding to climate change expectations

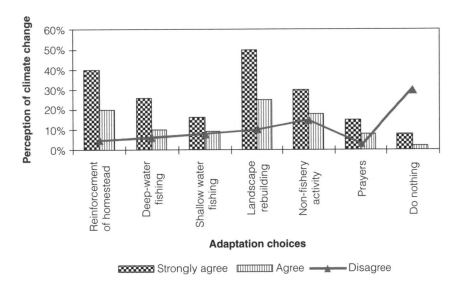

Figure 17.6 Correlation of perception of climate change and adaptive response

reduce vulnerability of livelihoods is observed with those who perceive climate change. About 25 per cent and 15 per cent of respondents who move into deep-water fishing and further exploit shallow waters, respectively, strongly agree that that they do this partly because climate change has taken place. However, those who disagree that climate change has not taken place are also observed to be adjusting their homesteads and economic activity. This adjustment could either be due to the increased economic activity from the growing population, increasing urbanization and improving incomes or adjusting to environmental changes that may not necessarily be linked to climate.

Perception of climate change and welfare

Analytical framework

To better understand the perception of climate change and review the economic importance of adaptive choices, we study the utility derived from mitigation effort. We characterize the problem of resource allocation in terms of maximizing utility, subject to the constraints on the availability and substitutability of resources. We assume that households derive utility as:

$$U_i = U_i(a_i, x_i, q_i, s_i) \tag{1}$$

Where U_i represents the utility of individuals, a_i is the adaptation efforts of individuals, x_i is goods bought by individuals, q_i is the individual perception of climate change, and s_i is a vector of socio-economic and spatial variables that affect utility. The benefit of adaptation embarked upon is represented in the following function as:

$$a_i = f(m_i, a_0, s_i) \tag{2}$$

Where m_i is a vector of activities employed for adaptation and a_0 the noted initial levels of natural adaptation that the community is predisposed towards. Utility is maximized subject to the following constraints:

$$I_i = P_{xi}x_i + P_{mi}m_i \tag{3}$$

Where I_i represents the exogenously given income of individual i, P_{xi} is a vector of private goods prices faced by individual i, and P_{mi} is a vector of prices paid by individual I in purchasing items for adaptation. This leads to the following indirect utility function:

$$V_i = V_i(a_i(I_i, P_{xi}, P_{mi}, a_0, S_i), I_i, P_{xi}, S_i) \tag{4}$$

Where V_i represents utility or satisfaction derived from the effort put into adapting to exogenous environmental variables. The exogenous variables (I_i, P_{xi}, S_i) may influence utility directly or indirectly. This suggests two alternative approaches for estimating the utility models. The first approach is to estimate the intervening adaptation variable in the following system of equation:

$$V_i = \beta_1 + \beta_2 I_i + \beta_3 P_{xi} + \beta_4 a_i + \beta_5 S_i + \varepsilon_1 \tag{5}$$

$$a_i = \beta_6 + \beta_7 I_i + \beta_8 P_{xi} + \beta_9 P_{mi} + \beta_{10} S_i + \varepsilon_2 \tag{6}$$

Alternatively, Equation (6) can be substituted for a_i in Equation (5) and the following reduced form model estimated:

$$V_i = \beta_{11} + \beta_{12} I_i + \beta_{13} P_{xi} + \beta_{14} P_{mi} + \beta_{15} a_{01} + \beta_{16} S_i + \varepsilon_3 \tag{7}$$

In the above models, β_1 through β_{16} represents coefficients to be estimated and ε_1 through ε_3 are error terms, assumed to have zero mean and constant variance. It is also assumed that $\text{cov}(\varepsilon_1 \varepsilon_2) = 0$. The full structural approach of Equations (5) and (6) distinguishes between the direct effects of the exogenous variables working through adaptation and indirect effects of the exogenous variables after controlling for adaptation. In other words, the model identifies the process underlying the effects of the exogenous variables. Equation (7) captures only the total (direct and indirect) effects of the exogenous variables in the reduced form equation. We employ both approaches to evaluate the direct and indirect effects of the variables (see Dustman, 1996). Since the dependent variables are ordered probit responses, we estimate an ordered probit model. Ordered probit or logit models are appropriate techniques for relationships involving ordered dependent variables (Cameron and Trivedi, 1986; Greene, 1993).

Measurement of variables

Dependent variables
The dependent variables are the categorical variables of: (i) adaptation is measured as 2 if adaptation effort is structural and planned in advance, 1 if adaptation is ad hoc and reactive, and 0 for not adapting; (ii) benefit of adaptation is measured as 2 if adaptation effort *regularly* overcomes the perceived effects of climate change, 1 if adaptation *sometimes* allows the household to withstand the perceived effects of climate change, and 0 if adaptation *does not* cushion against the perceived effects of climate change.[12]

Independent variables
The independent variables include gender (1 if male), age (if age of household head is 25–54), age-2 (greater than 55 years), employment (1 if unemployed), education (1 if more than secondary education), income (1 if gross monthly income is more than 90,000 Francs CFA),[13] years of residence (1 if more than 15 years of residence in the community), amenities (1 if there is a hospital or health centre in the village of residence), neighbourhood (1 if satisfied with the village as a place to live), spatial effect (1 if homestead is located in marshy land),

perception (1 if climate change is acknowledged or observed), environment (1 if respondent is concerned with the quality of environment) and household expenditure for adaptation.

Empirical results

The empirical results presented in Table 17.2 suggest that the demographic variables of age, gender and marital status are associated with both an ability to adapt and satisfaction obtained from productive and adaptive efforts. The coefficient of the age variable is positive and statistically significant. This implies older individuals are more able to adapt and are seemingly satisfied with the

Table 17.2 *Ordered probit maximum likelihood estimation: structural form equations*

Variables	Adaptation		Benefit of adaptation	
	Coefficient	t-ratio	Coefficient	t-ratio
Gender	0.062 *	1.790	0.069 *	1.927
Age	0.051 *	1.892	0.085 *	1.978
Age-2	−0.022	−1.579	−0.099	−1.763
Employment	0.083 **	2.282	0.058 **	2.243
Education	0.113 ***	4.109	0.231 ***	3.112
Income	0.413 ***	3.923	0.520 ***	4.123
Duration of residence	0.079 *	1.809	0.093 *	1.987
Amenities	0.061 *	1.947	0.072 *	1.995
Neighbourhood	0.231	1.392	0.185 *	1.981
Spatial	−0.324 *	−1.879	−0.426 **	−2.117
Perception	–	–	0.184 **	2.919
Environment	0.265 *	1.998	0.129 **	2.285
Expenditure	0.008 *	1.946	0.019 *	1.898
μ	1.315 ***	6.433	1.336 ***	5.072
Log-L	−628.3		−677.6	
Model χ^2	36.11		29.35	
Pseudo-R^2	0.273		0.438	
DF	588		589	
Interactions completed	15		17	
Sample size	597		598	

Note: *** $p < 0.01$, ** $p < 0.05$, * $p < 0.10$.

Source: Author's computation.

beneficial outcomes of the adaptive efforts. The effect of age-2 is negative indicating an inverted U-shape relationship between age and adaptive capacity. Educated males with higher incomes are better able to adapt and experience satisfaction with meaningful adaptive efforts. The spatial variable is significantly important and negative, indicating that residents in marshy creeks and year-round wetlands are likely to report that their adaptive efforts are not successful and they are dissatisfied with the environmental benefits derived.[14]

While the marine and freshwater biodiversity provide direct and indirect benefits to coastal and riverine residents in Southwestern Cameroon, Table 17.2 reiterates that the benefits derived by economic agents and households depend strongly on their socio-economic characteristics. This adds to a priori expectations that household income, education level, size and labour availability of households are important variables that influence livelihood. The benefits to livelihood of coastal communities include the direct and indirect fisheries function of the mangroves and deep and shallow waters, tourism related benefits, browsing of livestock, landscape and environmental benefits, coastal protection and sediment regulation functions.

Concluding remarks

With a significant number of households reporting stronger perceptions and observations of climate change, this calls for better policy and programmes dealing with agriculture, zoning and protection, and fisheries management within the coastal region. The findings indicate not only the need to conserve and protect the ecosystems in the face of climate change, but to build resilience in coastal assets and communities (WRI, 2000). Given the available scientific information from weather stations indicating increased warming and wetness in the coastal region of Cameroon, the attendant effects on marine resources on which livelihoods depend and the corresponding effort by communities to cushion negative consequences, there is a greater need than ever for public action to assist the adaptive capacity of communities.

A Biodiversity and Marine Fisheries Programme that recognizes the need to protect ecosystems, as well as target and non-target species, and advocating for a precautionary approach where there is a threat of significant reduction or loss of biodiversity, will be a catalyst to promote adaptation at the tiers of households, local communities and nationwide. In sum, building individual and institutional capacity to enhance adaptive resource management along the coast would be a major step forward both in achieving the nation's development goals and in preparing for potential climate change. There is a need for increased partnerships to harness formal and indigenous knowledge and empower community and stakeholder participation in ecosystem management processes while applying and reinforcing cultural heritage. The inclusion of traditional management into an integrated strategy should occur in partnership with government and community leaders. Investing in peer-to-peer learning among communities would be an effective means to develop and support the capacities needed to adapt and adopt best practices. Finally, the implementation and integration of ecological and socio-economic monitoring in tropical marine ecosystems management and more effective communication of the results will significantly contribute to enhancing the adaptive capacity of communities and households. The risks in awaiting unambiguous climate change signals are real, since neither climate change nor its impacts can be reversed quickly. Delaying actions by communities and governments might increase both the rate and magnitude of climate change and hence adaptation and damage costs.

Notes

1.   Global warming is affecting oceans, changing ocean currents and influencing wave climates, which in turn changes shoreline stability (IPCC, 2007).
2.   In addition to climatic factors, growth in domestic and external demand, the scale and rate of exploitation of marine products has expanded and is approaching unsustainable thresholds in many locations across the coastline. Overexploitation and the eventual disappearance are of both local and global concerns, because they may impact on local diet, economy of coastal households and induce the risk of irreplaceable loss of species and genetic biodiversity.
3.   The republics of Congo, Gabon and Equatorial Guinea border it to the south, and Chad and the republic of Central Africa to the northeast. While Lake Chad is in the north of Cameroon, Nigeria and the Atlantic Ocean border it to the west and southwest, respectively.
4.   The southern part of the country, which includes: the South (headquarters – Ebolowa), Centre (Yaoundé), East (Bertoua), Southwest (Buea) and Littoral (Douala) provinces, is lowland humid forest (below 800m above sea level except Mount Cameroon, which is 4100m above sea level). In the northwestern and central parts of the country, the West (Bafoussam), Northwest (Bamenda) and Adamawa (Ngaoundéré) provinces are mid-altitude (800–1200m above sea level) to highlands (above 1200–over 3000m above sea level). In the northern part of the country, the North (Garoua) and Far North (Maroua) provinces are dominated by lowland Sudano-sahelian savannah (below 600m above sea level).
5.   The principal commercial and staple food crops include coffee, cocoa, timber, cotton, rubber, bananas, oilseed, grains, livestock and root starches. Natural resources include petroleum, bauxite, iron ore and timber
6.   In Central Africa where Cameroon is situated, climate change is directly felt in terms of higher temperatures, changes in the timing and quality of rains, increase in the frequency of climate hazards, e.g. floods, droughts; tropical storms; and sea level rise. These climate impacts increase the country's vulnerability to coastal erosion, coral bleaching and degradation of mangroves.
7.   Melting glaciers in northern latitudes will have substantial impacts on tropical river flows and water availability downstream, coupled with altered precipitation, which will significantly impact water and food security.

8. More challenges posed to ecosystem well-being include: effects on distribution and stocks; effects on the timing of life cycle events; effects on physiology and behaviour; and more importantly the effects on communities and productivity.

9. After the field interviews and collation of questionnaires, the enumerators returned to the field with uncompleted questionnaires and updated them for missing information. This ensured that the sample of 600 questionnaires was properly completed assuring a response rate of 100%, and of sufficiently good quality to be used for analysis.

10. Other threats include the practice of gas flaring, the use of poison and dynamite for fishing, canalization, discharge of sewage and other pollutants, siltation, sand mining, erosion, construction of embankments, and growing population pressure in the coastal zone.

11. Prayers as adaptation choice relates to increased invocation of Divine intervention through formal religious prayers or animist incantations; non-fishery activities cited by respondents include wood-splitting, arts and craft production, dressmaking and micro grocery-trading; landscape rebuilding refers to the construction of protective walls and embankments and planting of trees in courtyard; shallow water fishing refers to the exploitation of the surrounding waters within the depth range of 1–10m; deep-water fishing refers to moving out of the creeks further into the deep Atlantic Ocean water in search of better catch; reinforcement of homestead includes structural amendments made to roofs, walls, floors, windows and doors. 'Do nothing' relates to household heads that do not employ any method or technique to adapt to perceived changes in climate.

12. Households were grouped based on the nature of adaptation. The groups are households that employed (i) structural and planned; and (ii) ad hoc and reactive measures. The benefits of adaptation are responses of households that strongly agreed that the expenses on adaptation have allowed the homestead to *regularly* overcome their perceived effects of climate change.

13. This is about US$225 or €137.4. The local currency, Francs CFA (*communautaire financier en Afrique*), is used by 15 former colonies of France in Africa. It is pegged to the euro at the exchange rate of FCFA655.657 to €1.

14. The models explain a substantial amount of the variations in the dependent variables. The goodness of fit (pseudo R^2) is 0.273 and 0.438 in the adaptation and benefit of adaptation structural equations, respectively.

References

Adams, W. M. (1990) *Green Development: Environment and Sustainability in the Third World*, Biddles Ltd., Guildford and King's Lynn, London

Adegbehin, J. O. (1993) 'Mangroves in Nigeria', in E. D. Diop (ed.), *Conservation and Sustainable Utilization of Mangrove Forests in Latin America and Africa Regions*. Part II – Africa, International Society for Mangrove Ecosystems and Coastal Marine Project of UNESCO, Mangrove Ecosystems Technical Reports volume 3

Agyepong, G. T. K., Yankson, P. W. K., Ntiamoa-Baidu, Y. (1990) *Coastal Zone Indicative Management Plan*, E.P.C., Accra

Ajao, E. A. (1993) 'Mangrove ecosystems in Nigeria', in E. D. Diop (ed.), *Conservation and Sustainable Utilization of Mangrove Forests in Latin America and Africa Regions*, Part II – Africa, International Society for Mangrove Ecosystems and Coastal Marine Project of UNESCO, Mangrove Ecosystems Technical Reports volume 3

Alcamo, J., Henrichs, T., Rösch, T. (2000) *World Water in 2025 – Global Modeling and Scenario Analysis for the World Commission on Water for the 21st Century*, Report A0002, Kassel, Center for Environmental Systems Research, University of Kassel, Germany

Appolinaire, Z. (1993) 'Mangroves of Cameroun', in E.D. Diop (ed.) *Conservation and Sustainable Utilization of Mangrove Forests in Latin America and Africa Regions*, Part II – Africa, International Society for Mangrove Ecosystems and Coastal Marine Project of UNESCO, Mangrove Ecosystems Technical Reports volume 3

Avakyan, A. B. and Iakovleva, V. B. (1998) 'Status of global reservoirs: The position in the late twentieth century', *Lakes and Reservoirs: Research and Management*, vol 3, pp45–52

Barbier, E. B. and Thompson, J. R. (1998) 'The value of water: Floodplain versus large-scale irrigation benefits in Northern Nigeria', *Ambio*, vol 27, no 6, pp434–440

Benhin, J. K. A. and Barbier, E. B. (1999) 'A case study analysis of the effects of structural adjustment on agriculture and on forest cover in Cameroon', *Final Report for the Center for International Forestry Research (CIFOR) and the Central African Regional Program for the Environment (CAPE)*, Department of Environment, University of York, York, UK

Besley, T. (1995) 'Property rights and investment incentives: Theory and evidence from Ghana', *Journal of Political Economy*, vol 103, pp903–937

Cameron, C. and Trivedi, P. (1986) 'Econometric models based on count data: Comparisons and applications of some estimators and tests', *Journal of Econometrics*, vol 1, pp29–53

Carroll, T. F. (2001) *Social Capital, Local Capacity Building and Poverty Reduction*, Asian Development Bank Social Development Papers No. 3, Asian Development Bank, Manila

Chambers, R., Shah, T., Saxena, N. C. (1989) *To the Hands of the Poor: Water and Trees*, Oxford and IBH Publishing Co., New Delhi

Clark, S. and Edwards, A. J. (1994) 'Use of artificial reef structures to rehabilitate reef flats degraded by coral mining in the Maldives', *Bulletin of Marine Science*, vol 55, no 2–3, pp724–744

Clark, S. and Edwards, A. J. (1995) 'Coral transplantation as an aid to reef rehabilitation: Evaluation of a case study in Maldive Islands', *Coral Reefs*, no 14, pp201–213

Cragg, M. I. and Kahn, M. E. (1997) 'New estimates of climate demand: Evidence from location choice', *Journal of Urban Economics*, no 42, pp261–284

Cragg, M. I. and Kahn, M. E. (1999) 'Climate consumption and climate pricing from 1940 to 1990', *Regional Science and Urban Economics*, no 29, pp519–539

Dercon, S. and Krishnan, P. (2000) 'In sickness and in health: Risk sharing within households in rural Ethiopia', *Journal of Political Economy*, vol 108, no 4, pp688–727

Diop, E. S. (1993) *Conservation and Sustainable Utilization of Mangrove Forests in Latin America and Africa Regions*, Part II – Africa, International Society for Mangrove Ecosystems and Coastal Marine Project of UNESCO, Mangrove Ecosystems Technical Reports volume 3

Doss, C. R. (2001) 'Is risk fully pooled within the household? Evidence from Ghana', *Economic Development and Cultural Change*, pp101–130

Dustman, C. (1996) 'The social assimilation of immigrants', *Journal of Population Economics*, vol 9, pp37–54

Edwards, A. J., Clark, S., Zahir, H., Rajasuriya, A., Naseer, A., Rubens, J. (2001) 'Coral bleaching and mortality on artificial and natural reefs in Maldives in 1998, sea surface temperature anomalies and initial recovery', *Marine Pollution Bulletin*, vol 42, no 1, pp7–15

EC (Commission of the European Communities), Directorate-General for Development (1992) 'Mangroves of Africa and Madagascar', Office for Official Publications of the European Communities, Brussels, Luxembourg

Falkenmark, M. and Widstrand, C. (1992) 'Population and water resources: A delicate balance', *Population Bulletin*, vol 47, no 3, pp1–36

Gartlan, S. (1989) *La Conservation des Ecosystèmes Forestiers du Cameroon*, IUCN, Gland and Cambridge

Gitay, H., Suárez, A., Watson, R. T., Anisimov, O., Chapin, F. S., Cruz, R. V., Finlayson, M., Hohenstein, W. G., Insarov, G., Kundzewicz, Z., Leemans, R., Magadza, C., Nurse, L., Noble, I., Price, J., Ravindranath, N. H., Root, T. L., Scholes, B., Villamizar, A., Rumei, X. (2002) *Climate Change and Biodiversity*, Intergovernmental Panel on Climate Change, Geneva, 77pp

Gliessman, S. R. (1990) *Agroecology: Researching the Ecological Basis for Sustainable Agriculture*, Springer-Verlag, New York

Greene, H. W. (1993) *Econometric Analysis*, Second Edition, Macmillan Publishing Company, New York

Hughes, R. H. and Hughes, J. S. (1992) *A Directory of African Wetlands*, IUCN, Gland Switzerland and Cambridge, UK/UNEP, Nairobi, Kenya/WCMC, Cambridge, UK

IPCC (Intergovernmental Panel on Climate Change) (2001) *Africa Climate Change 2001: Impacts, Adaptation, and Vulnerability*, (ch. 10) Report of IPCC Working Group II, IPCC, Geneva

IPCC (Intergovernmental Panel on Climate Change) (2007) *Climate Change 2007: The Scientific Basis*, Report of IPCC Working Group I, IPCC, Geneva

Isebor, C. E. and Awosika, L. F. (1993) 'Nigerian mangrove resources, status and management', in E. D. Diop (ed.), *Conservation and Sustainable Utilization of Mangrove Forests in Latin America and Africa Regions*, Part II – Africa, International Society for Mangrove Ecosystems and Coastal Marine Project of UNESCO, Mangrove Ecosystems Technical Reports volume 3

Jones, P. J. (1994) 'Biodiversity in the Gulf of Guinea: An overview', *Biodiversity and Conservation*, vol 3, pp772–784

Leemans, R. and Eickhout, B. (2004) 'Another reason for concern: Regional and global impacts on ecosystems for different levels of climate change', *Global Environmental Change*, vol 14, pp219–228

McAllister, D. E., Hamilton, A. L., Harvey, B. (1997) 'Global freshwater biodiversity: Striving for the integrity of freshwater ecosystems', *Sea Wind – Bulletin of Ocean Voice International*, vol 11, no 3, pp1–140

Maddison, D. J. (2001) *The Amenity Value of the Global Climate*, Earthscan, London

Makaya, J. F. (1993) 'Mangroves in Congo', in E. D. Diop (ed.), *Conservation and Sustainable Utilization of Mangrove Forests in Latin America and Africa Regions*, Part II – Africa. International Society for Mangrove Ecosystems and Coastal Marine Project of UNESCO, Mangrove Ecosystems Technical Reports volume 3

Molua, E. L. (2006) 'Climate trends in Cameroon: Implications for agricultural management', *Climate Research*, vol 30, pp255–262

Moyle, P. B. and Leidy, R. A. (1992) 'Loss of biodiversity in aquatic ecosystems: Evidence from fish faunas', in P. L. Fiedler and S. K. Jain (eds), *Conservation Biology: The Theory and Practice of Nature Conservation, Preservation and Management*, Chapman and Hall, New York, pp127–169

Myers, N. (1997) 'The rich diversity of biodiversity issues', in M. L. Reaka-Kudla, D. E. Wilson, E. O. Wilson (eds), *Biodiversity II: Understanding and Protecting our Biological Resources*, Joseph Henry Press, Washington, DC, pp125–138

Ngantou, D. and Braund, R. (1999) 'Waza-Logobe: Restoring the good life', *World Conservation*, vol 30, no 2, pp19–20

Parmesan, C. and Yohe, G. (2003) 'A globally coherent fingerprint of climate change impacts across natural systems', *Nature*, vol 421, pp37–42

Pearce, D., Barbier, E., Markhandya, A. (1990) *Sustainable Development: Economics and Environment in the Third World*, Earthscan, London

Pender, J. and Kerr, J. (1999) 'The effect of transferable land rights on credit, land investment and use: Evidence from south India', *Agricultural Economics*, vol 21, pp279–294

Postel, S. and Carpenter, S. (1997) 'Freshwater ecosystem services', in G.C. Daily (ed.), *Nature's Services: Societal Dependence on Natural Ecosystems*, Island Press, Washington, DC, pp195–214

Reid, W. V., Mooney, H. A., Cropper, A., Capistrano, D., Carpenter, S. R., Chopra, K., Dasgupta, P., Dietz, T., Duraiappah, A. K., Hassan, R., Kasperson, R., Leemans, R., May, R. M., McMichael, A. J., Pingali, P., Samper, C., Scholes, R., Watson, R. T., Zakri, A. H., Shidong, Z., Ash, N. J., Bennett, E., Kumar, P., Lee, M. J., Raudsepp-Hearne, C., Simons, H., Thonell, J., Zurek, M. B. (2005) *Millennium Ecosystem Assessment Synthesis report*, Island Press, Washington DC, 160pp

Sackey, I., Laing, E., Adomako, J. K. (1993) 'Status of the mangroves of Ghana', in E. D. Diop (ed.), *Conservation and Sustainable Utilization of Mangrove Forests in Latin America and Africa Regions*, Part II – Africa, International Society for Mangrove Ecosystems and Coastal Marine Project of UNESCO, Mangrove Ecosystems Technical Reports volume 3

Shumway, C. A. (1999) *Forgotten Waters: Freshwater and Marine Ecosystems in Africa. Strategies for Biodiversity Conservation and Sustainable Development*, The Biodiversity Support Program, Boston University, New England Aquarium, US Agency for International Development

UNDP (2006) *Human Development Report 2006*, United Nations Development Programme, Oxford University Press, New York

UNICEF (2006) *Statistics for Cameroon*, United Nations International Children Emergency Fund, New York. www.unicef.org/statis/, last accessed 23 July 2006

World Bank (1992) *Development and the Environment*, World Development Report 1992, Oxford University Press, London

World Resources Institute, United Nations Development Program, United Nations Environment Programme and the World Bank (2000) *World Resources 2000–2001: People and Ecosystems, the Fraying Web of Life*, World Resources Institute, Washington, DC

Index